EAST ASIAN LAW – UNIVERSAL NORMS AND LOCAL CULTURES

This book explores the tension in East Asia between, on the one hand, the trend toward a convergence of legal practices in the direction of a universal model, and, on the other hand, a reassertion of local cultural practices, including those which define different group identities, and which give substance to different ideas about what constitutes 'justice'. The trend towards convergence arises in part from 'globalization', from 'rule of law programs' promulgated by institutions such as the International Monetary Fund and the Asian Development Bank, who are keen to ensure a reasonable level of global conformity in the legal underpinnings of commercial activity, and from widespread migration in the region, whilst the opposing trend arises in part from moves to resist such 'globalization'. This book explores a wide range of issues related to this key problem, covering especially well China, where resolving differences in conceptions about the rule of law is a key issue as China begins to integrate itself into the World Trade Organization regime.

Arthur Rosett is Professor of Law at the University of California at Los Angeles. **Lucie Cheng** is Professor of Sociology at the University of California at Los Angeles. **Margaret Y. K. Woo** is Professor of Law at Northeastern University, Boston.

EAST ASIAN LAW – UNIVERSAL NORMS AND LOCAL CULTURES

Edited by Arthur Rosett, Lucie Cheng and Margaret Y. K. Woo

Routledge
Taylor & Francis Group
LONDON AND NEW YORK

First published 2003
by Routledge

2 Park Square, Milton Park, Abingdon, Oxfordshire OX14 4RN
711 Third Avenue, New York, NY 10017

Routledge is an imprint of the Taylor & Francis Group, an informa business

First issued in paperback 2018

Transferred to Digital Printing 2008

Typeset in Galliard by Taylor and Francis Books Ltd

British Library Cataloguing in Publication Data
A catalogue record for this book is available from the British Library

Library of Congress Cataloging in Publication Data
A Catalog record for this book has been requested

ISBN 978-0-415-29735-6 (hbk)
ISBN 978-0-367-02692-9 (pbk)

CONTENTS

Notes on contributors vii
Preface xi

1 Finding a role for law in Asian development 1
LUCIE CHENG, MARGARET Y. K. WOO AND ARTHUR ROSETT

2 Property rights and indigenous tradition among early twentieth-century Japanese firms 22
YOSHIRO MIWA AND J. MARK RAMSEYER

3 Markets, democracy and ethnicity 33
AMY L. CHUA

4 Competing conceptions of 'rule of law' in China 51
RANDALL PEERENBOOM

5 Transnational labor, citizenship and the Taiwan state 85
LUCIE CHENG

6 'Us' and 'them' in Korean law: the creation, accommodation and exclusion of outsiders in South Korea 106
CHULWOO LEE

7 Internal migrants and the challenge of the 'floating population' in the PRC 137
DOROTHY J. SOLINGER

8 The historical roots of stasis and change in Japanese legal education 156
KAHEI ROKUMOTO

9 Of lawyers lost and found: searching for legal professionalism in the People's Republic of China 182
WILLIAM P. ALFORD

10 Chinese courts and law reform in post-Mao China 205
STANLEY LUBMAN

Index 234

CONTRIBUTORS

William P. Alford is the Henry L. Stimson Professor of Law and Director of East Asian Legal Studies at Harvard Law School. He is the author of *To Steal a Book is an Elegant Offense* and articles concerning China, international law, US/East Asian relations, intellectual property and other subjects. He is an honorary professor of Renmin University and Zhejiang University (PRC).

Lucie Cheng is Professor of Sociology and Urban Planning at the University of California, Los Angeles. She is the Founding Dean of the School for Social Transformation Studies, Shih Hsin University, Taipei; and Permanent Visiting Professor of International Relations, Nankai University, Tianjin. Her publications are in the areas of migration and development, and gender, race and class.

Amy L. Chua is Professor of Law at Yale University. She received her A.B. from Harvard College in 1984 and her J.D. from Harvard Law School in 1987. Professor Chua was executive editor of the *Harvard Law Review*, and after graduating from law school clerked for Judge Patricia Wald of the United States Court of Appeals for the DC circuit. Professor Chua's publications include *Collision: Markets, Democracy, and Ethnonationalism in the Coming Global Order* (Doubleday, forthcoming 2002), 'The Paradox of Free Market Democracy: Rethinking Development Policy' (*Harvard International Law Journal*, 2000), and 'Markets, Democracy, and Ethnicity: Toward a New Paradigm for Law and Development' (*Yale Law Journal*, 1998).

Chulwoo Lee is an assistant professor at the College of Law, Sungkyunkwan University, Korea, where he teaches the sociology of law and legal history. He has published articles on law and colonialism, law and development, sociological approaches to legal culture, and social-scientific method in studying law. His current research themes include law and ethnic identity and the socio-cultural contexts of the rule of law in East Asia.

Stanley Lubman is Lecturer in Law at the University of California (Berkeley). For over thirty-five years he has been both a scholar of Chinese law and a practicing lawyer advising foreign clients in China. He is also advisor on

Chinese legal projects to the Asia Foundation. His publications include *Bird in a Cage: Legal Reform in China After Mao* (Stanford University Press, 1999)

Yoshiro Miwa is Professor of Economics at the University of Tokyo. An author, co-author, or co-editor of over a dozen books and numerous articles, Professor Miwa has written widely on economic issues – most recently on corporate finance, corporate governance and government regulation. He is currently collaborating with Mark Ramseyer on a series of books and articles exploring the ties between corporate governance and corporate finance in Japan. A graduate of the University of Tokyo (B.A. and Ph.D.), he taught at Shinshu University before joining the University of Tokyo faculty in 1986.

Randall Peerenboom obtained a B.A. in Philosophy, M.A. in Chinese Religion and Ph.D. in Philosophy before obtaining a J.D. from Columbia Law School. He has written extensively on Chinese law and philosophy, including *China's Long March Toward Rule of Law* (Cambridge University Press, 2002). From 1994 to 1998 he practiced law with a major international law firm in Beijing. He currently teaches Chinese law at the University of California Los Angeles. In addition to advising on various aspects of foreign investment in China, he often serves as an expert witness on PRC legal issues, and is Of Counsel at Yiwen Law Firm.

J. Mark Ramseyer is Mitsubishi Professor of Japanese Legal Studies at Harvard University. Educated at Goshen College (B.A., 1976), the University of Michigan (A.M., 1978), and Harvard (J.D. magna cum laude, 1982), Ramseyer has also practiced law at a Chicago law firm and clerked for Justice Stephen Breyer (on the US Court of Appeals at the time). Ramseyer's current research (with Professor Yoshiro Miwa) involves the connection between corporate finance and corporate governance in Japan. Prior to moving to Harvard, he taught at UCLA and the University of Chicago.

Kahei Rokumoto After completing his Ph.D. work at the University of Tokyo, Faculty of Law, Professor Rokumoto held the chair for the sociology of law for thirty years in the same faculty, retired because of the age limit, and presently teaches at the University of the Air, Japan's distance higher education institution. He has published a comprehensive textbook of the sociology of law, and has carried out extensive empirical research on such topics in law and society as the Japanese legal culture and its transformations, civil dispute processes, the legal profession and its reform, and medical malpractice litigation.

Arthur Rosett has been a Professor of Law at the University of California, Los Angeles School of Law (UCLA) since 1967. For more than twenty years he has taught a variety of Asian law courses as well as contract law and international business transactions. Among his Asian law publications are 'Contract with a Chinese Face: Socially Embedded Factors in the Transformation from Hierarchy to Market, 1978–1989', *Journal of Chinese Law*, vol. 5, p. 143 (with Lucie Cheng, 1991) and 'The Implications of Apology: Law and Culture in Japan and the United States', *Law and Society Review*, vol. 20, p. 461 (with Hiroshi Wagatsuma, 1986).

Dorothy J. Solinger is Professor of Political Science in the School of Social Sciences at the University of California, Irvine, and Adjunct Senior Research Scholar at the East Asian Institute at Columbia University. She is the author of five single-authored books on contemporary China, the most recent of which is *Contesting Citizenship In Urban China: Peasant Migrants, The State, And The Logic Of The Market* (University of California Press, 1999), and of numerous articles, one edited book, and one co-edited book.

Margaret Y. K. Woo is Professor of Law at Northeastern University School of Law. She earned her B.A. at Brown University, magna cum laude, her J.D. from New York University School of Law, and her LL.M. from Georgetown University Law Center. At Northeastern, Professor Woo teaches civil procedure, administrative law, and comparative law. In 1997 she was named the law school's Distinguished Professor of Public Policy. She was formerly a Fellow at the Bunting Institute of Radcliffe College, and is presently an Associate in Research at the East Asian Legal Studies Center of Harvard Law School and the Fairbank Center of Harvard College. Professor Woo has published and spoken widely on China's legal reforms, as well as on domestic legal issues involving Asian Americans and gender equality in America. She is the co-author of *American Civil Litigation in Historical, Empirical and Social Context* (Beijing: Law Publishing, Inc; 2001).

PREFACE

The debate over the remarkable economic growth in East Asian societies has tended to emphasize the importance of universal values, such as 'rule of law', in contrast to traditional, and other culturally specific mechanisms of social and economic organization. It is far from clear what is connoted by such terms, in particular societies. It seems safe to suggest that the use of such terms as 'rule of law' is linked in the minds of many observers to the particular needs of global economic markets. Some observers complain that such heavy emphasis on universalisms denies or denigrates the role of law in traditional society. Others respond that this emphasis overstates the role of law in modern Western social organization. The heart of the matter is that universalisms and localisms do not operate in inevitable contradiction. The tensions between them are balanced as each society gives rise to particular collections of social norms and institutions, including law. By comparing how East Asian societies have accommodated these tensions in dealing with different, specific problems, we hope to learn useful lessons about the potential of law, in all its forms.

This collection of essays, exploring the interactions between law and cultural values, was written in commemoration of the seventy-fifth anniversary of the birth of the late Professor Hiroshi Wagatsuma. Professor Wagatsuma was an anthropologist and social psychologist who devoted his career to the study of comparative identities and legal institutions in East Asia. Sponsored by the Hiroshi Wagatsuma Memorial Fund, the UCLA Asia-Pacific Institute and the UCLA School of Law, a symposium was held in Los Angeles in January 2001 entitled '"Rule of Law" and Group Identities Embedded in Asian Traditions and Cultures'. The symposium at UCLA brought together scholars in sociology, political science, anthropology, economics and law from Japan, Korea, China, Taiwan and the United States. Papers presented at the symposium reflect the interdisciplinary shape of the group, as well as different national perspectives. This book includes nine essays originally presented at the symposium and subsequently revised to take into account the discussions among the participants at the symposium. In addition, an introductory chapter has been written explicitly for this collection to provide greater cohesion while raising further questions.

The elder son of Sakae Wagatsuma, a distinguished legal scholar and Dean of the Tokyo University Law Faculty, Hiroshi received his education at the University of Tokyo, Harvard University and the University of Michigan. He taught in the United States and Japan before joining the Anthropology Department of the University of California, Los Angeles in the early 1970s. While at UCLA, Professor Wagatsuma developed a collaborative relationship with its School of Law, co-teaching courses on Japanese Law and Legal Institutions, as well as writing with Professor Arthur Rosett. Articles co-authored by the two include 'Cultural Attitudes Towards Contract Law: Japan and the United States Compared', *UCLA Pacific Basin Law Journal*, vol. 2, p. 77 (1983) and 'The Implications of Apology: Law and Culture in Japan and the United States', *Law and Society Review*, vol. 20, p. 461 (1986). The collaboration continued after Professor Wagatsuma returned to his native Japan to teach at Tsukuba University in 1983. He died in Tokyo on 25 July 1985.

In remembrance of Professor Hiroshi Wagatsuma, his widow Reiko, other family members, colleagues and friends established a permanent fund at the Center for Pacific Rim Studies at UCLA to further his scholarly interests in Japanese and comparative legal studies. The Hiroshi Wagatsuma Memorial Fund has supported more than a score of doctoral student and faculty research involving field studies in Japan.

We thank all the participants in this very stimulating symposium, who so generously contributed their time and talent. In addition to the authors whose work is included in this volume, Professors Kye Young Park of the UCLA Anthropology Department and Harry Scheiber of the Law Faculty of the University of California, Berkeley helped enormously as discussants.

Charles Cannon and Leigh Iwanaga of the UCLA Law Library and Leslie Evens of the Center for Pacific Rim Studies were indispensable in organizing the project and contributed remarkable skill to the execution of the symposium. Ellis Green contributed professionally to the prepartion of the final manuscript.

Finally, we are grateful for the generous support given this project by the UCLA School of Law, The UCLA Academic Senate Committee on Research, the UCLA International Studies and Overseas Programs, and the UCLA Hiroshi Wagatsuma Memorial Fund.

Arthur Rosett
Lucie Cheng
Margaret Y. K. Woo

1

FINDING A ROLE FOR LAW IN ASIAN DEVELOPMENT

Lucie Cheng, Margaret Y. K. Woo and Arthur Rosett

Introduction

Around the world in recent years there have been two somewhat divergent trends in the role of law in economic and social development. One is the remarkable growth in the use of legal institutions and an apparent global convergence of legal norms in the direction of a universal model. The contrasting trend has been the reassertion of local cultural practices that define group memberships, individual identities and community concepts of justice. How these trends interact and the tensions they represent are telling, not only of the role of law in development, but also of the possible new values and/or institutions that may emerge.

The global/local dichotomy is particularly relevant in light of the continued assertion of conventional myths about the East's distinctive cultures. While the recent wave of law and development activities assumes the centrality of law in economic growth, the generally accepted account for East Asia is that its persistent culture, rather than universal law, contributed more to the East Asian economic miracle. Early evidence on the course of economic development in East Asia seems to challenge the utility of a 'one size fits all' universal legal framework. Yet even in East Asia, global legal reforms are proceeding with unprecedented pace in the face of re-emerging local culture.

The tension between the local and the universal has a further dimension in East Asia, where nations that have in the past shared a common language and culture, in recent times have experienced divided histories, politics and economies. These divided communities assign different roles to law in dealing with global and local forces. In such a transitional flux, it is often uncertain whether the new sense of the centrality of law is redefining group identities in East Asia, or whether culturally embedded identities are reshaping law and legal institutions. Will the future be marked by legal uniformity, or particularization?

The thesis underlying this volume is that these two trends – global legal convergence and reassertion of local cultural practices – are not only intertwined, but that there are also supportive connections between the global and local approaches to legal development. Culturally embedded modes of organization are not polar opposites to a rule of law; instead, they are interacting aspects of a dynamic society. Both local culture and a universal rule of law are features in contemporary social development. Their interplay is the critical foundation from which new and more adaptive values and institutions can emerge.

Precisely because law is not simply juxtaposed to culture, but can instead be a particularly 'active locus for the contestation of cultural meanings',[1] law is an appropriate site for examining the tenaciously claimed divide between East and West, and the creation of specific cultural identities. Similarly, precisely because law can also be a codification of 'universal' ideals, law is an appropriate site for examining the force of global and universal forces, and the strength of law in development. Chapters in this volume focus specifically on law in selected East Asian countries, on how the law defines and redefines cultural identities, and on how legal institutions defy global/local forces.

Importantly, what we can learn from the East Asian legal regimes may be instructive of legal transformation not simply in East Asia, but in other areas as well. Rather than the one-way flow of legal institutions that was characteristic of imperial powers and their colonies, there can be reciprocal exchange between Asia and the rest of the world. The East Asian context can add to the picture, rendering our understanding of universal values richer, fuller and more 'universal'. East Asia can add a more pluralistic and contextual understanding of 'rule of law'.

Global convergence and local practices

Proponents of global markets and the expansion of international capital flows predict the convergence of values and cultures, the adoption of universal rights over particular traditions and beliefs, and the development of new global norms in place of local values.[2] Markets, they argue, are the panacea for the ills associated with economic development; and law, with its ability to ensure a stable property regime, is necessary to sustain developing markets. The legal regime and the values associated with the promotion of markets, in turn, are most often based on the perspective of the self-interested, unencumbered individual. The assumption is that economic development for most countries is accompanied by a progression to markets with the adoption of impartial, rational self- over group identities and the assertion of universal laws over local customs. In such a way, free markets are often deemed synonymous with democracy, universal rights and rule of law. Hence we see a variety of market development and rule of law programs around the world promulgated by such institutions as the World Bank, the International Monetary Fund, and the Asian Development Bank.[3]

Moreover, the practicalities of a global marketplace compel the convergence of legal norms with greater urgency. Some observers claim that economic convergence means legal convergence as well. As international economic transactions aided by technology increasingly lead to complex legal problems without borders, these scholars predict a globalization of legal practice.[4] They call for a paradigmatic shift in the ways that legal systems learn from each other. The eventual result would be that ancient distinctions between systems, such as the role assigned to the judge in stating and interpreting the law, and the differing approach taken to such procedural issues as the use of juries and the allocation of costs of litigation including legal fees, the relative availability to judges of effective judicial remedies and workable rules of proof all would fade or merge.[5] A project of the American Law Institute even seeks to develop a model set of transnational litigation rules, drawing on consensus from other systems, to be adopted by all nations.[6] Judges in this new regime will cooperate in 'equal but distinct legal spheres, to the presumption of an integrated global legal system'.[7]

Yet the persistence of bubbling ethnic, racial and national tensions in many parts of the world suggests that other forces are at work. Globalist ideas are reflected in the numerous efforts toward economic and political integration. Particularist ideas can be seen in resurgent nationalism and the rise of political movements based on identity politics, multiculturalism and communitarian ideals.[8] Challenges to the universalist claims of rule of law, markets and the unencumbered self range from those who question whether certain values are truly universal to those who question the validity of universalism itself. These critiques and arguments take the form of communitarian theorist debates, nationalist government policies, and even religious fundamentalist movements.

The debate between universalism and local values takes its most tangible form in the human rights arena, where supporters of the universalist school have argued for the force of law, the impartial self, and the universality of certain basic rights.[9] The argument is that if one has rights simply because one is a human being, then these rights are universal by definition.[10] Critics of the universalist school, in contrast, challenge the assumptions that the human in 'human rights' is necessarily an individual and that the rights are protections against the collective. They point out that '[o]ne cannot have a right as an abstract individual. Rather, one has a right as a member of a particular group and tradition within a given context'.[11] Others argue against the idea of a 'universal' foundational narrative serving as the standard by which all progress must be judged, and that progress is understood as a 'spiral where there is continual convergence concerning groups and where differences are ultimately transcended'.[12]

Underlying the discussion is, of course, a more fundamental philosophical difference between global humanists who believe in willed and idealistic individual conduct and an impartial morality,[13] and cultural theorists who speak of embedded selves. Universalist moral philosophers believe that some common ideas and principles are shared by humanity, although these ideas and principles work themselves out in different ways in different societies. By contrast, cultural theorists maintain that moral codes and principles always arise within a particular culture and are always addressed to members with particular identities and roles within that culture.[14]

We see an extreme form of the debate in a nascent political movement spurred by communitarians, who urge the re-elevation of community values and social duties that allegedly have been devalued by an ethos of individual rights in US law. Sometimes the debate aligns communitarianism with nationalism, and universalism with liberal values. Thus, as Robert Goodin has written:

> Nationalists, like communitarians, emphasize the various and nefarious ways in which individuals are embedded within particular communities – communities constituted in turn by self-consciously shared identities, defined in terms of race or place or history or religion or whatever. Liberals, like cosmopolitans more generally, emphasize what is common across all those communities – universal standards and a shared humanity.[15]

A more specific criticism challenges the supposed link between markets and rule of law as universal values.[16] For such critics, the associated emphasis on individualism amounts simply to a preference for Western values, no more and no less. Modernization theorists project an inevitable progression toward formal, rational law and the unfettered pursuit of self-interest by all players in market economies. Others deny that such links are inevitable. They point out that the value of rationality, along with the concept of an impartial law, has as its object the unencumbered individual and is traceable to Enlightenment roots and the liberal Western tradition.[17] Imposition of these Western values on other societies would represent cultural insensitivity at best, and imperialistic hegemony at worst. Such critiques have spurred leading liberal political philosophers such as John Rawls to reconsider whether their conceptions of justice are something particularly Western and liberal, or are universal.[18]

Still others challenge the hypothesis that global competitive pressures will lead to a convergence toward efficient rules and broader regulatory regimes.[19] The danger here is that 'efficient' rules may paradoxically foster mono-cultural conformity or force a 'be more like us' scenario. Yet if we take the contrary view to argue for implicit cultural essentialism, we may become prisoners of our own legal history and tradition. Will it be local configurations or external pressures that will dictate the trajectory of legal transplantation, reforms and convergence?

East Asia as a special case?

In the context of East Asia, these questions take on added relevance in light of the continued assertion of the conventional myth about the East's distinctive and unique culture. Numerous articles from both sides of the Pacific have argued that East Asia is fundamentally different from the West in culture, history and tradition. The Chinese government, in particular, has argued for the cultural divide as it proclaims a reform based on 'socialism with Chinese characteristics'.[20] Other governments, such as Singapore's, have claimed exceptions to international standards based on Asian values, which are unique or distinctly different from Western norms. Will East Asia, with all its internal diversities, converge with the West as it develops, or will it resist Westernization in setting an alternative trajectory based upon its distinctive cultures?

An East/West divide has also been suggested with respect to the role of law. The popular assumption is that law has had a limited role in Asian cultures and economies. It was only in the nineteenth century that Western legal concepts were introduced to Asia, along with imperialism. The recent economic development boom of East Asia challenges the supposed relationship between the growth of capitalism and formal rational law. Confucian ethics are said to still dominate there, dictating an emphasis on duty over rights, custom over legislation, and a preference for discretion over legal rules. For such scholars as Carol Jones and Jane Kaufman Winn, the persistent East Asian cultural preference for *guanxi* (rule of relationship) and 'familism' (the family and clan bases that underlie many Asian businesses) in the face of a thriving market economy may mean that an alternative trajectory exists for East Asia, namely one based on the co-existence of rule of law and a rule of relationship.[21]

Despite the continuing influence of Confucian ethics and the rule of relationships, the debate over the path of economic development in East Asian societies has increasingly emphasized the growing importance of 'rule of law' and the diminution of traditional and other culturally specific mechanisms of social and economic control. There is an expectation that over time there will be a convergence with Western, more rule-based legal systems as Asia moves more toward a market economy. But it is far from clear what this convergence will look like, nor is it obvious what is connoted by the term 'rule of law' in various East Asian societies. Could there be an East Asian model of law and development as some, including Kanishka Jayasuriya, have argued – one that recognizes the strength of the state and the use of legal institutions in state building, rather than the assumed Western liberal model of a limited state?[22]

Culture and legal interpretation

Certainly, if law is an arena for the contestation of cultural meanings,[23] then law is an appropriate site for the examination of the tenacity of the claimed East/West divide. Whether law reflects global or local values, universal or particularistic norms, understanding law requires an appreciation of the context that lies in the minds and culture of those involved in fashioning an interpretation and implementation of the law. Law is said 'to be embedded in a culture's way of life and in the thinking processes of those who must administer and interpret and abide by the law'.[24]

Rule of law is often linked to the felt desire to better serve the particular needs of global economic markets. Observed local practices that are organized around traditional social links are frequently criticized as arbitrary, irrational and corrupt. However, this limited analysis either denies or denigrates the role of law in traditional Asian society, overstates the role of law in Western social organization, and understates the role of culturally embedded practices in all contemporary social and economic organizations.

Furthermore, one must remember that law is constitutive as well as expressive of culture and values. Apart from the debate over whether universal or local values are reflected in law, there is the question of whether law, as an institution, is a force in itself affecting the society around it. The idea is that 'it is not social norms of a particular type which give rise to specific institutions, but on the contrary, specific institutions that give rise to a particular collection of social norms'.[25] Social institutions, including law, are, as Robert Grafstein has lucidly put it, 'social forces in their own right'.[26]

Critical scholarship also treats law as a dimension of culture. Law is 'an arena for the performance and contestation of representation of self and as an influence on the roles and identities available to groups and individuals in portraying themselves'.[27] Law creates boundaries in the sense that 'it helps to shape the actions and activities of individuals and groups'. Legal institutions and processes, as distinct from substantive law, may be more embedded in local culture and may be the most resistant to convergence.[28]

The plan of the book

This collection of chapters explores the globalist, localist, universalist and particularist orientations to law in the context of East Asia. How does law contribute to national projects of governance, economic expansion and cultural identity? In so doing, is law the central universalizing principle, or does it reflect or shape particular cultural identities? Perhaps East Asia is just another site for reproducing imperialism and dependence. These essays cross boundaries by being both international and inter-disciplinary. They can be categorized into three groups: the role of law and culturally embedded identities in Asian development; law, national identity and migrant labor; and legal institutions, world norms and culturally embedded practices.

The role of law and culturally embedded identities in Asian development

This first group of chapters explores the theme that law reflects universal norms, encompasses market principles and the protection of individual rights, and is challenged by ethnic and local identities. These chapters then go on to discuss how rule of law may incorporate both global and local values.

In their chapter, 'Property Rights and Indigenous Tradition Among Early Twentieth-century Japanese firms', Yoshiro Miwa and Mark Ramseyer defend the rational choice person and challenge the conclusion that culture trumped formal law in early twentieth-century Japan. They argue for the primacy of rule of law by examining the cotton spinning industry and the practices of the Tokyo and Osaka stock exchanges in early twentieth-century Japan. Despite the generally accepted assumption that developing nations industrialize through banks and only turn to securities markets later, the early twentieth-century Japanese cotton industry secured capital for development through a thriving stock market. Contrary to popular assumptions, Japanese firms did not shy away from the formal legal regime. Firms used laws and courts to enforce corporate charters, and employment contracts to make broadly dispersed equity issues profitable.

Miwa and Ramseyer challenge the contingency of social science and the indeterminacy of institutional structures. They argue that the Japanese experience is consistent with the claim that modern legal institutions overwhelm indigenous organizational frameworks. It is only when modern institutions fail that people return to culturally embedded options. According to Miwa and Ramseyer, modern rational choice theory predicts how people respond to such institutions. Indeed, their thesis is that when a good legal regime is established ('good' meaning neither too much nor too little law), people use it and use it well. Economic incentives matter, and matter in ways that track universal principles. Miwa and Ramseyer conclude that the rule of law generally dominates culturally embedded practices, provided that it avoids the 'rent seeking detritus' of the modern regulatory state.

Underlying the argument, of course, is really a belief in the primacy and universality of economic principles across cultures. Too little law fails to provide basic property rights, and too much law limits choices for contracting parties. When laws parallel rational and universal market principles, they will be followed, but if there is too much law, then indigenous arrangements will be turned to that will better mimic market principles. Indigenous arrangements are therefore second best.

By contrast, Amy Chua, in 'Markets, Democracy and Ethnicity', points out the hidden ethnic identity that refuses to be submerged despite economic and market principles. Chua reminds us of the power of culturally embedded principles. She points out the inherent tension between market capitalism and democracy, particularly when they are overlaid on top of historical ethnic divisions. In many respects, markets and democracy mutually reinforce each other. Indeed, it is in part because markets and democracy appear, at least at first glance, so luxuriously compatible throughout the developing world that the neo-liberal consensus has such a grip. But there is also a deep tension inherent in free market democracy, Chua asserts. She suggests that in all the developed nations this tension has been alleviated by a host of material, political and ideological institutions and devices, not all of which have been admirable, and many of which may not be transferable. These mediating devices have included not just the welfare state (in its widely varying forms) and constitutional rule of law protections, but also various 'market compatible ideologies' such as racism and the myth of upward mobility, as well as historically, massive exclusions from the suffrage.

The second half of Chua's chapter turns to the developing world. Although rarely acknowledged by international policymakers, the conflict between markets and democracy in the developing world is real, combustible, and sometimes lethal. The mediating devices found in the developed world are generally absent from developing countries – an absence made especially problematic given the extent of poverty and the rapidity of democratization. In many developing countries, free market democracy faces an additional, formidable structural problem: the problem of market-dominant ethnic minorities. This distinctive mapping of ethnicity onto class – camouflage in the developed world today – pits an impoverished indigenous majority against an economically dominant outsider minority, converting the paradox of free market democracy into an engine of potentially catastrophic ethnonationalism.

Indeed, Chua reminds us of the inherent tension between markets and democracy, long recognized by leading political philosophers and economists. By making the rich richer and the poor poorer, markets, in conjunction with 'democracy, by empowering the poor majority, would inevitably lead to convulsive acts of expropriation and confiscation'. When these economic divisions occur along ethnic lines, we see the resumption of ethnic strife. This overlay of democratic empowerment to relatively impoverished 'indigenous' majority will lead to a potentially catastrophic form of ethnonationalism. As such, free market democracy is a paradox in terms.

Interestingly, Chua's thesis also depends in part on the universality of economic principles, that is, the poor, being motivated by rational self-interest, would seek to expropriate property for themselves. But unlike Marx or Engels, Chua asserts the power of ethnic identities (and hence cultural alliances) even over class. For her argument, Chua cites a global survey suggesting that markets tend to benefit the economic dominance of certain resented ethnic minorities, while democracy increases the power of relatively impoverished 'indigenous' majorities. Chua predicts that this is likely to result in either actions aimed at eliminating the market-dominant minority, or a pro-market retreat from democracy.

Statistical reports support Chua's proposition when they demonstrate that global capitalism has yet to produce universal prosperity, but instead is associated with greater economic disparities. The World Bank estimates that 1.2 billion people, or a fifth of the world's population, live on less than one US dollar a day. A property rights regime as guaranteed by rule of law is not the be-all and end-all of progress. Rather than market principles alone, what may exist are 'cultural economies'. People around the globe respond to economic rewards and penalties, but those rewards and penalties are seen differently in different cultural contexts.[29]

In sum, when Miwa and Ramseyer see the self-interested individual, Chua sees social identity. On the one hand is the rational actor, while on the other is sociality and group identity. Indeed, under certain institutional conditions, a strict economic rationality of the self-interested individual may prevail, while under others, social norms from a collective identity may achieve a critical importance. Certainly, as Amartya Sen has so aptly pointed out, 'exchange is not the only activity in a society, or even in an economy, and the efficient working even of exchange systems demands more than the basic motivation that drives the desire to buy and sell'.[30] The question, of course, is when does one force overtake the other? In some arenas, could there be other forces at work more powerful than the self-interested utility-maximizing individual?

All departures from self-interested individualism need not mean the automatic embrace of social identity, as defined by history and culture. Social identity may be a matter of discovery and choice, with each of us having a multiplicity of identities to choose from. Nor are all identity choices permanent. As Albert Hirschman has demonstrated, such choices can be 'shifting involvements'.[31] In this shifting involvement, law and legal institutions define and shape our ethnic and national identity.

Furthermore, the inquiry is not limited to whether economic principles dictate or ethnic identification supercedes, but also includes the institutional setup that leads one to dominate the other. For example, legal institutions may serve as a force themselves to protect substantive principles of democracy and justice, apart from their function of promoting economic transactions. Ethnic tensions may be diffused or strict economic criteria readjusted. If democracy means more than just 'representative government and majoritarian rule', then markets and democracy are more compatible and less susceptible to ethnic tensions. In that instance, legal institutions have a greater role to play. If democracy encompasses substantive values of equality and dignity and courts are imbued with the responsibility to protect those values, then the paradox of markets and democracy may not result in turmoil and explosion.

Randall Peerenboom's contribution, 'Competing Conceptions of Rule of Law in China', rounds off this group of chapters by focusing directly on the rule of law in institutions and in its ideal. Peerenboom proposes a skeletal framework for rule of law that seeks to be acceptable across national and cultural lines. Peerenboom's analysis is grounded on his distinction between 'thick' and 'thin' rule of law (analogous to similar conceptions of thin versus thick definitions of democracy).[32] According to Peerenboom, thin rule of law emphasizes procedural protection and hence is less subject to local and cultural values and bias. Thick rule of law, in contrast, encompasses substantive elements of political morality, and thus is more likely to run across cultural and historically embedded practices. Furthermore, Peerenboom suggests that in the context of present-day China, four conceptions or ideal types are dominant: liberal democratic, Chinese communitarian, neo-authoritarian and statist socialist. Each ideal type is characterized by a distinct economic and political regime and by distinctive institutions, rules and practices.

In his chapter, Peerenboom captures the debate in contemporary China on the nature of rule of law. Historically, the conception of rule of law is integrally related to the rise of liberal democracy in the West. Indeed, for many, ' rule of law' *means* a liberal democratic version of rule of law. There is, however, little support for liberal democracy, and hence a liberal democratic rule of law, among state leaders, legal scholars, intellectuals or the general public in China. Accordingly, if we are to understand the likely path of development of China's system and the reasons for the difference in its institutions, rules, practices and outcomes in particular cases, we need to rethink rule of law. We need to avoid assuming a Western liberal democratic framework, and explore alternative conceptions of rule of law that are more consistent with China's circumstances. Peerenboom concludes that China is in transition towards some version of rule of law that meets the minimal requirements of a thin theory.

Peerenboom's model limits the universal conception of rule of law to thin or procedural conceptions of rule of law. Thick conceptions, according to Peerenboom, must by necessity and definition sit in an inseparable political and economic context – e.g. liberal democratic, statist socialist, etc. One could question whether this effectively renders rule of law subject to cultural relativism, and thereby toothless to defend its most basic function, namely 'to impose meaningful restraints on the state and individual members of the ruling elite'. For example, the neo-authoritarian version of rule of law is one in which the political regime is a single state, whose purpose is to 'balance between law as a means of strengthening the state and limiting the state', but with the balance more in favor of strengthening the state.

A similar point may be made with regard to the thin rule of law – defined along procedural grounds as a fair, stable, prospective, transparent, enforceable legal system. As the thin conception of rule of law can grant discretion in the state through procedural formalities, does it provide a sufficient basis for protecting fundamental human rights? Rather than focusing on the integrity of the process, is there a conception of rule of law that would support motivations that, normatively speaking, are good in themselves or will lead to good and just outcomes? Is this something we should strive for?[33]

Importantly, Peerenboom's analysis documents the diversity of present debates among Chinese legal scholars and practitioners about the concept of rule of law. Peerenboom's more refined categories effectively capture the nuances surrounding the 'rule of law' debates, and bridge the gap between unquestioning universal claims of rule of law and contesting cultural particularism. In the flourishing of these discourses, we see that statist law is not always uncontested or uniform. Peerenboom's model brings out the complexities that are often ignored by the dichotomy of universalism and culture, and warns us about the dangers of neglecting the interplay between the two.

Law, national identity and migrant labor

Powerful global economic pressures have led to migrations within and without national borders. Transnational and national labor migration and global norms of human rights have forced law to redefine citizenship status and social identities. How are these legal responses mediated by culturally embedded practices and identities? In turn, how do legal institutions shape the boundaries of cultural definitions of identity? Answers to such questions necessarily implicate the antinomies of nationalism and localism, citizenship and foreignness, community and officialdom. The three chapters that follow consider the position and rights of outsiders, foreigners and minority group members in the East Asian labor market, and the cultural representation of who belongs and what belonging means in the migration and labor law setting.

Accelerated globalization and regional economic change in the last two decades have led to the development of an Asian market for transnational migrant labor. Far from being a transitory phenomenon, the persistent existence of foreign workers in many Asian cities has challenged both the state and society in terms of identity formation, racialism, citizenship and human rights. In those countries ruled by a form of market democracy, public discourses on the migrant labor issue have shaped the laws, regulations and practices *vis-à-vis* the employment and treatment of the foreign workers. These discourses often reflect deep-seated prejudice and xenophobia, as well as economic and political concerns. More recently, world cultural norms promoted by local and international non-government organizations (NGOs) have also come into play. The threat, however vague, of supra-state intervention in the forms of international legal institutions and transnational NGOs on behalf of migrant labor has become an element in progressive state policy formation.

At the same time, the need to regulate foreign labor also offers the state an opportunity to define itself. These labor laws and regulations take on expressive meaning for parties and observers against the background of legal norms that regulate or recognize identities. This line-drawing is even more challenging in divided nations such as North and South Korea analyzed by Chulwoo Lee, China and Taiwan by Lucie Cheng, and even in, as Dorothy Solinger points out in her chapter, the internally divided labor market of domestic China. We see in these chapters how nationality conflicts and competes with feelings of nationalism, local identities with national projects, and social practices with legal rhetoric.

International law scholars such as Thomas Franck have argued that, when free of unnecessary communal contracts, 'individuals will freely choose multilayered affinities and complex, variegated interpersonal loyalties that redefine community without the loss of social responsibility'.[34] The chapters suggest how national governments through law can redefine and circumscribe these voluntary associations in the context of such global forces as transnational law, as well as global human rights norms. Where law has variously been argued as an arena for 'composing, representing, and contesting identity',[35] national laws have redefined citizenship status and cultural identities.

The cases of Taiwan and South Korea present contrasting comparative opportunities. Because Taiwan and South Korea share many common cultural, political and economic characteristics, including a history of Japanese colonization, their respective legal framework, policies and treatment of foreign workers show considerable similarities. Generally speaking, in both countries, unskilled or semi-skilled foreign migrant workers became visible in the 1980s, after a period of sharp economic growth. Policies concerning these workers evolved gradually, with structured institutional mechanisms to insure their 'cheap labor' role. Faced with pressures to be 'modern', both governments then instituted laws and regulations more liberal than actual practice. There is considerable discrepancy between the letter of law and its implementation. The Nationality Acts of both countries until very recently (1997 in South Korea and 2000 in Taiwan) showed historical gender inequality by denying children of foreign fathers eligibility for citizenship.

More interestingly, however, there are differences among the similarities. Both Taiwan and South Korea face the problem of how to define the legal status of fellow ethnics migrating from their socialist halves. Yet, as pointed out by Lucie Cheng and Chulwoo Lee in their respective chapters, how each of these countries deals with this problem varies depending on the different state-building projects pursued in Taiwan and South Korea. While Taiwan is moving in the direction of exclusion by 'other-izing' mainland Chinese, South Korea by contrast is turning in the direction of inclusion by adopting a policy in which North Koreans are 'us'. By juxtaposing the two cases, Cheng and Lee's chapters help us gain a more refined understanding of the relationship between law and society, and the manner in which law balances the goal of national development with shaping ethnic and group identity.

Specifically, Lucie Cheng, in 'Transnational Labor, Citizenship and the Taiwan State', examines the legal status of transnational migrant labor in Taiwan. Her chapter traces the development of legal institutions, bureaucratic structures and private corporations that are charged with the control and regulation of foreign workers. Cheng analyzes how notions of nationality and rights help to differentiate 'us' from 'them', and how these differentiations are retained and changed under contemporary economic and political considerations in the treatment of migrant labor.

In the process, Cheng also points out how the traditional relationship between law and bureaucracy in Taiwan find expression in the context of a modern state. Taiwan's policies on foreign labor are a combination of capitalist competition, complex class struggles within a global economy, and a state steeped in economic developmentalism. According to Cheng, as Taiwan seeks to construct its own national identity and establish a new state, it has to 'other-ize' the Mainland Chinese that it originally purported to represent.

Addressing similar theoretical issues, Chulwoo Lee places emphasis on a comparison of the status of Korean nationals, 'overseas compatriots' and aliens in the South Korean labor market. In his chapter, '"Us" and "Them" in Korean Law: The Creation, Accommodation and Exclusion of Outsiders in South Korea', Lee points out the ambiguous provisions of the Nationality Act, and discusses how the presence of migrant workers has stimulated Koreans to rethink their national self-image and identity. This process has increased the pressure for an improvement in the treatment of ethnic Chinese residents in Korea, whose discontent has been neglected for many years. Recent efforts to stabilize the status of these residents may have implications for foreigners with different backgrounds and identities from other countries.

When South Koreans look at their treatment of foreign workers and Chinese ethnics in Korea, they often become self-critical of the exclusionary implications and consequences of their national identity and nationalism. Historically, nationalism has been the supreme value in modern Korean history, serving as the prime force in the struggle for liberation from Japanese rule and national unification. It derives much of its force from a strong tradition of proto-nationalism inculcated through past dynasties. Yet the concept is now shedding its primordialist mystifications and is being subjected to critical scrutiny. On the other hand, many approaches to overseas Koreans draw their inspiration from an ethnic nationalism, and it is when appealing to such an ideology that the greatest popular support can be enlisted in South Korea for improving the treatment of those people.

While Cheng and Lee focus their attention on transnational labor, Dorothy Solinger's chapter is concerned with the status of domestic migrant workers within China. In 'Internal Migrants and the Challenge of the "Floating Population" in the PRC', Solinger addresses six antinomies that Chinese peasant migrants to cities must navigate: nationalism and localism, citizenship and foreignness, community and officialdom, the rhetoric of rights and the reality of an absence of rights, the socialist superstructure and capitalism, and above all, the market and the law. In reviewing each of these conflicts, Solinger characterizes the challenges of the Chinese peasant migrant population or 'floating population', as they are called, and how they affect the triangular tie between state, local society and alien in Chinese cities today and over the past two decades.

Drawing on her many publications on the topic, Solinger argues that rural migrants in big cities of China, though they are citizens by Chinese law, are not 'true' citizens in that they do not enjoy the rights or benefits normally associated with citizenship. Chinese rural migrants do not enjoy a form of valid, official membership in or affiliation with the city, and consequently are not recipients of state-disbursed goods. Unprotected by Chinese laws, these urban residents of rural origin live by their own local community rules that lack any reference to the laws of the central state. Solinger concludes that because both the economic market and law are underdeveloped in China, they appear to be in conflict with each other. The nascent legal institutions cannot truly govern market transactions, nor can the marketplace mature into a site of safety until law in China develops further. As Solinger points out, 'Migrants [who are] ill treated and excluded economically cannot call upon a calculable politics or a stable law to bail them out'.

Although Solinger deals exclusively with domestic migrants, her conclusions are applicable to transnational migrants in Taiwan and South Korea. The lack of legal status leads to the same abuses and victimization by institutional structures and practices faced by domestic migrants in China, as those confronting illegally and legally admitted foreign workers in Taiwan and South Korea. In all three chapters, we see how law interacts with culture in defining and redefining the boundaries of citizenship, shaping and reshaping group identities in the context of global economic pressures.

Legal institutions, world norms and culturally embedded practices

The final chapters deal with legal institutions specifically and the associated culturally embedded practices in East Asia. While the emergence of world norms has undeniably put pressure on culturally embedded practices, these norms do not always displace traditional ways of doing things. World norms may be embodied in codified laws, but the actual application of these laws may not follow such global norms. This group of chapters, following on the previous chapters, discusses the possibility that local law may formally incorporate world norms, but actual applications of the law may depend on local institutions and practices in which the traditional and the local continue to exert strong influence. This can be seen in legal institutions such as the courts studied by Stanley Lubman, the legal profession examined by William Alford, and legal education as described by Kahei Rokumoto.

Rokumoto's chapter connects the current proposals in Japan for reform and expansion of legal education institutions and professional formation, with the resulting reformation of the judicial system. Academic writings often examine Japanese law and legal processes in terms of stasis and change. Traditional scholarship on Japanese law generally measures the progress of particular institutions and practices against the model of the modern legal order as prescribed in the Constitution of 1946. By contrast, Rokumoto links proposed changes in contemporary Japanese legal institutions to the origins of these institutions during the Meiji period of reconstruction in the last half of the nineteenth century. Rokumoto shifts the perspective from the yardstick of the 1947 Japanese Constitution to ask what is the source of the persistence and resistance to change in Japanese legal institutions. He calls attention to the importance of the historically conditioned structure of the body politic, drawing on the critical needs of late Tokugawa Japan and the early Meiji years. During this time Japanese society was forced to react to foreign pressure, and to create new structures capable of effective governance.

Rokumoto first describes a proposal, currently under discussion, for fundamental reform of Japanese legal education that would have a profound long-term impact on the legal profession as a whole. He summarizes the main features of Japanese legal education and the judicial system that are undergoing change, and then returns to the pre- and post- Meiji Restoration period to sketch the political circumstances in which the modern judicial system was fashioned and its basic characteristics were implanted. The significance of the present efforts to overhaul legal education in Japan is not to be underestimated. This reform project is part of more comprehensive efforts to refurbish the judicial system commissioned by the Judicial Reform Council, established directly in the Cabinet in July 1999. The Council, based on its own intensive research and deliberations, announced in an interim report of November 2000 the recommendation to establish by the year 2003 a new regime of legal education, called the 'Japanese style law school'. The reform aims at expanding the number of new recruits to the legal profession from the present 1,000 to 3,000 annually. Even though this recommendation is only part of the interim report, the Council President declared that it represents a conclusive agreement of the Council members and urged the government and other organizations concerned to begin preparing for its realization.[36]

According to the reform plan, this 'Japanese style law school' would be introduced at graduate level with a three-year program, successful completion of which would be a prerequisite to taking the National Legal Examination. The existing Institute of Legal Research and Training would continue to admit those who have passed the Legal Examination and will confer upon its graduates the opportunity to qualify as judges, prosecutors and private attorneys. The present law faculties with their undergraduate law programs would also be preserved, but their curricula would be modified to fit the new scheme. It is contemplated that an average of 70–80 per cent of the annual graduates from law schools would be admitted to the Institute, a big leap from the current pass rate of 3 per cent on the Legal Examination. The proposed reform provides an example of how traditional legal institutions can be modified to meet the needs of a global economy and to fit international norms.

In 'Of Lawyers Lost and Found: Searching for Legal Professionalism in the People's Republic of China', William Alford focuses on the growth of the legal profession in China. There has been an exponential increase in the size of the Chinese legal profession over the past twenty years. This growth has been accompanied by important changes in the organization, formation, education, functional role and relationship to officialdom since the end of the Mao era in the mid-1970s. In the intervening years the Chinese bar has expanded from 3,000 members to more than 175,000, with the announced goal of 300,000 lawyers by the end of the current decade. The few lawyers that existed in 1981 were referred to as 'state legal workers' but the current statute describes lawyers as professionals, with duties to society as well as to the state. All law firms were under direct state ownership at the beginning of the period, and now about a third are organized as partnerships or collectives run by their owners.

Alford takes issue with the conventional wisdom that has equated the expansion of the bar and of enacted laws with the growth of rule of law and respect for legality. He points out that resort to law and lawyers is still very much the exception in Chinese affairs. The Communist Party continues to be the repository of political power and is the single most consequential actor economically, yet it also remains above the law. The Party remains involved in the selection and supervision of judicial personnel and sometimes in the decision of individual suits. China remains fundamentally an administrative state, still dependent upon administrative processes in which lawyers have little, if any, part to play representing clients.

Based on his fieldwork in China, Alford points out that the rise of the legal profession is a more complex phenomenon with the potential to retard, as well as promote, legality. He suggests that the expansion of the Chinese bar has been accompanied by increased corruption, with lawyers often a conduit for, if not the instigators of such behavior. Some outside observers believe such problems will decline in importance as lawyers are increasingly professionalized. That may happen, but then again it may not. The Chinese legal profession remains interwoven with the party-state, which is far more involved with the professional lives of lawyers than most foreign observers acknowledge. At least some lawyers benefit from the economic and political status quo and have little reason to welcome further reform. The profit motive of lawyers may sap the ideological content of the party-state's efforts at political control, but we need to consider the possibility that the activity of lawyers may reinforce the Party's hold on power and impede rather than facilitate the movement toward a liberal rule of law in China. Alford suggests that at least some in the Chinese bar, and particularly elite business legal practitioners in the capital, have struck a Faustian bargain with the party-state, accepting a good material life, prestige and security in return for forgoing some of the attributes of professionalism as it is understood in the West.

Alford suggests that the failure of American scholars to better understand the Chinese legal profession has three principal causes. The first lies in a failure to examine Chinese society with adequate care, in part owing to hubris about the universality of American models. The second lies in a broader lack of familiarity with legal systems beyond the common law. The third has to do with the simplistic and romanticized vision of the history of the American bar that informs many activists in exporting American models of lawyering. Alford sums up the argument by asking:

> Why is [it], then, that we are so inclined to see lawyers in the PRC as, in effect, junior colleagues – cut from the same cloth as their American brethren, but needing a bit more tailoring before their professional attire fits them as smartly as we like to think ours fits us (or at least once did)? The answer is in some respects quite obvious, in others appreciably less so. Ironically, the more obvious respects are those concerning the supposedly exotic Orient, the less apparent those much closer to home, linked to the ways in which we American lawyers and legal academics think of the very profession we seek to propagate.

Most of the chapters in this book look at tension between local and global influences on the legal system in operation from the perspective of the actors in the Asian country who must accommodate conflicting pressures in the course of development. Alford's analysis considers some of the same conflicts, but from the perspective of the non-Asian observer whose vision is obscured by his or her particular ideological, historical and cultural baggage. What is embedded is in the eyes of the observer, instead of in the eyes of the observed actor. The task of the observer is thus more complex than it originally seemed.

Stanley Lubman, in 'Chinese Courts and Law Reform in Post-Mao China', summarizes the state of Chinese courts after twenty years of reform to speculate on the prospects for further necessary reforms of the judicial system. Economic reforms that began in 1979 and have continued at a varying pace have propelled law into a more prominent role than it has held at any time in Chinese history: Law has been incorporated into governance of the Chinese party-state, a legal framework for the market economy has been constructed by an astounding outpouring of legislation, and courts and the legal profession have been rebuilt.

As impressive as the efforts to build new institutions, the tasks of deepening their power and broadening their reach continue to face critical difficulties. According to Lubman, residual Maoist ideology and unreformed Maoist institutions, and new forces unleashed by the economic reforms themselves, as well as traditional Chinese legal culture, have conspired to retard further legal reforms. Chinese courts operate against a background of extraordinary confusion regarding the hierarchy of norms that are issued at both central and local level. Courts also must operate in the face of vast discretion exercised by the Chinese bureaucracy at all levels.

Most visible, Lubman contends, is the current atmosphere of legislative chaos. The reform era has seen the expansion of the legislative power of provincial governments, and more than twenty functional bureaucracies of the central government. The State Council, which heads the central government bureaucracy, supervises more than sixty departments including ministries, commissions, administrations and offices. Each of these levels of government exercises authority to issue regulations that implement specific legislation, either under a specific grant of power by a legislative body such as the National Peoples Congress Standing Committee, or by wielding a general rule-making power that is deemed to be inherent in the agencies and enables them to issue any rule that is necessary to carry out their functions in the hesitantly developing field of administrative law.

Lubman concludes that on balance, the overall thrust of the past twenty years of reform efforts has been positive, and further encouraging efforts are underway to advance judicial reform. These efforts add coherence to Chinese law-making and continue the development of administrative law. Chinese legal institutions are slowly becoming increasingly differentiated and functionally specialized, changes that promise to expand rights and rights-consciousness. Further reform continues to be deterred or slowed, however, by formidable obstacles that arise out of both the Chinese party-state and Chinese society.

Conclusion: bringing universal norms and local practices together

When the notion of rule of law is too closely connected to the particular needs of global economic markets, there is a tendency to criticize local practices organized around traditional social links as arbitrary, irrational and corrupt. This tendency inaccurately denies the role played by law in traditional and modern Asian societies. It also overstates the role of law in Western social organization. Most importantly, it fails to place adequate weight or recognition on the potential role of culturally embedded practices in all modern social and economic organizations.

The message of this book is that the successful use of law and legal institutions requires an appreciation of the social context and the local cultures of those who use the law, and who therefore must interpret and implement it. Formal codes are made by persons who respond primarily to global and national concerns. These laws take on meaning, however, only when they are interpreted in the context of specific transactions, typically by persons whose concerns are more local.

East Asian societies are under pressure to make their legal attitudes conform to global expectations. They may formally adopt laws and legal institutions that will satisfy the demands of their partners, but the application of such norms, no matter how they are formally stated in codes and conventions, will not always reflect the law in practice or action, which will continue to reflect local values and methods.

The result of this gap between formal law and law in practice, is that law is not homogenous in practice, although it may be universally identical in formal statement. Global markets and politics pressurize developing societies into converging toward universal norms. When the global solution to a problem does not satisfy cultural values, however, people will be led to seek familiar and local solutions that conform to their sense of justice and right.

Law is not just reflective of social attitudes, but constitutes them as well.[37] Law is an agent of change and shapes political practices and identities. Law decides who is 'us' and who belongs to 'them'. The East Asian experience indicates both the opportunities and the limits of law. That experience also suggests that striking a balance between global and embedded local interests is not a task that can be accomplished once and for all. Rather, the interplay of the two is iterative and dynamic.

Notes

1 Anthony G. Amsterdam and Jerome Bruner, *Minding The Law* (Cambridge MA: Harvard University Press, 2000) p. 15.

2 There is even a Global Citizen Millenium Award that is presented to an 'outstanding individual who transcends national boundaries; works tirelessly for all peoples and their universal human rights; focuses the world's attention on pressing human and social conditions by being a moral witness to the process of peace and reconciliation'.

The award recipient is supposed to embody the leadership, responsibility and promise of global citizenship.

3 See World Bank, 'Legal Institutions and the Rule of Law', in *World Development Report 1996: From Plan to Market* (New York: Oxford University Press, 1996); Asian Development Bank, *Law and Development at the Asian Development Bank* (Asian Development Bank, 1998). For a good critique of some of the aid programmes in the United States, see Thomas Carothers, *Aiding Democracy: The Learning Curve* (Carnegie Endowment for International Peace, 1999).

4 For example, Anne-Marie Slaughter calls it 'judicial globalization', a process of judicial interaction across, above and below borders, exchanging ideas and cooperating in cases involving national as much as international courts. Anne-Marie Slaughter, 'Judicial Convergence', *Virginia Journal of International Law*, vol. 40 (2000) pp. 1103–4.

5 See e.g. Linda S. Mullenix, 'Lessons From Abroad: Complexity and Convergence', *Villanova Law Review*, vol. 46 (2001) p. 1.

6 American Law Institute, UNIDROIT, Principles and Rules of 'Transnational Civil Procedure, Discussion Draft' No. 3 (8 April 2002) (Professors Geoffrey C. Hazard Jr and Michele Taruffo, reporters).

7 Anne-Marie Slaughter, 'Judicial Globalization', *Virginia Journal of International Law*, vol. 40 (2000) p. 1115.

8

> Particularist ideas are reflected not only in the recent resurgence of nationalism as a political force but also in the idea of multiculturalism, in the emergence of communitarianism as a nascent political movement and in the tendency toward ethnic or communal fragmentation and conflict in many parts of the world. Globalist ideas are reflected in the various steps toward greater economic, technological and political integration that have been trumpeted with such fanfare in recent years.
>
> (Samuel Scheffler, 'Liberalism, Nationalism and Egalitarianism', in Robert McKim and Jeff McMahan, *The Morality of Nationalism* [New York: Oxford University Press, 1997] p. 192)

9 In discussing the tensions between universal human rights and sovereignty, Thomas Franck outlined the historical role of the United Nations in promoting global values. As recently as last year, Kofi Annan, Secretary-General of the United Nations, called on states to redefine national interests that will encourage the pursuit of such UN Charter values as 'democracy, pluralism, human rights, and the rule of law'. Thomas M. Franck, 'Are Human Rights Universal?', *Foreign Affairs*, vol. 80, no. 1 (January-February 2001) p. 194.

10 For good discussions of the theories underlying human rights, see Charles Beits, *Political Theory and International Relations* (Princeton: Princeton University Press, 1979); Jack Donnelly, *International Human Rights: Theory and Practice*, 2nd edn (Boulder: Westview Press, 1998); Alison Dundes Renteln, *International Human Rights: Universalism versus Relativism* (Newbury Park CA: Sage, 1990).

11 See e.g. Adeno Addis, 'Rights, Individualism, Communitarianism and the Ethnic Minorities', *Notre Dame Law Review*, vol. 67 (1991) p. 615; Mary Ann Glendon, *Rights Talk: The Impoverishment of Political Discourse* (Cambridge MA: Harvard University Press, 1991) p. 109.

12 Adeno Addis, 'On Human Diversity and the Limits of Toleration', in Will Kymlicka and Ian Shapiro (eds) *Ethnicity and Group Rights* (New York: New York University Press, 1997) pp. 69–104.

13 Stephen Nathanson, 'Nationalism and the Limits of Global Humanism', in Robert McKim and Jeff McMahan (eds) *The Morality of Nationalism* (New York: Oxford University Press, 1997) p. 176.

14 Thus, while Kantians philosophers typically insist that justice springs from reason and only reason can impose universal and unconditional moral obligations, Hegelian-Marxists proposes the idea that the so-called moral law is, at best, a handy abbreviation for a concrete web of social practices. Ron Bontekoe and Marietta Stepaniants, *Justice and Democracy: Cross-Cultural Perspectives* (Honolulu: University of Hawaii Press, 1997) pp. 11, 13.

15 Robert E. Goodin, 'Conventions and Conversions, or Why is Nationalism Sometimes So Nasty?', in Robert McKim and Jeff McMahan (eds) *The Morality of Nationalism* (New York: Oxford University Press, 1997) p. 88.

16 See e.g. Kanishka Jayasuriya (ed.) *Law, Capitalism and Power in Asia: The Rule of Law and Legal Institutions* (New York: Routledge, 1999); Carol A. G. Jones, 'Capitalism, Globalization and Rule of Law: An Alternative Trajectory of Legal Change in China', *Social and Legal Studies*, vol. 3 (1994) pp. 195–220.

17 John D. Ver der Vyver, 'Constitutional Options for Post-Apartheid South Africa', *Emory Law Journal*, vol. 50 (1991) pp. 774–7; Michel Rosenfeld, 'Can Human Rights Bridge The Gap Between Universalism and Cultural Relativism? A Pluralist Assessment Based on Rights of minorities', *Columbia Human Rights Law Review*, vol. 30 (1990) pp. 249–284.

18 John Rawls, 'The Law of Peoples', in Stephen Shute and Susan Hurley (eds) *On Human Rights: The Oxford Amnesty Lectures 1993* (New York: Basic Books, 1993).

19 See discussion in Steven K. Vogel, *Freer Markets, More Rules: Regulatory Reform in Advanced Industrial Countries* (Ithaca NY: Cornell University Press, 1996).

20 For a discussion of China and the global human rights regime, see e.g. Rosemary Foot, *Rights Beyond Borders: The Global Community and the Struggle Over Human Rights in China* (Oxford: Oxford University Press, 2000); Melanne Andromecca, 'Comparative Analysis of International and Chinese Human Rights Law: Universalism versus Cultural Relativism', *Buffalo Journal of International Law*, vol. 2 (winter 1995–6) p. 285.

21 See Carol A. G. Jones, 'Capitalism, Globalization and Rule of Law: An Alternative Trajectory of Legal Change in China', *Social and Legal Studies*, vol. 3 (1994) pp. 195–220; Jane Kaufman Winn, 'Relational Practices and the Marginalization of Law: Informal Financial Practices of Small Businesses in Taiwan', *Law and Society Review*, vol. 28, no. 2 (1994) pp. 193–232. See also 'Pitman Potter, Guanxi and the PRC Legal system: From Contradiction to Complementarity', paper prepared for the Wilson Center for Scholars Seminar on Civil Society in China, February 9, 2000, Washington DC; Teemu Ruskola, 'Conceptualization Corporations and Kinship: Comparative Law and Development Theory in a Chinese Perspective', *Stanford Law Review*, vol. 52 (2000) p. 1599.

22 Jayasuriya Kanishka, 'Introduction: A Framework For Analysis', in Jayasuriya Kanishka (ed.) *Law, Capitalism and Power in Asia: The Rule of Law and Legal Institutions* (New York: Routledge, 1999) p. 13.

23 Of course, anthropologists themselves are divided as to the meaning of culture. Some regard it 'as a set of institutional arrangements that provide the consensual pattern for the commonplace exchanges constituting communal life in a society', and others see it 'as an ensemble of ways of thinking, feeling, and believing shared by the members of the society'. But both forms of description – outside in institutional and inside out subjective – are indispensable. 'Neither institutional arrangements alone nor shared subjectivity can capture the curious complexity of human cultures'. Anthony G. Amsterdam and Jerome Bruner, *Minding The Law* (Cambridge MA: Harvard University Press, 2000) p. 15.

24 Anthony G. Amsterdam and Jerome Bruner, *Minding The Law* (Cambridge MA: Harvard University Press, 2000) p. 287.
25 Bo Rothstein, *Just Institutions Matter: The Moral and Political Logic of the Universal Welfare State* (Cambridge: Cambridge University Press, 1998) p. 139.
26 Robert Grafstein, *Institutional Realism: Social and Politcal Constraints on Rational Actors* (New Haven: Yale University Press, 1992) p. 1.
27 Guyora Binder and Robert Weisberg, 'Cultural Criticism of Law', *Stanford Law Review*, vol. 49 (May 1997) p. 1152.
28 Katharina Pistor and Philip A. Wellons, *The Role of Law and Legal Institutions in Asian Economic Development 1960–1995* (Oxford: Oxford University Press, 1999) pp. 280–4.
29 Review essay, Robert F. Samuelson, 'The Spirit of Capitalism', *Foreign Affairs*, vol. 80, no. 1 (January-February 2001) p. 210.
30 Amartya Sen, 'Reason Before Identity', the Romanes Lecture for 1998 (New York: Oxford University Press, 1999).
31 Amartya Sen, 'Reason Before Identity', the Romanes Lecture for 1998 (New York: Oxford University Press, 1999), citing Albert Hirschman who criticized the parsimonious position of a 'self-interested, isolated individual' to argue for a new focus on values and on noninstrumental action. See Albert O. Hirschman, 'Against Parsimony', *Economics and Philosophy*, vol. 1, pp. 7–21 (1985).
32 See e.g. Michael Walzer, *On Toleration* (New Haven: Yale University Press, 1997); John Rawls, *A Theory of Justice* (Cambridge MA: Belknap Press of Harvard University Press, 1999) (discussing the 'thin' and 'thick' theory of the good); Bernard Williams, *Morality: An Introduction to Ethics* (New York: Harper & Row, 1972) (discussing 'thick' and 'thin' moral concepts).
33 The questions paraphrased those posed by Jane J. Mansbridge, 'Self-Interest in the Explanation of Political Life', in *Beyond Self-Interest* (Chicago: University of Chicago Press, 1990) p. 21.
34 Thomas M. Franck, 'Are Human Rights Universal?', *Foreign Affairs*, vol. 80, no. 1 (January-February 2001) p. 191–204.
35 Guyora Binder and Robert Weisberg, 'Cultural Criticism of Law', *Stanford Law Review*, vol. 49 (1997) p. 1149.
36 Interim Report, 2.(3) *Shiho Kaikaku*, no. 15 (2000) p. 175.
37 Clifford Geertz, Local Knowledge: Furthter Essays in Interpretive Anthropology (New York: Basic Books, 1993).

2

PROPERTY RIGHTS AND INDIGENOUS TRADITION AMONG EARLY TWENTIETH-CENTURY JAPANESE FIRMS

Yoshiro Miwa and J. Mark Ramseyer[1]

Old habits die hard. We heard in college if not before that all we know is culturally contingent. Now, we find it hard to make the objective cross-cultural comparisons inherent in serious social science. We heard with all the moral confidence of Jonathan Edwards that only orientalist boors make transnational value judgments. Now, we find it hard to admit that some economic systems consistently outperform others.

But of course they do. Over a decade has passed since the collapse of Eastern Europe. Over a decade has passed since it forced most of us to come to terms with the socialist disaster, with the way it showed how economic incentives matter – and matter in ways that track universal principles.

Usually cited for the opposite argument to be sure, Japanese management history illustrates the same point: institutional constraints (the 'rule of law', in the organizing terminology of this conference) have effects that largely track a cross-cultural, pan-historical logic ('global norms', by the conference language). In this chapter, we draw on empirical research in Japanese economic history to illustrate that logic.

We admit we do not prove the universality of the phenomenon. We confess we do not know how to prove that a universal logic governs societies about which we know nothing. Indeed, one of us still remembers the hostile respondent on a Law and Society Association panel years ago who seemed convinced he had proven that economics could not explain Japanese traffic accident data by showing it did not explain Indian religious practices. Knowing nothing about Indian religion and jetlagged besides, the one of us was at a loss to say much in response.

We may not know Indian religion, but we do know the Japanese and US economies. In this chapter we discuss the effect of institutional constraints on early twentieth-century Japan. In the process, we illustrate two points. First, we show how modern institutional frameworks generally dominate indigenous arrangements (in the language of the conference, again, 'culturally embedded practices'). Second, we show how our susceptibility to the relativist canon can lead to profound mistakes of fact. In our eagerness to avoid chauvinist bias, too often we take local stereotypes at face value, and too often the local stereotypes are wrong. Only by asking hard questions will we get the facts straight, but without good theory we seldom know what questions to ask.

We start by canvassing the capital and governance structures of turn-of-the-century Japanese firms. Second, we outline the legal institutional basis for the arrangements, and third, we discuss one aspect of the role the government played (or did not play) in economic growth. We conclude by suggesting some of the implications this history poses for understanding the role of law in economic development.

Corporate investment

Equity

During the 1960s, in several sectors Japanese firms are said to have raised much of the money they needed from banks. From this well known (but quite possibly wrong) fact, many scholars extrapolate to firms pre-war. If equity markets did not provide the funds firms needed in the 1960s, they reason, equity markets must not have done so at the turn of the century either. Did not Alexander Gerschenkron[2] teach us that 'backward' countries will industrialize through bank finance and turn to securities markets only later? Does not modern theory teach us that banks mitigate informational asymmetries more effectively than securities markets, and do we not know that informational problems plague the less developed world?

One could extrapolate in this way. But if one did, one would be wrong. Firms in turn-of-the-century Japan did not raise their funds through banks. Overwhelmingly, they raised them on the stock market. Take the flagship industry of the period, cotton textiles. Most of the firms that would eventually dominate this industry had already begun to operate in the 1880s. By 1930, they produced a quarter of all manufactured goods in Japan and employed 40 per cent of all factory workers.

All this the spinning firms did without banks. On its balance sheets, the typical spinning firm in 1898 (there were fifty-two firms) had equity of 58 per cent, and bank debt of only 11 per cent. On average, it had 300–500 shareholders. The largest shareholder held about 8 per cent of the stock, and the largest five collectively held 24 per cent.

Nor was this reliance on equity peculiar to cotton spinning. Take railroads. In 1898, the forty-one railroad firms in operation had equity capital of 94 per cent and bank debt of 1 per cent. On average they had over 1,000 shareholders, and again the shareholdings seemed widely dispersed. Or take electrical utilities. Until the 1930s, the utilities were private, unregulated firms operating in highly competitive markets. In 1910, the 178 firms in the industry had equity capital of 88 per cent and bank debt of only 8 per cent.

Finally, take the stock exchanges themselves. Both the Tokyo and Osaka stock exchanges began operations in 1878. By 1900 the TSE listed the shares of 113 firms. Ten years later it listed 142 stocks, and by 1920, 569 stocks. Similarly founded in 1878, by 1900 the OSE listed the shares of fifty firms, by 1910 sixty-four firms, and by 1920, 206 firms. What the firms listed, investors traded. Together, investors on the two exchanges traded stocks worth 512 million yen in 1900, 2.09 billion in 1910, and 8.13 billion in 1920. As a percentage of GDP, these figures amounted to 21.2 per cent, 53.3 per cent, and 51.1 per cent – comparable to the amounts traded in advanced capitalist economies today.

Corporate law and governance

Introduction

All this the turn-of-the-century firms accomplished with neither a regulatory apparatus nor corporate law. Japan had no securities regulation until the Americans imposed one in the late 1940s. It had no corporate law until it passed a Commercial Code in 1890. Even that one did not last. Legislators promptly decided they disliked it, and replaced it with another in 1899.

Nor did investors and managers rely on local norms or indigenous traditions. To be sure, spinning-firm shareholders were often local. Presumably, through geographical proximity they obtained information to which out-of-towners would not have had access. Beyond geography, however, in operating and governing their firms investors and managers primarily relied on institutional arrangements based on the modern legal system.

Labor policy

For these new firms, entrepreneurs needed managers with expertise, and needed both managers and workers with the right incentives. To obtain the people they wanted and to motivate them to maximize profits, they (we focus here on the spinning firms) took basic, straightforward steps. First, they recruited from the universities. Notwithstanding the need for engineering and managerial sophistication, Lancashire firms had trained their own men. Not so in Japan. Instead, the Japanese firms turned to university graduates. The giant Kanebo spinning firm, for example, brought in Keio-University-trained Sanji Muto to run the firm in 1893, and Muto immediately began hiring other university graduates.

Sometimes, the firms recruited their new educated managers from competitors. So much for the bromides about how Japanese firms cultivate Confucian norms of loyalty by operating as a 'family'. Shamelessly, the spinning firms stole talented managers from their rivals.

Yet sometimes they hired their managers from the schools directly. By 1914 Kanebo was hiring a dozen a year, and had placed university graduates in nearly all branch manager posts. At the outset, the firms recruited mostly engineering students. Soon they were hiring men with managerial education as well.

Generally, the strategy worked. Managers from universities apparently brought an expertise others lacked. Other firm characteristics held constant, enterprises that hired university graduates earned significantly higher profits than their competitors.

Second, to motivate these managers to maximize profits, firms paid them a compensation package keyed to profitability. Although they did not use stock options, they used a variety of arrangements to similar effect. The Mie Boseki firm, for example, explicitly provided by charter that officers would earn 13 per cent of the corporation's net profits, and blue-collar workers another 7 per cent. Other firms included similar provisions.

Third, to motivate the workers on the shop floor firms paid them 'efficiency wages'. So much for the tales about 'exploited' female workers. Most of the employees were young girls off the farm, but to induce them to work hard and not quit, firms paid them wages significantly above market levels. In 1898 a girl at a spinning firm could earn 1.2 times the annual wage women earned in agriculture. By 1908 she could earn 1.9 times the female agricultural wage.

Agency slack

To police the inherent potential for agency slack between managers and investors, entrepreneurs again took several steps. First, they recruited to their boards men with substantial business experience. They did not hire these men because they brought banking or industry connections, for banking and spinning connections did not add value. Instead, they hired the men because they brought basic good business sense. They were men who knew how to monitor large firms. Through their presence on the board, they significantly boosted firm profitability.

Second, through explicit dividend policy the firms subjected new investments to the test of the market. By corporate charter, many promised to pay out a large fraction of the earnings as dividends. As Frank Easterbrook[3] shows, large dividend policies reduce the free cash managers can spend, and thereby force them to return to the stock market for large projects. Disproportionately, the firms that paid high dividends were those that listed their stock on an exchange. The greater the potential agency slack between managers and investors, in other words, the greater likelihood that the firms would commit themselves to market constraints on new investments.

Third, once the Diet passed a corporate law, the firms used it and charter provisions to limit managerial discretion more directly. The Kurashiki firm, for example, specified the number of spindles it would use by charter. The new corporate law imposed still other constraints. By the 1899 Commercial Code, managers had to call a special shareholders' meeting if they lost half the firm's stated capital. They needed a shareholder vote if they wanted to issue bonds.

Corporate market control

The most efficient spinning firms relentlessly acquired their less successful rivals. So much again for the notion that cultural values prevent Japanese firms from masterminding takeovers. In turn-of-the-century Japan, the most successful firms steadily acquired their less successful competitors.

Results

Generally, these strategies worked, and worked to make equity issues advantageous. Too often, we hear that firms in primitive environments should avoid stock market financing. In fact, firm size held constant, in turn-of-the-century Japan (a) those firms with more shareholders were significantly more profitable than those with fewer, and (b) firms with stock listed on the national exchanges were more profitable than those not listed. Even at the very onset of the modern legal regime, firms used court-enforceable corporate charters and employment contracts to make broadly dispersed equity issues profitable.

Legal structure and growth

To run this system, entrepreneurs needed a functioning legal system. They did not need a complicated one. Instead, they needed a system that let contracting parties define their rights to scarce property, that protected the property rights they defined, and that enforced any trades they negotiated in such property rights. For this, they needed an elementary private law regime of property, tort and contract, along with basic criminal law enforcement. This the new Japanese government offered.

Within a few years of taking power, the new Japanese government had a functioning police force and court system. Although it did not have a Civil Code in place until 1896–8, judges understood from the start that enforcing private property rights was their business. This is not rocket science. As much as law school professors enjoy the ambiguities, most disputes do not involve ambiguities. Most are simple. And simple rules go a long way toward providing the legal infrastructure contracting parties need. As Richard Epstein[4] put it – in what he calls 'Blum's Law' – the optimal rule is not one designed to get every case right. It is a simple rule designed merely to get most of the cases right.

If courts just try to enforce private deals straightforwardly, 'the rest' is not 'gravy'. Instead, the rest will likely do more harm than good. One does not, for example, need a Securities and Exchange Commission to run a stock market. As George Stigler[5] showed four decades ago, securities regulation instead imposes on investors a net harm. It raises the costs investors bear to little offsetting benefit.

Corporate law is less nefarious, but only if legislators are willing to limit it to a set of default contracts for investors.[6] If designed as a standard form contract with 'off-the-rack' governance schemes, corporate law can indeed facilitate investment. As such, it reduces the cost of arriving at the contractual solution that investors could have negotiated anyway. Presumably, however, it facilitates investment more effectively among the smaller firms, where incorporation costs would loom relatively larger. Among larger firms, where incorporation costs would be relatively small, it would have only trivial consequence.

If such is the theory, such is not the practice. Courts and legislatures in modern capitalist economies frequently try to do more. In trying to do more, they dramatically lower aggregate welfare. When courts and legislatures impose mandatory terms through corporate law, they raise the costs to participants in the firm of reaching the contract they would most prefer. Even when the participants can maneuver around the ostensibly mandatory terms, they necessarily increase the cost of reaching the most preferred solution.

None of this is peculiar to corporate law, of course. Whether by the dynamics of modern democracy or the idiosyncrasies of judicial ideology, modern capitalist governments routinely impose mandatory terms. Often, they do so with disastrous results. Whole bodies of law reduce the choice sets available to investors, consumers and workers, to little positive effect: labor law and landlord-tenant law are perhaps the most obvious examples, but much the same could be said of medical malpractice and products liability law.

Because they will be subject to contractual terms they would not have chosen (else the 'mandatory' nature of the term has no bite), private parties will now find the legal regimes costly. Necessarily, to the extent they stay within the ambit of the legal system, they will find it harder than before to reach the contractual arrangement that maximizes their joint welfare. Necessarily, they will now have greater incentives than before to try to 'opt out' of the legal system. If possible, they will look to other ways of structuring their relationships. To the extent that indigenous customs and norms provide that structure, these inefficient legal rules should increase the extent to which the parties 'opt in' to such customs and norms.

The role of government – the IBJ example

Of course, scholars skeptical of any transcultural generalizations based on claims that Japan looks 'Western' have long dismissed the country as a 'special case'. To do so, often they cite the putatively crucial role the Japanese government played in the economy. Famously ascribing 'Japan's post war economic triumph' to its 'state-guided market system', Chalmers Johnson[7] is the best known of this the-government-grew-the-economy school. In fact, this misreads both the Japanese experience and major swaths of economic and political theory.[8]

Yet in the context of corporate finance, the issue is narrower. The question is not whether the government guided the economy generally. It is whether it helped route funds to growth-oriented firms. Claims that it did are not hard to find, and usually involve the Industrial Bank of Japan (IBJ). William Lockwood,[9] for example, claimed early on that government-controlled banks like the IBJ 'played a large part in mobilizing resources for the introduction of modern techniques in commerce and industry'.

From its founding in 1900, sympathetic observers had dubbed the IBJ the 'central bank of manufacturing'. The bank, according to observers like Lockwood, 'specialized in financing large-scale industry and public undertakings'.[10] Fundamentally, however, the IBJ never had either the wherewithal nor the independence to play this role. Largely, it faced the same regulatory and competitive constraints as other banks.

What special benefits the government granted the IBJ were modest. It bought enough of any IBJ bond offerings to let it raise funds through bonds rather than deposits – except that the bank did not need bonds to raise funds. Large banks faced such a surplus of deposits over good loan applications that some (like the Mitsui Bank) regularly turned depositors away. The government also guaranteed IBJ dividends at 5 per cent of capital – except that the bank never had trouble issuing dividends. Throughout the period, it regularly posted profits higher than its dividends.

Even had the IBJ hoped to promote growth, it answered to the cabinet, and the cabinet had other priorities. By the terms of the IBJ's implementing statute, the Finance Minister appointed the bank's CEO; could veto bond issues, dividends and new branches; and supervised bank policy and actions generally. Through these powers, he regularly forced the bank to invest in unprofitable and decidedly non-growth-promoting projects.

In the wake of the 1905–6 Russo-Japanese war, for instance, the government decided it needed more foreign exchange. At the time, that meant more gold and silver, so it ordered the IBJ to lend up to 4 million yen to the Hasami gold mine on an unsecured basis (all the bank's loans that year totaled 12 million). Alas, the mine could not repay the money, and the bank eventually dropped the loan from its books after a 1921 government-run bail-out (costing 11 million yen).

In the midst of the Hasami fiasco, the government decided to use the IBJ to subsidize shipbuilding and ocean shipping. It apparently wanted solvent ocean shipping firms; the military wanted solvent shipbuilding firms; and the Kawasaki shipbuilding firm – headed by Kojiro Matsukata, the eminently well connected son of a former Finance Minister – wanted a place to unload the firm's inventory left unsold at the end of World War I.[11] As a receptacle for those unsold Kawasaki ships, in 1919 the government helped coordinate the creation of the Kokusai Kisen shipping firm.

To make Kokusai Kisen operational, the government wanted the IBJ to lend the firm 20 million yen (when the bank's loan portfolio totaled 81 million). It did, but that was not enough. Soon, the firm needed another 57 million, and obtained it from a syndicate of the IBJ and three other banks.

Several more attempts to refinance the firm followed, along with additional subsidies from the government to the IBJ.

Yet it was all to no avail. Like the Hasami mine, Kokusai Kisen never made money. In 1937 its assets passed to the Osaka Shosen shipping firm, and the IBJ took a loss. Ironically, however, the escalating war in China had substantially increased the demand for ships. Although the bank lost money, in the end it did not lose as much as one might have expected a few years earlier.

By the 1930s, the government was heavily pushing munitions firms. Not surprisingly, it used the IBJ to lend to them. And lend the IBJ did. In 1936 it loaned firms in the (overwhelmingly military-related) machinery industry 5 per cent of its total loan base. By 1940 it was lending them 30 per cent of its loans, and by 1945 45 per cent.

Despite its reputation as 'the central bank to manufacturing', other than to munitions firms the IBJ never lent heavily to manufacturers. In the mid-1920s, the government declared that the bank should lend to small manufacturers, but by 1930 it was still lending them only 6 per cent of its loans. Instead, more than to any other industrial sector it lent to electric utility firms (13 per cent of its loan base in 1929), textile firms (9 per cent), and foodstuffs firms (8 per cent). Even to these sectors, however, it loaned (in 1929) less than Kokusai Kisen's outstanding syndicated debt. Indeed, even in 1936 it loaned manufacturing firms less than 28 per cent of all loans.

Nor did the IBJ promote manufacturing through the bond market, where it did play a key underwriting role. During 1930–6, the two manufacturers raising the most through the bond market were the Nippon Chisso fertilizer firm (60 million yen) and Oji Paper (25 million). They were dwarfed by the Tokyo Electrical Utility (303 million yen), Tokyo City (330 million), and the infamous Southern Manchuria Railway (700 million). By this point, however, it should come as no surprise that the IBJ mostly underwrote the bonds of entities like the Southern Manchuria Railway, Tokyo City, and the public utilities.

Over the last decade, several prominent economists have found in the wartime IBJ the basis of what they call Japan's modern 'main-bank system'. Tetsuji Okazaki and Masahiro Okuno-Fujiwara, for example, claim:[12]

> [T]he high monitoring capability of banks these days owes much to an improvement of the monitoring practices established pre-war mostly by the Industrial Bank of Japan (IBJ), and the spread of these techniques from IBJ to other banks (mainly government lending institutions) since the war.

In fact, during the late 1930s and early 1940s, the IBJ had no incentive to monitor the firms to which it lent. Like other banks, it lent to the firms because the military told it to lend to them. Whether it monitored or not, it had no choice but to ignore any default and to renew any loan as the government urged. Any effort it expended on monitoring a firm would have been pure waste.

Law and custom

Too little law, too much law

By the logic of the above section, private parties will structure their relationships by indigenous norms primarily in two contexts: when the legal regime provides 'too little' law, and when it provides 'too much'. In Tokugawa Japan, courts only haphazardly protected property rights. Predictably, investors chose other ways of structuring their arrangements. A wide variety of their trades they kept within the family. If a successful merchant had a smart and enterprising son, he passed the business on to him. If he did not, he found a good young man and adopted him into the family.

In modern Russia, the police and courts arguably protect property rights even less. When they can, businessmen make do with extra-legal arrangements. Much the same thing happens in the less developed countries the world over. The legal systems provide too little law, and investors and entrepreneurs make their own arrangements.

The private arrangements reappear in worlds with 'too much' law. Where courts try to stop private parties from reaching their desired contractual outcome, the parties concerned will either opt for the second-best solution within the legal regime, or leave the regime altogether. In American cities where urban governments try to cap rents, some landlords convert apartments to condominiums. Others let the apartments deteriorate to the point where the legal rent equals the market rental. If labor law in northern states requires firms to negotiate with a cartelized labor force, firms try to relocate in the south. If even there restrictions on labor arrangements prevent mutually beneficial arrangements, they move to Mexico. If legislatures in Western Europe require firms to place labor representatives on the board, they shift decision-making out of the boardroom.

Comparative statics

In some industries in some countries in some periods, contracting parties abandon the legal system for private, indigenous arrangements. But when do they make these choices, and why? The discussion above should give us some clues – for the private, indigenous arrangements generally substitute for formal, court-enforceable arrangements.

Suppose that we observe the indigenous arrangements only in worlds where the legal system either fails to provide basic property rights protection (too little law), or where courts and legislatures try to use the legal system to limit the choice set available to contracting parties (too much law). If we observe the indigenous arrangements only in such worlds, it suggests that private parties see them as distinctly second-best. They choose the indigenous arrangements only when the legal system does not work.

On the other hand, suppose that private parties choose the indigenous arrangements even where the legal system cheaply enforces the desired arrangements. If even here they avoid the legal system, it suggests they prefer the indigenous arrangements to the courts. Crucially, however, only in such contexts could we reach that conclusion.

In short, a sensible comparison of modern and indigenous arrangements requires that we compare them in contexts where both are available. Academics fascinated by the idiosyncratic and foreign typically extol the marvelous benefits of the indigenous systems, while at the same time preaching the culturally contingent nature of modern law. Yet if private contracting parties routinely choose the former only where legal options are unavailable or over-regulatory, that very fact suggests ordinary humans see less merit in the indigenous arrangements than do academics.

As with much that matters, this is ultimately an empirical exercise. But at least the evidence from Japan suggests that when the legal system offers private parties to business arrangements a workable option, they choose it. Throughout the Tokugawa period, they formed firms through kin and fictive-kin ties. Once courts protected private contractual arrangements, they switched with blinding speed to formal court-enforced arrangements. In doing so, they also learned – with equal alacrity – how to manipulate those arrangements to reach contractual arrangements that protected their private interests.

Conclusions

When sensible, legal policy is not about redistributing rents to politically favored interest groups. And it should not be about facilitating indigenous business practices. It should be about facilitating consensual deals, whether indigenous or not, 'occidental' or not. Whether those deals involve management contracts, labor arrangements, consumer credit contracts, or corporate capital structure, they take place among consenting adults. Necessarily (not generally or usually, but *necessarily* – as Kaplow and Shavell[13] show), the legal regime that maximizes social welfare is the regime that enforces the deal these consenting adults want.

Japanese courts at the turn of the last century understood this. Imperfectly to be sure, they let private parties define claims to scarce resources; they enforced those claims; and they enforced most contracts the parties negotiated over those claims. They enforced, in short, a basic set of property rights. The earlier courts had not done so, and entrepreneurs had used a wide variety of informal indigenous arrangements instead. Faced now with a working modern court system, entrepreneurs invoked it voraciously. In virtually all business arrangements they used the modern legal machinery. The economy boomed, and the rest – as they say – is history.

Provided a legal regime both (a) cheaply defines and enforces property rights, and (b) cheaply enforces consensual deals involving those rights, the Japanese experience suggests (though it obviously does not prove) that businessmen will generally use it. Generally, the experience implies, legal regimes that enforce such rights trump indigenous customs. To return to the organizing language of this conference, provided it avoids the rent-seeking detritus of the modern regulatory state, the 'rule of law' generally dominates 'culturally embedded practices'. There is progress in science. There can be progress in law. Provided we avoid the Saidian bog where departments whole have sunk, there may yet be progress in social science too.

Notes

1 This chapter draws on: Yoshiro Miwa and J. Mark Ramseyer (2000) 'Corporate Governance in Transitional Economies: Lessons from the Pre-War Japanese Cotton Textile Industry', *Journal of Legal Studies*, 29: 171; (forthcoming 2002) 'The Value of Prominent Directors: Lessons in Corporate Governance from Transitional Japan', *Journal of Legal Studies*; (forthcoming 2000) 'Banks and Economic Growth: Implications from Japanese History', *Journal of Law and Economics*; (2000) 'Seisaku kin'yu to keizai hatten: Senzenki Nihon kogyo ginko no keesu' [Financial Policy and Economic Development: The Case of the Pre-War Industrial Bank of Japan], *Keizaigaku Ronshu*, 66: 2.

2 Alexander Gerschenkron (1962) *Economic Backwardness in Historical Perspective*, Cambridge MA: Harvard University Press.

3 Frank Easterbrook (1984) 'Two Agency-Cost Explanations of Dividends', *American Economic Review*, 74: 650.

4 Richard A. Epstein (1995) *Simple Rules for a Complex World*, Cambridge MA: Harvard University Press.

5 George Stigler (1964) 'Public Regulation of the Securities Market', *Journal of Business*, 37: 117.

6 Frank Easterbrook and Daniel Fischel (1991) *Corporate Law*, Cambridge MA: Harvard University Press.

7 Chalmers Johnson (1982) *MITI and the Japanese Miracle*, Stanford: Stanford University Press, vii.

8 Yoshiro Miwa (1996) *Firms and Industrial Organization in Japan*, London: Macmillan; (1998) *Seifu no noryoku* [The Competance of the State], Tokyo: Yuhikaku; J. Mark Ramseyer and Frances McCall Rosenbluth (1993) *Japan's Political Marketplace*, Cambridge MA: Harvard University Press.

9 William W. Lockwood (1955) *The Economic Development of Japan*, London: Oxford University Press, 250.

10 *Ibid.*, 249.

11 In addition, Kawasaki shipbuilding's principal creditor, the 15th Bank, was headed by another son of the former Finance Minister.

12 Juro Teranishi (1994) 'Loan Syndication in War-time Japan and the Origins of the Main Bank System', in Masahiko Aoki and Hugh Patrick (eds) *The Japanese Main Bank System*, Oxford: Oxford University Press. Teranishi (1994: 51) argued that the particular pattern of corporate control (characterized by the main bank system) which utilizes the monitoring activity of a bank in loan syndication traces its origins to the wartime loan syndications. However, he explicitly notes that these syndications did not involve monitoring (*ibid.*, 75).

13 Louis Kaplow and Steven Shavell (2001) 'Fairness versus Welfare', *Harvard Law Review*, 114: 961.

3

MARKETS, DEMOCRACY AND ETHNICITY

Amy L. Chua[1]

Over the last two decades, Western lawyers and legal academics have been called upon to help restructure the fundamental institutions of the developing world, to an extent unprecedented since decolonization after the Second World War. This restructuring has been driven by two principal goals: marketization and democratization. In fact, these two forces, markets and democracy, have come to be seen as global solutions to the intransigent problem of development.

But as anyone who reads the newspapers knows, there is another force, much older and often darker, that plays an equally elemental role in shaping the societies of the developing world (and for that matter, the developed world) – the force of ethnicity, or ethnic hatred. To date, there has been almost no systematic study of the interplay among these three forces: markets, democracy, and ethnicity. It is this interplay that I would like to focus on in this essay.

As Professors Cheng, Rosett and Woo note in Chapter 1 of this volume, markets are viewed as 'the panacea for the ills associated with economic development. ... [and] are often deemed synonymous with democracy, universal rights and rule of law'. This essay will make three main points, each of which challenges prevailing international development orthodoxy. First, contrary to conventional wisdom, markets and democracy in the developing world are not always mutually reinforcing. Second, virtually everywhere in the world, markets tend to benefit not just some people over others, but also some ethnic groups over others. In the developing countries, moreover, markets often favor certain ethnic minorities over the rest of the population. This phenomenon is potentially very destabilizing, yet it is almost uniformly disregarded by lawyers and scholars involved in marketization and rule-of-law projects. Third, like markets, democratization too often benefits some ethnic groups over others. Further, in developing societies, the ethnic groups favored by global markets are frequently different from the ethnic groups favored by majority rule. As a result, in many developing countries, the combined pursuit of marketization and democratization will not alleviate, but often catalyze ethnic tensions, in highly determinate and predictable ways, with potentially very serious consequences, including the subversion of markets and democracy themselves.

A note on terminology before continuing. 'Markets', 'democracy', and 'ethnicity' are notoriously difficult concepts to define. Indeed, I hope in this essay precisely to remind us that the 'market systems' currently being urged on developing countries are very different from the ones now in place in the Western nations; that the process of 'democratization' currently being promoted in the developing world (i.e. rapid, sudden implementation of universal suffrage) is not the same as the one that Western countries themselves went through at analogous periods in their history; and that 'ethnicity' is a fluid, constructed, and dangerously manipulable concept.

Nevertheless, some clarification of my usage of these terms is in order. In the advanced industrialized nations, terms like 'market economy' or 'market system' refer to a broad spectrum of economic systems based primarily on private property and competition, with government regulation and redistribution ranging from substantial (as in the United States) to extensive (as in the Scandinavian countries). Ironically, however, the version of capitalism currently being exported to developing countries more closely resembles the laissez-faire regimes characteristic of the Western nations during an earlier period, when property qualifications and other stringent suffrage limitations were in place. Thus in this essay, unless otherwise indicated, terms like 'marketization' and 'markets' will refer to the kinds of measures actually being implemented today in the developing world in the effort to create or promote the basic institutions of a capitalist economy. These measures characteristically include privatization, liberalization of restraints on foreign investment and trade, and the elimination of state economic controls and subsidies. As a practical matter, they rarely, if ever, include any substantial redistribution measures or social safety nets.

Similarly, while 'democracy' can take many forms, I will use the term 'democratization' to refer to the political reforms actually being promoted and implemented in the developing world today. Thus, 'democratization' will refer broadly to concerted efforts to introduce greater electoral competition and increased majoritarianism in the political process. Needless to say, an ideal democratic society would surely include more substantive principles, such as equality under law or minority protections, but to build such principles into the definition of democracy would be to confuse aspiration with reality.

Ethnicity is another controversial concept that has generated much debate among social scientists. For purposes of this essay, I adopt a broad conception of ethnicity, which acknowledges the importance of subjective perceptions of belonging and encompasses differences along racial lines; lines of geographic origin; and linguistic, religious, tribal or other cultural lines. While subjective perceptions of identity often depend on more 'objective' traits assigned to individuals (based on, for example, perceived morphological characteristics, language differences or ancestry), the crucial point here is that ethnic identity is not static but shifting and deeply unstable.

The paradox of free market democracy

Markets and democracy are the 'twin pillars' of prevailing development orthodoxy. Many have explored the ways – 'theoretical, historical, and empirical' – in which these two pillars are said to reinforce each other.[2] It has to be remembered, however, that there is also an inherent instability in free market democracy.

For a long time, leading political philosophers and economists held that market capitalism and democracy could coexist, if at all, only in fundamental tension with one another.[3] Markets would produce enormous concentrations of wealth in the hands of a few, while democracy, by empowering the poor majority, would inevitably lead to convulsive acts of expropriation and confiscation. In Adam Smith's words, 'For one very rich man, there must be at least five hundred poor. ... The affluence of the rich excites the indignation of the poor, who are often both driven by want, and prompted by envy, to invade his possessions'.[4] For this reason, Smith, along with David Ricardo, James Madison and many others, all opposed universal suffrage, which in Thomas Babington Macaulay's words, was 'incompatible with property' and thus 'with civilization' itself.[5] From this point of view, free market democracy is a paradox, a contradiction in terms.

As it turned out, of course, the paradox of free market democracy did not prove insuperable. On the contrary, in all the Western nations and Japan, this paradox has been successfully mediated by a host of institutions, defusing the conflict between market-generated wealth disparities and majoritarian politics. One of the most important challenges facing international policymakers today is to identify these mediating institutions and to think much more carefully about whether analogous institutions could – or should – exist in the developing world.

Paradox lost: markets and democracy in the developed world

Why, then, haven't poor majorities in the advanced democratic nations used their political power to equalize wealth far more than they have done, to an extent that would undermine the functioning of a market system?

I want to suggest that the tensions between markets and democracy have been substantially alleviated throughout the developed world by institutions and devices that, while varying widely across countries, generally fall into three categories: material, political and ideological. It goes without saying that the literatures implicated here are too vast to even be summarized in this essay. I will instead be very brief.

Materially, the less well-off in the developed world have essentially been bought out, in part through market-generated material prosperity, but also in significant part through redistributive institutions, such as progressive taxation, social security, minimum wage laws, antitrust regulation, labor laws, and so on.

Politically, the most obvious device for mediating the conflict between markets and democracy is the existence of constitutional checks on the confiscation of property. But, far more important (although rarely mentioned), another reason that the poor in the developed world have not used their political power to equalize wealth is because, trappings of democracy aside, they have not actually possessed such political power. Historically, all of the Western democracies had massive exclusions from the suffrage, including explicit property qualifications and, after they were eliminated, tax-paying requirements and pauper exclusions. Arguably, these longstanding political exclusions were instrumental to the success of Western nations in establishing stable free market democracies.

But these material and political devices are only part of the picture. Indeed, they are premised on a flat view of the world in which the poor want only one thing from democracy – to appropriate wealth from the rich – which is simply not the case (especially not today in the United States). Throughout the developed world, these redistributive and political devices have been supplemented, perhaps crucially, by various market-compatible ideologies – belief-systems that, if held with sufficient strength by sufficient numbers, make the relatively worse-off majority more inclined to accept (or at least not to rebel against) the extreme income disparities inevitably produced in a market economy.

Probably the most prominent of these ideologies in the United States is the ideology of upward mobility. Ideally, upward mobility gives everyone a stake in the continuing success of the market economy.[6] At its extreme, it teaches the worse-off that their plight is the result not of an unfair or invidious economic system, but rather of their own deficiencies. In both these ways, upward mobility makes the income disparities of a market system less likely to provoke popular furor. Among Western countries, the ideology of upward mobility has probably been most successful in the United States.

Elsewhere I describe a number of other market-compatible ideologies, some of which are more prominent in Western Europe and Japan. Rather than recapitulate these here, I want instead to highlight a final market-compatible ideology that has operated in the United States and undoubtedly many other developed nations as well: racism. Racism is not inherently market-compatible. But in many developed countries racism has arguably been a powerful force fracturing the 'lower class' and inducing large numbers of the less well-off majority to vote in defiance of what might be expected to be their rational economic self-interest.[7] In the United States, it is well documented that racism has historically hindered the formation of political alliances between poor and working-class whites on one hand, and poor and working-class minorities on the other hand.[8]

In short, these material, political and ideological mediating devices have played a critical role in helping to neutralize the tension between majoritarian politics and market economies in the developed world. In canvassing these devices, my objective is not to offer a comprehensive theory explaining the success of free market democracy in the developed world. Rather, my goals are far more limited: to initiate reflection on the institutions and devices that have helped to overcome the tensions between market and democracy; and to suggest that the story behind the success of free market democracy in the developed world is much more complex – and in many respects much darker – than is commonly supposed, including not just noble-sounding constitutional rule-of-law protections, but also longstanding disenfranchisment of the poor and racism.

The developing world's absence of institutions to mediate the paradox of free market democracy

Let me turn now to the developing world, where, rather remarkably, we have been vigorously exporting markets and democracy almost without the slightest consciousness of the tension between them. Again, in other work I have described at length the general absence in the developing world of the kinds of material, political and ideological mediating devices just described. Once more, I will only briefly summarize.

First, with some exceptions, there is painfully little material redistribution in developing societies, together with much more pervasive poverty. Almost by definition, the poor are far more numerous (and generally speaking far poorer) in the developing world than in the developed world. The ongoing population explosion in the developing world – one of the greatest sources of pessimism for developmental economists – contrasts markedly 'with the history of the presently rich industrial nations when they were in earlier phases of their development'. For example, 'in their nineteenth-century pre-industrial phase, the countries of western Europe had a population growth that was generally less than half the rate now existing in the poor countries'.[9] If current World Bank projections are correct, the population in countries now classified as developing is expected to increase from roughly four billion today to roughly eight billion by the year 2050.[10] As a result, throughout the developing world, it is much more difficult for market-generated wealth to 'buy out' the poor either through 'trickle-down' or redistribution because, to put it mildly, there is much less to be spread across many more.

To be clear, 'buy-outs' occur all the time in the developing world; they are a part of daily life. But in contrast to the developed world, these buy-outs rarely take the form of welfare payments to the needy or transfers to poor workers and farmers. Rather, these buy-outs far more typically go to corrupt officials and bureaucrats who are in a position to extract rents from the wealthy (including foreign investors), whether through bribes, speed money, kickbacks, embezzlement, extortion or other forms of illicit activity.

The problem, therefore, is not only that of insufficient funds. It is no secret that most developing countries lack strong, accountable institutions capable of administering a regulatory welfare state. It was often hoped that privatization, by eliminating bloated bureaucracies and state-owned enterprises, would both substantially reduce corruption and leave behind a pared-down and better-functioning state apparatus, capable of administering regulatory and redistributive institutions. Unfortunately, to date privatization generally has done neither. Instead, in many developing countries, the privatization process itself has been corrupted, with transfers of wealth going not to the relatively poor but rather to those rich enough to bid and bribe, to corporate insiders, to government officials and their families and friends, and, in some cases, to criminal organizations.

Second, with respect to political mediating devices, while most developing nations have on paper constitutional property protections, they lack the institutions necessary to make such protections effective. More important, it is crucial to recognize that the process of democratization that developing societies are being asked to embrace is not the same as that which the Western democracies themselves went through. While enfranchisement in Western nations generally took place only gradually and incrementally, universal suffrage is being implemented in the developing world today on a massive scale and almost (by comparison) overnight. This sudden, unmediated process of democratization makes the transition to free market democracy particularly volatile, and the need for other mediating devices more pressing.

On the other hand, many developing countries do have one highly effective restraint on democracy: systemic political corruption. Even in nominally democratic countries, rigged elections, rampant bribery and, more subtly, extensive patron-clientelism often create substantial obstacles to genuine democracy in the developing world. For this reason, anti-corruption campaigns have been a major thrust of international development policy. These initiatives are long overdue and of the utmost importance, but to the extent that they succeed, they will sharpen the conflict between markets and democracy.

Finally, for obvious reasons, market-compatible ideologies such as upward mobility do not exist robustly among the chronically poor, malnourished majorities of the developing world. 'People whose physical survival is imperiled cannot think about the future'[11] – let alone experience an enriching sense of having a stake in the marketplace. It is important here to distinguish periodic bursts of pro-market euphoria, and dangerously inflated market expectations, which are common enough in the developing world, from an historically rooted, sustaining ideology of upward mobility. Far from being capable of maintaining support for markets among the less well-off even in the face of ongoing, market-generated, extreme income disparities, dangerously unrealistic expectations can be expected to do just the opposite – produce widespread disappointment, anger and rebellion when it becomes clear that rapid riches will not come.

Unfortunately, the problem facing free market democracy in the developing world is not just the lack of mediating devices. The next two sections will elaborate.

The link between markets and ethnicity

The idea that the invisible hand of the market will benefit some people over others is hardly new. Proponents of laissez-faire capitalism respect and relish the anonymous justice of the market insofar as it promises to reward anyone who is sufficiently entrepreneurial, hardworking and lucky. The problem I wish to highlight here, however, is that virtually everywhere in the world, markets tend to favor not just some people over others, but also some ethnic groups over others. In other words, in the terminology I have coined elsewhere, some ethnic groups are market-dominant, meaning that they will tend under market conditions to economically dominate other ethnic groups around them.

Countries with market-dominant majorities

In China, for example, the Han Chinese, comprising 95 per cent of the population, have represented an economically and politically dominant majority *vis-à-vis* ethnic minorities like the Tibetans, Uighers and Miao for three millennia.[12] Recent evidence, moreover, suggests that the Han Chinese are generally market-dominant *vis-à-vis* the country's ethnic minorities as well. Starting in the 1980s, China's recent economic liberalization policies have starkly favored the country's coastal regions, leaving 'inland provinces, and in particular the areas inhabited by ethnic minorities, far behind'. To address 'this imbalance and assuage minority feelings that they were being exploited by the majority Han group, minorities were permitted to trade across borders', and 'tourism from abroad was encouraged'. At least in the case of Tibet, however, the benefits of tourism frequently ended up in the hands of entrepreneurial new Han 'arrivals, often young people from impoverished areas of nearby Sichuan province', who 'flooded into Lhasa to profit from the tourist trade and take advantage of … preferential taxes'.[13]

In China's case, market-oriented policies have tended to benefit an ethnic majority over historically oppressed ethnic minorities. This dynamic, although found in China, is much more common to the developed world as opposed to the developing world. In the United States, for example, markets have also tended to reinforce the economic dominance of a perceived ethnic majority over the countries' most salient ethnic minorities – hence the controversial calls for (and backlash against) market-'correcting' affirmative action for blacks and Hispanics. Likewise, in Australia, Canada, New Zealand and all the Scandinavian and Western European nations, the core ethnic problem is one that pits an economically and politically dominant white majority against economically and politically weaker ethnic minorities.[14]

Interestingly, the same basic ethnoeconomic dynamic holds in all of the more economically developed societies of East Asia. As in the West, in each of the 'Asian tigers', the ethnic majority – the Japanese in Japan, the Koreans in South Korea, and the Chinese in Hong Kong, Singapore and Taiwan – is economically and politically dominant. In Singapore, for example, the Chinese constitute roughly 77 per cent of the population and are an economically, politically, and culturally dominant majority *vis-à-vis* the country's Indian and Malaysian minorities. In Japan and Korea, ethnic minorities are not merely economically disadvantaged, but practically nonexistent. (In fact, it was only in 1997 that the Japanese formally acknowledged the existence of an indigenous ethnic minority, the Ainu.) In Hong Kong, the English and Chinese are both prosperous, but the numeric strength of the latter (who constitute 99 per cent of the population) makes them the economically dominant majority. In Taiwan, Han Chinese (including both the Taiwanese Chinese and the Mainland Chinese) constitute roughly 99 per cent of the population, with non-Han aborigines (*yuan-chu min*) composing the other 1 per cent. Even if the Taiwanese (roughly 85 per cent of the population) and the Mainlanders (14 per cent) were viewed as distinct ethnic groups (which in my view would be a mistake, especially given the high rates of intermarriage), the Taiwanese 'majority' is economically dominant.[15]

The pervasiveness of market-dominant minorities in the developing world

By contrast to China, the East Asian tigers, and all the Western nations, the ethnoeconomic dynamic tends to be just the reverse in most developing countries: Markets often favor, or reinforce the economic dominance of, certain resented ethnic minorities. If history is any guide, in country after country throughout the developing world, one or more ethnic minorities, along with foreign investors, can be expected with privatization, economic liberalization and other market-oriented reforms, to economically dominate the 'indigenous' majorities around them, at least in the near to mid-term future.

Examples of such market-dominant minorities have included the Chinese throughout Southeast Asia, Indians throughout East Africa and parts of the Caribbean, the Lebanese in West Africa and parts of the Caribbean, the Ibo in Nigeria, the Bamileke in Cameroon, Tutsi in Rwanda, Kikuyu in Kenya, whites in South Africa, whites in Zimbabwe, Tamils in Sri Lanka, Bengalis in Assam – the list goes on, quite strikingly, as I have documented in detail.[16] (Needless to say, groups can be market-dominant for very different reasons, ranging from superior 'entrepreneurialism' to a history of apartheid or colonial oppression. If, as with whites in South Africa, you use force to relegate the majority to inferior 'Bantu' education and generally inhumane conditions for seventy years – you're likely to be market-dominant, and this has nothing to do with 'culture'.)

To be clear, by 'economic dominance' I am referring not to vague stereotypes, but rather to actual, starkly disproportionate control over major sectors of the economy. In Indonesia, for example, the Chinese comprise only roughly 3 per cent of the population, but until recently controlled up to 70 per cent (or even more) of the private economy under a number of different measures.[17] Similarly, in South Africa, the white minority constitutes roughly 13 per cent of the population, but, at least until recently, owned over 85 per cent of the country's arable land and controlled all of the country's largest conglomerates.[18] In Guatemala (as in a number of Latin American countries), 'a tiny minority of generally light-skinned elites' controls most of the nation's wealth, while Mayan Indians, comprising two thirds of the population, live in abject poverty.[19]

In some cases, for example when a particular ethnic group owes its economic dominance in part to political favoritism or military force, market reforms might in theory be expected to undercut the economic dominance of such groups. In reality, however, in part because of historical or 'path dependent' reasons, many economically dominant minorities will also tend to be market-dominant – meaning that their economic dominance will not dissipate but rather persist or even increase with privatization and other market-oriented reforms, at least in the near to mid-term future. There are a number of reasons for this.

To begin with, 'economic liberalization naturally favors private business while reducing the role and influence of bureaucrats and the state'.[20] Thus in the many developing societies in which the private sector is overwhelmingly dominated by a particular ethnic minority, economic liberalization is likely to disproportionately benefit that minority, at least in the earlier years (or decades) of marketization. In Indonesia, the Philippines and Thailand, for example, the 'liberal, market-oriented economic reform programs' of the 1980s appear to have 'greatly increased the wealth and relative power' of those countries' Chinese-dominated private business communities.[21] Most recently, economic liberalization in Vietnam and Burma has led to a resurgence of Chinese commercial dominance in those countries' major cities.[22]

Relatedly, because economically dominant minorities frequently control (or at least are disproportionately represented in) those sectors of the economy that are most attractive to foreign investors – for example, finance, technology, industry, transport, and mining and other natural resources – they often are better positioned to benefit from foreign investment liberalization (for example, in the form of lucrative joint ventures). Again, this has been strikingly true of the Chinese minorities of Southeast Asia. Some of this market dominance may reflect 'superior entrepreneurialism', which itself can result from a number of factors, from culture to a history of political favoritism by colonial authorities. At the same time, more invidiously, some economically dominant minorities may be market-dominant because, like whites in apartheid South Africa, they have oppressed the indigenous majorities around them for so long that it will be decades before education levels and entrepreneurial experience come close to being equalized.

In any event, throughout much of the developing world, and especially throughout Southeast Asia, the awkward but persisting reality is this. Rather than markets 'lifting all boats' and encouraging 'the assertion of the impartial, rational self over group identities', marketization instead reinforces or exacerbates the disproportionate wealth of an 'outsider' market-dominant minority, thereby fomenting intense ethnic resentment among the impoverished, 'indigenous' majority.

Paradox unleashed: markets, democracy and ethnonationalist conflict

The phenomenon of market-dominant minorities has sobering implications for free market democracy in the developing world. Most crucially, in developing countries with a market-dominant minority, markets and democracy will tend to favor not just different people, or different classes, but different ethnic groups. Markets will tend to benefit the market-dominant minority, while democracy will increase the power of the relatively impoverished 'indigenous' majority. In such circumstances, where the wealthy minority is a resented, ethnically distinct 'outsider' group – the paradox of free market democracy becomes an engine of potentially catastrophic ethnonationalism, pitting a poor 'indigenous' majority, easily aroused by opportunistic vote-seeking politicians, against wealthy outsiders, including both foreign investors and the market-dominant 'foreigners within'.

To put it another way, whereas racism or ethnic animosities in countries like the United States help to defuse the conflict between democracy and markets, in the developing world they tend to catalyze that conflict.

More specifically, as I have modeled elsewhere, in developing countries satisfying certain specified conditions, rapid democratization in the face of a market-dominant ethnic minority will tend to produce an ethnically charged and highly unstable situation in which one of three non-mutually-exclusive outcomes become highly probable. The three probable outcomes are:

1 an anti-market backlash targeting the market-dominant minority (for example through ethnically targeted nationalizations or economic restrictions);
2 actions aimed at eliminating the market-dominant minority (for example, through expulsion or atrocity); and
3 a pro-market retreat from democracy.

These three outcomes have occurred repeatedly throughout the history of the developing world. Here I will use Indonesia as just one particularly vivid illustration.

Indonesia

As in all the Southeast Asian countries, the ethnic Chinese in Indonesia have long represented an economically dominant minority *vis-à-vis* the indigenous majority around them – in this case, the *pribumi* ('of the earth').[23] Since at least the early 1910s, the Indonesian Chinese have been the frequent targets of popular anti-Chinese violence. As many scholars have noted, the emergence of Indonesian nationalism at the turn of the century was inextricably bound up with 'the sudden increased impingement of aggressively competitive Chinese entrepreneurs upon the interests of the vestigial Javanese merchant class'.[24] After independence, President Sukarno's sweeping nationalizations in the 1950s and 1960s targeted not just the Dutch but also, very explicitly, the ethnic Chinese – an instance of the first outcome noted above (ethnically targeted anti-market backlash). It is crucial to distinguish these ethnically targeted nationalizations from socialism. Unlike the former Soviet Union or China, when Sukarno nationalized, his goal was never to eliminate private property or to level the class structure. Rather, Sukarno used nationalization and other measures of economic nationalism to 'indigenize' much of Indonesia's financial, mining, import-export, rice, batik and modern industrial sectors – all formerly dominated by Chinese and Europeans.[25]

By contrast, the thirty-year 'capitalist-style' autocracy of General Suharto is a paradigmatic example of the third outcome noted above (pro-market retreat from democracy). After seizing power militarily in 1965, Suharto proceeded to quash rival political parties and to extinguish opposition of all kinds. In return for the support of the World Bank and the IMF, Suharto adopted aggressive privatization and economic liberalization policies to encourage foreign investment and rapid economic growth. To that end, Suharto reached out to the Chinese business community. Throughout his rule, Suharto not only protected the Chinese politically, but also affirmatively directed lucrative business opportunities to them. In exchange, the Indonesian Chinese, with their 'business expertise, international connections, and preexisting business links with the armed forces', returned these favors, both by fueling the country's economy and by adding enormously to the personal wealth of the Suharto family.[26]

As already mentioned, by the end of the Suharto regime, Sino-Indonesians occupied a position of economic dominance wildly disproportionate to their numbers (roughly 3 per cent of the population). All of Indonesia's billionaires reportedly have been ethnically Chinese, and, until very recently, almost all of the country's largest conglomerates were owned by Sino-Indonesian families. The major exception to this rule was companies owned by the children of President Suharto, which themselves 'depended for their success on state favors and links with Sino-Indonesians'. On a smaller scale, although of course not all Sino-Indonesians were well-off, ethnic Chinese dominated petty trading occupations in rural areas and retail and wholesale trade in urban areas, as well as the country's informal credit sector. Indeed, '[p]ractically every tiny town [had] an ethnic Chinese-run general store that [was] the center of local economic life'.[27]

As recent events have made clear, this state of affairs provoked massive, widespread hostility among the *pribumi* majority. Suharto's resignation in May 1998 was accompanied by discriminatory ethnically targeted market interventions[28] and an eruption of vicious anti-Chinese violence, in which nearly 5,000 shops and homes of ethnic Chinese were burned and looted, over 2,000 people died, and many ethnic Chinese women were raped.[29] Many Sino-Indonesian families (including some of the wealthiest) left the country,[30] along with massive amounts of Chinese-controlled capital, estimated at $40–100 billion,[31] making Indonesia during this period an illustration of the second (eliminationist) outcome noted above.

Recent elections brought to power a new president, Abdurrahman Wahid, who was initially widely praised for his tolerance and commitment to human rights, but who has recently been superceded by Megawati Sukarnoputri. Like Wahid, Megawati supports both 'democratic reforms' and IMF-dictated pro-free-market policies. In other words, the combined pursuit of markets and democracy is once again the prevailing prescription.

Unfortunately, the conflict between these two goals is likely to be intense and combustible. With poverty pervasive, and 'its banks and largest corporations still mired in delinquent debts', Indonesia remains 'in its worst economic crisis in a generation'. The point of pro-market reforms is explicitly to procure the return of foreign investment and Chinese-controlled capital, without which, experts agree, the Indonesian economy cannot be restarted. But for these policies to succeed would require a degree of assurance of Chinese economic security that may be not be compatible with genuine democratic politics, in a country where, just fifteen months ago, many reportedly felt that 'it would be worthwhile to lose ten years of growth to "get rid of the [Chinese] problem once and for all"'.[32]

Other developing countries

Indonesia is in no sense exceptional. As I have documented in detail elsewhere, ethnically targeted nationalizations or confiscations (outcome one) have occurred in postcolonial Burma, Kenya, Pakistan, the Philippines, Sri Lanka, Thailand, Uganda and Vietnam, and most recently have been championed by indigenous politicians in Eritrea, Russia, South Africa and Zimbabwe. Suharto-style symbiotic relationships between autocratic governments and entrepreneurial minorities (outcome three) have been pursued by the Nguyen emperors in Vietnam, many Thai kings, Marcos in the Philippines, and a host of rulers in Africa. Finally, economically dominant minorities have been killed *en masse* in, expelled from, or pressured to leave Burma, Cambodia, Kenya, the Philippines, Rwanda, Uganda and Vietnam, and most recently many of the Central Asian republics of the former Soviet Union (outcome two).[33]

Law, culture and development

The paradox of free market democracy, once fully recognized, demands serious rethinking of current international development policy. This is particularly, but by no means only, true in developing countries with a market-dominant minority, where there is a very real danger that the paradox will be ethnicized. I explore specific policy proposals at length elsewhere,[34] but here will simply state five broad policy observations.

First, all developing countries – even countries (like China) without market-dominant minorities – will, if they choose to pursue both markets and democracy, have to find ways to mediate the basic conflict between market-generated wealth disparities and majoritarian politics. Needless to say, there can be no 'one-size-fits-all' solution. Some countries are much further along than others in the marketization or democratization process; each will have to find a balance of mediating institutions appropriate to its own history and cultural traditions.

Second, the design of all the latest legal reform measures in the developing world (including promotion of the rule of law, state-building, free and fair elections, independent judiciary and civil society) must be reexamined in this light. These measures are of great importance for the developing world. Moreover, if properly designed, they could ultimately play a valuable role in mediating the paradox of free market democracy. (Ideally, for example, rule-of-law initiatives can strengthen the rights and position of the less well-off as well as help legitimize the state.) But if care is not taken, these measures may inadvertently heighten the conflict between markets and democracy. For example, as a practical matter, the main thrust of today's rule-of-law initiatives in the developing world is to facilitate market activity (by strengthening legislative and judicial protections of property and contract). To the extent that such initiatives succeed, they will accomplish very significant achievements, but in the process they may intensify the contest between unequal wealth and majoritarian politics.

Third, there are many versions of 'market capitalism' on which developing countries might draw. Sweden and the United Kingdom, for example, are both 'market economics', but very different from the United States. Moreover, there is no Western country today that has anything close to a laissez-faire system. Ironically, however, the version of capitalism being exported today to many developing countries more closely resembles the relatively laissez-faire regimes characteristic of the developed world during an earlier period, when property qualifications and other stringent suffrage limitations were in place. This anachronism is especially questionable given the much more pervasive poverty and political instability of the developing world.

Fourth, there are similarly many different forms of democracy. Taking universal suffrage as a given, democratization can vary along a large number of axes relevant to the paradox of free market democracy: to name a few, presidentialism versus parliamentarism; first-past-the-post versus proportional representation; starting locally versus starting nationally. Much more consideration needs to be given to the question of what kind of democracy is suitable to particular developing nations in light of the tensions that will inevitably arise between markets and majoritarian politics.

Fifth, regarding ideology, as market institutions are exported to the developing world, there is a tendency to assume that the generally market-supportive beliefs and cultural attitudes familiar to us in the West will be exported along with them. This assumption is deeply problematic. While Cheng *et al.* are surely right that 'law is constitutive as well as expressive of culture and values', ideologies do not come 'attached' to institutions in a simplistic way. Are the poor of the developing world really to be expected to support a market economy, with its phenomenal wealth disparities, out of a belief in an American-style, rags-to-riches ideology of upward mobility, which does not travel particularly well even to Europe? If not, are they expected to support markets because they are rational maximizers of the society's long-term gross national product? It should not be assumed that any of the developed world's market-compatible ideologies will spontaneously come into being with market reforms in the developing world. The question, then, is how the poor in the developing world can be given a genuine, sufficient stake – material, political and psychological – in a market economy.

In conclusion, as the editors of this volume observe in their chapter,

> The rise of global markets and the expansion of international capital flows have led to predictions of the convergence of values and cultures, the adoption of universal rights over particular traditions and beliefs, and the development of new global norms in place of local values.[35]

Specifically, as the authors also note, a fundamental assumption among influential institutions such as the World Bank and the International Monetary Fund 'is that economic development for most countries is accompanied by the progression to markets and the adoption of law over custom, the assertion of the impartial, rational self over group identities'.

I would push the point further. Prevailing international development orthodoxy effectively presumes that ethnic conflict is just another (irrational) aspect of under-development that the universal prescription of markets and democracy will cure. By contrast, this chapter urges lawyers and policymakers to recognize that marketization and democratization – to the extent that they are successful, to the extent that they do just what they are supposed to do – will in fact tend in many developing countries to catalyze ethnic conflict in a highly predictable and combustible fashion.

Markets and democracy cannot be regarded as antidotes to the intensifying nationalism, the 'rise of political movements based on identity politics', and the ethnic tensions and conflagrations that persist in the developing world. With respect to these dangers, markets and democracy are not solutions. They are, at least in the short and mid-term, part of the problem.

Notes

1 Professor of Law, Yale University. This chapter is based extensively on three previous works: Amy L. Chua, 'The Paradox of Free Market Democracy: Rethinking Development Policy', *Harvard International Law Journal*, vol. 41, 287 (2000); 'Depoliticizing Ethnicity', *American Journal of Competition Law*, vol. 48, 181 (1998); 'Markets, Democracy, and Ethnicity: Toward a New Paradigm for Law and Development', *Yale Law Journal*, vol. 108, no. 1 (1998).

2 Larry Diamond, 'Democracy and Economic Reform: Tensions, Compatibilities, and Strategies for Reconciliation', in Edward P. Lazear (ed.) *Economic Transition in*

Eastern Europe and Russia: Realities of Reform, 107, 108 (Stanford: Hoover Institution Press, 1995); see e.g. Peter Berger, *The Capitalist Revolution*, 73 (New York: Basic Books, 1986) (describing the contemporaneous rise of capitalism and democracy in Europe and the United States); Robert Dahl, *On Democracy*, 168 (New Haven and London: Yale University Press, 1998) (suggesting that market-capitalism 'creates a large middling stratum of property owners' who 'are the natural allies of democratic ideas and institutions'); Diamond, *supra*, 108 (observing that both capitalism and democracy rest on 'fundamental principles of competition and choice' and are threatened by 'excessive concentration of power in the state'); Owen M. Fiss, 'Capitalism and Democracy', *Michigan Journal of International Law*, vol. 13, 908, 911 (1992) ('Both notions are rooted in assumption of human rationality and self-interest, and thus rely on individual freedom and autonomy as the means for achieving their ends').

3 See e.g. James Madison, 'Notes of Debates in the Federal Convention of 1787', 403–4 (New York and London: W. W. Norton, 1976); *The Works and Correspondence of David Ricardo*, vol. 7, 369–70 (ed. Peiro Sraffa, Cambridge; University Press for Royal Economic Society 1973); Karl Marx, *The Class Struggles in France* 69–70 (New York: International Publishers, 1934 [1848–50]).

4 Adam Smith, *An Inquiry Into the Nature and Causes of The Wealth of Nations*, bk. V, ch. I, pt. II, 232 (Chicago: univerisity of Chicago Press, 1976 [1776]).

5 Thomas Babington Macaulay, *Complete Writings*, vol. 17, 263–76 (Boston and New York: Houghton, Mifflin & Company, 1900).

6 Some economists have described this dynamic in terms of uncertainty. See e.g. Anthony Downs, *An Economic Theory of Democracy*, 200 (New York: Addison-Wesley, 1957) ('[U]ncertainty allows low-income citizens to believe that someday they too may have high-incomes; hence their desire to "soak the rich" is mitigated by the hope that they themselves will be rich').

7 See Michael Goldfield, *The Color of Politics: Race and the Mainsprings of American Politics*, 30–1, 308–9 (New York: New Press, 1997); Jill Quadagno, *The Color of Welfare*, 7, 191–3 (Oxford: Oxford University Press, 1996).

8 See Frances Fox Piven and Richard Cloward, *The Breaking of the American Compact*, 12, 29, 92 (New York: New Press, 1998). Thus, after the second World War, the CIO's mass unionism campaign in the southern states ('Operation Dixie') failed dismally, unable to overcome 'the insuperable task of forming unified workplace movements between white workers, who attended Klan meetings after work, and black workers'. Mark Barenberg, 'Federalism and American Labor Law: Toward a Critical Mapping of the "Social Dumping" Question', in Ingolf Oernice (ed.) *Harmonization of Legislation in Federal Systems*, 93, 110 (Baden-Baden: Nomos Verlagsgesellschaft, 1996). More generally, '[t]he "identity politics" of white supremacy in the South and of white ethnic parochialism in northern cities, was the glue of Democratic constituency building' (Fox Piven and Cloward, *supra*, 91–2); Barenberg, *supra*, 110–11. In recent years, not just in the United States but in many developed countries, political elites have played on racism and xenophobia, seeking to gain advantage from popular division. Thus

> Le Pen's National Front in France, the Christian Right in the United States, the Freedom Party in Austria, the Falangists in Spain, the Lombardy League in Italy, or the Republicans in Germany where half a million immigrants arrived in 1992 alone – work to stoke the anger against outsiders. They draw popular attention away from the economic transformation underway, and try to hold or win anxious voters by directing resentment against outsiders.

(Frances Fox Piven and Richard Cloward, *The Breaking of the American Compact*, 53 [New York: New Press, 1998])

9 Gerald Meier, *Leading Issues in Economic Development*, 276–7 (6th edn, New York and Oxford: Oxford University Press, 1995).
10 Nancy Birdsall, 'Population Growth', *Finance and Development*, Sept. 1984, 10–14.
11 Adam Przeworski, *Sustainable Democracy*, 76 (Cambridge: Cambridge University Press, 1995).
12 For the purposes of this chapter, I assume, along with most Sinologists, that the 'Han' Chinese in China may be viewed appropriately as a single ethnic group. This is not to deny important differences within China along provincial, north/south and rural/urban lines.
13 June Teufel Dreyer, 'Assimilation and Accommodation in China', in Michael E. Brown and Sumit Ganguly (eds) *Government Policies and Ethnic Relations in Asia and the Pacific*, 351 (Cambridge MA: MIT Press, 1997).
14 See Christine Fletcher, 'Federalism and Indigenous Peoples in Australia', in *ibid.*, 395, 401; Andrew Sharp, 'Civil Rights, Amelioration, and Reparation in New Zealand', in *ibid.*, 421, 441–7; Amy L. Chua, 'Markets, Democracy, and Ethnicity: Toward a New Paradigm for Law and Development', *Yale Law Journal*, vol. 108, no. 1, 27–8 (1998).
15 See *ibid.*, 28.
16 See *ibid.*, 21–6.
17 See e.g. Leo Surydinata, 'Indonesian Policies Toward the Chinese Minority Under the New Order', *Asian Survey*, vol. 16, 770, (1976); 'A Taxing Dilemma', *Asiaweek*, 20 Oct. 1993, 53.
18 See Amy L. Chua, 'Markets, Democracy, and Ethnicity: Toward a New Paradigm for Law and Development', *Yale Law Journal*, vol. 108, no. 1, 65 (1998). A 1994 study showed that black South Africans, representing over 80 per cent of the country's population, held only 3 per cent of total jobs in management. See 'Affirmative Action', *SAM Advanced Management Journal*, vol. 63, 28 (22 June 1998).
19 Jacobo Finkelman, 'Towards Equity in Guatemala', *World Health*, vol. 47, 12 (Nov. 1994).
20 Linda Y. C. Lim and L. A. Peter Gosling, 'Strengths and Weaknesses of Minority Status for Southeast Asian Chinese at a Time of Economic Growth and Liberalization', in Daniel Chirot and Anthony Reid (eds) *Essential Outsiders: Chinese and Jews in the Modern Transformation of Southeast Asia and Central Europe*, 285, 295 (Seattle and London: University of Washington Press, 1997).
21 *Ibid.*, 295, 298, 301.
22 See David I. Steinberg, *Burma: The State of Myanmar*, 227–30 (Washington DC: Georgetown University Press, 2001); Amy L. Chua, 'Markets, Democracy, and Ethnicity: Toward a New Paradigm for Law and Development', *Yale Law Journal*, vol. 108, no. 1, 22–3 (1998).
23 This is by no means to suggest that indigenous Indonesians are homogeneous – nothing could be further from the truth. Indonesia's 'nearly 200 million people are divided into hundreds of distinct cultural groups living for the most part in regional homelands … from Aceh on the northern tip of Sumatra to Irian Jaya'. R. William Liddle, 'Coercion, Co-optation, and the Management of Ethnic Relations in Indonesia', in Michael E. Brown and Sumit Ganguly (eds) *Government Policies and Ethnic Relations in Asia and the Pacific*, 273, 274 (Cambridge MA: MIT Press, 1997).
24 George M. Kahin, *Nationalism and Revolution in Indonesia*, 67 (Ithaca; Cornell University Press1952).
25 See Amy L. Chua, 'The Paradox of Free Market Democracy: Rethinking Development Policy', *Harvard International Law Journal*, vol. 41, 321–4 (2000). Despite his 'indigenization' campaign, Sukarno was criticized by ethnic Indonesians

for 'his protective attitude to the Chinese minority', perhaps reflecting the gradual rapprochement under Sukarno between Indonesia and China.

26 See Michael R. J. Vatikiotis, *Indonesian Politics Under Suharto*, 39–41 (3rd edn, London and New York: Routledge, 1993); William Liddle, 'Coercion, Co-optation, and the Management of Ethnic Relations in Indonesia', in Michael E. Brown and Sumit Ganguly (eds) *Government Policies and Ethnic Relations in Asia and the Pacific*, 300–1 (Cambridge MA: MIT Press, 1997); William Ascher, 'From Oil to Timber: The Political Economy of Off-Budget Development Financing in Indonesia', *Indonesia*, vol. 65: 37, 53 (1998); Amy L. Chua, 'The Paradox of Free Market Democracy: Rethinking Development Policy', *Harvard International Law Journal*, vol. 41, 321–4 (2000).

27 Michael Shari and Jonathan Moore, 'The Plight of the Ethnic Chinese', *Business Week*, 3 Aug. 1998, 48; see Michael R. J. Vatikiotis, *Indonesian Politics Under Suharto*, 101 (3rd edn, London and New York: Routledge, 1993); William Liddle, 'Coercion, Co-optation, and the Management of Ethnic Relations in Indonesia', in Michael E. Brown and Sumit Ganguly (eds) *Government Policies and Ethnic Relations in Asia and the Pacific*, 300–1 (Cambridge MA: MIT Press, 1997).

28 Indonesia's rice industry provides one illustration. Until May 1998, Indonesia's rice distribution network was dominated by ethnic Chinese traders, who operated a fairly efficient system, 'despite some profiteering on their part and despite the pay-offs they had to make to an increasingly venal indigenous bureaucracy' (*ibid.*). After Suharto's resignation, the Habibie government, in an openly ethnonationalist move supported by majoritarian sentiment, canceled rice distribution contracts with hundreds of ethnic Chinese businessmen and awarded them instead to indigenous Indonesians, some of whom had little or no experience in the field. The results were disastrous, part of a food crisis in which tens of millions of Indonesians were at one time reportedly eating only one meal a day. See 'Indonesia's Anguish', *New York Times*, 16 Oct. 1998, A26. The new state-run rice cooperatives were immediately saturated with corruption, inefficiency and scandal (one official was accused of trying to export illegally 1,900 tons of rice to Malaysia while his own constituents were starving). Predictably, indigenous officials and businessmen began secretly to subcontract work out to Chinese traders again.

29 See Gregg Jones, 'Fear Overwhelming Indonesia's Chinese', *Dallas Morning News*, 4 Oct. 1998, 1A. Most of those who died were 'non-Chinese looters trapped in burning shopping malls' (*ibid.*). According to local human rights workers, ' "more than 168 women" – most of them ethnic Chinese – were gang-raped during the riots' (*ibid.*). The Habibie government denied these allegations, claiming that they were 'exaggerated' (*ibid.*).

30 See Jay Solomon, 'Indonesia's Chinese Move to Increase Civil Rights After a Decades-Long Ban on Political Activities', *Wall Street Journal*, 9 June 1998, A14 (reporting that 110,000 Sino-Indonesian families left the country).

31 See Ravi Velloor, 'Fix Chinese Issue, Indonesia Told', *Straits Times*, 10 Oct. 1998, 2; Kafil Yamin, 'Economy – Indonesia: Not Too Happy With Very Strong Currency', Inter Press Service, 2 July 1999.

32 Ravi Velloor, 'Fix Chinese Issue, Indonesia Told', *Straits Times*, 10 Oct. 1998, 2; see Wayne Arnold, 'New Indonesian Leadership Stirs Financiers' Skepticism', *New York Times*, 27 Oct. 1999, C4; Jay Solomon, 'Indonesia's Chinese Move to Increase Civil Rights After a Decades-Long Ban on Political Activities', *Wall Street Journal*, 9 June 1998, A14; Kafil Yamin, 'Economy – Indonesia: Not Too Happy With Very Strong Currency', Inter Press Service, 2 July 1999. It is no coincidence that President Wahid's first official visit was to China, where one of his primary

goals was to secure Beijing's blessing for the return of 'overseas Chinese' capital to Indonesia.

33 See Amy L. Chua, 'Markets, Democracy, and Ethnicity: Toward a New Paradigm for Law and Development', *Yale Law Journal*, vol. 108, no. 1, 47–63 (1998).

34 Amy L. Chua, 'The Paradox of Free Market Democracy: Rethinking Development Policy', *Harvard International Law Journal*, vol. 41, 338–79 (2000).

35 Lucie Cheng, Margaret Y. K. Woo and Arthur Rosett, 'Finding a Role for Law in Asian Development', this volume, Chapter 1.

4

COMPETING CONCEPTIONS OF 'RULE OF LAW' IN CHINA[1]

Randall Peerenboom

Rule of law, like any other important political concept such as justice or equality, is an 'essentially contested concept'.[2] Yet the fact that there is room for debate about the proper interpretation of 'rule of law' should not blind us to the broad consensus as to its core meaning and basic elements. At its most basic, rule of law refers to a system in which law is able to impose meaningful restraints on the state and individual members of the ruling elite, as captured in the rhetorically powerful if overly simplistic notions of a government of laws, the supremacy of the law, and equality of all before the law.[3]

Theories of rule of law can be divided into two general types, thin and thick. A thin theory stresses the formal or instrumental aspects of rule of law – those features that any legal system allegedly must possess to function effectively as a system of laws, regardless of whether the legal system is part of a democratic or non-democratic society, capitalist or socialist, liberal or theocratic.[4] Although proponents of thin interpretations of rule of law define it in slightly different ways, there is considerable common ground.[5] For present purposes, the constitutive elements of a thin conception include, in addition to meaningful restraints on state actors, the following:

- There must be procedural rules for law-making, and laws must be made by an entity with the authority to make laws in accordance with such rules to be valid.
- Transparency: laws must be made public and readily accessible.
- Law must be generally applicable: that is, law must not be aimed at a particular person and must treat similarly situated people equally.
- Laws must be relatively clear.
- Laws generally must be prospective rather than retroactive.
- Laws must be consistent on the whole.
- Laws must be relatively stable.
- Laws must be fairly applied.
- Laws must be enforced: the gap between the law on books and law in practice should be narrow.

- Laws must be reasonably acceptable to a majority of the populace or people affected (or at least the key groups affected) by the laws.[6]

In contrast to thin versions, thick or substantive conceptions begin with the basic elements of a thin conception but then incorporate elements of political morality such as particular economic arrangements (free market capitalism, central planning, etc.), forms of government (democratic, single-party socialism, etc.) or conceptions of human rights (liberal, communitarian, 'Asian values', etc.).

Thus the liberal democratic version of rule of law incorporates free market capitalism (subject to qualifications that would allow various degrees of 'legitimate' government regulation of the market), multiparty democracy in which citizens may choose their representatives at all levels of government, and a liberal interpretation of human rights that gives priority to civil and political rights over economic, social, cultural and collective or group rights.

Although rule of law has ancient roots and may be traced back to Aristotle, the modern conception of rule of law is integrally related to the rise of liberal democracy in the West. Indeed, for many, 'the rule of law' means a liberal democratic version of rule of law.[7] In striking contrast to the many volumes on rule of law in the Western literature, relatively little work has been done on clarifying alternative conceptions of rule of law in other parts of the world.[8]

Significantly, however, there is relatively little support for liberal democracy, and hence a liberal democratic rule of law, among state leaders, legal scholars, intellectuals or the general public in China. On the contrary, study after study shows most people are more concerned about stability and economic growth than democracy and civil and political liberties.[9] Moreover, although China's leaders have officially endorsed rule of law, they have not sanctioned the liberal democratic version. In 1996, Jiang Zemin adopted the new *tifa* or official policy formulation of ruling the country in accordance with law and establishing a socialist rule-of-law state (*yifa zhiguo, jianshe shuhui zhuyi fazhiguo*), which was subsequently incorporated into the Constitution in 1999.

Accordingly, if we are to understand the likely path of development of China's system, and the reasons for differences in its institutions, rules, practices and outcomes in particular cases, we need to rethink rule of law. We need to theorize rule of law in ways that do not assume a liberal democratic framework, and explore alternative conceptions of rule of law that are consistent with China's own circumstances.

To that end, I describe four competing thick conceptions of rule of law: statist socialism, neo-authoritarian, communitarian and liberal democratic.[10] In contrast to liberal democratic rule of law, Jiang Zemin and other statist socialists endorse a state-centered socialist rule of law defined by, *inter alia*, a socialist form of economy (which in today's China means an increasingly market-based economy, but one in which public ownership still plays a somewhat larger role than in other market economies); a non-democratic system in which the Party plays a leading role; and an interpretation of rights that emphasizes stability, collective rights over individual rights, and subsistence as the basic right rather than civil and political rights.

There is also support for various forms of rule of law that fall between the statist socialism type championed by Jiang Zemin and other central leaders and the liberal democratic version. For example, there is some support for a democratic but non-liberal (new Confucian) communitarian variant built on market capitalism, perhaps with a somewhat greater degree of government intervention than in the liberal version; some genuine form of multiparty democracy in which citizens choose their representatives at all levels of government; and 'Asian values' or communitarian interpretation of rights that attaches relatively greater weight to the interests of the majority, and collective rights as opposed to the civil and political rights of individuals.[11]

Another variant is a neo-authoritarian or soft authoritarian form of rule of law that, like the communitarian version, rejects a liberal interpretation of rights, but unlike its communitarian cousin also rejects democracy. Whereas communitarians adopt a genuine multiparty democracy in which citizens choose their representatives at all levels of government, neo-authoritarians permit democracy only at lower levels of government or not at all.[12]

Four ideal types: statist socialist, neo-authoritarian, communitarian, liberal democratic

Given the wide variety of political beliefs and conceptions of a just socio-political order, it is in theory possible to categorize thick rule-of-law theories in any number of ways. In order to facilitate discussion, however, I have divided PRC views into four schools: statist socialist, neo-authoritarian, communitarian and liberal democratic. A few preliminary observations about these conceptions may help avoid misunderstandings.

First, a full elaboration of any of these types requires a more detailed account of the purposes or goals the regime is intended to serve and its institutions, practices, rules and outcomes, as provided in the rest of this chapter and more fully elsewhere.[13] Second, these four ideal types were constructed with the present realities of China in mind. For instance, I attribute to statist socialism a belief in a market economy. This is not to rule out the possibility of a statist socialist rule of law that adopts a centrally planned economy. However, China can no longer be described in such terms. My purpose is not to create an exhaustive set of categories that can be applied to all countries and legal systems, or even to all Asian countries.[14] The categories may not be applicable at all to other countries, or even if applicable in a general sense, they may need to be redefined in light of the particular circumstances and issues.

Nor are these categories exhaustive with respect to China. For instance, given the wide regional differences and the importance of religion and non-Han values in some areas such as Tibet and Xinjiang, a form of semi-religious rule of law might be more appropriate.[15] Moreover, the ideal types could be further subdivided. Thus communitarian rule of law could come in a more statist 'Asian values' version, a pragmatic new Confucian version, or a Deweyean civic republicanism version that assumes much of the value structure and institutional framework of a liberal democratic order.[16] Indeed, one could create an ever-expanding taxonomy by making finer specifications of any of the variables or introducing new ones. However, at some point, one begins to lose the forest for the trees.[17] For present purposes, these four types are sufficient to capture the main differences in the dominant prevailing political and legal views.

The four variants are ideal types in the sense that they are representative models. As such, they are intended to reflect real positions. It is therefore possible to identify schools of thought and individuals that fall into each of the categories.[18] At the same time, they are a distillation of the views of many different individuals, drawn from not only written sources but also thousands of conversations with scholars, legal academics, judges, lawyers and citizens over the years.[19] Consequently, no one type may fit exactly the position of any one person or group. For instance, while most new conservatives would support neo-authoritarianism, some might favor statist socialism or communitarianism.[20] Others might not fit easily into any category, but rather endorse elements from different schools. Moreover, although certain individuals may have expressed general support for some of the central tenets of the various ideal types, they will not have addressed all of the specific issues that I address. At times, therefore, the positions attributed to their variant of rule of law are a logical extension of their ideas based on inferences from their general principles.

Each of the various types is compatible with a variety of institutions, practices, rules and, to some extent, outcomes. Within Western liberal democratic legal orders, for example, there is considerable variation along each of these dimensions. Take such a basic issue as separation of powers. In the US, 'separation of powers' refers to a system in which the legislature, executive and judiciary are constitutionally independent and equal branches. In contrast, the UK and Belgium, among others, are parliamentary supreme states. On the other hand, despite these structural differences, no country – not even the US – adheres to the simplistic separation of powers where the legislature passes laws, the executive implements them and the courts interpret and enforce them by adjudicating disputes. For better or worse, administrative agencies everywhere make, implement and adjudicate laws.[21]

Similarly, some liberal states have written constitutions while others such as the UK do not. Some are common law systems, and others are civil. Civil law countries tend to prefer broadly drafted laws; common law countries, more narrowly drafted laws.[22] In some liberal states, judges are elected; in others, judges are appointed; in still others, some judges are elected and some are appointed. In some, the legal profession is self-regulating. In others, the legal profession is subject to supervision by a government body such as a ministry of justice.

Conversely, different regimes may share similar purposes, institutions, practices and rules. Given a general consensus on the purposes and elements of a thin theory, one would expect of course a certain amount of convergence in institutions, practices and rules. For instance, in order to enhance predictability and limit government arbitrariness, China has established many of the same mechanisms for controlling administrative discretion, as have other regimes.[23] It has also enacted a number of administrative laws modeled on comparable laws in the US and Europe.

Notwithstanding the wide variation within particular regime types on the one hand and the overlap among different regime types on the other, the ideological differences that underlie different thick conceptions of rule of law tend to be reflected in variations in institutional arrangements, practices, rules and most importantly in outcomes. Indeed, even were China to import wholesale the institutions and legal doctrines of the US, the outcomes in particular cases would still differ as a result of fundamental differences in values, political beliefs and philosophies. The four ideal types, therefore, serve a heuristic purpose in capturing some of the basic differences between alternative thick conceptions of rule of law in the PRC.

For comparison purposes, I refer to a rule-by-law regime where relevant. Of course, rule-by-law systems come in different varieties as well. There are more moderate and more extreme versions. The legal system during the Mao era, particularly during the Cultural Revolution, was a good example of an extreme version, to the point where at times it hardly could be described as even a rule-by-law legal system, which after all implies some form of law-based order.[24] Notwithstanding variation within the category of rule by law, rule by law is distinguishable from rule of law in that the former rejects the central premise of rule of law, namely that law is to impose meaningful limits on even the highest government officials. Nevertheless, a rule-by-law system, especially a more moderate form than that of the Mao era, may share some features with some versions of rule of law, particularly the statist socialist and neo-authoritarian ones: for example, the rejection of elections in favor of single-party rule. This is hardly surprising given that institutions, rules or practices may serve more than one purpose or end. On the other hand, in some cases, certain features appear to be the same but differ in degree or the role they play in rule-of-law and rule-by-law regimes. For instance, while communitarians accept some limits on civil society, the limits are much more restrictive in a rule-by-law system, even a moderate rule-by-law regime. Similarly, a rule-by-law system aims at a much higher degree of thought control than the others.[25]

The economic regime

Although all four rule-of-law variants favor a market economy, they differ with respect to the degree, nature and manner of government intervention. Notwithstanding the significant differences in the economies of Western liberal democracies that have led neo-institutionalists and political economists to posit varieties of capitalism even within Europe,[26] economies in liberal democratic states tend to be characterized by minimal government regulation intended primarily to correct market failures; a clear distinction between the public sphere and private commercial sphere; and limited administration discretion to interfere in private business. In contrast, economic growth in many Asian countries, including China, has been attributed to a form of managed capitalism in which the state actively intervenes in the market, government officials blur the line between public and private spheres by establishing clientelist or corporatist relationships with private businesses, and universal laws are complemented, and sometimes supplanted, by administrative guidance, vertical and horizontal relationships, and informal mechanisms for resolving disputes.[27] In these Asian development states, the government relies on its licensing power and control over access to loans, technology and other information and inputs to steer companies in the direction determined by the state. In some cases, the government will champion particular companies or sectors of the economy. The government may also have a direct or indirect economic interest in certain companies. Of course there is considerable variation in the amount, nature and form of government intervention in Asian countries. Surely Hong Kong's economy has been as laissez-faire as any in the West. On the whole, however, Asian governments have taken a more interventionist approach to managing the economy.

China's economy is currently heavily regulated and characterized by clientelism and corporatism.[28] Moreover, governments at all levels have both direct and indirect economic interests in companies. To be sure, there is considerable debate about the merits of such heavy government intervention and close government/business relations. While a more laissez-faire economy has its supporters, there is ample support for the view that China's transition from a centrally planned economy to a market economy that requires a strong (neo-authoritarian) government able to make tough decisions without fear of having to appease the electorate.[29] Although statist socialists and neo-authoritarians (and rule-by-law proponents) are most likely to adopt such views, many if not most communitarians also support them. The difference between them is that statist socialists arguably favor a higher degree of government regulation than neo-authoritarians and communitarians.

Statist socialists and neo-authoritarians are also somewhat more likely to favor corporatist or clientelist relationships between government and businesses than are communitarians, on the grounds that it increases the state's control over economic activities. However, all are concerned about the negative effects of corporatism and clientelism, in terms of both economic efficiency and increased corruption. Thus some shift away from such relationships as they currently exist toward a more open, transparent process based on generally applicable laws is likely, even if in the end there remains a higher degree of interaction between government and business than in the West.

Public ownership is one pillar, albeit a shaky one, of Jiang Zemin's socialist rule-of-law state. To be sure, all states allow for some public ownership. Nonetheless, in comparison to the others, statist socialists can be expected to favor somewhat higher levels of public ownership, more limitations on the kinds of shares that can be held by private and foreign investors, and more restrictions on the industries in which private and foreign companies may hold majority shares.

The political order

Liberal democracies are characterized by genuine democratic elections for even the highest level of government office. Thus a liberal democractic state is a neutral one in which the normative agenda for society is determined by the people through elections and a limited state with an expansive private sphere and robust civil society independent of the state.[30] In contrast, statist socialism is defined by single-party rule, elections at only the lowest level of government and at present a nomenclatural system of appointments whereby the highest-level personnel in all government organs including the courts are chosen or approved by the Party. Rather than a neutral state, the Party in its role as vanguard sets the normative agenda for society, which currently consists of the four cardinal principles: the leading role of the Party, adherence to socialism, the dictatorship of the proletariat, and adherence to Marxism-Leninism-Mao Zedong thought. In addition, there is a smaller private sphere and a correspondingly larger role for the state in supervising and guiding social activities. If statist socialists had their way, there would be at most a limited civil society characterized by a high level of corporatist and clientelist relationships with government.[31] In these respects, there is little to distinguish statist socialists from rule-by-law advocates, although the latter might favor an even more totalitarian form of government.

Neo-authoritarians prefer single-party rule to a genuine democracy. They would either do away with elections, or were that not politically feasible, limit elections to lower levels of government. If forced to hold national-level elections, they would attempt to control the outcome of the elections by imposing limits on the opposition party or through their monopoly on major media channels. Like the statist socialists, they reject the neutral state and favor a large role for government in controlling social activities. Nevertheless, they would tolerate a somewhat smaller role for government and a correspondingly larger civil society, albeit one still subject to restrictions and characterized by clientelism and corporatism.

In contrast, communitarians favor genuine multiparty democratic elections at all levels of government, though not necessarily right at the moment. Given their fear of chaos, distrust of the allegedly ignorant masses, and lack of requisite institutions, they are willing to postpone elections for the moment and to accept a gradual step-by-step process where elections are permitted at successively higher levels of government. Like the statist socialists and neo-authoritarians, they believe state leaders should determine the normative agenda for society, and hence allow a larger role for the state in managing social activities than in a liberal democratic state. However, they prefer a somewhat more expansive civil society. Although some groups, particularly commercial associations, might find close relationships with the government helpful, other more social or spiritual groups might not. The latter would be permitted to go their own way, subject to concerns about social order, public morality and specific harms to members of the group or society at large. Rather than hard or statist corporatism, communitarians favor a soft or societal version.[32]

Perspective on rights

Liberal democrats favor a liberal understanding of rights that gives priority to civil and political rights over economic, social, cultural and collective or group rights. Rights are conceived of in deontological terms as distinct from and normatively superior to interests.[33] Rights are considered to be prior to the good (and interests) both in the sense that rights 'trump' the good/interests, and in that rights are based not on utility, interests or consequences, but on moral principles whose justification is derived independent of the good.[34] To protect individuals and minorities against the tyranny of the majority, rights impose limits on the interests of others, the good of society and the will of the majority. Substantively, freedom is privileged over order, individual autonomy takes precedence over social solidarity and harmony, and freedom of thought and the right to think win out over the need for common ground and right thinking on important social issues.[35] In addition, rights are emphasized rather than duties or virtues.

In contrast, communitarians endorse a communitarian or 'Asian values' interpretation of human rights that emphasizes the indivisibility of rights.[36] Greater emphasis is placed on collective rights and the need for economic growth, even if at the expense of individual civil and political rights.[37] Rather than a deontological conception of rights as anti-majoritarian trumps on the social good, rights are conceived of in utilitarian or pragmatic terms as another type of interest to be weighed against other interests, including the interests of groups and society as a whole.[38] Accordingly, stability is privileged over freedom; social solidarity and harmony are as important, if not more so, than autonomy and freedom of thought; and the right to think is limited by the need for common ground and consensus on important social issues. Communitarians, neo-authoritarians, statist socialists and rule-by-law advocates also pay more attention than liberal democrats to the development of moral character and virtues and the need to be aware of one's duties to other individuals, one's family, members of the community and the nation.

Like communitarians, neo-authoritarians and statist socialists conceive of rights in utilitarian or pragmatic terms. However, they have a more state-centered view than communitarians. Statist socialists in particular are likely to conceive of rights as positivist grants of the state and useful tools for strengthening the nation and the ruling regime.[39] They are also more likely than neo-authoritarians to invoke state sovereignty, 'Asian values' and the threat of cultural imperialism, to prevent other countries from interfering in their internal affairs while overseeing the destruction of the communities and traditional cultures and value systems that they were allegedly defending.[40] Nevertheless, communitarians and neo-authoritarians in China are also likely to object to strong-arm politics and the use of rights to impose culture-specific values on China or to extract trade concessions in the form of greater access to Chinese markets.[41] Moreover, like communitarians, neo-authoritarians and statist socialists privilege order over freedom. They go even farther than communitarians, however, in tilting the scales toward social solidarity and harmony rather than autonomy, and are willing to impose more limits on freedom of thought and the right to think. While neo-authoritarians would restrict the right of citizens to criticize the government, statist socialists would impose such broad restrictions that criticism of the government would be for all practical purposes prohibited. Indeed, statist socialists much prefer unity of thought to freedom of thought, and right thinking to the right to think.[42] Were it possible (without undermining their other goals such as economic growth), they would return to the strict thought-control rule-by-law regime of the Mao era. At minimum, they draw the line at public attacks on the ruling party or challenges to single-party socialism. Despite the changes in society over the last twenty years that have greatly reduced the effectiveness of 'thought work', they continue to emphasize its important role of ensuring common ground and consensus on important social issues defined by the Party line.[43]

The rule-by-law regime of the Mao era differed from any of these rule-of-law regimes in considering the concept of rights as a bourgeois liberal device to induce false consciousness in the proletariat. Although the Mao regime did include some rights in its various constitutions, such rights were considered programmatic goals to be realized at some future date. In addition, duties were privileged over rights (especially duties to the state), civil society was extremely limited, and efforts at thought control were pervasive.

Purposes of rule of law

Proponents of the various conceptions see rule of law serving certain similar purposes: enhancing predictability and certainty, which promotes economic growth and allows individuals to plan their affairs; preventing government arbitrariness; increasing government efficiency and rationality; providing a mechanism for dispute resolution; protecting individual rights; and bolstering regime legitimacy. They differ, however, with respect to the priorities of the various purposes, their degree of support or enthusiasm for any given purpose and the details of how the goals are interpreted. Broadly stated, liberal democrats emphasize the role of rule of law in limiting the state and protecting the individual against government arbitrariness, whereas communitarians favor a more balanced role for rule of law as a means of both limiting and strengthening the state. In contrast, neo-authoritarians place somewhat greater emphasis on the state-strengthening aspect, which is assigned an even higher priority by statist socialists.

Indeed, although statist socialists accept – at least in theory – the primary requirement of rule of law, namely that government officials and citizens alike are subject to law and must act in accordance with it, they accept such limits grudgingly. Not surprisingly, the reach of the law has been limited to date, with high-level government officials typically subject to a separate system of Party discipline rather than to the formal legal process. Moreover, while statist socialists appreciate the benefits of limiting government arbitrariness, they also prefer a system that allows them sufficient flexibility to pursue their legitimate (and sometimes illegitimate) ends. And while they regularly declare that rule of law is necessary to protect individual rights, it is not a high priority. In any case, the ability of the legal system to protect individual rights is severely hampered by their statist conception of rights and the extreme emphasis on stability and order over freedom.

Differences in the purposes of rule of law are evident in the weights attached to stability. All – even liberal democrats – agree that stability is important. Clearly, one purpose of law in Western traditions has been to prevent anarchy and a Hobbesian war of all against all. China, for its part, has suffered tremendous upheaval in the last 150 years, from the uprisings against and eventual collapse of the Qing, to the chaos and internal struggles of the republican period, the turbulence of the anti-rightist movement, the Great Leap Forward, and the Cultural Revolution of the Mao era. With a quarter of the world's population, many of them below or near the poverty level, China (and the rest of the world) can hardly afford political chaos or anarchy. The current economic reforms have already resulted in massive unemployment and rising unrest. As the reforms continue and the number of unemployed shoots up, the potential for traumatic disruptions of the social order increase accordingly.[44]

Rule of law could serve the goal of stability in a variety of ways. First, it could limit the arbitrary acts of government. One of the biggest sources of instability in the last fifty years has been the Party itself and the arbitrariness of senior leaders. One of the main reasons for promoting rule of law after the death of Mao was to avoid the chaos of the Cultural Revolution, where the whims of Party leaders substituted for laws. Rule of law is meant to make governance more regular and predictable. It is also needed to address the perennial problem confronting socialist regimes of political succession.[45] Whereas the death of Mao set off a struggle for power, rule of law is supposed to ensure a more seemly and seamless transition of power.[46]

In addition, rule of law serves stability by regularizing central/local relations. Conflicts between the central and local governments have increased dramatically as a result of economic reforms that have given local governments both more authority and responsibility. In their desire to promote local economic development, local governments regularly ignore central laws and policies, issue regulations that are inconsistent with national-level laws, or engage in local protectionism. While there seems little chance of the central government losing control over local governments to the point where local governments emerge as republican-era type warlords, as some alarmists have suggested, authority has become fragmented to such an extent that China arguably now has a *de facto* federalist form of government.[47] Predictably, Jiang Zemin and other statist socialists emphasize the value of rule of law as a means of disciplining local governments and recentralizing power.

On the other hand, some scholars have noted that stability is often a code word in Chinese politics for greater centralization of power, an emphasis on collective over individual rights, and the continued dominance of the Party.[48] In this view, the government's emphasis on stability is overstated and is really just an attempt to limit challenges to Party rule. Former Vice Director of the Chinese Academy of Social Sciences Li Shenzhi, for instance, argues that subsistence is no longer such a major problem. Accordingly, more emphasis should be paid to political reform and citizens' civil and political rights.[49] Similarly, Yu Keping has argued that political reform need not lead to instability.[50] To some extent, the differences turn on empirical issues. How unstable is China? How likely is it that the activities of any one dissident or even a group of dissidents could endanger national security? But they also reflect fundamental differences in values. Although all appreciate the need for stability, liberals would place greater importance on freedom, whereas statist socialists, neo-authoritarians and communitarians would privilege, to varying degrees, order over freedom.

Broad agreement over other purposes also gives way to subtle differences upon further probing. All agree, for instance, that predictability and certainty are crucial for economic growth. But predictability and certainty may serve other purposes as well. Liberal democrats value predictability because it enhances freedom by allowing people to plan their affairs and realize their ends in life, and thus promotes human dignity.[51] Underlying this view is a liberal view of the self as moral agent that emphasizes autonomy and the importance of making moral choices. But not all ethical traditions share this view of the self or place such importance on choice-making. The dominant Chinese view of the self as social, and the Confucian emphasis on doing what is right rather than the right to choose, call into question justifications of rule of law that appeal to this interpretation of human dignity.[52] Of course, the ability to plan one's affairs is valuable to some degree in China.[53] However, the weight attached to the ability to plan one's affairs and the reasons given in support are likely to differ between liberal democrats and the others, with statist socialists assigning it the least weight.[54]

Similarly, all hope that rule of law will enhance the legitimacy of the ruling regime. However, by allowing elections and ample opportunities for public participation in lawmaking, administrative rulemaking, interpretation and implementation processes, legitimacy for liberal democrats and communitarians is based on consent. In contrast, in the absence of elections and with only limited opportunities for public participation, legitimacy for statist socialists and neo-authoritarians is primarily performance based: that is, legitimacy depends on whether the laws, the legal system and the regime as a whole produce good results.[55]

In contrast, in a rule-by-law regime, law is merely a tool to serve the interests of the state, and there are no meaningful legal limits on the rulers. Law serves the state by enhancing government efficiency, although that goal is often compromised by the heavily politicized nature of law and the dominance of policy. Law is not meant to protect the rights of individuals. Whereas rule-of-law regimes rely on the courts to resolve disputes, in the Mao era, for instance, the formal legal system was used primarily to suppress enemies. Disputes among the people were settled through mediation, and economic conflicts between state-owned entities were resolved administratively or by Party organs.

Institutions and practices

According to Max Weber, the defining feature of a modern legal system that merits the label 'rule of law' is autonomy. Law is distinct from politics, and independent judges decide cases impartially in accordance with generally applicable laws using a distinct type of legal reasoning. To be sure, the line between politics and law is not always a clear one, as critical legal scholars repeatedly remind us.[56] Nevertheless, as Alice Tay observes:

> The difference between law and decree, between government proclamation and administrative power on the one hand and the genuine rule of law on the other, is perfectly well understood in all those countries where rule of law is seriously threatened or has been abolished.[57]

While the outer extremes of a system dominated by politics – such as the legal system in the Mao era, particularly during the Cultural Revolution – and those of a rule-of-law system – in which legal institutions and actors enjoy a high degree of autonomy – are reasonably clear, there is considerable room for variation in the middle. Advocates of alternative conceptions of rule of law are likely to disagree over where to draw the line between law and politics, due in part to their divergent views about the economy, the political order, the nature and limits of rights and the purposes that law is meant to serve.

Liberal democrats favor a high degree of independence and autonomy. The legislature that makes laws is freely elected rather than appointed by the ruling party. The judiciary as a whole and individual judges are independent. Judges generally enjoy lifetime tenure and can be removed only for limited reasons and in accordance with strict procedures. The appointment process is relatively non-politicized.[58] There is a variety of mechanisms for reining-in administrative discretion, and the legal system is capable of holding even top-level government officials accountable. The legal profession is independent and often self-governing.

At the other end of the spectrum, statist socialists favor only a moderate to low level of separation between law and politics. In keeping with the minimal requirements of rule of law, Chinese Communist Party policy is now to be transformed into laws and regulations by entities authorized to make law in accordance with the stipulated procedures for lawmaking,[59] whereas in the Mao era CCP policies substituted for or trumped laws.[60] Although the legislature is not freely elected, Party influence on the lawmaking processes has diminished radically since the beginning of reforms.[61] To be sure, like ruling parties in parliamentary systems in other countries, the Party is able to ensure that major policy initiatives become law when it is united and willing to expend the political capital to do so.[62]

Statist socialists also favor a more limited judicial independence. Courts have a functional independence in the sense that other branches of government are not to interfere in the way courts handle specific cases. Unlike the Mao era, courts may decide cases without Party approval of the judgment.[63] However, the courts may still be subject to macro-supervision by the NPC, the procuracy and other state organs, and even Party organs. While the courts as a whole enjoy limited functional independence, the autonomy and independence of individual judges is even more restricted. Accordingly, most cases are decided by a panel of judges, and a special adjudicative supervision committee within the court has the right to review particular decisions in case of manifest error.

The legal profession is granted a similar partial independence. Although not the 'workers of the state' of the Mao era, lawyers still must meet political correctness standards to practice law and pass the annual inspection test.[64] While the Ministry of Justice shares responsibility for supervising the legal profession with lawyers associations, the MOJ retains most of the authority, including the power to punish lawyers. In part because of such political reasons, but mainly due simply to corruption and rent-seeking by the MOJ and its local affiliates, lawyers try to forge close clientelist relations with the MOJ.[65]

In the administrative law area, government officials are granted considerable discretion, in part so that they may be more responsive to shifts in Party policy, but mainly for other reasons, including the need to respond quickly and flexibly to a rapidly changing economic environment.[66] Limits on civil society, freedom of the press and public participation in the law making, interpretation and implementation processes make it difficult for the public to monitor government officials. The lack of elections eliminates whatever leverage the public has over officials resulting from the possibility of voting the current government out of office.

Neo-authoritarians prefer a moderate separation between law and politics. As with statist socialism, the legislature is not elected. However, neo-authoritarians favor greater judicial independence than do statist socialists, although many would still limit the independence of the courts and individual judges in various ways. For instance, they may prefer China's unitary system, in which the NPC is supreme and exercises supervision over the courts, to a US-style separation of powers system. On the other hand, they support the development of a more professional and honest civil service, and an administrative law system capable of reining-in wayward government officials and combating corruption.[67] They also advocate greater public participation and more expansive, though still limited, freedom of association, speech and the press, so that the public can play a greater role in the monitoring of government officials. The primary purpose of administrative law, however, remains rational and efficient governance rather than the protection of individual rights. The elite corps of civil servants are to be given considerable flexibility in formulating and implementing administrative rules, which are the main form of legislation in daily governance. The legal profession would be granted limited independence and subject to supervision by the MOJ, albeit a cleaner and more professional one. Nevertheless, lawyers would still seek to establish clientelist ties to the MOJ due to its control over licensing for special forms of business and other commercial reasons.[68]

Communitarians prefer a moderate to high degree of separation between law and politics. The legislature would be freely elected. There would be ample opportunities for public participation in rule making, interpretation and implementation. The public would also be able to throw out a government that is corrupt or performs poorly; as a whole, the administrative law system would be sufficiently strong to hold even top-level government officials accountable. Although communitarians are sympathetic to the argument that a strong economy, particularly in times of transition, requires a strong executive, they balance the need for efficient government against the need to protect individual rights. Moreover, like the liberal democrats, they support an autonomous judiciary, with life tenure for judges and relatively apolitical processes for appointing and removing judges. At the same time, they reject the liberal notion of a neutral state. Accordingly, they favor the practice whereby courts decide cases in light of a substantive moral agenda for society determined by the ruling elite. In that sense, they do not differ from statist socialists or neo-authoritarians.[69] Rather, what distinguishes them is their particular normative agenda. The communitarians believe that judges should emphasize harmony, stability and the interests of the community over the interests of individuals as well as economic development. Neo-authoritarians and statist socialists agree in general but place more emphasis on economic development and upholding the authority of the state. In particular, statist socialists insist that the courts uphold the four cardinal principles – a position not supported by either neo-authoritarians or communitarians.

Rules

Although there is room for disagreement among liberal democrats on specific issues, on the whole liberal democrats prefer liberal laws. For instance, liberal laws provide strong protections for broadly defined civil and political rights. For some, free speech may be subject to only narrow time, place and manner restrictions. Social groups are free to organize without having to register with government authorities. Persons accused of crimes have the right to a lawyer, who may be present at all stages of formal interrogation; the accused may only be held for a very limited time without being charged; and the state may not rely on illegally obtained evidence in making its case. Euthanasia laws may allow individuals to choose to end their life or to ask others to assist them in doing so. Parents may keep their children out of the schools and educate them at home if they choose.

Communitarians, neo-authoritarians and statist socialists all endorse laws that limit individual freedom to one extent or another. For instance, all allow registration requirements for social groups to ensure public order. All accept substantive limits on speech as well as those of time, place and manner. No one is free to walk into a courtroom with a jacket that says 'Fuck the Draft' on it.[70] Flag burning is outlawed. The accused have a right to a lawyer but only after the police have had an initial opportunity to question them. The accused may be held for longer periods without being charged, and the period may be extended upon approval of the authorities. Illegally obtained evidence may be used in certain instances, though forced confessions and police torture are not allowed. Children are required to attend state-authorized schools, and to study a curriculum approved by the Ministry of Education. More controversially, statist socialists and neo-authoritarians, and perhaps even communitarians, endorse broadly drafted laws to protect the state and social order, such as state secrets laws and prohibitions against endangering the state.

Outcomes in specific cases

Institutions, in a broad sense, include ideology, purposes, organizational structures and cultures, norms, practices, rules and outcomes in specific cases.[71] Although I have separated them for the sake of a clearer exposition, in reality they overlap and blend together, as evident from the following examples concerning constitutional, administrative and criminal law.[72]

In general, constitutions in socialist countries have played a very different role than constitutions in liberal democratic rule-of-law states, in part because socialist states have made little pretense of abiding by the basic requirements of rule of law or of accepting any constitutional limits on the ruling regime's power.[73] Reflecting their origins in Enlightenment theories of social contract, liberal constitutions emphasize a limited state and a separation between state and society. Rule of law plays a central role in imposing limits on the state and protecting the individual against an over-reaching government, by ensuring that the state does not encroach on the fundamental rights of individuals set out in the constitution. Liberal constitutions set out fundamental principles that are supposed to stand the test of time, including the basic rights of citizens.

In contrast, socialist constitutions are characterized by frequent change. The frequent change in socialist constitutions is consistent with socialist legal theory, which conceives of law as a superstructure that reflects the economic basis of society and in particular the ownership of the material modes of production. When the economic base changes, law – and the constitution – must change accordingly. Moreover, since Marxism posits an evolution toward an ideal state, when the economy passes through various stages, amendment of the constitution is to be expected. In the PRC, the 1978 constitution was replaced in 1982 by a more market-oriented constitution that reflected Deng Xiaoping's economic open-door and reform policies. The 1982 constitution has subsequently been amended three times, as economic reforms have deepened and the economy has steadily moved away from a centrally planned economy toward a more market-oriented economy. Each time the amendments incorporated the more market-oriented policies.

Although changes in PRC constitutions reflect transformations in the economic base of society, they also reflect fundamental shifts in political power. Again, this is entirely consistent with socialist legal theory, which conceives of law as a tool of the ruling class. Whereas in a capitalist society law serves the bourgeoisie, in a socialist state law allegedly serves the people. However, in a Leninist socialist state, the Party acts as the vanguard of the people. Thus law becomes a tool of the Party. The constitution changes when there are major changes in Party leadership or Party policy.[74] The 1954 constitution therefore reflected the victory of the CCP and the Party's consolidation of power. The 1975 Cultural Revolution constitution codified Mao's victory over his opponents and embodied his radical vision for a society that must engage in permanent revolution and ceaseless class struggle to defend socialism against the enemy within and abroad. The short-lived 1978 constitution signaled Deng's victory over Mao loyalists, the turn toward a more law-based order and the need to concentrate on economic development rather than class struggle. However, Deng had yet to consolidate his power. By 1982, he was firmly in control. Thus the 1982 constitution confirmed the new emphasis on economic development. It also continued the trend, begun in the 1978 constitution, to downplay the dominance of the CCP, separate the Party from government, and turn over the functions of day-to-day governance to state organs.[75] Although the 1982 constitution incorporated Deng's four cardinal principles, they were placed in the preamble. In contrast, the principles of the supremacy of the law and that no individual or party is beyond the law were incorporated into the body of the constitution. Nevertheless, the constitution did not explicitly endorse rule of law, even a socialist rule of law, until the amendment in 1999.

What role the constitution will play in the future depends in part on which version of rule of law prevails. Should statist socialism win out, given the relatively low level of separation between law and politics, the constitution is likely to continue to change frequently to reflect major changes in policies as determined by state leaders. Because statist socialists see rule of law as a means to strengthen the state, the role of the constitution in protecting rights will remain limited. The constitution might not be directly justiciable; individuals would generally be able to avail themselves of the rights provided in the constitution only if such rights are implemented by specific legislation. On the other hand, even if statist socialism prevails, the constitution is likely to play a more important role as a baseline for measuring the legitimacy of state actions. To maintain credibility, the ruling regime will have to take the constitution more seriously. As a result, the ruling regime will appeal to the constitution more often to justify its acts. Indicative of the transition toward rule of law, Beijing has already begun to appeal to the constitution at critical times, for example when the government imposed martial law in 1989, and when it banned the Falungong in 1999.

The constitution will play an even more important role if a neo-authoritarian or communitarian form of rule of law is adopted. Although the tension between strengthening and limiting the state would still be manifest in constitutional law, at minimum there would be greater emphasis on individual rights. As a result, the constitution would probably become directly justiciable.[76] It might also be subject to less change. The process of amending the constitution would differ, at least for communitarians. Whereas non-elected state leaders would make the decision to amend the constitution for statist socialists and neo-authoritarians, democratically elected representatives would make the decision in a communitarian state.

Like constitutional law, the administrative law regime will vary depending on which version of rule of law wins out. Until recently in China, the main purpose of administrative law was considered to be to facilitate efficient administration. This view has now largely given way to the belief that administrative law must strike a balance between protecting the rights of individuals and promoting government efficiency.[77] Although the tension between the two goals is evident in every system, how China balances the two will depend on which of the various alternatives of rule of law is adopted. To date, there is very limited public participation in the administrative law process. An Administrative Procedure Law is being drafted, however, that will increase opportunities for public participation. Should the communitarian or even the neo-authoritarian conception prevail, one should expect the law to allow for greater public participation than if the statist socialist conception prevailed.

Differences in conceptions of rule of law are also evident in the outcomes of administrative litigation cases. PRC courts have been reluctant to aggressively review administrative decisions. On the whole, they have shown considerable deference to administrative agencies, for example by interpreting very narrowly the abuse of authority standard for quashing administrative decisions. In particular, they have been reluctant to interpret abuse of authority to include a concept of fundamental rights, as have courts in some Western liberal democracies.[78] There are many reasons for the courts' deference other than ideology, including institutional limits on the power of the courts.[79] But even setting aside the various institutional obstacles, given the weak support for liberalism in China, PRC courts are less likely than their counterparts in liberal democratic states to take full advantage of the abuse of authority standard as a means to protect individual rights and rein-in government officials at the expense of government efficiency.

Criminal law is another area where outcomes are especially sensitive to differences in ideology and in the conception of rule of law. In light of the importance of stability to most Chinese,[80] civil and political rights are likely to be subject to more limits than in liberal democratic states. Statist socialists in particular will object to criticisms of the government that challenge single-party socialism. Accordingly, the continued persecution of dissidents is likely to continue if statist socialists (and perhaps if neo-authoritarians) prevail. At present, the authorities often rely on re-education through labor (*lao jiao*), an administrative sanction whereby dissidents may be detained for one to three years, with a possible extension for another year, without many of the procedural rights afforded criminal suspects under the Criminal Procedure Law.[81] Although liberal democrats object to re-education through labor, others are likely to support it as necessary for social stability. Hence the complete elimination of re-education through labor does not appear to be politically feasible at this point. Arguably the best that liberal democrats can hope for is that the process is changed to incorporate more procedural protections of the kind incorporated in the Criminal Procedure Law.

On the other hand, rule of law is not infinitely elastic. Any supporter of rule of law will question the manner in which the government has suppressed dissidents. Even in criminal cases, dissidents are often denied their rights under the Criminal Procedure Law, including a right to an open trial, to communicate with their lawyers and families, and so on.[82]

In short, the outcomes of many particular issues will turn on the specific substantive moral, political and economic beliefs that define a particular thick conception of rule of law. How much criticism of government should be allowed and under what circumstances? Should one be able to use offensive language in public? Should beggars be allowed on the street? Under what circumstances can someone be stopped and searched? Do the police need a warrant to enter your house and, if so, how and when can they obtain one? Must individuals carry an identification card? Is the 'anger of the people' a legitimate basis for meting out capital punishment? Should adultery be a crime? Are gay marriages consistent with family values, a way of strengthening a newly envisioned family or a threat to the very notion of family? Liberal democrats, communitarians, neo-authoritarians and statist socialists will disagree over these issues, and indeed there will be many disagreements within any given school, just as there are many disagreements over such issues in countries known for a liberal democratic rule of law.

Nevertheless, despite such disagreements, there is also considerable common ground about the basic requirements of rule of law as captured in thin theories, and general acceptance that rule of law differs from rule by law in that the former entails meaningful legal limits on government actors.

Conclusion

Given that 'rule of law' has become associated with liberal democratic rule of law, one might argue that the term should not be stretched to include other variants. When talking about China, one should simply forgo use of rule of law in favor of other terms. Obviously, one is free to reserve the label 'rule of law' for a particular version if one so chooses. However, one problem with this approach is that forcing PRC ideas about rule of law into our prevailing yet contingent categories smacks of cultural imperialism. Second, the debate about legal reform in China has been couched in terms of rule of law, both in China and abroad. Of course, one could protest every time the term rule of law is used, or at least point out that the term is being misused. But given that 'rule of law' is a contested concept even in the West, any attempt to appropriate the term for a particular usage will be futile: the debate will continue to be posed in terms of rule of law, both by those inside and outside of China. Rather than restricting the use of the term with respect to China, it might be more useful to try to figure out what those who use the term mean by it and why they want to invoke it. How one defines rule of law will depend on what one's purpose is. Investors, governments and multilateral agencies, NGOs, moral philosophers and political scientists all have different purposes for invoking rule of law, and may therefore find some ways of defining or measuring it more suitable to their particular purpose than others. That does not mean that they are free to define rule of law as they like. Enough people in the relevant discourse community must accept the usage for the speech act to be meaningful and for the definition to serve a useful purpose. There is, however, enough common ground to the various conceptions of rule of law, provided by the basic requirements of a thin rule of law, to render the invocation of rule of law in the Chinese context intelligible and useful.

Third, many reformers in China want the debate couched in terms of rule of law for strategic reasons: rule of law entails at minimum some restraints on government leaders, and opens up other possibilities for political reform.

Fourth, simply relying on either liberal democratic rule of law or rule by law is no longer sufficient to capture what is happening in China. It is descriptively incorrect – the legal system is no longer a pure rule by law. Nor can we capture all of the nuances in the PRC debates about rule of law if we only have the overly simplistic categories of rule of law (i.e. our liberal democratic version) or else rule by law.[83] Without more refined categories, we simply will not be able to understand what is happening, either in terms of the evolution of PRC discourse, or in practice with respect to the development of the legal system.

Fifth, the practical import of forcing PRC discourse and practice into our preconceived boxes of liberal democratic rule of law or authoritarian rule by law is that we are likely to come to the wrong conclusions about reforms. We are likely to be either too pessimistic or too optimistic – either there is no fundamental change, or China is becoming 'like us'. But neither seems to be the case. Misreading what is happening is likely to lead to bad policy choices. Foreign governments and aid agencies could miss opportunities to support reforms that would improve the PRC system, for example, by failing to provide adequate resources for certain reforms because they do not believe such changes could possibly work in a rule-by-law system meant to serve the interests of the Party and nothing more. Alternatively, time and resources could be wasted on projects that are not consistent with the form of rule of law likely to emerge in China. Some rules or practices that work in the context of a liberal democratic rule of law might require liberal institutions and perhaps liberal values to succeed. They may fail to take hold in a different legal order, exacerbating the gap between law and practice.

Sixth, objecting to the application of rule of law to China and other states that are not liberal democracies, overstates the differences and fails to capture the considerable agreement with respect to the basic elements of a thin rule of law. Despite considerable variation, all four variants of rule of law accept the basic benchmark that law must impose meaningful limits on the ruler, and all are compatible with a thin conception of rule of law. Predictably, as legal reforms have progressed in China, the legal system has converged in many respects with the legal systems of well developed countries, and it is likely to continue to converge in the future.

At the same time, however, there will inevitably be some variations in rule-of-law regimes, even with respect to the basic requirements of a thin conception, due to the context in which they are embedded. Hence signs of both divergence and convergence are to be expected. Indeed, whether one finds convergence or divergence depends to a large extent on the particular indicators that one chooses, the time frame, and the degree of abstraction or focus. The closer one looks, the more likely one is to find divergence. That is, however, a natural result of narrowing the focus.

A second frequent and related objection is that, while it is possible conceptually to distinguish between these different types of rule of law legal systems, in reality rule of law is only sustainable in countries that adopt liberal democratic institutions and values. Yet Singapore and Hong Kong, among others, are examples of non-democratic, non-liberal countries that have enjoyed rule of law,[84] and contemporary Japan, Taiwan and South Korea to some extent seem to be examples of a communitarian rule of law, although an adequate discussion of whether or not these categories do in fact apply to these countries, and if so whether they are the best way to characterize the legal systems, would take us far afield.

To be sure, skeptics might argue that the use of the legal system to harass opposition politicians demonstrates that Singapore does not merit the label of rule of law, and calls into question whether a non-democratic rule of law is in fact possible. As for Hong Kong, it may be a special case, having had the benefit, as it were, of colonial rule by the British. Thus one could still claim that, as a general rule, establishing and maintaining rule of law requires democracy.[85] Indeed, one could argue that whatever the general practice, China is an unlikely candidate to implement and sustain rule of law without democracy, given the limits of socialist ideology and the Party's commitment to single-party socialism and maintaining its grip on power. Ultimately, the key to the future realization of rule of law in China is power. How is power to be controlled and allocated in a single-party socialist state? To the extent that law is to limit the Party, how does the legal system obtain sufficient authority to control a party that has been above the law? In a democracy, the final check on government power is the ability of the people to throw the government out and elect a new one. In the absence of multiparty democracy, an authoritarian government must either voluntarily relinquish some of its power or else have it taken away by force. Naturally, Party leaders will resist giving up power so readily. They may therefore be disinclined to support reforms that would strengthen rule of law but also allow institutions to become so powerful that they could then provide the basis for challenging Party rule. The result may be that, at least on those issues that threaten the Party's ability to survive, the needs of the Party will continue to trump rule of law for some time (though it bears noting that most issues do not threaten the Party).

I have argued elsewhere that there are reasons to believe that the issue of power can be resolved in favor of rule of law, and that law will come to impose ever more meaningful restraints on Party and government leaders.[86] It is possible that the ruling regime will be forced to accept limitations on its power as a condition for staying in power. At the same time, while China is not likely to embrace democracy in the near future, in the long run it may need to allow genuine democratic elections to enhance accountability and to provide a peaceful mechanism for alleviating growing social cleavages. Yet even if China becomes democratic, that does not mean it will necessarily become a liberal democracy or adopt a liberal democratic form of rule of law.

Notes

1 A draft of this article was presented at Columbia University Law School, the Sinology Department of the Catholic University in Lueven, and at a conference on 'Rule of Law and Group Identities Embedded in Asian Traditions and Cultures', held at UCLA School of Law. I would like to thank William Alford, Joseph Chan, Stanley Lubman, Herbert Morris, Stephen Munzer, Arthur Rosett, Richard Steinberg, Margarett Woo, Xia Yong and the participants at the talks at Columbia, Lueven and UCLA for their helpful comments.

2 Margaret Jane Radin, 'Reconsidering the Rule of Law', *Boston University Law Review*, vol. 69, no.4 (1989) pp. 781–819.

3 Notwithstanding such general agreement, there are areas of controversy. For instance, the emphasis on law's role in limiting the state is based on the liberal

Lockean tradition that emphasizes the supremacy of the law and the equality of all before the law (though even Locke allows that government authorities have considerable discretion and thus may act outside the law, even against it, provided they do so for the public good). In contrast, Hobbes and Austin favored the view that whatever the sovereign (or CCP) says is the law is the law. Thus for Hobbes, the sovereign authority had to be above the law. See Leslie Friedman Goldstein, 'The Rule of Law: Do We Know It When We See It?', unpublished manuscript presented at the 'Law and Society' conference (Budapest, 2001). Similarly, the emperor in the Imperial Chinese legal system had the power to make law; and, at least in the view of some commentators, the Party's leading role means that it must to some extent be above the law in that Party plays an important role in determining what the laws will be.

In all systems, the entities with power to make or change laws are in some sense beyond the law. However, there may still be laws that limit their authority to make or change laws. The view that the sovereign is above the law and determines the law was modified slightly but significantly by positivists such as H. L. A. Hart, for whom the touchstone for what constitutes a valid law is whether the rule was promulgated in accordance with proper procedures. Such procedures, and thus the authority for law, can be traced back to a basic legal norm or a 'rule of recognition' to use Hart's terminology. A dictatorial regime therefore could exercise legal authority and make law, as long as it complied with the procedural requirements for making law. Moreover, the rulers could be required to follow laws once made. Such a system is compatible with rule of law. On the other hand, a system in which the ruling regime's pronouncements simply have the force of law and the regime is not itself bound by such laws is better characterized as a rule by law or *rechtsstaat*. For the concept of rule of recognition, see H. L. A. Hart, *The Concept of Law* (Oxford: Clarendon Press, 1961).

A second concern is that it is not clear how meaningful the limits on state actors must be to qualify as 'rule of law'. For a discussion of this issue and the related issue of how to define the minimal conditions for rule of law, see R. Peerenboom, *China's Long March toward Rule of Law* (Cambridge: Cambridge University Press, forthcoming 2002).

4 See, for example, Joseph Raz, 'The Rule of Law and Its Virtue', in Joseph Raz (ed.) *The Authority of Law* (Oxford: Clarendon Press, 1979); Robert Summers, 'The Ideal Socio-Legal Order: Its "Rule of Law" Dimension', *Ratio Juris*, vol. 1, no. 2 (1988) pp. 154–61; Robert Summers, 'A Formal Theory of Rule of Law', *Ratio Juris*, vol. 6, no. 2 (1993) pp. 127–42.

5 A quick comparison of the lists of rule-of-law elements of Lon Fuller, Geoffrey de Q. Walker, Joseph Raz, Robert Summers, Richard Fallon, John Finnis and various PRC scholars reveals both common ground and some differences. See Lon Fuller, *The Morality of Law* (New Haven: Yale University Press, 1976) p. 39; Geoffrey de Q. Walker, *The Rule of Law* (Carlton, Victoria: Melbourne Press, 1988) pp. 23–42; Joseph Raz, 'The Rule of Law and Its Virtue', in Joseph Raz (ed.) *The Authority of Law* (Oxford: Clarendon Press, 1979) pp. 214–19; Robert Summers, 'A Formal Theory of Rule of Law', *Ratio Juris*, vol. 6, no. 2, pp. 127–42 ; Richard Fallon, '"The Rule of Law" as a Concept in Constitutional Discourse', *Columbia Law Review*, vol. 97, no.1 (1997) pp. 1–56; and John Finnis, *Natural Law and Natural Rights* (Oxford: Clarendon Press, 1980) pp. 270–1. Preferring thick to thin theories, several PRC scholars begin with a list similar to Fuller's and then add various elements, some of them substantive. See Xu Xianming, 'Lun "Fazhi" de Goucheng Yaojian' [On the Constitutive Elements of Rule of Law], *Faxue Yanjiu*, vol. 18, no. 3 (1996) pp. 37–44; Liu Junning, 'Cong fazhiguo dao fazhi' [From Rechstaat to Rule of Law], in Dong Yuyu and Shi Binhai (eds) *Zhengzhi Zhongguo* [Political

China] (Beijing: Jinri Zhongguo Chubanshe, 1998) pp. 254–6. Xia Yong, 'Fazhi shi shenme' [What is the rule of law?], *Zhongguo Shehui Kexue*, vol. 4 (1999) p. 117, for example, adds supremacy of the law, judicial authority and judicial justice to the list.

6 Of course a thin theory requires more than just these elements. A fully articulated thin theory would also specify the goals and purposes of the system as well as its institutions, rules, practices and outcomes.

7 See, for example, the influential statement of rule of law in the report of Committee I of the International Congress of Jurists (New Delhi, 1959). Given the many possible conceptions of rule of law, I avoid reference to 'the rule of law', which suggests that there is a single type of rule of law. Alternatively, one could refer to the concept of 'the rule of law', for which there are different possible conceptions. The thin theory of rule of law would define the core concept of rule of law, with the various thick theories constituting different conceptions. Yet from the perspective of philosophical pragmatism, how one defines a term depends on one's purposes and the consequences that attach to defining a term in a particular way. As thick and thin theories serve different purposes, I do not want to privilege thin theories over thick theories by declaring the thin version to be 'the rule of law'.

8 For a welcome exception, see the essays in Kanishka Jayasuriya, 'Introduction: Framework for the Analysis of Legal Institutions in East Asia', in Kanishka Jayasuriya (ed.) *Law, Capitalism and Power in Asia* (London: Routledge, 1999).

9 See, for example, Yali Peng, 'Democracy and Chinese Political Discourses', *Modern China*, vol. 24, no. 4 (1998) pp. 408–44; see also Minxin Pei, 'Racing Against Time: Institutional Decay and Renewal in China', in William A. Joseph (ed.) *China Briefing: The Contradictions of Change* (Armonk: M. E. Sharpe, 1997) pp. 11–49. Pei cites polls showing that two thirds of the people thought that the economic situation was improving while half thought their own living standards were improving and that that the majority of respondents (54 per cent) placed a higher priority on economic development than democracy. Over two thirds of those polled supported the government's policy of promoting economic growth and social stability, and 63 per cent agreed that 'it would be a disaster for China to experience a similar change as that in the former Soviet Union' (*ibid.*, 18). Even 40 per cent of non-CCP member respondents said they voluntarily supported the same political position as the CCP (*ibid.*, 18). See also Xia Li Lollar, *China's Transition toward a Market Economy, Civil Society and Democracy* (Bristol IN: Wyndham Hall Press, 1997) p. 74, citing results of poll in which 60 per cent of respondents assigned highest priority to maintaining order, while another 30 per cent chose controlling inflation, whereas only 8 per cent chose giving people more say in political decisions and free elections, and only 2 per cent chose protecting free speech. Wan Ming cites survey data showing growing support for the Party, and concludes that a development consensus that emphasizes stability has emerged. See 'Chinese Opinion on Human Rights', *Orbis*, vol. 42, no. 3 (1998) pp. 361–74. Another study showed Chinese to be the least tolerant of diverse viewpoints among all of the countries surveyed. It also found little support for a free press and the publishing of alternative views. See Andrew Nathan and Shi Tianjian, 'Cultural Requisites for Democracy in China: Findings from a Survey', *Daedalus*, vol. 122, no. 2 (1993) pp. 95–123. Granted, polling results must be used with caution. Often, the design of the question influences the outcome, as may be the case when people are simply asked to choose between economic growth and democracy. Moreover, respondents may feel inhibited, and provide what they feel are safe answers or the answers desired by the pollsters. On the other hand, PRC nationals living abroad often make similar arguments about democracy and economic growth and exhibit similar values. Nor are such views limited to mainland PRC citizens. When asked to choose between democracy and economic prosperity and political stability, 71 per cent of Hong Kong residents chose the latter,

and only 20 per cent chose democracy. Similarly, almost 90 per cent preferred a stable and peaceful handover to insisting on increasing the pace of democracy. Cited in Daniel Bell, *East Meets West* (Princeton: Princeton University Press, 2000) p. 119.

10 While thin and thick versions of rule of law are analytically distinct, in the real world there are no free-standing thin rule-of-law legal systems that exist independently of a particular political, economic, social and cultural context. Put differently, any legal system that meets the standards of a thin rule of law is inevitably embedded in a particular institutional, cultural and values complex, whether that be liberal democratic, statist socialist, neo-authoritarian, communitarian, some combination of them or some other alternative.

One way of conceiving of the relationship between a thin rule of law, particular thick conceptions of rule of law, and the broader context is in terms of concentric circles. The smallest circle consists of the core elements of a thin rule of law, which is embedded within a thick rule-of-law conception or framework. The thick conception is in turn part of a broader social and political philosophy that addresses a range of issues beyond those relating to the legal system and rule of law. This broader social and political philosophy would be one aspect of a more comprehensive general philosophy or worldview that might include metaphysics, aesthetics, religious beliefs, and so on.

Relying on a thin rule of law as a benchmark to assess China's legal system does not allow one to completely avoid all substantive issues of the type that must be addressed by advocates of a thick theory of rule of law. It merely reduces the range of issues where such substantive values will be relevant, and hence the scope of possible conflict. Although the features of a thin of rule of law are common to all rule-of-law systems, they will vary to some extent in the way they are interpreted and implemented depending on one's substantive political views and values. For instance, socialists and liberals may agree that one of the purposes of a thin rule of law is to protect individual rights and interests, but disagree about what those rights and interests are. Or they may agree that rule of law requires that laws be made by an entity with the authority to make laws, but disagree as to whether members of that entity must be democratically elected. Accordingly, legal systems that meet the standards of a thin rule of law will still diverge to some extent with respect to purposes, institutions, rules and outcomes, due to the different contexts in which they are embedded.

11 The debate over 'Asian values' has tended to produce more heat than light. Supporters of universal human rights dismiss the claims of Asian governments as the self-serving rhetoric of dictators and misrepresent their position as a morally reprehensible and philosophically absurd anything-goes cultural relativism. Defenders of 'Asian values' respond by attacking Western governments for past and present violations of human rights, and accuse them of cultural imperialism and ethnocentricity. Clearly, authoritarian regimes have at times used the rhetoric of 'Asian values' for self-serving ends, playing the culture card to deny citizens their rights and then to fend off foreign criticism. Just as clearly there are many different voices within Asia, and anyone professing to speak for all Asians or of 'Asian values' runs the danger of discounting these voices. Yet we need to be careful not to dismiss 'Asian values' as merely a cynical strategy seized on by authoritarian regimes to deny Asian citizens their rights. That some Asian governments use culture as an excuse to deny citizens their rights speaks to the motives of the governments but tells us little about the substantive merits of their position. A government's invocation of 'Asian values' may be politically motivated and yet still accurately reflect the views of the majority of the people. Indeed, Asian governments would not appeal to 'Asian values' unless such values resonated with the attitudes of their constituency. More philosophical and nuanced accounts point out that whatever Asian governments' political motivations,

there are legitimate differences in values at stake. See for example Joseph Chan, 'The Asian Challenge to Universal Human Rights: A Philosophical Critique', in James T. H. Tang (ed.) *Human Rights and International Relations in the Asia-Pacific Region* (New York: St Martin's Press, 1995) pp. 25–38; Randall Peerenboom, 'Human Rights and Asian Values: The Limits of Universalism', *China Review International*, vol. 7, no. 2 (2001) pp. 295–320. See generally the essays in Joanne R. Bauer and Daniel A. Bell, *The East Asian Challenge for Human Rights* (Cambridge: Cambridge University Press, 1999).

12 Alternatively, the neo-authoritarian state might give the appearance of allowing genuine multiparty elections at all levels but in fact control the outcome by limiting the ability of opposition parties to campaign (as in Singapore).

13 See Randall Peerenboom, *China's Long March toward Rule of Law* (Cambridge: Cambridge University Press, forthcoming 2002).

14 Jayasuriya's commendable effort to develop an alternative to a liberal conception of rule of law is, in my view, marred by his strong-arm attempt to force all Asian countries into his statist model. As several of the other contributors point out, his model fails to capture the diversity within Asia. The model is even less applicable to two countries conspicuously missing from the volume – Japan and South Korea.

15 I am indebted for this point to Xia Yong, Director of the China Academy of Social Sciences (CASS) Law Institute.

16 As Michael Davis notes, communitarianism in Asia is different than in the West, in that Western communitarians assume a liberal democratic framework. Michael C. Davis, 'Constitutionalism and Political Culture: The Debate Over Human Rights and Asian Values', *Harvard Human Rights Journal*, vol. 11 (1998) pp. 109–47. In contrast, Asian communitarians tend to be more conservative and authoritarian. Asian neo-conservative communitarians emphasize hierarchy and order rather than pluralism and a vibrant social discourse. Western communitarians put more stress on equality and liberation of the members of the community. For an attempt to develop a Deweyean-Confucian alternative to liberalism, see David Hall and Roger Ames, *Democracy of the Dead: Dewey, Confucius and the Hope for Democracy in China* (Chicago: Open Court, 1999). Wm Theodore de Bary, *Asian Values and Human Rights: A Confucian communitarian Perspective* (Cambridge MA: Harvard University Press, 1998) argues for a more liberal form of Confucian communitarianism. While admirable preliminary attempts to sketch a philosophical theory of Confucian communitarianism, neither account addresses in any detail the issue of rule of law, nor provides details regarding political or legal institutions, legal rules or outcomes with respect to particular controversial issues. In *East Meets West* (Princeton: Princeton University Press, 2000) Daniel Bell assesses the arguments for and against a communitarian system based on nonliberal democratic traditions and values, suggesting that such a system may suit certain states. Critics of Asian communitarian have pointed out that often citizens in Asian countries exhibit precious little concern for the community. Indeed, in China today the principal units of normative concern and allegiance appear to be the family and the state, with little regard shown for what falls between the family and state. Accordingly, 'collectivism' might be a better descriptive term than communitarianism. On normative grounds, however, communitarianism provides a better foundation for establishing a normatively attractive social and political order than collectivism.

17 If China's legal system does at some point reach a stable equilibrium state, for example coming to rest in some form of communitarian rule of law, it would become necessary to draw increasingly fine distinctions between the various forms of communitarian rule of law. By way of comparison, the category of liberal democratic rule of law, while useful for comparative purposes with respect to competing conceptions of rule of law in China, is of little use without further specification for capturing

competing conceptions of rule of law in Western developed liberal democracies. With respect to the US for instance, one would need to distinguish between libertarians, conservatives, communitarians and liberals, and then between various schools of liberals, including traditional liberal, social liberals, postmodern liberals, and so on. Moreover, particular issues might be more important in one context than another. For example, in the US, the fault lines for competing conceptions of rule of law tend to run along the lines of different theories of constitutional interpretation. See Richard Fallon, '"The Rule of Law" as a Concept in Constitutional Discourse', *Columbia Law Review*, vol. 97, no. 1 (1997) pp. 1–56.

18 Jiang Zemin's report at the fifteenth Party Congress is an excellent example of statist socialism. See 'Jiang Zemin's Congress Report', *FBIS-CHI-97-266* (23 September 1997). Neo-authoritarianism is generally associated with Zhao Ziyang and members of his think tank. See for example Barry Sautman, 'Sirens of the Strongman: Neo-authoritarianism in Recent Chinese Political Theory', *China Quarterly*, no. 129 (1992) pp. 72–102. However, I use the term in a more inclusive way. For instance, neo-authoritarianism has resurfaced in the form of new conservatism and elitist democracy. See Edward X. Gu, 'Elitist Democracy and China's Democratization', *Democratization*, vol. 4, no. 2 (1997) pp. 84–112, who notes that despite some differences new conservatives and elitist democrats share the same basic views with respect to democracy and the role of the elite in bringing about social order and harmony. Pan Wei, a political scientist at Beijing University, has put forth a 'consultative rule of law' that incorporates and builds on the basic principles of neo-authoritarianism, including the rejection of democracy in favor of strong state, albeit with a much reduced role for the Party. See Pan Wei, 'Democracy or Rule of Law: China's Political Future' (unpublished manuscript presented at the conference on 'China's Political Options', 19–20 May 2000, Vail, Colorado). Liberal democratic rule of law is well represented by Liu Junning and many living abroad in exile, such as Baogang He. See Liu Junning, 'Cong Fazhiguo dao Fazhi' [From Rechstaat to Rule of Law], in Dong Yuyu and Shi Binhai (eds) *Zhengzhi Zhongguo* [Political China] (Beijing: Jinri Zhongguo Chubanshe, 1998) pp. 254–6, at 233; Baogang He, *The Democratization of China* (New York: Routledge, 1996). No PRC scholar has articulated a comprehensive theory of a communitarian rule of law. However, PRC scholars have criticized aspects of the current system, taken exception to various features of a liberal democratic order, and developed pieces of a communitarian alternative. For instance, Xia Yong has attempted to construct a virtue-based theory of rights. Similarly, scholars in China and abroad have defended communitarian positions against liberal democratic critics, but generally on highly abstract philosophical grounds, and primarily with respect to alternatives to democracy and liberal human rights, as noted in note 17 above. The communitarian position captures the views of the majority of Chinese citizens who may wish for democracy, but not right now, as reflected in the polling data cited previously. They value individual rights but even more they fear disorder and chaos. Accordingly, they draw a different balance than do liberals between individual rights and group interests. This position is evident in the legal and philosophical literature in the long running debates over collectivism and the relation between rights and duties. See for example Chih-yu Shih, *Collective Democracy: Political and Legal Reform in China* (Hong Kong: The Chinese University Press, 1999) discussing such debates. The four positions also track the result of Peng's survey of political discourse in China. Peng's four categories overlap to a large extent with the four positions I have identified, with radical democracy representing the liberal democratic view; established conservativism representing statist socialism; concerned traditionalism representing neo-authoritarianism; and alienated populism aligning to some degree with communitarianism, albeit a jaded and somewhat cynical communitarian view. One of the striking features is that

despite radically divergent views on democracy, all four groups strongly support rule of law. See Yali Peng, 'Democracy and Chinese Political Discourses', *Modern China*, vol. 24, no. 4 (1998) pp. 408–44.

19 In some cases, I have drawn on current institutions, rules, practices and outcomes to demonstrate features of the various positions, particularly statist socialism and neo-authoritarianism, but also to some extent communitarianism and rule by law. Similarly, while the current system does not exhibit many features of a liberal democratic order, it is possible to appeal to Western countries for concrete 'real life' examples. The communitarian variant is the most hypothetical (in the sense of not being grounded in existing institutions and practices) of the positions, as the current system remains more state-dominated than the communitarian view would allow. One advantage of defining a communitarian rule of law in a rigorous way is that it becomes possible to design a survey instrument to gauge the degree of support for it among the populace.

20 Xiao Gongqin, one of the leading new conservative theorists, considers himself a neo-authoritarian. However, his support for the Party also aligns him with statist socialists. On new conservatives, see Merle Goldman, 'The Potential for Instability Among Alienated Intellectuals and Students in Post-Mao China', in David Shambaugh (ed.) *Is China Unstable?* (Armonk: M. E. Sharpe, 2000); Barret McCormick and David Kelly, 'The Limits of Anti-Liberalism', *Journal of Asian Studies*, vol. 53, no. 3 (1994) pp. 804–31.

21 Kenneth Warren notes that 'administrative agencies, much to the dismay of those who endorse a clear separation of powers in government, have legislative, judicial and administrative powers'. Kenneth F. Warren, *Administrative Law in the American Political System* (St Paul: West Publishing Co., 1982) p. 310.

22 Mary Ann Glendon, Michael Wallace Gordon and Christopher Osakwe (eds) *Comparative Legal Traditions*, 2nd edn (St Paul: West Group, 1999) p. 56.

23 Randall Peerenboom, 'Globalization, Path Dependency and the Limits of Law: Administrative Law Reform and Rule of Law in the People's Republic of China', *Berkeley Journal of International Law*, vol. 19, no. 2 (2001).

24 Chinese commentators often describe the Mao era, or at least the Cultural Revolution period, as rule by man (*renzhi*). However, even during the Cultural Revolution, the legal system continued to exist and limp along. Claims that China fell into a state of legal anarchy and of legal nihilism are overstated. In any event, my concern here is not with the distinction between rule of man and Mao-era rule by law. More relevant for present purposes is the opposite end of the rule by law spectrum, where rule by law arguably butts up against rule of law.

25 Many skeptics question whether the China's ruling regime accepts the principle that law binds the state and state actors. Some argue that many of the reforms are actually consistent with a more efficient rule by law, especially a softer authoritarian version than that of the Mao era. Chen Jianfu, for instance, suggests that legal reforms are not meant to change the nature of law as a tool but just to make law a better tool. Chen Jianfu, 'Market Economy and the Internationalisation of Civil and Commercial Law in the People's Republic of China', in Kanishka Jayasuriya (ed.) *Law, Capitalism and Power in Asia* (London: Routledge, 1999) pp. 69–94. Yet there are good reasons to be skeptical about the skeptics' view. Undeniably, some of the recent reforms and developments, such as a certain amount of institution-building, greater reliance on law rather than policy, and even some devolution of power, are consistent with the view that the purpose of legal reforms is a more efficient rule by law. However, they are also consistent with a transition to rule of law. As is often the case, much turns on which side bears the burden of proof. Those who see reforms as supporting rule by law insist that those who perceive a transition toward rule of law provide conclusive proof of the transition. Turning the tables, however, why assume

the skeptics' view is correct? Taken to the extreme, diehard skeptics will be satisfied with nothing less than the full realization of the rule of law ideal. Yet the establishment of rule of law is a long-term process. No legal system can transform itself from rule by law into a fully implemented rule-of-law system overnight. All countries now known for rule of law initially went through a period in which legal institutions were weak and rule of law only imperfectly implemented at best. Although it may be impossible to pinpoint the exact moment the tide turned toward rule of law, at some point preceding the actual implementation of some reasonable approximation of the ideal of rule of law, there was inevitably a credible commitment to it. Moreover, while skeptics can explain away some reforms as consistent with a more efficient rule by law, other reforms cannot be dismissed so readily. The express commitment to rule of law and the efforts to establish a viable administrative law system that aims to both protect individual rights and enhance government efficiency, for instance, are at odds with the establishment of a more efficient rule by law. For a fuller discussion, see Randall Peerenboom, *China's Long March toward Rule of Law* (Cambridge: Cambridge University Press, forthcoming 2002).

26 For an assessment of the variety of capitalism literature, see Peter Hall, 'The Political Economy of Europe in an Era of Independence', in Herbert Kitschelt, Peter Lange, Gary Marks and John D. Stephens (eds) *Continuity and Change in Contemporary Capitalism* (New York: Cambridge University Press, 1999) pp. 135–63; J. Roger Hollingsworth and Robert Boyer, 'Coordination of Economic Actors and Social Systems of Production', in J. Rogers Hollingsworth and Robert Boyer (eds) *Contemporary Capitalism: The Embeddedness of Institutions* (New York: Cambridge University Press, 1999). On the importance of institutions to economic development, see generally Douglass C. North, *Institutions, Institutional Change, and Economic Performance* (New York: Cambridge University Press, 1990).

27 See, for example, John Gillespie, 'Law and Development in "the Market Place": An East Asian Perspective', in Kanishka Jayasuriya (ed.) *Law, Capitalism and Power in Asia* (London: Routledge, 1999) pp. 118–50; Carol A. G. Jones, 'Capitalism, Globalization and Rule of Law: An Alternative Trajectory of Legal Change in China', *Social and Legal Studies*, vol. 3, no. 2 (1994) pp. 195–221. Whether Asian countries grew because of or in spite of such practices is of course much contested.

28 See, for example, David Wank, *Commodifying Communism: Business, Trust, and Politics in a Chinese City* (New York: Cambridge University Press, 1999), describing the importance of clientelism for private businesses in Xiamen. Corporatism has been put to three main, quite different uses, in China. Some analysts have used it as it is has been used elsewhere – as a way of looking at state/society relations and a measure of civil society. See, for example, Jonathan Unger and Anita Chan, 'China, Corporatism, and the East Asian Model', *Australian Journal of Chinese Affairs* (January 1995) p. 29. Others have used it as a way of understanding East Asian statist models of economic development. See for example Margaret Pearson, *China's New Business Elite: The Political Consequences of Economic Reform* (Berkeley: University of California Press, 1997). Still others have used it to explain local forms of government/business relations. Jean Oi, *Rural China Takes Off* (Berkeley: University of California Press, 1999), for instance, uses corporatism to capture the way in which local governments have treated the local economy as a single corporate entity. See also Andrew G. Walder, 'The County Government as an Industrial Corporation', in Andrew G. Walder (ed.) *Zouping in Transition* (Cambridge MA: Harvard University Press, 1998) pp. 62–85.

29 See Barry Sautman, 'Sirens of the Strongman: Neo-authoritarianism in Recent Chinese Political Theory', *China Quarterly*, no. 129 (1992). For a critique of the alleged advantage of authoritarianism, see Jose Maria Maravall, 'The Myth of the Authoritarian Advantage', *Journal of Democracy*, vol. 5 (1994) pp. 17–31.

30 For a defense of the neutral state, see, for example, Ronald Dworkin, 'Liberalism', in Stuart Hampshire (ed.) *Public and Private Morality* (New York: Cambridge University Press, 1978) p. 127; *West Virginia Board of Education v. Barnette, 319 U.S. 624* (1943). For a critique of the claim that liberal democracy is neutral, see Michael J. Perry, *Morality, Politics, and Law* (New York: Oxford University Press, 1988) pp. 57–73. That democracy should be neutral is contested by both communitarians and conservatives. See for example Michael Sandel's invocation of John Dewey in 'Dewey Rides Again', a review of Alan Ryan's *John Dewey and the High Tide of American Liberalism*, in the *New York Review of Books*, 9 May 1996, p. 35; see also Michael Sandel, *Democracy's Discontent: America in Search of A Public Philosophy* (Cambridge MA: Belknap Press of Harvard University Press, 1996).

31 See Edward X. Gu, '"Non-establishment" Intellectuals, Public Space, and the Creation of Non-governmental Organizations in China: The Chen Ziming-Wang Juntao Saga', *China Journal*, vol. 39 (1998) p. 40, noting the limited space for civil society; see also Gordon White, Jude Howell and Shang Xiaoyuan, *In Search of Civil Society: Market Reform and Social Change in Contemporary China* (Oxford: Clarendon Press, 1996) describing the close relations of many civil organizations with the state; Tony Saich, 'Negotiating the State: The Development of Social Organizations in China', *China Quarterly*, vol. 161 (2000) pp. 124–41, pointing out that the Leninist tendency to thwart organizational plurality is compounded by the fear of the potential for social unrest resulting from economic reforms, but also observing that the state's capacity to exert formal control is increasingly limited.

32 For a discussion of hard or statist corporatism versus soft or societal corporatism, see Philippe C. Schmitter, 'Still the Century of Corporatism?', in Frederick Pike and Thomas Stritch (eds) *The New Corporatism* (Notre Dame: University of Notre Dame Press, 1974); Howard J. Wiarda, *Corporatism and Comparative Politics: The Other Great 'Ism'* (Armonk: M. E. Sharpe, 1997).

33 Randall P. Peerenboom, 'Rights, Interests, and the Interest in Rights in China', *Stanford Journal of International Law*, vol. 31, no. 2 (1995) pp. 359–86.

34 John Rawls, *A Theory of Justice* (Cambridge MA: Harvard University Press, 1971); Ronald Dworkin, *Taking Rights Seriously* (Cambridge MA: Harvard University Press, 1977).

35 Randall P. Peerenboom, 'Confucian Harmony and Freedom of Thought', in Wm Theordore de Bary and Tu Weiming (eds) *Confucianism and Human Rights* (New York: Columbia University Press, 1998) pp. 234–60.

36 On the Asian Values debate, see generally Joanne Bauer and Daniel Bell, *The East Asian Challenge for Human Rights* (Cambridge: Cambridge University Press, 1999); Yash Ghai, 'Human Rights and Governance: The Asia Debate', Asia Foundation's Center for Asian Pacific Affairs Occasional Paper no. 4 (1994); Randall Peerenboom, 'Human Rights and Asian Values: The Limits of Universalism' *China Review International*, vol. 7, no. 2 (2001) pp. 295–320; Joseph Chan, 'The Asian Challenge to Universal Human Rights: A Philosophical Critique', in James T. H. Tang (ed.) *Human Rights and International Relations in the Asia-Pacific Region* (New York: Pinter, 1995); Michael Davis, 'Constitutionalism and Political Culture: The Debate over Human Rights and Asian Values', *Harvard Human Rights Journal*, vol. 11 (1998) pp. 109–47.

37 Jack Donelley refers to the perceived need to limit individual civil and political rights to ensure development as the liberty tradeoff. See 'Human Rights and Asian Values: A Defense of "Western" Universalism', in Joanne Bauer and Daniel Bell (eds) *The East Asian Challenge for Human Rights* (Cambridge: Cambridge University Press, 1999) pp. 60–87.

38 Randall Peerenboom, 'Rights, Interests and the Interest in Rights in China', *Stanford Journal of International Law*, vol. 31, no. 2 (1995) pp. 359–86.

39 Andrew Nathan, 'Sources of Chinese Rights Thinking', in R. Randle Edwards, Louis Henkin and Andrew Nathan (eds) *Human Rights in Contemporary China* (New York: Columbia University Press, 1986) pp. 77–124; R. Randle Edwards, 'Civil and Social Rights: Theory and Practice in Chinese Law Today', in R. Randle Edwards, Louis Henkin and Andrew Nathan (eds) *Human Rights in Contemporary China* (New York: Columbia University Press, 1986) pp. 41–75.

40 Yash Ghai, 'Human Rights and Governance: The Asia Debate', Asia Foundation's Center for Asian Pacific Affairs Occasional Paper no. 4.

41 In a survey of 547 students from thirteen universities in China, 82 percent claimed that for other countries to initiate anti-China motions before the UN Commission on Human Rights constituted interference in China's internal affairs; 71 percent believed that the true aim of the United States and other countries in censuring China was to use the human rights issue to attack China and impose sanctions on it, with 69 percent maintaining that this constituted a form of power politics. See 'Students' Attitudes toward Human Rights Surveyed', *BBC Summary of World Broadcasts*, 4 May 1999.

42 Randall Peerenboom, 'Confucian Harmony and Freedom of Thought: Right Thinking Versus the Right to Think', in Wm Theodore de Bary and Tu Weiming (eds) *Confucianism and Human Rights* (New York: Columbia University Press, 1998) pp. 234–60.

43 Daniel Lynch, *After the Propaganda State: Media, Politics, and 'Thought Work' in Reformed China* (Stanford: Stanford University Press, 1999).

44 For an analysis of the likelihood of China becoming unstable and the factors that might contribute to it, see David Shambaugh (ed.) *Is China Unstable?* (Armonk: M. E. Sharpe, 2000). The contributors discuss conflicts among the ruling elite and government/military relations, the declining role of the Party at the grassroots level, economic reforms, urban and rural unrest and minority regions.

45 Wang Jiafu, 'Lun Yifa Zhiguo' [On Governing the Country in Accordance with Law], *Faxue Yanjiu*, vol. 18, no. 2 (1996) pp. 3–9.

46 In fact, the transition from Deng to Jiang was relatively smooth, as has been the recent shuffling of top leaders, including Li Peng's move from the State Council to the NPC when his term expired. To be sure, one could question what, if anything, rule of law had to do with it. Nevertheless, the fact that there are term limits does provide the backdrop against which political maneuvering occurs. In any event, the hope is that in the future succession will proceed in accordance with legal rules, and that when senior officials reach the end of their terms they will step down or move to another post as required by law.

47 Yasheng Huang, *Inflation and Investment Controls in China* (Cambridge: Cambridge University Press, 1996).

48 Noting that stability entails the continued dominance of the Party, Stanley Lubman, in *Bird in a Cage*, contends that the rule of law co-exists in the Constitution with the thought of Mao Zedong and Deng Xiaoping. See Stanley B. Lubman, *Bird in a Cage* (Stanford: Stanford University Press, 1999). Shi Qinfeng asserts that whereas the purpose of rule of law is to limit the state, in China the purpose of rule of law is stability to ensure that the current regime remains in power. This view is typical of the statist socialist variety but not of the others. 'Yifa zhiguo jianshe shehuizhuyi fazhi guojia xueshu yantaohui jiyao' [Excerpts from the Academic Conference on Ruling the Country According to Law, Establish a Socialist Rule of Law State], *Faxue Yanjiu*, vol. 18, no. 3 (1996) pp. 13–23.

49 Li Shenzhi, 'Yei yao tuidong zhengzhi gaige' [Push Ahead with Political Reforms Too], in Dong Yuyu and Shi Binhai (eds) *Zhengzhi Zhongguo* (Beijing: Jinri Zhongguo Chubanshe, 1998) p. 21.

50 Yu Keping, 'Zouchu "Zhengzhi gaige – shehuiwending" de liangnan jingdi' [A Way Out of the Two Trouble Areas: 'Political Reform – Social Stability'], in Dong Yuyu and Shi Binhai (eds) *Political China* (Beijing: Jinri Zhongguo Chubanshe, 1998) pp. 49–53.

51 Joseph Raz, 'The Rule of Law and Its Virtue', in Joseph Raz (ed.) *The Authority of Law* (Oxford: Clarendon Press, 1979) p. 221; John Finnis, *Natural Law and Natural Rights* (Oxford: Clarendon Press, 1980) p. 272.

52 Randall Peerenboom, 'Confucian Harmony and Freedom of Thought: Right Thinking Versus the Right to Think', in Wm Theodore de Bary and Tu Weiming (eds) *Confucianism and Human Rights* (New York: Columbia University Press, 1998). Joseph Chan, for example, develops a Confucian alternative to a liberal or Kantian conception of moral autonomy. The former is a more minimal conception of autonomy than the latter, and supports civil liberties to a lesser degree. Joseph Chan, 'Moral Autonomy, Civil Liberties, and Confucianism', *Philosophy East and West*, vol. 52 (forthcoming 2002).

53 See for example Liu Hainian, 'Beilun Shehuizhuyi Fazhi Yuanze' [General Discussion of Socialist Rule of Law Principles], *Zhongguo Faxue*, no. 1 (1998) pp. 5–15.

54 A survey of academics, think tank experts, officials, businesspeople, journalists and religious and cultural leaders found significant differences between Asians and Americans. The former chose an orderly society, harmony and accountability of public values, in descending order, as the three most important societal values. In contrast, the Americans chose freedom of expression, personal freedom and the rights of the individual. See Susan Sim, 'Human Rights: Bridging the Gulf', *Straits Times* (Singapore) 21 October 1995, p. 32.

55 Jiang Zemin seems to believe that rule of law can help shore up the regime's legitimacy in a more direct way by providing a normative basis for a market economy.

56 See, generally, David Kairys (ed.) *The Politics of Law*, 3rd edn (New York: Basic Books, 1998).

57 Alice Ehr-Soon Tay, 'Communist Visions, Communist Realities, and the Role of Law', *Journal of Law and Society*, vol. 17, no. 2 (1990) pp. 155–69.

58 In practice, the degree of politicization varies widely from country to country. See Shimon Shetreet and Jules Deschenes, *Judicial Independence: The Contemporary Debate* (Boston MA: Martinus Nijhoff, 1985).

59 The greater reliance on laws rather than CCP policy is widely acknowledged to be one of the hallmarks of the post-Mao era. See for example Thomas Jones and Susan Finder, 'PRC Law: A Millenium Retrospective', *China Law and Practice* (December/January 1999–2000) pp. 53–4.

60 Michel Oksenberg, 'Policy Making Under Mao, 1949–68: An Overview', in John M. H. Lindbeck (ed.) *China: Management of a Revolutionary Society* (Seattle: University of Washington Press, 1971); Kenneth Lieberthal and Michel Oksenberg, *Policy Making in China: Leaders, Structures and Processes* (Princeton: Princeton University Press, 1988).

61 Michael Dowdle, 'The Constitutional Development and Operations of the National People's Congress', *Columbia Journal of Asian Law*, vol. 11, no. 1 (1997); Murray Scott Tanner, *The Politics of Lawmaking in China* (Oxford: Clarendon Press, 1999).

62 See P. P. Craig, *Administrative Law*, 3rd edn (London: Sweet and Maxwell, 1994) p. 74, for the idea that 'the government can always ensure that its policies become law in much the way that it desires'. G. Craenen, 'Legislators', in G. Craenen (ed.) *The Institutions of Federal Belgium* (Leuven: Acco, 1996) pp. 71, 77, describes a change in center of gravity away from the parliament to the executive such that the latter is able to 'push its initiatives to the foreground and to obtain from Parliament what it considers necessary' and argues that parliament's main function is now less legislative

and more to keep the government in check. This is not to claim of course that the Party is on all fours with ruling parties in parliamentary liberal democracies.

63 In fact, Party interference in specific cases is rare; interference by government officials motivated by local protectionism is much more common. See Gong Xiangrui (ed.) *Fazhi de Lixiang yu Xianshi* [The Ideal and Reality of the Rule of Law] (Beijing: China University of Law and Politics Press, 1993) p. 33. Of course, it is often difficult to draw a clear line between the Party and state, as government officials generally wear two hats. However, the primary allegiance of government officials may in some cases be to their government post rather than to the Party. See Shiping Zheng, *Party vs. State in Post-1949 China* (Cambridge: Cambridge University Press, 1997).

64 See Randall P. Peerenboom, *Lawyers in China* (New York: Lawyers Committee on Human Rights, 1998) noting there are no reported cases in which a political litmus test was invoked to deny a license.

65 See Randall P. Peerenboom, 'Law Enforcement and the Legal Profession', in Chen Jianfu, Yuwen Li and Jan Michael Otto (eds) *Implementation of Law in the People's Republic of China* (The Hague: Kluwer Law International, 2001) discussing rent-seeking and importance of clientelist ties to justice ministry and bureaus.

66 This paragraph depicts the current situation. See Randall Peerenboom, 'Globalization, Path Dependency and the Limits of Law: Administrative Law Reform and the Rule of Law in the People's Republic of China', *Berkeley Journal of International Law*, vol. 19, no. 2 (2001).

67 See, for example, Pan Wei, 'Democracy or Rule of Law – China's Political Future' (unpublished manuscript presented at the conference on 'China's Political Options', 19–20 May 2000, Vail, Colorado). Statist socialists might also favor an honest and professional civil service, though they may put greater emphasis on ideology and political factors in appointing civil servants, and prefer that Party disciplinary committees be responsible for dealing with corruption among senior officials.

68 Communitarians share a similar view of the legal profession as the neo-authoritarians, though they view the legal profession's obligations as being more toward society than the state, and differ over specific issues such as when lawyers' obligations to the state and society will trump their obligations to their clients.

69 Kanishka Jayasuriya, 'Introduction: Framework for the Analysis of Legal Institutions in East Asia', in Kanisha Jayasuriya (ed.) *Law, Capitalism and Power in Asia* (London: Routledge, 1999) p. 19, argues that judicial independence in East Asia is influenced by a statist ideology that rejects the liberal notion of a neutral state, in favor of a paternalist state which grounds its legitimacy in its superior ability to fathom what constitutes 'the good' for society. Thus, he claims, courts are more likely to serve as an instrument for the implementation of the policy objectives of the state and ruling elite.

70 In *Cohen v. California, 403 U.S. 15* (1971) the US Supreme Court held that an individual's right to free speech extends to wearing a jacket with 'Fuck the Draft' on it in court, even though others may find such language offensive.

71 Douglass C. North, *Institutions, Institutional Change, and Economic Performance* (New York: Cambridge University Press, 1990).

72 Indeed, focusing on each dimension separately is somewhat misleading. While different regime types tend to be correlated with different institutions and rules, in some cases advocates of alternative conceptions of rule of law might espouse seemingly similar purposes or adopt similar institutions or rules. Yet in practice the outcomes will still differ widely. This is to be expected in that there is generally some degree of indeterminacy to legal rules. Thus, even in the US, for example, conservative judges are likely to come to different conclusions in some cases than liberal judges, notwithstanding the fact that they share the same institutional context.

73 Yash Ghai, 'Constitutions and Governance in Africa: A Prolegomenon', in Sammy Adelman and Abdul Paliwala (eds) *Law and Crisis in the Third World* (London: Hans Zell Publishers, 1993).

74 See, generally, Jerome Cohen, 'China's Changing Constitution', *China Quarterly*, no. 76 (1978) pp. 794–841; William Jones, 'The Constitution of the People's Republic of China', *Washington University Law Quarterly*, vol. 63 (1985).

75 Andrew Nathan, 'Political Rights in Chinese Constitutions', in R. Randle Edwards, Louis Henkin and Andrew Nathan (eds) *Human Rights in Contemporary China* (New York: Columbia University Press, 1986).

76 Many PRC scholars maintain that the constitution should be justiciable. See for example Wang Chenguang, 'Falu de Kesuxing: Xiandai Fazhi Guojia Zhong Falu de Tezheng Zhiyi' [Justiciability of Law- One Characteristic of a Modern Rule of Law Country], *Faxue Yanjiu*, no. 8 (1998). Interestingly, the Supreme People's Court recently issued a potential landmark interpretation in its reply to an inquiry from Shandong High People's Court. The Supreme Court stated that the plaintiff's basic right to an education as provided in the constitution should be protected even though there was no implementing law regarding the right to education. While a number of questions remain as to the court's interpretation, it would appear that the decision opens the door to parties to directly invoke the constitution when at least their basic (*jiben*) constitutional rights have been violated, even in the absence of implementing legislation, thus making the constitution directly justiciable. See the Supreme Court's Reply, no. 25, issued on 13 August 2001.

77 See for example Luo Haocai (ed.) *Xiandai Xingzhengfa de Pingheng Lun* [The Balance Theory of Modern Administrative Law] (Beijing: Beijing University Press, 1997).

78 Compare P. P. Craig, *Administrative Law*, 3rd edn (London: Sweet and Maxwell, 1994) pp. 17–18, claiming that the standard of *ultra vires* is being reinterpreted along lines consistent with respect for fundamental rights in the UK, with Minxin Pei ('Citizens v. Mandarins: Administrative Litigation in China', *China Quarterly*, no. 152 [1997] pp. 832–62, 856 table 12) reporting that abuse of authority was invoked in only sixteen of 219 cases where PRC courts quashed the illegal acts of agencies in comparison to sixty times for exceeding legal authority, forty-eight for insufficient principal evidence, forty for incorrect application of law and even thirty-two for violation of legal procedures.

79 Randall Peerenboom, 'Globalization, Path Dependency and the Limits of Law: Administrative Law Reform and the Rule of Law in the People's Republic of China', *Berkeley Journal of International Law*, vol. 19, no. 2 (2001).

80 See the surveys by Pei and Lollar: Minxin Pei, 'Racing Against Time: Institutional Decay and Renewal in China', in William A. Joseph (ed.) *China Briefing: The Contradictions of Change* (Armonk: M. E. Sharpe, 1997) pp. 11–49; Xia Li Lollar, *China's Transition toward a Market Economy, Civil Society and Democracy* (Bristol IN: Wyndham Hall Press, 1997) p. 74.

81 Jonathan Hecht, *Opening to Reform: An Analysis of China's Revised Criminal Procedure Law* (New York: Lawyer's Committee for Human Rights, 1996) pp. 65–7.

82 *Ibid.* See also 'Human Rights Watch World Report 1998: China' (8 December 1998) online at www.hrw.org/hrw/campaigns/china-98/chn-wr98.htm.

83 Nor is it possible to simply rely on Jayasuriya's statist rule of law as an alternative. The statist version fails to capture the differences between the statist socialist and neo-authoritarian versions, and is at odds in significant respects with the communitarian variant.

84 See Daniel Bell, *East Meets West: Human Rights and Democracy in East Asia* (Princeton: Princeton University Press, 2000); Pan Wei 'Democracy or Rule of Law – China's Political Future' (unpublished manuscript presented at the conference on

'China's Political Options', 19–20 May 2000, Vail, Colorado). Minxin Pei, 'Political Institutions, Democracy and Development', in Farrukh Iqbal and Jong-Il You (eds) *Democracy, Market Economics and Development* (Washington DC: World Bank, 2001) cites as further examples in addition to Hong Kong and Singapore, Kaiser Germany, pre-1945 Japan, Pinochet's Chile, Franco's Spain and 'nearly all Western European countries before they became democratic in the mid-1800's. To be sure, full implementation of rule of law generally goes hand-in-hand with democracy. For instance, it was only after Taiwan and South Korea democratized that the judiciary acquired enough independence and authority to handle virtually all politically sensitive cases in an impartial manner according to law. Nevertheless, rule of law and impartial treatment in politically sensitive cases do not necessarily require democracy, as evidenced by Hong Kong. Pei argues that the key to autocracies maintaining rule of law is the existence of political constraints that oblige rulers to exercise political moderation. These restraints may come from an independent aristocracy, the church, a rising urban capitalist class or external threats.

85 Of course, the absence of any example of a non-democratic rule-of-law state would not prove that such a state is not possible or that the PRC could not become one, though it certainly would give pause to those who believe it possible.

86 See Randall Peerenboom, *China's Long March toward Rule of Law* (Cambridge: Cambridge University Press, 2002).

5

TRANSNATIONAL LABOR, CITIZENSHIP AND THE TAIWAN STATE[1]

Lucie Cheng

Introduction

Accelerated globalization in the last decade has reoriented our thinking on the relationship between international law, state sovereignty, and individual rights and duties.[2] This is especially true in relation to international migration, which is affecting an ever-larger proportion of the world's population. Changes in the flow of people are not merely expressed by the increase in the number and frequency of people who move across state borders, but by the number of states involved in the flow, and the complexity of migrant composition and patterns of their movement. As a result of this global dispersion, myriad social networks and civil organizations emerge that span territories under the jurisdiction of sovereign states. A transnational society, alongside an international system of states and a globalized market, is in the process of formation.[3] What, then, is the political status of the individual embedded in a transnational system of governance involving divergent cultures and institutions? Who is a citizen, and to whom does she make her claim of deprivation of rights, and for whom does she fulfill obligations? What are the rights and obligations of citizenship beyond those granted by the nation-state? From the point of view of the nation-states, how and by what means will the flow of citizens and others be promoted and regulated so as to maintain and enhance national competitiveness in a global economy? And how can such national interests be coordinated without serious inequality and conflict in an interstate system? These are some of the questions being raised in the literature.[4]

This chapter addresses the issue of the political status of transnational workers, a new form of migrant labor. They differ from both the immigrants and conventional migrants in aim and intention. Although migrant and transnational workers may end up settling permanently in the host country, that is not why they move. Students of international migration have seen the phenomenon in terms of immigration and emigration, with clear destinations and origins. The assumption is that people are uprooted from their country of birth to settle in a country of their choice. As a great majority of international migration has been from economically underdeveloped countries to the more developed ones, questions are often raised when migrants do not become settlers. A debate has raged among scholars, for example, over whether Chinese migrants to the United States in the nineteenth century were willing sojourners never intending to stay, maladjusted individuals who failed to fit in, or people forced to leave because they were rejected by the dominant white society. The sojourner/settler dichotomy has been a major theme in international migration, and sojourning is an indication of failure of either society or individual requiring explanation. This conception is challenged by the global and multi-directional flow of workers, whose stay in any particular country is temporary and contractual. Unlike seasonal migrant workers in the past, today's transnational workers travel far and wide. Since the concept of international migration conjures up definite destinations, the current pattern of migration is more suitably conceptualized as a transnational diaspora, and the people who move as transnational workers.[5]

The political status of transnational migrant labor has been a source of heated debates in recent times. All countries that receive significant numbers of such laborers, together with their originating states, have wrestled with this issue. Should the migrants come under the jurisdiction of the sending country, the receiving country, both, or a third international party such as the European Union? Which will be more effective in answering the claims of the migrant worker? In other words, what form of citizenship should apply to the category of people defined as migrant labor? So far, a variety of practices exist that range from an extremely limited form with only minimal rights to nearly full citizenship short of national voting rights.

Theoretically and normatively, there are also a number of formulations regarding citizenship within a globalized world. For instance, Castles[6] identifies three models of citizenship: republican, exclusionary and multicultural; Soysal[7] has argued for a conception of citizenship which is not confined within the borders of any nation-state, and was criticized by Faist[8] as akin to academic musing. In the various existing formulations and practices, the relation between nation and state, including their criss-cross, remains a crucial consideration. The likely mode of incorporating transnational migrant workers is determined by a combination of the migrant's orientation, the ideology of the state-building project, the strength of a transnational civil society, and international politics.

In the following pages I will analyze the political status of transnational migrant labor in Taiwan, and argue that the particular ideological heritage that guides current state-building efforts is insufficiently articulated to allow the formulation of a consistent and clear policy on the political incorporation of transnational workers. Indigenous migrant rights advocates, faced with popular racism and local labor resistance, are forced to seek support from abroad. Their calls have brought to Taiwan a number of transnational organizations committed to further migrant labor rights worldwide. As migrant labor increasingly becomes a permanent rather than transient phenomenon, both the state and the society will have to come to terms with the migrants' claim for citizenship, however limited in scope that claim may be.

The state-building project and ideologies of incorporation

All countries today allow the incorporation of migrants into their citizenry through naturalization, although the criteria that they use vary. Three principles and their combinations describe extant practices: descent (*jus sanguinis*), place of birth (*jus soli*) and place of residence (*jus domicili*).[9] The specific pattern adopted is reflective of the ideology of the state-building project. I distinguish between five ideologies of state-building: exclusion, assimilation, multiculturalism, multinationalism and transnationalism (see Table 5.1). Countries that adopt almost solely the descent principle of citizenship are exclusionists. Germany and Japan, especially before World War II, typify this mode. The assimilation mode is represented by 'nations of immigrants' such as the United States, Canada and Australia before the 1960s, and emphasizes individual integration into a common culture. While immigrants believed to be assimilable are welcome, cultural pluralism is only a transitory phenomenon. It may take a long time for an individual to melt into the receiving society, but the long-term outcome is clearly anticipated. The third mode, multiculturalism, differs from assimilation in that cultural pluralism is not seen as a transitory stage, but a desired outcome. Differences between groups and individuals are not a marker for strangeness and separation, but rather an opportunity for informed choices among many possibilities. With the rise of national minorities rights in North America and Australia, countries that have subscribed to the idea of a single unifying national culture have been moving gradually toward a multicultural project. However, as many scholars point out, multiculturalism assumes a dominant culture, or the dominance of a common culture. It argues for the respect of differences, but tends to marginalize cultures that are different from the common core. Multinationalism, on the other hand, not only recognizes and respects differences but also embodies those differences in a political structure that gives the same rights to all groups with autonomous rule. The former

Table 5.1 International migration, migrant rtights and the state

Migrant identity	*State-building ideology*	*Territoriality*	*Rights claimed*
Foreign workers	Exclusion	Territorially bound	Local (municipal, etc.)
Settlers	Assimilation	Porous borders	Citizenship (national)
Transnationals	Multiculturalism	Borderless	Dual/multiple citizenship
	Multinationalism		Basic human rights
	Transnationalism		

Soviet Union and the People's Republic of China have formally adopted this ideology of state-building, but their practices are very much in question.[10] The last mode is transnationalism, which is not yet a conscious strategy of any state-building project but, as globalization speeds up, has in recent years become a topic of much discussion and thought. At least two forms of transnationalism have been identified, both of which underline the importance of a transnational civil society. The difference is, whereas one is based on the notion of non-territoriality or borderless states, the other sees the state as the locus of citizen claims and argues for its continuing legitimacy and strength.[11] Yet the question that both address is: As societies are no longer contained within territorial states, what should their relationship be?

East Asian countries such as China, Japan, and Korea all adopt *jus sanguinis* as the dominant principle of citizenship, which is inclusive of people who can claim a common ancestral origin, real or imagined, and somewhat exclusive of people who do not share that commonality. The three countries differ in the way this dominant principle is combined with the other two principles of birthplace and residence. Japan, for instance, tends to treat those who claim a common ancestry but have settled abroad very differently from China. During the 1990s, the Japanese government created a category of sub-citizens or denizens to accommodate and attract ethnic Japanese from Latin America to work in Japan.[12] Two concerns have brought about this new reverse immigration code: a severe labor shortage, especially in 3-D type (dirty, difficult, dangerous) industries, and the reluctance of Japanese establishments to employ non-Japanese unskilled workers.[13] Japan is also more exclusive of people who are perceived as not sharing the same blood even though they may have been born on the same soil or have lived there most of their lives, such as the ethnic Koreans in Japan. Children of Japanese nationals who have been posted abroad for a long time receive much more government attention than children of ethnic Koreans and foreigners. While the Japanese Constitution provides no clear definition of the status of foreign workers, the dominant interpretation is that certain social rights, such as the right to receive education, apply only to Japanese citizens.[14]

As Chulwoo Lee's chapter in this book indicates, South Korea is similar to Japan in some ways and closer to China (Taiwan) in other ways. Ethnic Chinese in South Korea are treated in much the same legal terms as ethnic Koreans in Japan, who are marginal to the country where they have settled. Overseas compatriots in all three countries have a legal status different from that of foreigners, but their situations are in flux, and very much dependent on the political and economic needs of the mother countries for capital or labor.

Since the beginning of its modern statehood, indicated by the founding of the Republic out of its imperial past, China has always considered ethnic Chinese in other countries as *Zhongguoren*, i.e. Chinese, allowing them to participate in national representative bodies in their mother country. The role that overseas Chinese played in the 1911 Revolution that established the Republic of China, in the Anti-Japanese War and the Civil War are familiar chapters in modern history. This concept of Chinese nationality was constructed through discourses during the late nineteenth and early twentieth centuries,[15] and is manifested in the constitutions of the Republic of China, or Taiwan, and the People's Republic of China, as well as held widely by the Chinese people as a whole.[16] The difference between Chinese and Japanese conceptions of nationality is reflected in the expressions 'once a Chinese always a Chinese', and 'one cannot be a Japanese unless one is a Japanese'.

The descent principle of incorporation in all three countries is being challenged by the persistent presence of foreign migrant workers. The United Nations Convention on the Protection of the Rights of All Migrant Workers and their Families entitles all foreign workers certain minimal forms of human rights regardless of their status, and additional rights are granted to legally registered guest workers and their families. The UN and other international organs, including many religious and non-governmental organizations such as Migrante International, are creating norms that demand responses, if not compliance, from individual states. Such pressures from the international system of states and transnational civil society have led to each of the three countries to draw on their cultural and historical resources to restructure institutions and develop alternative practices to meet the challenge.

The recent election of a sixty-one year-old naturalized Japanese citizen of Finnish heritage to the parliament indicates how the conceptions of the relationships between race, nationality and citizenship are changing in Japan.[17] Marutei Tsurunen arrived in Japan in 1967, became a naturalized citizen in 1979 after marrying a Japanese woman, won a local assembly seat in 1992, and ran for national office four times before elected in January 2002. The *Los Angeles Times* correspondent in Japan reported that the first Caucasian lawmaker there considered himself a champion for foreign residents, including ethnic Koreans who have lived in Japan for generations: 'There are almost two million foreigners who are not citizens of Japan, and their situation is still very weak compared to the Japanese. I want to make their life better'.

Nation and state in Chinese discourse

The coupling of national identity and political unit established nearly a century ago by Sun Yat-sen, the founder of the Republic of China (ROC), reflects a traditional Chinese emphasis on lineage and ancestry in the context of Manchurian minority rule and foreign imperialism.[18] This nationalist thinking has legitimated the mutual claims that the People's Republic of China (PRC) and Taiwan have made against each other for five decades since 1948, when the ROC government retreated to Taiwan after losing a civil war to the communists. However, Taiwan's rapid economic growth and slow but impressive democratization have raised skepticism concerning the nationalist ideology and have led to a variety of alternative conceptualizations vying for dominance in a new nation-state building project currently in progress.

Throughout the recent history of Chinese discourse on the past, present or future relations between mainland China and Taiwan, the conception of nation and state has been fluid and complex. Shaped by changing domestic and international circumstances, this relationship has gone from early twentieth-century coupling, to decoupling, and finally recoupling, but in a different configuration.

Briefly stated, the Chinese Communist Party (CCP) and the Nationalist Party or Kuomintang (KMT) both adopted the nationalist principle of state-building in their early years, albeit with some ambivalence toward Taiwan.[19] However, that ambivalence dissolved in 1943 when both explicitly claimed Taiwan, which was under Japanese rule at the time, as an integral part of China. From 1948 to the 1970s, using the same nationalist principle, both the PRC and the ROC claimed sovereignty over territories held by the other. Thus recovery of the mainland became the rallying cry of the ROC in Taiwan; and liberation of fellow compatriots in Taiwan became the slogan of the PRC on the mainland. The unification of Taiwan and mainland China has continued to be an over-riding issue for the two regimes, as well as an issue in international politics.

In the meantime there have always been voices both within and without the island calling for the independence of Taiwan.[20] Although rationales vary for different political groups, the independence claim is usually based on one or more of the following arguments.

1 Taiwan has never really been an integral part of China. The Qing government decision in 1895 to cede Taiwan to Japan despite local opposition was a clear indication. Since Taiwan was considered a dispensable part of the Empire, it should not surprise anyone that the people of Taiwan do not feel that they belong. One cannot claim a child whom one has abandoned.
2 Taiwan people are racially and ethnically distinct from mainland Chinese. They are children of mixed races including various indigenous tribes, mainland Chinese immigrants, Dutch, Portuguese and Japanese. Since 'Taiwanese' are not part of the Chinese nationality, China should have no claim to Taiwan.
3 Just because most Taiwan people are descendants of mainland immigrants in the eighteenth century, and therefore share the same 'flesh and blood' does not mean that they should come under one state. People should be allowed to determine which state they want to identify with. Singapore is often cited by those who use this rationale as an example. With over 90 per cent of her population being ethnic Chinese, Singapore is a sovereign city-state.
4 The shared history and experience of the people in Taiwan in the last hundred years or so has made Taiwan quite distinct from China. There are more differences than similarities between the two. It is natural for children (or siblings if China is seen as an elder brother) to form separate households when they grow up. Therefore China should not continue to claim Taiwan.

5 Taiwan is superior to China in economic achievement. Taiwan would have to shoulder debts that she did not incur should she be integrated with the poorer state.
6 Taiwan has a democratic form of government, whereas China is a one-party state committed to socialism. These are different systems and imply different ways of life. People in Taiwan should be able to decide how they want to live, regardless of their nationality.

As we can see, for many pro-independence advocates, national identity and state identity are quite independent of each other. Adhering to the democracy principle which underlies the Western concept of nation-state, they de-coupled nation and state, allowing people who claim the same nationality to establish more than one state, and many nationalities develop a common state identity. When independence was the goal, disassociating nationality and state served the purpose of identifying the enemy in the interstate system – a foreign power seeking the right to rule illegitimately. But after 'they' has been identified the polity must decide who 'we' are. Here the nationalist principle is revived in Taiwan, and nation and state are re-coupled in a different configuration.

Peng Ming-min, a law professor at the National Taiwan University and a native Taiwanese, first challenged the coupling of nation and state in 1964, when he and two students published the *Declaration of Taiwanese Self-Salvation*, for which they were arrested and imprisoned. In it and his 1972 autobiography, Peng questioned the links between nation, state and polity:

> the Chinese must learn to distinguish between ethnic origin, culture and language on the one hand, and politics and law on the other. They must give up the idea that those who are ethnically, culturally and linguistically Chinese must be politically and legally Chinese as well. Individuals should be able to be proud of their Chinese culture and ancestry, but at the same time divorce their status from China politically and legally.[21]

What then will be the principle of incorporation of the new state in Taiwan? Writing in the early 1970s, Peng did not mention cultural and ancestral affinities, but emphasized the ideas of political community and democracy. Whether he thought the former to be insignificant, or simply took them for granted, is not known. At first glance, Peng's pronouncement seems to be in line with what Benedict Anderson had described as 'forward-looking' construction, which imagined a civic nationalism that would turn segmented subjects into collective-oriented citizens.[22] However, so far, Peng's silence on the incorporation of foreign labor into Taiwan's polity does not seem to bear this out.

The discussions above point to two aspects of the discourses on the relationship between nation and state that underlie the current politics of migrant labor incorporation. One is the continuing operation of the descent and ancestry principle, which is primarily exclusionist of those who presumably do not share the same 'blood', real or imagined. Recent changes in the Nationality Law notwithstanding, it remains extremely difficult for those excluded from nationality to become citizens of Taiwan. But this does not mean that all those who are recognized as sharing the same 'blood' are included as potential citizens of Taiwan. While everyone would agree that except for those identified with national minority groups, citizens of the PRC are Chinese by descent, they are still excluded from both the new Taiwan nation and the state in formation.

Recognizing this paradox, the government saw the necessity to give an explanation:

> Nationals of [M]ainland China are also nationals of the Republic of China. Although they have the freedom to enter Taiwan to live and work, yet considering the population pressure, national security and social stability, it is necessary to impose certain limitations.[23]

Though descent and ancestry is still the primary principle of inclusion, it is mediated by political concerns.

The principle of descent and ancestry gave the Taiwan state a rationale for claiming special affinity with Chinese in the diaspora, but political and economic considerations operate to differentiate among them. While mainland Chinese are excluded, overseas Chinese, especially those who are highly trained or from whom Taiwan can benefit, are given preferential treatment in law and in practice. The fact that the Nationality Law specifically allows some highly skilled occupational positions to be held by Chinese with dual citizenship, while excluding other positions, is a clear example.

This principle of descent and ancestry has been relaxed in the current Nationality Law, passed only in 2000 in response to the increasing number of foreign spouses and the modernizing project of the Taiwan state. Residence or *jus domicili* is explicitly recognized as a condition for nationality for those who cannot claim Chinese ancestry. This would seem to indicate a shift of Taiwan's state-building ideology away from exclusionism. However, as we shall see below, such a conclusion is perhaps premature.

Migrant (foreign) labor in Taiwan

In the everyday vocabulary of people in Taiwan, only two kinds of labor are distinguished: *benlao*, meaning local labor, and *wailao*, meaning foreign labor; the term 'migrant labor' has no equivalent in colloquial Chinese language. Foreign labor is presumed to be migrant: temporary, outside, and different. Taiwan workers who move from one place to another within the Islands are considered 'local' regardless of their regular domicile. This distinction between local and foreign appeared to have worked well until labor from the

People's Republic of China began to appear in Taiwan. By the Constitution of the Republic of China, i.e. Taiwan, mainland Chinese are compatriots and therefore cannot be considered as 'foreign'. Yet in reality, since their entry and departure are severely circumscribed, their status is closer to 'foreigners' than 'locals'. The government of Taiwan has explicitly excluded mainland Chinese from certain regulations governing the employment of foreign labor, but seems to be at a loss on how to deal with them. One might think that as the labor shortage developed, Taiwan Chinese would prefer mainland Chinese workers with whom they share language and cultural tradition. But in fact the Taiwan state's fear of being overrun by mainland Chinese workers has led them to prefer foreigners over ethnic Chinese from the PRC. As I pointed out earlier, Chinese in the diaspora have a special status in Taiwan, but class is also a strong mediating factor. While ethnic Chinese with skills and money are courted as overseas compatriots, those without resources are not clearly differentiated in treatment from foreign labor. For this reason, I will use the tern 'foreign labor' to denote labor from foreign countries who may or may not be of Chinese ancestry, and 'mainland labor' to refer to Chinese labor from the PRC.

Demographics of foreign labor

Economists generally consider that Taiwan was a labor-surplus area before the mid-1950s. Rapid economic development led to a competition for labor between the agricultural and industrial sectors, and later among different industries. A shortage of labor resulted, especially in low-skilled jobs in construction and certain segments of manufacturing. While a small number of foreigners have always worked in Taiwan as technical and professional advisers, low-skilled foreign workers began to appear in the labor force sometime in the early 1980s. By 1986 the latter had become one of the most popular topics of media reports. Just how many foreign workers were present in Taiwan in the late 1980s is uncertain. Estimates vary from 10,000 to 300,000.[24]

Table 5.2 shows the official number of foreign workers from 1991 to 1999 by country of origin. Two points can be made from the table. First, Filipino and Thai workers dominate the makeup of all foreign labor throughout the decade; and second, as Thai labor decreased Filipino labor increased. The latter pattern of ethnic replacement is found in many countries and requires further analysis. If we examine the occupational distribution of foreign workers in Taiwan at the end of the decade (see Table 5.3), we find that both Thai and Filipino labor are concentrated in manufacturing work, especially Thai. A major difference between the two groups is that while Thai workers are found in large numbers in public construction work, most Filipinos are in domestic and care-giving service. The need for domestic and care-giving help also accounts for more than half of the large increase in 1999 of Indonesian workers. The difference in occupational distribution parallels a gender division of labor. While most Thai

Table 5.2 Foreign Workers in Taiwan by country of origin, 1991—1999

Year	*Number*	*Indonesia*	*Malaysia*	*Phillipines*	*Thailand*
1991	1,610				
1992	15,924				
1993	97,565				
1994	151,989	2%	4%	25%	69%
1995	189,051	3%	1%	29%	67%
1996	236,555	4%	1%	35%	60%
1997	248,396	6%		40%	53%
1998	270,620	8%		42%	49%
1999	298,106	12%		41%	47%

Source: Council of Labor Affairs, Executive Yuan, ROC

workers are male, most Filipino and Indonesian workers are female. This pattern has significant implications for government policy as well as their different reception in the society.

Foreign workers are not distributed evenly in Taiwan. The Taipei City-region accounts for more than half of the total. Two reasons explain this skewed distribution. The Taipei City-region includes the Hsin-chu Science Park, where thousands of foreign assembly workers are hired to do electronic assembly work. Not content to be just the political capital and economic center of Taiwan, Taipei aspires to be a global city. Over the last two decades, Taipei City has absorbed a large number of nearby cities and towns into its orbit, creating a network of dependencies.

Table 5.3 Foreign workers by industrial category and country of origin, 1999

Categories	*Total*	*Indonesia*	*Phillipines*	*Thailand*
Total	298,106	34,604	121,442	141,712
Public construction	47,282	2,064	9,974	35,120
Care givers *	61,547	19,294	39,491	2,757
Domestic help	9,214	1,224	7,500	485
Major manufacturing	64,000	3,665	36,019	24,286
Restructured manufacturing	73,208	5,437	16,460	51,273

Source: Council of Labor Affairs, Executive Yuan, ROC.

Note:
*includes domestic care givers

Background on the importation of foreign labor

Foreign labor in Taiwan was illegal until 1992, when the government formulated its first policy to permit its importation under pressure from industries in need of cheap labor.[25] The presence of foreign labor resulted from the state-led capitalist development of Taiwan during the two previous decades, and from the relative economic stagnation of some neighboring countries. Several consequences of Taiwan's economic growth are especially significant for the change in government policy toward the importation of foreign labor. These are summarized in Figure 5.1. As we can see, the export-oriented growth strategy adopted by the state led to the growth of manufacturing industries from the 1960s to the 1980s. This then led to rising labor costs, which cut into capitalists' profits. At the same time, as demand for skilled labor increased, educational opportunities expanded, more people spent more time in school, and they consequently became less interested in low-skilled or unskilled work, which frequently was 'difficult, dangerous and dirty'. Furthermore, due to the success of the economy, and to insure its continuous growth, the state embarked on an ambitious program to build infrastructure that increased the demand for certain categories of labor. These factors propelled capitalists in the affected industries to seek cheap labor abroad.

Political development in Taiwan also contributed to this process. Under the period of martial law between 1948 and 1988, labor was organized into a government-controlled union and forbidden to strike. But labor dissatisfaction began to surface toward the end of the 1980s, and militancy increased soon after the lifting of martial law. Actual and potential labor unrest and growing organized strength presented a serious threat to industrial capitalists. Foreign labor, under strict government control, seemed to be the answer.

But not all industries have been equally affected by the so-called labor shortage. As we have seen in Table 5.3, foreign labor is heavily concentrated in manufacturing, construction, and domestic and care services. Industries not so affected by manpower shortage were against importing labor, citing potential social costs such as crime, overcrowding, etc. Ironically, joining them in opposition to labor importation were the native workers in affected industries, who saw foreign labor as a potential threat to their jobs and wage levels (Table 5.4).

The legalization of foreign labor

The Labor Standards Act promulgated in 1981 says nothing about foreign labor. Throughout the 1980s, as increasing numbers of foreigners were working illegally under various pretenses, domestic labor began to feel threatened. Furthermore, reports of crimes committed by foreign labor in other countries such as Singapore, as well as their health problems, were played up in the Taiwan media. The general public became worried about potential security and health risks. Those industries in need of foreign labor clashed with those concerned about

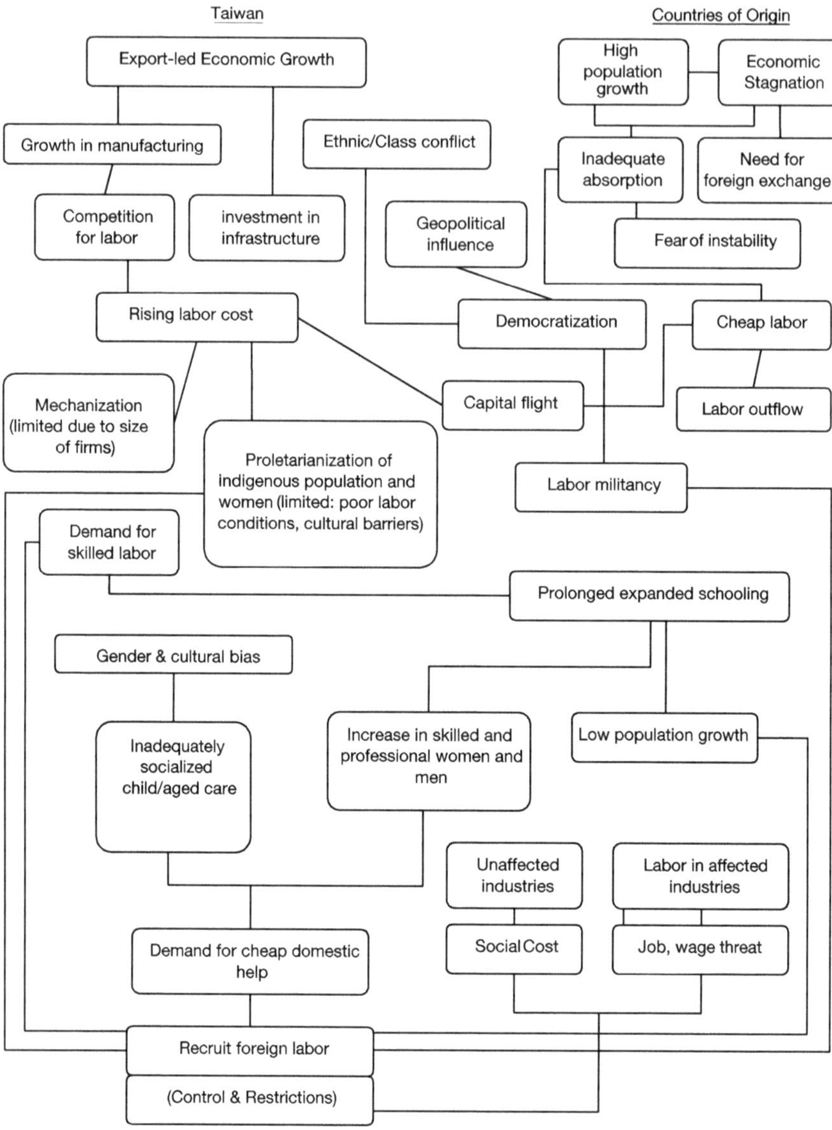

Figure 5.1 The recruitment of foreign labor: a framework of analysis

domestic labor rights and social issues. Explicit and implicit racism also entered into the public discourse, eventually influencing the way that specific laws, regulations and practices concerning foreign labor were framed.

Table 5.4 Wage differentials between native and foreign workers, 1993 –9, by industry

	1994		*1996*		*1998*		*2000*	
	F	*F/N*	*F*	*F/N*	*F*	*F/N*	*F*	*F/N*
Manufacturing	18,186	66.6	20,102	67.2	21,006	66.1	21,083	62.5
Construction	18,305	56.8	19,954	59.3	21,909	63.3	20,372	57.5
Domestic	13,812	64.3	15,889	66.1	17,651	68.7	17,935	68.0

Source: Wages of foreign labor from Council of Labor Affairs, ROC, *Report on the Foreign Workers Administration and Utilization Survey*, 1993–2000. Wages of local labor from Bureau of Accounting and Statistics, *Annual Report of Wages and Productivity*, 2000. Wages for domestics are estimated from wages of non-supervisory workers in 'other personal services'.

Debates on the legalization of foreign labor heated up in the late 1980s, and reached a climax in 1991. To facilitate understanding of the issue, the Legislative Yuan published a volume of newspaper clippings in October for internal use by the lawmakers.[26] Despite strong opposition from politically weak labor and aboriginal groups, the legislature passed a law in 1992 that permits, with certain restrictions, the importation of foreign workers.[27] The government unit responsible for its implementation at national level is the Council on Labor Affairs of the Executive Yuan. The Employment Services Act can be seen as an official attempt to provide a legal framework for national incorporation and to differentiate 'us' from 'them' in the Taiwan's new state-building project.

The Act makes a clear distinction between *guomin* and *waiguoren. Guomin* is sometimes translated as 'nationals' and sometimes as 'citizens'. A closer look at those who are to be treated as *waiguoren* or aliens may be instructive. Article 67 stipulates that the law applies to aliens, including also individuals without nationality, Chinese persons (*Zhongguoren*) who hold a foreign nationality and entered the ROC with a foreign passport, or entered with a ROC passport but did not establish legal residence. In other words, a person of Chinese ancestry can be regarded as a *guomin* regardless of what other nationality she possesses, if that person entered the ROC with a Chinese passport and is a permanent resident of Taiwan. The fact that this is explicitly recognized speaks to the importance of both the *jus sanguinis* and *jus domicili* principles in differentiating 'us' from 'them'.

However, immediately following the above is Article 68, which does not allow us to reach a neat conclusion on the issue. This Article stipulates that unless otherwise prescribed by other laws, the hiring and regulating of 'people of the mainland region' will follow the same law as that which applies to alien workers. It seems clear that political and security concerns have made the application of the concept 'Chinese' problematic. Are 'people of the mainland region' Chinese just like the Chinese in Taiwan? Are they like the Chinese in other countries? Or are they Chinese of still another kind? Is 'mainland region' part of the ROC, so that Chinese who live there can be considered to have established permanent residence in the ROC? Are 'they' part of 'us'?

As Taiwan seeks to construct its own national identity and establish a new state, it has to 'other-ize' the Chinese that it originally purported to represent. One strategy, followed by the old KMT, was to claim that people in Taiwan are Chinese, but they are more Chinese than those of the mainland because they are the true agency or carrier of Chinese culture. A second strategy, advocated by the DPP before it took power and by the former President Li Denghui, is to deny that to be Taiwanese is to be Chinese. The third strategy, followed by the current ruling DPP, is to argue that both are Chinese, but 'we' are not 'them'. Just why that is the case is more assumed than demonstrated. One often-repeated claim is based on collective experience and collective fate, which sidesteps the nationality or ethnic issue. This view argues that regardless of birthplace (assumed to be either China or Taiwan) or date of arrival, all those who have lived through Taiwan's recent history and who collectively are forced to share the same fate are bona-fide Taiwanese, entitled to the same rights and obligations. This argument does not include people designated as foreign workers.

Foreign workers are subject to specific restrictions regarding the jobs they can hold, the number of years they can work in Taiwan (usually no longer than three), and so forth. Employers in designated industries, including domestic service, must apply for a quota permit before they can hire a foreign worker. Foreign workers are not permitted to apply for a job on their own without the approval of the employer who brought them to Taiwan. Furthermore, they are required to have regular physical examinations.

Taiwan does not treat all foreign workers alike. Differentiation in the treatment of foreign workers by class, race and gender is discernible in the laws and regulations. For instance, professionals and the highly trained foreign workers are not subject to the same restrictions as the unskilled; white and darker colored foreign workers are not treated the same; women workers are subject to more restrictions and abuse.

The Employment Services Act provides for the Council on Labor Affairs to develop and issue rules and regulations regarding the employment and management of foreign labor. Many details were developed to deal with two problems that have arisen. One has to do with employer abuse, such as withholding wages, retaining the passport and residence permit of the worker, bringing the worker in under false pretenses, etc. Another has to do with the general public's fears of contamination and competition. These actions by employers were later prohibited by rules promulgated on 7 July 1999. The same rules also stipulate that foreign workers may not bring their spouses and may not get married while in Taiwan, measures that were intended to prevent settlement. Regular health examinations are underlined; failure of compliance is cause for deportation. A pregnancy test is one of the nine items in mandated regular health examinations, and is treated as a disease, the carrier of which is not allowed to enter Taiwan, and if already there, is to be deported.

Although these restrictions have racial overtones and may indeed be motivated by racism, Taiwan does not have an anti-miscegenation law. In fact, foreign brides, mostly from Thailand, Vietnam and Indonesia are a rather common phenomenon in rural areas, although their integration has been an issue frequently addressed by the media. Due to the efforts of community activists, the issue has gained significance in the national political arena, and has led to the recent elimination of many restrictive rules.[28]

Supplementary or alternative labor

A central issue in legalizing foreign labor is its necessity. Does foreign labor fill a real shortage or is it artificial and created by wage suppression? Some Taiwan observers argue that, as living standards rise and work opportunities expand, there are simply not enough workers interested in taking up certain types of job, such as the 3-Ds and domestic service. Others maintain that it is the continuous search for cheap labor dictated by capitalism that underlies the cry of labor shortage. The Employment Services Act originally may have reflected more of the former view, when only a limited number of industries were allowed to recruit foreign labor, and vacancies had to be advertised in local newspapers before employers could petition to import workers from abroad. But as the years went by, the list of industries permitted to import labor expanded, and the wage disparities between domestic and foreign labor increased, creating a serious issue. Taiwan employers preferred to hire foreign workers because of their much lower wages and flexibility, not because of some sheer shortage of local people willing to do the work. Foreign labor was no longer supplementary but alternative. Table 5.4 above lists wage differentials between native and foreign workers, by industry.

State, employer and *wailao* rights

Since *wailao* are concentrated in manufacturing and domestic services, let us examine their situations. Perhaps the most significant difference between the two categories of labor is that the former is under the protection of the Labor Standards Law, and therefore theoretically should be treated the same as local labor or *benlao*. In contrast, domestic service providers are not protected by the same law regardless of their foreign or local status. The working conditions and wages of the latter are negotiated between employer and worker.

The laws have little to say on the rights of foreign workers, but much to say about their obligations and restrictions. As I have pointed out before, foreign workers are subjected to many restrictions. They are forbidden to hold jobs other than those stipulated by law, to overstay the two- or three-year limit, to change employer without the permission of both current and future employer, and so forth. Their work permit will be forfeited if they are absent from work for three days without maintaining contact with their employer, if they work for another employer, work at another job, refuse to submit to a regular health examination, etc.

Actual abuses and pressure from foreign labor advocates have forced the government to establish in 2000 a few rules and regulations circumscribing the power of employers over their foreign workers. However, the same rules impose additional prohibitions on the foreign worker, such as on getting married while being employed. A later attempt by the Council on Labor Affairs to lift this rule failed. The Council forwarded proposed changes in the Rules to the Executive Yuan. The latter turned these down, claiming that it was premature to consider them.[29] In conjunction with several new attempts to circumscribe migrant rights, Taiwan seems to be extending fewer, and not more rights to foreign workers.

Laws and bureaucratic practices: mutually reinforcing or contradicting?

The Labor Standards Act of Taiwan is well known for its advanced state, following closely to standards set by the International Labor Organization. Many employers have complained that Taiwan is ahead of its own economic development and that the advantages that labor enjoys are more than they can accommodate. This view provides one explanation for the discrepancy between the laws and their implementation by the bureaucracy.

An alternative view locates this discrepancy in the political anxiety of the Taiwan state. One important way by which Taiwan distinguishes itself from China is in its claim of being a good member of the interstate system, even though it is not recognized by most countries as a sovereign state. Taiwan proclaims itself more modern, more democratic, more humane and more rational than China. The laws that are enacted in its legislature are in line with those of the most advanced countries, with the legislators and government officials fully aware that they will not be implemented under current circumstances. Once the laws are in the books, the bureaucracy is left to develop rules and regulations to deal with the daily chores of implementation.

The bureaucracy, on the other hand, is managed by entrenched civil servants whose outlook is famously conservative. This is why the rules that the bureaucracy goes by are often not in the same spirit as the laws from which they are derived. In the case of foreign labor, the Council on Labor Affairs has proclaimed that the Labor Standards Act applies equally to local and foreign workers in the same industries. Yet the Council clearly violated this position by prohibiting foreign workers from organizing unions or going on strike, rights that are accorded local labor. According to law, foreign workers should be paid the same wages as locals, work the same hours, enjoy the same number of days off, and have the same mobility. But in actuality none of the above obtain. Such inconsistencies abound but are almost never challenged, partly due to the underdevelopment of administrative law and partly to the way the legal profession is structured. So it is perhaps fair to say that it is the bureaucracy and not the law that really matters in Taiwan.

The fact that this gap exists between the law and the bureaucracy makes the status of foreign labor in Taiwan unstable. During an economic downturn, government can easily back away from implementing the law. As I write in August 2001, President Chen Shui-bian has just approved a recommendation by his hastily appointed Economic Development Advisory Conference to de-couple the minimum wage requirement in the Labor Standards Act from foreign worker employment.

As foreign workers become a permanent fixture in Taiwan, there is increasing concern about their rights and obligations. Human rights and migrant worker rights advocates are targeting Taiwan's foreign labor for change.[30]

Migrant identity, state-building ideology and rights

Current concerns about global migration reflect an uneasiness over the relationship between group identity and the nation-state, since the memberships of families, nations and groups of today's migrants tend to traverse the state boundaries of the 'host' and/or 'home' countries.[31] Depending on the ideology underlying the individual state-building project, various strategies for dealing with migrant workers have been developed. Table 5.1 links migrant identity, state-building ideology, territoriality, and the basis of rights claimed by the migrants in a framework of analysis. These dimensions are not static, but instead must be historicized.

As I have pointed out previously, globalization has reconfigured patterns of international migration. The lines of immigration and emigration are much less clear-cut than before. Migrant identity, a result of interaction between experiences in departing and receiving countries, is more fluid. Today we observe three distinct types of migrant identity: foreign workers, settlers and transnationals. Foreign workers do not stay longer than the prescribed period of work, either because of rules governing their circumstances in one or both of the countries involved, or because of personal preference. They retain close relationships with their country of origin and are not politically or socially involved with the host society. Settlers are just the opposite. Although they do not sever all ties with their originating country, they are eager to become part of the host society. While the first two types of migrant identity are well established concepts, the third type, the transnational, is a product of globalization and a mode of adaptation to globalization. Transnationals are simultaneously oriented toward, and carry on sustained and constant contact between, country of origin and destination. This concept has been applied to the diaspora of Chinese professionals and bourgeoisie.[32]

Another set of considerations refers to the originating country's concept of territoriality. Three basic orientations of state territoriality are identified in Table 5.1. Most states are territorially bound in that sovereignty is claimed within physical demarcations. This notion of the territorial state has come under scrutiny in recent years, partly because certain powers of the state over its subjects often extend beyond state borders. State borders are now more porous. Some scholars even go so far as to argue for a concept of the state as territorially unbounded or borderless.

Table 5.1 also shows four types of rights that may be claimed by the migrant:

1 local rights, including civil rights such as the right to vote in local elections, and social rights such as housing, education, etc.;
2 national citizenship rights, those claimed by all nationals and citizens of the host country;
3 dual or multiple citizenship rights, where a person may have the full rights prescribed by both country of origin and country of destination;
4 the basic human rights of all human beings.

Combining migrant identity, state-building ideology and state territoriality, I shall hypothesize the kind of migrant rights movements that are most likely to spring up. Take the United States and Germany as examples. Migrants to the US, a country known for its assimilationist ideology, are assumed to aspire to citizen status and see citizenship as a potential goal. Thus, they tend to claim the right to naturalize, to receive nationality or citizenship with the least hassle and in the shortest time. The large number of non-government organizations that lobby and mobilize for immigrant causes often focus on their civil rights and on the rights to citizenship as crucial to fair treatment. Germany, on the other hand, is known for her racial nationalism and exclusionist ideology. A recent government plan to adjust the 1913 nationality law to grant citizenship to second-generation immigrants born in Germany met with an unprecedented defeat.[33] Migrant workers in Germany, well aware of the *jus sanguinis* principle of German nationality, tend to focus their struggles for fair treatment on social rights such as housing, health care, etc.

The Taiwan state has primarily continued with a traditional exclusionist ideology in its new state-building project, though with some ambiguities. On the surface, foreign workers are those workers without Chinese nationality. But in actuality the definition is ambiguous, due to political considerations regarding the status of China. Before January 2000, the ROC law (promulgated in 1929) had no specific provision for the naturalization of foreigners except through marriage. The recently amended Nationality Act stipulates explicitly the conditions for naturalization, which include five years of continuous legal residency in the ROC, being over twenty years of age, having no criminal record, and possessing a certain amount of property or professional skills. In the new law, which is still dominated by the notion that 'Blood is a very special juice',[34] elements of *jus soli* and *jus domicili* are also evident. So are considerations of national needs and the economic and human capital of the petitioner.

When we juxtapose the Nationality Act with the Employment Services Act, we find that in fact it is impossible for a designated foreign worker to acquire ROC nationality, since she is prohibited from marrying or residing in Taiwan for more than three years! As a Chinese adage goes: 'For every policy issued by the state, there is a way to circumscribe it by the people'. A foreign worker who intends to marry a Chinese national will leave Taiwan according to the legal requirement and return as his spouse. Quite a large proportion of so-called 'foreign brides' are a result of this arrangement.

The intention to prevent foreign workers becoming citizens of the ROC is explicitly stated in the most recent revision of the Employment Services Act (24 January 2002). Article 52 extended the length of employment from three to six years. However to guard against foreign workers applying for naturalization on the grounds that they have met the residence requirement stipulated in the Nationality Act, the revised Employment Services Act mandates a forty-day break in residence after the first three years of employment.[35]

Conclusion

As globalization proceeds, the state gradually reduces its responsibilities towards its citizens. At the same time, the increasing multidirectional flows of people have made territorial borders less significant. Two normative visions emerge. One envisages the formation of a global society and polity, where people of the world are all citizens of the same union, and although there would still be rights and obligations in relation to their respective state, citizens have a different, if not higher authority to whom claims may be successfully made. A second vision sees the emergence of a transnational civil society, albeit with the persistence of state structures. Supra-state organizations may exist and even proliferate, but their effectiveness in answering the claims of the citizens of any state is dependent on state cooperation. To a limited extent both visions are already beginning to appear. Taiwan, as a state-in-formation in need of outside labor, must re-evaluate its state-building ideology. The analysis above points to two potential routes: to privilege transnational foreign labor over mainland Chinese and change its descent-centered exclusionist policy; or to privilege ethnic Chinese and relax its political vigilance toward PRC residents. Both would call for the construction of a forward-looking conception of nationhood, and a new mode of incorporation to meet the humanistic, social and economic challenges of globalization.

Notes

1 Research for this chapter was funded by the National Science Council, Taipei. A number of rules regulating the status of foreign labor were changed in early 2002 after this chapter was completed. I have tried to note the changes when these may strengthen or contradict my argument.

2 David Held, 'International Law', in David Held and Anthony McGrew (eds) *The Global Transformations Reader* (Cambridge: Polity, 2000) pp. 167–71.
3 John Agnew, 'The Territorial Trap: The Geographical Assumptions of International Relations Theory?', *Review of International Political Economy*, vol. 1, no. 1 (1994) pp. 53–80; Richard Falk, *Predatory Globalization: A Critique* (Cambridge: Polity, 1999).
4 Thomas Faist, *The Volume and Dynamics of International Migration and Transnational Social Spaces* (Oxford: Oxford University Press, 2000); Stephen Castles and Alastair Davidson (eds) *Citizenship and Migration: Globalization and the Politics of Belonging* (New York: Routledge, 2000).
5 John Lie, 'From International Migration to Transnational Diaspora', *Contemporary Sociology*, vol. 5, no. 3 (1996) pp. 303–6.
6 Stephen Castles and Alastair Davidson (eds) *Citizenship and Migration: Globalization and the Politics of Belonging* (New York: Routledge, 2000)
7 Yasemin Soysal, *The Limits of Citizenship* (Chicago: University of Chicago Press, 1994).
8 Thomas Faist, *The Volume and Dynamics of International Migration and Transnational Social Spaces* (Oxford: Oxford University Press, 2000) pp. 274–6.
9 *Ibid.*
10 Arthur Rosett, 'Legal Structures for Special Treatment of Minorities in the People's Republic of China', *Notre Dame Law Review*, vol. 66 (1991) p. 1503.
11 Richard Falk, *Predatory Globalization: A Critique* (Cambridge: Polity, 1999).
12 Hiromi Mori, *Immigration Policy and Foreign Workers in Japan* (Basingstoke: Macmillan, 1997).
13 Takashi Oka, *Prying Open the Door: Foreign Workers in Japan* (Washington DC: Carnegie Endowment for International Peace, 1994). Many of the 230,000 Brazilians of Japanese origin who returned to Japan to work are reportedly returning to Brazil in 2001, due to Japan's stagnant economy and increasing hostility to foreigners, including those with Japanese 'blood'. *Asian Migration News*, August 2001, pp. 16–31.
14 Kaon Okano and Motonori Tsuchiya, *Education in Contemporary Japan: Inequality and Diversity* (Cambridge: Cambridge University Press, 1999) pp. 110–37.
15 Qichao Liang, 'The Renovation of the People, 1902', trans. in Ssu-yu Teng and J. K. Fairbank (eds) *China's Response to the West: A Documentary Survey 1839–1923* (New York: Atheneum 1966); Kai-wing Chow, 'Imagining Boundaries of Blood: Zhang Binglin and the Invention of the Han 'Race' in Modern China', in Fran Dikotter (ed.) *The Construction of Racial Identities in China and Japan* (Honolulu: University of Hawaii Press, 1997) pp. 34–52.
16 Sung-chiao Shen, 'The Myth of Huang-ti (Yellow Emperor) and the Construction of Chinese Nationhood in Late Qing', *Taiwan Shehui Yanjiu Jikan*, vol. 28 (December 1997) pp. 1–77 (in Chinese).
17 *Los Angeles Times*, 16 February 2002. For a discussion of debates on the relationships between race, nationality and culture in Japan, see Yoshio Sugimoto, 'Making Sense of Nihonjinron', *Thesis Eleven*, vol. 57, (May 1999) pp. 81–96.
18 Wen Sun (SunYat-sen) *Sanmin Zhuyi* [The Three Principles of the People] (Taipei: Zhongguo Guomindang Zhongyang Weiyuanhui, 1985) pp. 1–88 (in Chinese).
19 Christopher Hughes, *Taiwan and Chinese Nationalism: National Identity and Status in International Society* (London: Routledge, 1997).
20 Hughes *ibid.*; Alan Wachman, *Taiwan: National Identity and Democratization* (Armonk: M. E. Sharpe, 1994).
21 Christopher Hughes, *Taiwan and Chinese Nationalism: National Identity and Status in International Society* (London: Routledge, 1997) pp. 37–8.

22 Benedict Anderson, *Imagined Communities: Reflections on the Origin and Spread of Nationalism*, revised edn (London: Verso, 1991).
23 Mainland Affairs Council, Executive Yuan, Republic of China, Document 5253 (18 November 1992).
24 Hui-lin Wu and Ching-hsi Chang, *A Study of the Labor Shortage and Foreign Workers in Taiwan* (Taipei: Chung-hua Institution for Economic Research, 1991) (in Chinese).
25 Raymond Chan, 'Taiwan's Policy Towards Foreign Workers', *Journal of Contemporary Asia*, vol. 29, no. 3 (1999) pp. 383–400.
26 Legislative Yuan, Republic of China, *Alien Labor* (Taipei: Legislative Yuan Library, 1991) (in Chinese).
27 Employment Services Act, Republic of China, 2000 (in Chinese).
28 Hsiao-chuan Hsia, 'Selfing and Othering in the "Foreign Bride" phenomenon: A Study of Class, Gender and Ethnicity in the Transnational Marriages Between Taiwanese men and Indonesian Women', University of Florida doctoral dissertation, 1997.
29 *China Times*, December 2000 (in Chinese).
30 For example, the Asia Pacific Mission for Migrant Filipinos and the Catholic Church Migrant Advocates are organizations active in Taiwan.
31 Lucie Cheng and Marian Katz, 'Migration and the Diaspora Communities', in Richard Maidment and Colin McKerras (eds) *Culture and Society in the Asia-Pacific* (London: Routledge, 1998).
32 Lucie Cheng, 'Chinese Americans and the Formation of the Pacific Rim Regional Economy', in Evelyn Hu-DeHart (ed.) *Across the Pacific* (Philadelphia: Temple University Press, 1999); Aihwa Ong, *Flexible Citizenship* (Durham NC: Duke University Press, 1999).
33 F. El-Tayeb, '"Blood is a Very Special Juice": Racialized Bodies and Citizenship in Twentieth-century Germany', *International Review of Social History*, vol. 44, supp. 7 (1999) pp. 149–69.
34 *Faust*, I, verse 1740, quoted in *ibid.*
35 *Economic Daily News*, 23 January 2002 (in Chinese).

6

'US' AND 'THEM' IN KOREAN LAW

The creation, accommodation and exclusion of outsiders in South Korea

Chulwoo Lee[1]

Introduction

Those I describe in this study as 'outsiders' to South Korean society are ethnic Koreans from China, migrant workers from various Asian countries, and Chinese residents. They are more deeply involved than other *étrangers* in Korea in the process in which Koreans of today ascertain and renegotiate their conception of ethnic and national identity. The influx of ethnic Koreans from China and migrant workers was a product of the 1990s, amidst the melting down of the Cold War in East Asia and an increasing globalization of labor supply. In coming to terms with this novel experience, Koreans have also awakened to the erstwhile neglected discontent of the Chinese residents who have been with them for generations. Cries for human rights voiced in respect of the treatment of these groups have shaken Koreans' complacency with the nation's transition from authoritarianism to democracy. Furthermore, problems arising from the presence of the three groups have stimulated critical reflection on the opacity and incoherence of Korean law in instituting distinctions between 'us' and 'them'. These problems also pose challenges to the glorification by the Koreans of the assumed homogeneity of their culture and society, and their hitherto unquestioned belief that cultural identity, ethnic boundaries, membership of society and state borders should coincide with one another.

This study canvasses how each of the above groups of outsiders has been treated in Korean law. It brings into light the structures of the laws that give them the places they occupy in South Korean society, and examines the changes brought to the law and administrative practice during the last decade and their consequences. It also shows how the responses to problems arising from the treatment of the outsiders have in turn transformed the Korean conception of national identity, by looking into the legal definition of nationality with reference to gender. The study will demonstrate what limitations there are in the legal devices and policies that have been implemented in response to the discontent of the outsiders. The study points to the potential tension in the divergent rationales and proposals for accommodating those groups. These groups have different historical relationships with Korea, and differing backgrounds of presence in the country, despite efforts to find a common ground between them and to cater to their common grievances.

Nationals, 'overseas compatriots' and aliens

The Roh Tae-woo administration's *Nordpolitik* opened the way for Korean emigrants to China and the Soviet Union and their descendants to rebuild their broken ties with Koreans in South Korea. South Korean contacts with people of Korean descent in China and the Soviet Union, and the latter's influx into South Korea, began in the late 1980s, and remarkably expanded in the 1990s, as the Republic of Korea entered into full diplomatic relationships with the Soviet Union in 1990 and with China, Kazakhstan and Uzbekistan in 1992. Almost 1,800,000 ethnic Koreans, called *chaoxianzu* in Chinese and *joseonjok* in Korean, are known to be living in China, while there are 520,000 *goryeoin* (Koreans) in all of the CIS countries.[2] These are treated by the host states as their nationals and differ from the approximately 7,000 nationals of North Korea known to be living in China.[3]

If *joseonjok* and *goryeoin* are nationals of the host states under the domestic laws of those states, are they aliens under Korean law? Article 15 of the present Nationality Act and Article 12 of the same Act before its revision in 1997 provide that if a person voluntarily acquires the nationality of another state his/her Korean nationality shall terminate. Before the Nationality Act came into force in December 1948, questions regarding nationality were governed by the Provisional Rules on Nationality enacted in May 1948 by the South Korean Interim Government, the governmental organization of Koreans under the auspices of the US Military Government. It stipulated that those who had acquired the nationality of another state were regarded as having recovered their Korean nationality as of 9 August 1945 upon renouncing their nationality of the foreign state.[4] Many problems arose with regard to those who had emigrated to other countries before the above rules came into force, or before the birth of the Republic of Korea on 15 August 1948. Suppose a Korean man emigrated to China during Japanese rule and became a member of the *chaoxianzu*. Is he not a national of the Republic of Korea because he became a Chinese national? Some legal commentators suggest that Korean nationality may extend to that person. Why? For one thing, both the law of traditional Korea and the rules that applied to Koreans under Japanese rule did not allow Koreans to give up their nationality.[5] For another, the person probably did not acquire Chinese nationality voluntarily.[6] Yet decisions of the courts differ with respect to whether a person who acquired the nationality of another state before 1948 retains Korean nationality and whether to adopt the voluntariness test in answering the question.[7]

In any case, the South Korean government has taken an ambiguous stance as to the nationality issue. With its preoccupation with preventing an unlimited number of *joseonjok* flowing into and settling in Korea, the government has taken a functional attitude, eschewing putting the nationality issue on the agenda. Its words and deeds initially were so shaped as not to be taken as denying that *joseonjok* were Korean nationals, although it discussed the *joseonjok* issue in line with its policy regarding overseas Koreans in general, which was geared toward encouraging and supporting overseas Koreans to become 'respectable citizens of the host states'.[8] When *joseonjok* began to visit South Korea in the mid-1980s, via third-state territories such as Hong Kong, the South Korean government did not allow their entry on Chinese passports, but issued travel certificates, which were explained to be substitutes for Korean passports, and allowed the entry of over 300 *joseonjok* in that way by the end of 1987. Although the government began to issue visas to *joseonjok* traveling on Chinese passports, following President Roh Tae-woo's Declaration of 7 July 1988 signaling South Korea's rapprochement with communist states, this change of policy did not necessarily indicate a change in the government's view of the nationality question. The government's position at this stage was illustrated by its recognition of a small number of *joseonjok* as Korean nationals.

Since the Declaration of 7 July, *joseonjok* entry greatly expanded – from 1,660 in 1988 to 36,135 in 1991.[9] Among these people were former independence activists and their descendants, who were invited and treated as Korean nationals. In accommodating them, the government did not act as if those people had newly obtained Korean nationality. Instead, it introduced, without a clear ground in the Nationality Act, a 'nationality adjudication' (*gukjeok panjeong*) procedure, the purpose of which it said was to ascertain the erstwhile unclear Korean nationality of the invitees, who were called 'permanent resident returnees' (*yeongjugwigukja*). The nationality adjudication procedure was not available to all *joseonjok*, but was only a formality to avoid admitting that the 'permanent resident returnees' were aliens. The rest were not even referred to the adjudication procedure and were treated as aliens. Therefore, despite the intention of the government to avoid giving an impression that it regarded *joseonjok* as aliens, many confused the ascertainment of the Korean nationality of 'permanent resident returnees' through the nationality adjudication procedure with naturalization, and the press commonly used the term 'acquisition of Korean nationality' in describing the procedure. The government gradually extended eligibility for 'permanent resident returnee' status to other categories of *joseonjok*, namely those who came to join their spouses, lineal ancestors or lineal descendants in South Korea, *joseonjok* women married to Korean farmers, and fifty people who had entered Korea between 1985 and 1991 to meet their families and had stayed since.[10]

In the meantime, the expansion of *joseonjok* entry made it increasingly difficult for the government to maintain its hazy use of the nationality adjudication procedure unfounded in law, and to justify its selective referral of *joseonjok* incomers to the procedure. This prompted a change in both law and practice. As for law, the 1997 amendment of the Nationality Act formally introduced the nationality adjudication procedure.[11] As for practice, the Ministry of Justice laid down an internal guideline assuming that those who are classified by China as *chaoxianzu* had acquired Chinese nationality on 1 October 1949, the day when the People's Republic of China was inaugurated. The guideline excludes the question whether one's acquisition of Chinese nationality was voluntary, and treats *joseonjok* who were born before 1 October 1949 as if their Korean nationality terminated on 1 October 1949 upon their acquisition of Chinese nationality. Those born after that day, are treated as having never been Korean nationals. Theoretically, this guideline within the Ministry of Justice has no force of law, and is not necessarily followed by the courts and other departments of the government. Nevertheless, according to the practice of the Ministry of Justice, two different avenues are available to *joseonjok* who wish to acquire Korean nationality: the nationality recovery procedure for those who used to be Korean nationals and the naturalization procedure for the younger ones.

In the end, the *joseonjok* are in practice no more Korean nationals than are Korean emigrants to North America who have voluntarily acquired US or Canadian citizenship over the last five decades. Yet the two groups were differentiated as a result of the 1999 Act on the Immigration and Legal Status of Overseas Koreans (Overseas Koreans Act), which was enacted in response to the grievances of overseas Korean communities, particularly those in North America after the Los Angeles riot in 1992, against the South Korean government's apparent lack of interest in the well-being of Korean emigrants. The Kim Young-Sam government began to cater for those grievances in its New Overseas Koreans Policy. The first consideration was whether to amend the Nationality Act so as to allow dual nationality. Those who rallied for such an amendment, including Korean communities in North America, emphasized the need to entice talents and successful businessmen of Korean descent to return and contribute to development back home, whereas arguments against the idea pointed to the danger of conflict with neighboring states, possible misuse, and the negative public opinion which often compared those seeking dual nationality to 'bats moving back and forth between birds and mammals'. In 1996 the Kim Young-Sam administration decided to rule out the idea, and reconfirmed the government's traditional stance that 'overseas Koreans policy should be geared towards encouraging overseas Koreans to become decent and respectable citizens of the host states'.[12]

Instead of allowing dual nationality by revising the Nationality Act, the government tried to placate the discontent of Korean emigrants by improving their visa status and relaxing some of the restrictions regarding foreign exchange and real property rights. It also set up the Overseas Koreans Foundation to serve overseas Koreans in cultural and educational fields. Simultaneously, some members of the National Assembly proposed a law that would give overseas Koreans a few special rights and streamline overseas Koreans policy.[13] In the meantime, the opposition party came to power, and the new administration under Kim Dae-jung set out to design a special law granting overseas Koreans, including nationals of foreign states, rights not available to aliens of non-Korean descent. The Ministry of Justice drafted the bill to the effect of extending to *hangukgye oegugin* (aliens of Korean descent) national treatment in economic activity, some social entitlements, and, with exceptions, civil-service eligibility. The category 'aliens of Korean descent' closely resembles the Chinese concept of *huaren* (ethnic Chinese) and the Japanese *nikkeijin* (people of Japanese descent) in contrast to *huaqiao* (overseas Chinese nationals) and *kaigai zairyū hōjin* (overseas nationals) respectively.

The bill, however, faced opposition from the Ministry of Foreign Affairs and Trade, which was more sensitive than any other government department to the reactions of the countries with ethnic Korean minorities. China strongly protested that Korea was seeking to control its Korean minority. The foreign ministry criticized the idea of the bill as a 'blood-centered approach' based on a 'narrow-minded nationalism' which was incompatible with 'the universal globalism that President Kim was striving for'.[14] After a year's vicissitudes, the National Assembly passed the Act under the title Act on the Immigration and Legal Status of Overseas Koreans.

The phrase 'overseas Koreans' is a translation of *jaeoe dongpo* literally meaning 'overseas compatriots'. The Overseas Koreans Act stipulates for two categories of 'overseas compatriots' – *jaeoe gungmin* (overseas Korean nationals) and *haeoe gukjeok dongpo* (compatriots of foreign nationality). The former covers Korean nationals who are long-term residents in other countries, while the latter consists of (1) 'persons who have emigrated abroad after the establishment of the Republic of Korea and have relinquished their Korean nationality and their lineal descendants', and (2) 'persons who emigrated abroad before the establishment of the Republic of Korea and had their Korean nationality expressly ascertained before acquiring foreign nationality and their lineal descendants'.[15] The shift from 'aliens of Korean descent' to 'compatriots of foreign nationality' and the definition of the latter in the above way means that most *joseonjok* and *goryeoin* were removed from the ambit of the law.[16] The government explained that those people had never possessed the nationality of the Republic of Korea, which was at variance with the aforementioned guideline of the Ministry of Justice.[17] Even if it were admitted that they had once possessed Korean nationality, they would still be excluded because they failed to have their Korean nationality expressly ascertained before acquiring foreign nationality.

The Overseas Koreans Act provides *haeoe gukjeok dongpo* with a special visa status, considerable freedom in employment and economic activity, and national treatment with regard to real property rights and transactions, foreign exchange transactions, and health insurance and pensions. With all the blunting of the sharp edges of the law, however, critics continued to take issue with the main thrust of the law that prioritized ethnic belonging over the legal definition of nationality.[18] In another vein, it generated a good deal of vexation, as it refused to recognize as 'overseas compatriots' the 2.4 million Koreans in China and the former Soviet Union out of the 5.6 million Korean emigrants in total. Some *joseonjok* sojourning in Korea staged hunger strikes and sympathetic Koreans led by more than sixty non-government organizations launched protests against the government. Three *joseonjok* filed a constitutional complaint, which is still pending in the Constitutional Court. They highlighted the unfairness of the law by pointing out that, unlike most emigrants to North America, *joseonjok* and *goryeoin* had either left the homeland to fight against Japanese rule or been transported to remote areas against their will.[19] In their eyes, it is ironic that those who have chosen to discard Korean nationality are being favored, whereas those who have not been given the chance to choose their nationality are being discriminated against.

In reaction to the protests, the government announced 'supplementary measures', which expanded the scope of eligibility to apply for Korean nationality and relaxed entry qualifications. Now *joseonjok* who moved to China before 15 August 1948 but are or used to be registered on the Korean household register, those who desire to join their siblings in Korea, those who have contributed or are expected to contribute to Korea's national interests, and their spouses and unmarried offspring may apply for Korean nationality, that is, for either recovery of Korean nationality or naturalization, although, of course, they have to pass such additional tests as whether they have sufficient means to support themselves in Korea. As for the relaxation of conditions for entry, those who moved to China before 15 August 1948, or so-called first-generation *joseonjok*, but not their spouses or other family members, may enter Korea and stay for a maximum of one year without invitation by relatives in Korea. The age requirement for entry for visiting relatives upon their invitation has also been lowered from fifty-five or over to fifty or over, and those who enter Korea on this condition are now allowed to work if they provide a surety. Besides, the 'supplementary measures' contain a plan to increase the percentage of *joseonjok* among all 'industrial trainees' from 15 to 20 per cent.[20]

Foreigners in the labor market

As of 2000, over 22,000 *joseonjok* were registered as aliens in South Korea, accounting for 13 per cent of the 172,000 registered aliens from Asia, including 26,500 non-Korean Chinese, 16,700 Indonesians, 16,000 Filipinos, 15,500 Vietnamese, 7,900 from Bangladesh, 2,500 from Sri Lanka, 3,200 from Thailand, 3,200 Pakistanis, 2,000 Nepalese, and 800 from Myanmar. There were also a total of 5,100 from Uzbekistan and Kazakhstan, most of whom were *goryeoin*. While registration is required for aliens to stay for ninety days or more, registered aliens formed only a little over half of those who had been staying in the country longer than ninety days. In 2000, more than 143,000 people from Asia were staying in South Korea with illegal status, ignoring the expiry of their short-term visas (for less than ninety days). More than half of them had stayed longer than a year and 30 per cent of them longer than two years. Moreover, amongst the registered Asians, 38,300 were remaining in Korea despite the passage of their permitted periods of sojourn. Again, *joseonjok* were the greatest in number among these 'illegal sojourners' from Asia, accounting for over 32 per cent of the 143,000 short-term visa holders and 34 per cent of the 38,300 registered. And Asians made up 96 per cent of the 189,000 illegal sojourners in total.[21] Yet the number of illegal sojourners thus estimated by the government may be far smaller than in reality. Some estimate the total number to be between 200,000 and 300,000, and the number of illegal *joseonjok* to be almost 100,000.[22] Most of the illegal sojourners from Asia are engaged in manual labor, along with 105,000 'industrial trainees' recorded in 2000.[23]

How has Korea come to have such a large foreign workforce? The history can be traced back to 1991, when demand for labor exploded with the construction boom that President Roh Tae-woo had promised by way of his 'plan to build two million new houses'. Labor costs had already shot up as a result of democratization in industrial relations since 1987, and Korean workers tended to avoid the so-called 3-D (dirty, difficult and dangerous) jobs. Such job sectors began to be filled by foreigners, who had entered Korea on tourist or other short-term visas or without a visa if exempted. In mid-1992, when the government received voluntary reports from illegal sojourners in return for a postponement of their required departure, over 60,000 foreigners reported to the government their illegal status, and 42,500 of them were found to be employed in various industrial sectors. The 60,000 comprised 19,000 Filipinos, 8,950 from Bangladesh, 1,900 from Pakistan and 22,000 *joseonjok*.[24] An increasing number of *joseonjok* switched from peddling, mainly selling Chinese medicine, and other forms of informal economy to manual labor. In addition to the 42,500, an estimation of 30,000 unreported illegal sojourners were employed as manual workers.

In the meantime, the government introduced the 'industrial trainee scheme' in 1991. The original purpose of the scheme was to support Korean companies that had subsidiaries or joint-venture projects in foreign countries, exporters of industrial supplies, and companies that transferred technologies to foreign firms by facilitating their training of employees of the foreign subsidiaries and affiliates, who were expected to return to their original workplaces with improved skills. Yet the industrial trainee system was soon used for a different purpose, the purpose of recruiting cheap laborers. From the outset, government ministries could recommend enterprises that needed to train foreign workers. In 1992, the Ministry of Commerce and Industry decided to bring in 10,000 trainees in this way. The trainees were distributed to firms that did not necessarily have a foreign subsidiary or affiliate but firms mostly engaged in 3-D industries. Thanks to this shift in function, the trainee system expanded an intake of 1,275 in 1991 to over 9,000 at the end of 1993.[25] This was followed by the empowerment of the Federation of Small and Medium Enterprises (FSME), a union of cooperatives of private firms, to recommend companies that needed trainees, along with a lengthening of the maximum period of stay for trainees – from a single year to two years in 1994 – and an increase of the maximum size of annual intake – from 10,000 to 20,000 in 1993 and to 30,000 in 1994. Hence the industrial trainee scheme came to operate in a number of ways, of which the two most important were, first, through companies that invested in foreign countries or exported industrial supplies or technologies to foreign firms; and second, through the FSME. Although the former scheme is also used to provide cheap labor, the latter more directly serves that purpose. It covered 66 per cent of all trainees in 1994, and 74 per cent in 2000. The number of industrial trainees under the two schemes combined increased from 28,800 in 1994 to 103,000 in 2000, excluding those who broke out of the scheme and became illegal sojourners. They were distributed to small firms in either declining industrial sectors or sectors that involved heavy physical work, such as the textile, footwear and leatherware industries, dyeing, the manufacture of rubber and plastic goods, automobile parts manufacturing, and metallic assembly.[26]

According to the government, one of the objectives of the introduction of the FSME-operated industrial trainee program was to replace illegal workers with legal trainees. The result has been, however, quite the opposite. As many as 34 per cent of all trainees brought in through the FSME between 1994 and 1997 broke out of the scheme and joined the army of illegal workers.[27] The main reason for this was income. What trainees receive is termed an allowance and not a wage, so as to get round the Immigration Control Act's prohibition of the employment of aliens other than holders of certain kinds of visa. In the initial stage, trainee allowances differed according to country of origin; the basic monthly allowance for Chinese and Filipinos in 1994 was $260, while Indonesians received $250, those from Myanmar, Pakistan and Vietnam $230, the Nepalese $210, and those from Bangladesh $200. Trainees received extra pay for overtime work, but their income was nonetheless extremely low; their mean income in 1994 was 252,000 won, only 59 per cent of the estimated average wage for illegal workers.[28] Besides, trainees deserted simply in order to stay in Korea longer, as their permitted period of stay was limited to one or two years. While there was ample reason to escape from the trainee scheme, there was little deterrence against going illegal, since the government did not strictly enforce the Immigration Control Act, bowing to the cries of the businesses that employed the cheap workers.

The exodus of trainees from the scheme alarmed the companies that had invited them. Companies asked their trainees to deposit guarantee fees and kept their passports. Wardens were deployed to oversee them, and trainees were often prohibited from leaving their quarters on weekends. Bitterness caused by mistreatment exploded in early 1995, when thirteen trainees from Nepal staged a sit-in strike. They protested against six months' wage default, 12–13 hours work per day, and sexual assault against a female trainee, as well as the extreme degree of control over their daily lives. Activists from thirty-eight non-governmental organizations joined the protest and sympathetic public opinion turned the issue into a national concern.[29] The incident forced the government to reconsider its policy toward industrial trainees. The Ministry of Labor decided to apply to the trainees the national minimum wage, the statutory health insurance, the Industrial Accident Compensation Insurance Act, and the Industrial Safety and Health Act, despite opposition from business.

Industrial trainees find themselves in complex legal relations. The FSME-operated trainee scheme starts with the FSME receiving applications from companies that need trainees. Then the FSME requests designated dispatching firms in the sending countries to dispatch trainees, and the recruited trainees are distributed to applicant firms through the FSME. The inviting company in Korea and the dispatching company in the sending country enter into a 'training cooperation contract'. The dispatching company recruits trainees according to the specified tastes of the inviting company and concludes 'trainee dispatch contracts' with them. Finally, the dispatched trainee and the inviting company enter into a 'training contract'. The content of these contracts is fixed in standard form. The legal form is thus carefully designed to avoid giving the trainee the status as an employee under Korean law, and puts the dispatching company in the position of employer. The trainee is under the instruction of the dispatching company, while the inviting company trains and supervises the trainee. The dispatching company bears *respondeat superior* in connection with any tortious conduct of the trainee. In the early stage, trainees' allowances were even paid into the bank account of the dispatching company and the trainees collected their wages from the dispatching company and not from the training company in Korea. This practice changed after the 1995 protest, and now the training company has to pay the allowance directly into the trainee's bank account.[30]

With all the efforts to minimize the responsibility of Korean companies that hire trainees, the discrepancy between the legal form and the unmistakable fact that the trainee provides labor under the instruction of the training company and receives money in return is too obvious. The government's decision in 1995 to grant trainees some benefits to which previously only 'workers' had been entitled signaled a move from complacency with the fictitious nature of the legal cloak of the trainee scheme toward the recognition of trainees as 'workers'. A court decision in the same year confirmed that a trainee was a worker under the Labor Standards Act as long as the content of the contract was not confined to training and the trainee provided labor under the instruction of the company and received rewards in return.[31] The Ministry of Labor also instructed that certain provisions of the Labor Standards Act should apply to trainees.[32] To what extent does the Labor Standards Act apply, in both law and practice? Although Article 5 of the Labor Standards Act enshrines the principle against discrimination on account of gender, 'nationality', religion and social status, whether the wage gap is an infringement of the rule is problematic, because wages can vary according to productivity. Further, Korean wages depend heavily on seniority. As of 1999, trainees were found to receive two thirds of the average wage of Korean workers in the small- and medium enterprise sector.[33] Bonuses, annual and monthly paid leave, and severance pay are basically excluded from the benefits to which trainees are entitled, which signifies that trainees are 'workers' in a limited sense of the term.[34] Violations of the Labor Standards Act are widespread, even in matters in which trainees are regarded as workers, such as maximum hours of work and overtime pay.

Nevertheless, the application of the national minimum wage brought a change to the method of determining the size of allowances and, combined with other factors, gradually pushed up the trainee income. Allowances were no longer given in dollar terms but determined directly in Korean currency. Differences on the basis of country of origin were also eliminated. Allowances increased from roughly 300,000–400,000 won in 1994 to 450,000–550,000 won in 1995, to almost 600,000 won in 1996, and to over 600,000 won since then, almost double the national minimum wage.[35] The developments are, however, true only of the FMSE-operated trainee program, and not the scheme for foreign subsidiaries and affiliates. From the outset, allowances for trainees under the latter scheme have been far smaller than those for trainees under the former. Despite the explanation that the latter is for the genuine purpose of training, it is also frequently misused for the purpose of cutting labor costs.

The increase in allowances has narrowed the wage gap between trainees and illegal workers, as well as that between trainees and Korean workers.[36] In 1996, the government lengthened the maximum period of sojourn for industrial trainees to three years. This has weakened the trend of trainee flight, but there are still many reasons for desertion. First, despite the narrowed gap, trainees continue to earn less than illegal workers. Further, their legitimate status under immigration law does not necessarily put them in a better position than illegal workers in terms of social entitlements. As we shall see, illegal workers had secured some entitlements even before trainees attained them. Second, trainees are subject to a greater degree of control. Trainees are required to open savings accounts with the Industry Bank in which half of their monthly allowance is required to be deposited. Since the dispatching company is responsible for flight of trainees it has dispatched, it also exercises control through its Korean branch. Third, trainees have to pay management fees levied by the dispatching company and the FSME or companies performing outsourced management functions. Trainees are particularly indignant at excessive fees and recruitment commissions levied by the dispatching companies. A survey by the FSME in 1999 shows that 14.7 per cent of trainees spend over $3,000; 26.9 per cent spend $2,000–3,000; another 26.9 per cent $1,500–2,000; and 16.7 per cent $1,000–1,500 to cover recruitment commissions and other expenses before leaving their countries.[37] They are susceptible to the lure of higher incomes and tend to become illegal workers to make up for the expenditure. Fourth, many trainees find that the working conditions and treatment they experience are worse than they expected before leaving for Korea. This is partly due to misinformation, misrepresentation and fraudulent advertisement by the dispatching companies. Because the dispatching companies are foreign firms based abroad, Korean law cannot regulate their conduct and there are few means of deterrence other than contractual provisions against their excesses and penalizing by reducing or removing their quotas. Last, many companies have gone bankrupt and thrown out their trainees onto the streets. This problem was particularly serious during the financial crisis of 1997–8. Although such trainees can be switched to other companies, it is natural that their sense of instability should test their patience.

Flight from the trainee scheme is only one of many illegal routes into the labor market. Many illegally get jobs after the expiry of their tourist and other short-term visas. Nowadays an increasing number of people have themselves illegally transported across the sea from China to the Korean coast or enter Korea hiding in vessels. Thanks to the immense demand for entry into Korea, illegal networks have mushroomed in and out of the country. Forged passports are common. Many potential workers get themselves guided into Korea and into work by paying fees to recruitment brokers in Korea and their native land, and often fall victim to frauds. *Joseonjok* often enter the country on bogus invitations or by way of deceptive marriages. Marriage used to be particularly useful, because foreign brides immediately obtained Korean nationality until the Nationality Act was amended in 1997.

Once they have entered the labor market, illegal foreigners find themselves in the middle of the income ladder, between Korean workers and industrial trainees. Studies estimate that by 1997 wages for illegal workers had increased to roughly 90 per cent of those for Korean workers in the same industrial sector. According to a recent survey of 1,008 samples, illegal workers earn 790,000 won as an average monthly wage, compared with 648,000 won for industrial trainees.[38] Their freedom of movement from one employer to another gives them leverage unavailable to trainees. In respect of other labor standards, illegal workers are no less protected than trainees. Since 1993 the courts have recognized illegal workers as 'workers' entitled to accident compensation.[39] According to their rulings, one's status as an illegal sojourner under the Immigration Control Act does not make one's labor contract void. Pressed by such court decisions and growing public concern for the helpless victims of industrial accidents, the Ministry of Labor changed its negative position in 1994, and agreed that illegal workers were protected by the Industrial Accident Compensation Insurance Act and the Labor Standards Act.[40]

In practice, however, illegal workers find it difficult to claim their entitlements because of the danger of exposing their illegal status to the authorities. Therefore, and for other reasons, foreign victims of industrial accidents do not benefit as much as the law allows. Of the 1,008 workers in the aforementioned survey, 29.5 per cent have experienced injuries from accidents, but only 10.2 per cent of the injured have received compensation under the accident compensation insurance scheme. It should also be noted that the Industrial Accident Compensation Insurance Act applied until recently, and many provisions of the Labor Standards Act still apply, only to workplaces where there are five or more full-time employees. Whereas until recently industrial trainees could be distributed only to firms with five or more employees, illegal workers have flowed even into the smallest workplaces excluded from the benefits of the social and labor laws.

The greater freedom and higher income that illegal workers enjoy relative to industrial trainees is offset by their greater vulnerability to mistreatment and exploitation. The aforementioned survey of 1,008 workers shows that 50.7 per cent of those sampled have experienced wage default by employers. Illegal workers have to pay broker fees, which are exacted in large proportions from their monthly wages.[41] Besides, since illegal workers are unable to transmit money out of the country in their names, they often rely on recruitment brokers or other middlemen, and cases of embezzlement are not uncommon.[42]

What we have seen so far suggests that the maintenance of the migrant workforce in Korea rests on a structural discrepancy between law and practice. The inconsistent, and often arbitrary, enforcement of the Immigration Control Act is an example. Social activists and academics have proposed the adoption of a work and/or employment permit system as the best way to right the wrongs, pointing to the Taiwanese example. The Democratic Party for the New Millennium and the Ministry of Labor have set out to draft a bill entitled the Employment of Foreign Workers Act, incorporating the ideas of the campaigners. Yet government ministries are not at one in dealing with the problem.[43] Instead of a work/employment permit system, currently in force is the 'trainee employment scheme', under which industrial trainees may take an examination upon the recommendation of the chief executive of their training company after eighteen months' work. If they pass the examination, they can be employed for one year with the status of a sojourn, which allows them to work for income. The examination has been taken three times in 2000 and 1,076 persons passed.[44]

Problems arising from the presence of migrant workers have caused Koreans to rethink their national self-image and identity. That the migrant workforce includes ethnic Koreans complicates the issue. While *joseonjok*, who account for 15 per cent of industrial trainees and supposedly 30–35 per cent of illegal workers, are no different from workers from South and Southeast Asia in immigration status, they are treated a little differently in economic terms. When trainee allowances reflected national differences and were given in dollar terms, those from China received the greatest amount, along with Filipinos, which cannot be explained only by differences in national wage levels and per capita income, the official criteria for determining the level of allowance.[45] It is more obvious that *joseonjok* are paid more when wages are determined by market forces, although the gap has narrowed over the years. It is partly due to the different sectors where *joseonjok* and the others are mainly employed – construction and services for *joseonjok* and manufacturing for the others. Yet even within the same sector, *joseonjok* seem to earn more. They have no language barrier, and their looks and speech, which make them less vulnerable to police surveillance, as well as their wider connections in Korea, give them a better chance of finding alternative work, which forces employers to pay more to keep them.[46]

On the other hand, employers' attitudes towards *joseonjok* workers are ambivalent. While employers give credit to language and cultural affinities, they accuse *joseonjok* workers of switching jobs too freely. *Joseonjok* industrial trainees are among the groups known to have the strongest inclination to abscond from the training scheme. While the government has favored China in allocating trainee quotas, explaining that it takes the *joseonjok* factor into account, opinion surveys suggest that the frequent flight of *joseonjok* trainees has lowered their popularity among employers.[47]

The flight of *joseonjok* trainees is motivated by the large gap between their trainee allowances and their potential market wages; and the frequent move of illegal *joseonjok* workers from one company to another owes to the fact that they have wider job opportunities than others. Moreover, *joseonjok* seem to have a greater degree of dissatisfaction with the current situation and a more acute sense of being discriminated against than workers from any other country, mainly because they compare their condition with that of Korean workers, whereas workers from other countries compare theirs with that of other foreigners. *Joseonjok* are indignant at the very fact that they are treated as foreigners. Yet their attitudes are also ambivalent in that, of all foreign workers, they are the most willing to bring their friends and relatives to the Korean labor market, which is partly explained by the fact that *joseonjok* find Korea to be the only overseas land where they can work, whereas Korea is only one of many countries for the others.[48]

Korean workers also take on ambivalent attitudes towards *joseonjok* workers. According to Seol Donghun's extensive study, Korean workers have sympathy for *joseonjok* as compatriots, but this shared identity does not override the legal distinction. Korean workers are on the whole unfriendly, if not hostile, to the influx of migrant workers, and take wage discrimination by nationality for granted. Among the foreign workers, they are the most tolerant to *joseonjok* industrial trainees, who they say should get the highest wages, and the least tolerant to illegal workers from other countries. Between industrial trainees from other countries and illegal *joseonjok* workers, Korean workers find the former more acceptable. In short, ethnic backgrounds do play a role in shaping Korean workers' attitudes toward migrant workers, but only a secondary one.[49]

This attitude of the Korean workers explains their lack of enthusiasm for incorporating migrant workers into their unions. Again, Seol's study shows that Korean workers are more tolerant to opening their unions to *joseonjok* industrial trainees than to any other category of worker, but on the whole are indifferent to the idea of offering union membership to foreigners.[50] In theory industrial trainees and illegal workers have the right to organize and join unions, and the right of collective bargaining inasmuch as they are regarded as 'workers' under

Korean labor law. In practice, however, few foreign workers are union members or seek membership of Korean unions. Indeed, unions do not exist in most of their small workplaces. To be sure, unions have moved toward expressing concern about the situation of migrant workers. The Korean Confederation of Trade Unions (*Minju nochong*), one of the two national leagues of unions, cooperated with a number of NGOs in founding the Joint Committee for Migrant Workers in Korea in 1995. The Federation of Korean Trade Unions (*Hanguk nochong*), which used to oppose the influx of foreign workers, now calls for equal treatment of foreign workers.[51] Neither organization, however, seems to have made significant efforts to develop programs for foreign workers. Few references to foreign workers are to be found amongst the hundreds of declarations, resolutions and press releases from the two national leagues of unions during the year 2000.[52]

Migrant workers may find their interests best represented by organizations specially formed to deal with their problems. These are led and sponsored by social activists, religious workers, lawyers and intellectuals, and run by volunteers, some of whom are migrant workers. Their federation, the Joint Committee for Migrant Workers in Korea, was organized in 1995 in the wake of the aforementioned protest by Nepalese trainees. It now encompasses twenty-seven local organizations as full members and five affiliate associations.[53] These associations run shelters that offer advice, educational programs, medical services and accommodation to needy foreigners. Also within the ambit of their activities are problems related to *joseonjok*, as is exemplified by their campaign against the Overseas Koreans Act of 1999. Recently, some associations have taken up matters related to escapees from North Korea. Efforts are thus being made to bring various groups of outsiders under common agendas and to seek their common interests.

Such efforts are, however, not free from potential tension. It is natural to deal with the *joseonjok* question in conjunction with the problem of migrant workers in general, insofar as *joseonjok* form a large percentage of the migrant workforce. Arguments in support of the two groups, however, often draw on different rationales. *Segyehwa* (globalization) or global standards are invoked as the most powerful slogan in rallying for the protection of migrant workers in general. It is argued that Korea should reform its treatment of foreigners according to the universal values embodied in the international norms that Korea has declared itself to abide by, such as the International Covenant on Economic, Social and Cultural Rights and the International Convention on the Elimination of All Forms of Racial Discrimination.[54] When it comes to *joseonjok*, on the other hand, emphasis is given to the common ethnic identity, the historical background of Korean emigrations to China, and the significance of the *joseonjok* economy in the future integration of the two Koreas. Some say, 'How can you talk about globalization if you can't accommodate *joseonjok*, who are of the same ethnic stock and use the same language?'.[55] While campaigners for the rights of migrant workers and the sympathetic public agree that all workers in Korea should enjoy equal labor standards, insurance protection and union rights, most of them also agree that the size of the foreign workforce should be strictly controlled. They suggest that the invitation of *joseonjok* workers should be approached from the perspective of national integration. Further, they add that the size of the non-Korean foreign workforce should be controlled in conjunction with the prospects for incorporating North Korean workers into a pan-Korean labor market.[56] Not surprisingly, similar references to the 'nation' are made in an opposing context, in arguments against reforming the current system of treating migrant workers.[57]

Ethnic Chinese residents

The most stable status that can be enjoyed by aliens in South Korea is the F-2 (residence) visa status, which is granted *inter alia* to 'persons who continuously reside and have their living bases in the Republic of Korea and their spouses and offspring'. It allows the holder to stay in Korea for a maximum of five years and to work for income. Chinese residents or *hwagyo* (*huaqiao* in Chinese pronunciation) account for almost 97 per cent of F-2 visa holders. Among the 22,000 *hwagyo*, 18,000 are currently living in South Korea. Almost all of them are nationals of Taiwan. There is only a very small number of people who are Chinese in origin but Korean by nationality, whom the Chinese classify as *huaren*. Hence the Chinese community in Korea is tiny in view of Korea's contiguity with China and in comparison with many Southeast Asian countries, each of which has millions of ethnic Chinese. While the Chinese population in Korea has never been so large from the outset, even this small population has steadily diminished over the last few decades.

The historical origins of the present Chinese community in Korea can be traced back to 1882, when Korea and China signed a trade agreement that permitted Chinese merchants to own and lease land and houses in treaty port areas. The number of Chinese immigrants fluctuated during Japanese rule between 12,000 and 80,000, and less than 15,000 were living in the southern half of Korea when Korea became independent and divided. At that time, the *hwagyo* played a significant part in South Korea's economy, as trade with China accounted for 80 per cent of total trade and Chinese capital made up 70 per cent of total capital invested in China trade. Their success, however, came to a halt as the Korean War broke out and the Cold War severed South Korea's ties with mainland China. Refugees from North Korea increased the South Korean *hwagyo* population to 22,000 shortly after the Korean War, a figure which grew to 32,400 in the early 1970s thanks only to natural factors. Since then the *hwagyo* population has fallen to 22,000. North Korea is estimated to have less than 10,000 *hwagyo* residents.[58]

The small size of the *hwagyo* community and its further diminution can be attributed to many factors beyond the control of the Koreans. Yet Korea's unfavorable laws and policies have undoubtedly been responsible for the shrinking of the *hwagyo* population. The first blow came with the Aliens' Land Act of 1961, which prohibited foreign ownership of land without permission. Chinese farmers had to give up their farming and merchants had to sell their commercial premises or put their businesses in the names of their Korean friends. The law was amended in 1968 to relax the prohibition, but aliens were still prohibited to hold more than 660 square meters of residential land and 185 square meters of commercial property without government permission. This restriction, along with municipal development planning, caused Chinese commercial areas to disappear and rendered Korea arguably the world's only industrialized country without a Chinatown. The already crippled *hwagyo* businesses faced the extra difficulty of competing with Korean firms under the government-engineered allocation of credit. The discriminatory law and practice have affected the distribution of occupations. Operating Chinese restaurants has remained the only business where Chinese still have some advantage, although the land restriction and various other regulations have made the business increasingly unattractive. More than half of the families of 1,100 pupils in Seoul Overseas Chinese High School live by operating or cooking in Chinese restaurants.[59]

In contrast to such restrictive devices and policies as the Aliens' Land Act, South Korea has adopted a strikingly 'libertarian' policy in education. There are twenty-eight primary and four secondary *hwagyo* schools in Korea, accommodating more than 3,000 pupils. This contrasts with the draconian policies of Thailand and Indonesia against ethnic Chinese education. Ironically, this 'tolerance' has been another kind of exclusion. Until 1998, *hwagyo* schools were outside the purview of education laws, not recognized as educational institutions and excluded from subsidies. In fact, Korea's attitude towards the *hwagyo* in education has been a peculiar mixture of exclusion and inclusion. Despite the impression among some *hwagyo* that Korean primary and secondary schools do not admit their children, Korean schools have never placed such a barrier.[60] At the same time, Korean universities have admitted graduates of *hwagyo* schools as proper high-school graduates. Further, many universities have included *hwagyo*-school graduates in their extra quotas for foreign applicants so that they do not have to sit for the notoriously competitive entrance examination. This seemingly accommodating special entrance system has the unintended consequence of discouraging Chinese parents from sending their children to Korean secondary schools, whose graduates are ineligible for the benefit.[61]

The policy towards *hwagyo* education has helped to preserve a cultural space where the Chinese immigrants have reproduced their identity. *Hwagyo* education has also strengthened the *hwagyo*'s attachment to Taiwan, as their education programs are strictly in line with those of Taiwan. Many *hwagyo*-school graduates have chosen to further their studies in Taiwanese universities, and their presence in Taiwan has been an important channel through which Korean *hwagyo* have emigrated to Taiwan. On the other hand, ethnic education has contributed to the isolation of the Chinese immigrants in Korean society, where alumni networks are the greatest source of social capital.

Just as Korean *hwagyo* have a demonstrably high representation amongst university students in Taiwan, compared with *huaqiao/huaren* students from Southeast Asia, so they have recorded a higher frequency of visits to Taiwan than the ethnic Chinese of Thailand and Indonesia.[62] This reflects their low degree of incorporation into Korean society and strong Taiwanese identity, unparalleled in Chinese immigrant communities of other countries. Unlike most *huaqiao* and *huaren* in other parts of the world, no less than 95 per cent of Chinese immigrants in Korea are from Shandong. Their association with Taiwan is a double product of the political situation surrounding the Yellow Sea and Korea's exclusionary policy. They were totally dissociated from their homes in mainland China as the Cold War blocked the Yellow Sea, and have had no choice but to rely on Taiwan as their state of nationality and source of support. Living in South Korea, they have been baptized with a strong anti-communism, which has reinforced their political identification with Taiwan. Nevertheless, their condition as Taiwanese is problematic. Many *hwagyo* have left Korea for Taiwan since the 1970s and yet, with their Shandong background and unique identity formed while living in Korea, often find themselves to be 'a minority in their own country'.[63] The same is true of those who have emigrated to North America, who are neither part of the Korean community nor included among Chinese immigrants from elsewhere.

There has been a wave of reverse immigration since the beginning of the 1990s. Also on the increase is the percentage of high-school graduates who choose to go to Korean universities. These *hwagyo* may have realized that their identity is inseparably tied to Korea. Yet the main lure seems to be the wider job opportunities resulting from Korea's economic success and adjustment to globalization. Changes wrought by globalization have been in the direction of improving the treatment of the *hwagyo* and other long-term foreign residents in Korea. The Aliens' Land Act was revised in 1997 to remove the ceilings on ownership, partly in an attempt to attract *huaqiao* and *huaren* capital from Southeast Asia. *Hwagyo* are now able to become members of the Korean bar or certified public accountants under the same conditions as Koreans, as WTO- and OECD-led talks about the internationalization of professional services prompted Korea to remove the nationality requirement for those professions. Yet *hwagyo* still complain about barriers they continue to face and inconveniences they experience in daily life.[64] The most resented is the immigration policy.

Although the maximum period of sojourn under the F-2 visa was lengthened from three years to five years in 1999, *hwagyo* are regularly reminded that they are eternal strangers to Korean society, as they have to renew their F-2 visas periodically. The onerous immigration policy is blind to the fact that the *hwagyo* have developed increasing ties with Korean society. The level of intermarriage among mothers of all pupils in Seoul Overseas Chinese High School who are Korean has reached 30 percent. Some pupils are three-quarters Korean, as their grandmothers are also Korean.[65] Yet, as we shall see, the patrilateral *ius sanguinis* principle under the Nationality Act before its 1997 revision denied them Korean nationality, and most of them do not benefit from the bilateral *ius sanguinis* rule introduced by the 1997 amendment.

Naturalization may be the only option for Chinese residents seeking incorporation into Korean society. As we shall see, one has to meet many conditions for naturalization, which *hwagyo* often find prohibitive. It is, however, not Korean nationality that the *hwagyo* ultimately desire. They want above all a more stable right of abode. Progress is being made to that effect, as sympathetic intellectuals, lawyers and members of the National Assembly have come up with a legislative proposal that the *hwagyo* and other long-term foreign residents be given a right of permanent residence, and the idea has been translated into a bill entitled the Act on the Permanent Residence Right and the Legal Status of Long-term Foreign Sojourners (hereinafter the Permanent Residence Act). Within the purview of the Act are F-2 visa holders who have resided continuously in the Republic of Korea for five years, their offspring, and the foreign spouses of nationals of the Republic of Korea. The draft proposes to grant them permanent residence on condition that they satisfy certain requirements such as 'capability of maintaining livelihood' either with their own property or skills or by depending on their families. It also proposes to extend to permanent residents the national treatment regarding real property rights and transactions, foreign exchange transactions, health insurance, national pensions, education and tax obligations, on a par with overseas Koreans under the Overseas Koreans Act.

Before the introduction of the bill for the Permanent Residence Act, some National Assembly representatives from the ruling Democratic Party for the New Millennium tabled a bill named the Act for Granting Long-Term Foreign Residents the Right to Vote in Local Elections (hereinafter the Foreign Residents' Local Election Right Act). The bill aims at conferring the right to vote in local elections on F-2 visa holders who have resided in the Republic of Korea for five years or more. The government and the ruling party began to prepare the bill in the wake of President Kim Dae-jung's visit to Japan in 1999, where the President suggested that his government was considering granting foreign residents the right to vote in local elections, and requested Premier Obuchi of Japan to extend such a right to Korean residents in Japan. President Kim's suggestion reflected concern among Koreans that the unfavorable treatment of Chinese residents in Korea was being used as a pretext for Japanese indifference to calls for an improved treatment of Korean residents in Japan. Although President Kim's suggestion created some euphoria, the *hwagyo* community and campaigners for the permanent residence right commented that a voting right was meaningless without a stable right of residence, and that the initiative was putting the cart before the horse.[66] The campaigners nonetheless supported it in tandem with their crusade for the Permanent Residence Act. A potential hurdle for the Foreign Residents' Local Election Right Act is the question of whether the National Assembly can confer such a right on aliens under the present constitution. Those in favor of the bill are developing a rationale that distinguishes national and local elections, but controversy will be inevitable once the bill is put to discussion.[67]

The treatment of the *hwagyo* is being discussed in a number of different contexts. First, human rights campaigners approach the problem from a universalistic perspective and find a link between the *hwagyo* question and the treatment of migrant workers and other outsiders. Among those who drew up the draft for the Permanent Residence Act were public-interest lawyers in support of the rights of migrant workers. Campaigners for the rights of migrant workers call for greater attention to the Chinese residents alongside the *joseonjok* and migrant workers, the treatment of all of whom they say is a mirror reflecting the general human rights standard of Korea. They stress the significance of the *hwagyo* issue because migrant workers are likely to find themselves in the same situation as they prolong their presence in Korea.[68] Second, campaigners often come up with a utilitarian rationale in calling for better treatment of the *hwagyo*. As we have seen, one of the motives for the 1997 revision of the Aliens' Land Act was to invite Chinese capital into Southeast Asia. In the same vein, campaigns have been launched to build a Chinatown in Seoul, and a few other municipalities have set out similar plans with a view to attracting *huaqiao* and *huaren* investments. Utilitarian concern also straddles the argument that an improved treatment of foreign residents in Korea will strengthen the position of Korean residents in Japan in their fight against discrimination. The human rights perspective and the utilitarian rationale have compounded each other to generate impetus for the *hwagyo* rights campaign. On the other hand, the self-criticism that finds fault with the Korean attitude towards the *hwagyo* has created uneasiness among some sections of the Korean population. They feel particularly uneasy about the implication that the exclusionary attitude of the Korean public derives from the Korean *mentalité* itself. They point out that the Chinese immigrants chose to settle in Korea for their own benefit during the era of imperialism, and their current situation has much to do with the Cold War and South Korea's anti-communist policy. Therefore, they say, the *hwagyo*'s situation should not be compared to that of Korean residents in Japan. Nevertheless, they register little opposition against the human rights implications of the campaigns for the rights of foreigners in general. What they argue is that Asians in Korea, particularly the migrant workers, should be protected as victims of imperialism and neo-colonialism, and that anti-imperialism rather than rationales for globalization should be the supporting ground for their rights.[69]

Gender and nationality

Another change that occurred in parallel with the efforts to cope with the advent of novel groups of outsiders in the 1990s was the revision of the Nationality Act in 1997 toward greater equality between the sexes. It marked a transformation of the Korean sense of national identity in the face of increasing transnational migrations.

Korean nationality law is based on *ius sanguinis* and applies *ius soli* only in exceptional cases, that is, where one's parents are unidentified or stateless or he/she is an abandoned child discovered in the Republic of Korea without evidence that he/she was born in another state (Article 2, Nationality Act). Until 1997, the *ius sanguinis* rule was grounded on patrilateralism. Thus a child born of a Korean man and a foreign woman obtained Korean nationality at birth, whereas Korean nationality was not granted to the child of a Korean woman and her foreign spouse.

This male-centered system was buttressed by a peculiar notion of nationhood, namely the belief that the Korean state was constituted by a single *minjok*. The term *minjok* in Korean resembles *minzoku* in Japan in that it denotes simultaneously a *nation* and what Anthony Smith terms an *ethnie* – a community whose unity rests on a collective name, a common myth of descent, a shared history, a distinctive shared culture, an association with a specific territory, and a sense of solidarity – and also a *people* and even a *race*. Like *minzoku* in Japan, the *minjok* conception presupposes and conflates biological ties and cultural homogeneity.[70] An important rationale for patrilateral *ius sanguinis* in Korean nationality law was that it was the best way to preserve the purity of the *danil minjok gukka* (unitary *minjok* state). A typical argument goes as follows.

> From time immemorial our *minjok* has maintained its homogeneity and has made it its historical mission to build a unitary state consisting of a single *minjok*. ... [N]ationality in our country has more than legal-technical meaning. ... If we adopted bilateral *ius sanguinis*, a person who would be a foreign national under patrilateral *ius sanguinis* could be a dual national of Korea and a foreign state and obtain Korean nationality at birth. This will impair the *danil minjok gukka* nature of our state.[71]

Patrilateral *ius sanguinis* alone cannot guarantee the purity of blood, if there is any, unless transnational marriage itself is prohibited. Such a logical flaw lies in all sorts of patriarchal ideology and patrilineal organization of kinship, to which purity of blood is central but female blood is irrelevant. Not surprisingly, a *minjok* is regarded as a family writ large, insofar as the *minjok* notion centers on common descent.

Campaigners for gender equality began to struggle against the male-dominant ideology inherent in the Nationality Act in parallel with their strife for equality in family law. Their campaign gained momentum following South Korea's accession to the International Covenant on Civil and Political Rights in 1990. Another source of impetus was the change in the landscape of transnational marriage in Korea in the 1990s. Marriages began to involve aliens other than American servicemen, missionaries, and followers of the Unification Church. Many Korean men got married to *joseonjok* and, later,

Filipino women. The major pressure for the legal change, however, came from the failure to give Korean nationality to children born of marriages between Korean women and migrant workers from other Asian countries.

The Nationality Act was amended in 1997 under added pressure from a court decision. The case involved a man named Gim Gwangho, who was served a deportation order for having illegally sailed into Korea from China. Gim sued to have the deportation order declared void on account that the patrilateral *ius sanguinis* rule in the Nationality Act was an infringement of the constitutional principle of equality between the sexes. While the court found that Gim's father, originally a North Korean, was not a national of the Republic of Korea, because he had acquired Chinese nationality, Gim argued that his mother was a North Korean national at the time of his birth and, therefore, he was a son of a woman who was a national of the Republic of Korea insofar as North Korea was part of the republic's territory. He contended that the unconstitutional patrilateralism unduly denied him Korean nationality. The Seoul High Court found that the rule might be unconstitutional and referred the constitutional question to the Constitutional Court, and the National Assembly amended the Nationality Act before the Constitutional Court made its decision.[72]

Thanks to the bilateral *ius sanguinis* principle introduced by the 1997 amendment, a child born to parents of whom one is a Korean national is a Korean national. The law also enables children born during the previous ten years to women who are Korean nationals or were Korean nationals at the time of the birth of the child to acquire Korean nationality by reporting to the justice minister. Whereas the benefit of the new rule extends, at least in theory, to most children born to Korean women and migrant workers, many of those who were born to Korean mothers and *hwagyo* fathers cannot enjoy the benefit, because they were over ten years of age at the time when the new rule came into force. When the Constitutional Court made its decision regarding the above-mentioned Gim Gwangho case after the amendment of the Nationality Act, it ruled that the ten-year limitation was incompatible with the constitution, but, instead of setting it aside, recognized its effect until a subsequent legislative action by the National Assembly to correct the wrong.[73] The National Assembly has yet to change the rule.

Despite the progress, children whose fathers are illegal sojourners do not always find themselves in a better situation than the past, since it is difficult in practice for them either to have their marriages properly registered in Korea or get married under their country's law and live in Korea. In order to register his or her marriage, a foreigner has to submit an affidavit of eligibility for marriage, which some embassies do not issue particularly when it is requested by an illegal sojourner. Neither do these embassies offer services to illegal sojourners who wish to get married under their country's law. Therefore, illegal sojourners have to go to their own country either to get the right document for registering their marriage under Korean law or to get married under their country's law. This is risky because they might not get a visa or pass the immigration control on the way back to Korea. Therefore, many choose to cohabit without entering into legal marriage either under Korean or foreign law. A child born from such a relationship is either unregistered for many years, say, until school age, or recorded on the household register of the mother's family as an illegitimate child, given the mother's surname, and placed under the parental right of the mother. The child obtains Korean nationality, but at the cost of being a bastard. Considering the seriousness of the problem, the government now takes a generous attitude towards illegal sojourners who have reported their illegal status during a 'voluntary reporting period', during which the government waives penalties, when they apply for visas to return to Korea after getting married in their own country.[74]

The revision of the Nationality Act did not bring any change to the status of foreign men married to Korean women in terms of nationality, whereas it dropped the previous rule that accorded Korean nationality to foreign women upon marriage to Korean men unless they failed to renounce their original nationality within six months. As in the past, therefore, no foreigner automatically obtains Korean nationality upon marriage to a Korean woman. Foreign spouses of Korean nationals may apply for naturalization if they have been domiciled in Korea continuously for two years while maintaining the marital relationship, or have maintained the marital relationship for not less than three years and been domiciled in Korea continuously for one year. The applicant must meet additional conditions, which give the government wide room for discretion, such as 'decent behavior' and 'capability of maintaining the livelihood of the family and of him/herself'. The financial threshold is as high as a bank account or real property worth 30 million won or an equivalent amount of wealth. Also required are recommendations from two or more high-ranking people such as National Assembly representatives, mayors, local councilors, judges, public prosecutors, lawyers, school principals, university professors, high civil servants, bankers and journalists (Article 3, Rules for Implementing the Nationality Act). Few migrant workers can overcome these hurdles, and even *hwagyo* find the requirements prohibitive.

Legal marriage does not necessarily make life easier for foreign men married to Korean women. Although foreign spouses of Korean nationals are eligible to apply for an F-2 visa, it is rarely given to foreign men married to Korean women. They normally get F-1 visas (for visiting and joining the family). Although the F-1 visa allows the holder to stay in Korea for a maximum of two years, it is the immigration practice that such men rarely get the full two years, whereas foreign women married to Korean men are allowed lengthier periods of stay under F-1 and have better chances of obtaining F-2 visas. Worse, the F-1 visa does not allow the holder to work for income. Therefore, many foreigners continue to hold short-term visas instead of switching them to F-1. One who wishes to have his F-1 or short-term visa renewed must leave the country and reenter, which is not only cumbersome but financially costly as well. In short, notwithstanding the amendment of the Nationality Act, obstacles installed by the immigration law continue to penalize Korean women and their foreign spouses, and thereby keep alive the gender inequality in immigration policy. Since the foreign spouses of Korean women cannot work for income, their Korean wives have to work alone to support the family. Such difficulties naturally drive foreign husbands to violate the immigration law and find employment or hold on to their existing jobs in illegal status of sojourn. They have no choice but to go underground, because if they are caught and deported they cannot obtain a proper visa to reenter within five years, according to the Immigration Control Act. Naturally, Korean immigration law is being criticized for systematically creating illegal sojourners and producing separated and broken families.[75]

Social activists, religious workers and volunteers have set out to help couples in transnational marriages and their children, in tandem with their campaigns against the existing law and practice. The Ansan Migrant Shelter, an organization for migrant workers, has opened an advice and care program for those whom it calls 'Kosians' (Korean + Asians), namely the families of migrant workers and particularly children born of foreign workers or of foreign workers and Korean women.[76]

Their efforts bring into light the situation of such forgotten outsiders as mixed-blood children. Since the first baby born of an American serviceman and a Korean woman in 1947, a floating estimate of 20,000–60,000 children have been born in South Korea to Korean women and foreign men. Now 650 are registered with the Pearl Buck Foundation, an institution designed to promote the welfare of mixed-blood people, and roughly 1,000 are estimated to be living in Korea, after a huge exodus by way of adoption and emigration. Over 43 per cent of the mixed-blood people who registered with the Pearl Buck Foundation have been brought up by single mothers, compared with 8.4 per cent of all Koreans. A majority of the adults are engaged in manual labor, entertainment, and serving in bars and restaurants, and not a single one has become a civil servant, although they are Korean by nationality.[77] 'Kosians' will join them in urging a reconsideration of Korea's highly racialized sense of ethnicity and myth of *danil minjok gukka*.

Epilogue

The Korean situation is further complicated by the national division. Rapid economic deterioration in North Korea in the early 1990s has produced floods of *talbukja* (deserters from North Korea) crossing the northern borders into China and Russia. Because North Korea is part of the territory of the Republic of Korea under Article 3 of the Constitution, the Republic of Korea treats *talbukja* as its nationals without reservation, unlike *joseonjok* and *goryeoin*. Koreans are, however, experiencing a serious discrepancy between their constitutional order and the international reality, since North Korea is a sovereign state in the international arena, particularly *vis-à-vis* China and Russia. This has resulted in the record of only about 1,000 *talbukja* successfully settled in South Korea since 1990. The constitutional rule also conflicts with the social reality, as the incomers from North Korea find themselves to be an isolated minority in South Korean society, suffering from cultural differences, identity crisis and social discrimination. They have joined the other groups of outsiders in testing the Korean sense of identity.[78]

South Koreans have extended their rising awareness regarding the incorporation of outsiders to the *talbukja* as well. Non-governmental organizations and human rights campaigners have taken up the issue in tandem with their concerns over the treatment of the *joseonjok*, foreign workers and *hwagyo*. To be sure, there are overlaps between these groups, as *talbukja* are often indistinct from *joseonjok* when they come from China, *joseonjok* form a large section of the migrant workforce, and an improved treatment of the *hwagyo* may be a signpost for the future accommodation of foreign workers who have developed special bonds with Korean society. The universalistic appeals of human rights campaigners have successfully brought the problems faced by those groups into the same light, and will continue to serve as a catalyst for a more culturally diverse and inclusive Korean society. On the other hand, those groups are separated from one another by two dividing axes – ethnicity and nationality – and their aspirations and preoccupations, as well as the goals and rationales of the campaigns for their inclusion, are not the same.

In relation to the ethnic Koreans from/in China and fellow ethnics from North Korea, Koreans have found the assumed solidity of the Korean *ethnie* being shaken by both the stern forces of the international system of sovereign states and their reluctance to sacrifice the tranquility that economic development has brought to South Korea. Looking at the foreign workers and the *hwagyo*, they have become self-critical of the exclusionary implications and consequences of the putative seamlessness of their society. These challenges have impelled the Koreans to reconsider their notion of ethnic and national identity and nationalism, which is now shedding its primordialist mystifications and being subjected to critical scrutiny.[79] On the other hand, it is true that many approaches to *joseonjok* and *talbukja* draw their inspiration from an ethnic nationalism, and it is when appealing to the goal of national unification and the idea of building a pan-Korean economy that the greatest popular support can be enlisted for improving the treatment of those people. The prospects for the inclusion of the outsider groups described in this study rest on two forces in interplay – globalism and nationalism.

Postscript

On 29 November 2002, the Constitutional Court of Korea declared 'unconformable to the Constitution' those parts of Article 2 of the Overseas Koreans Act and Article 3 of the Order Implementing the Overseas Koreans Act which precluded from the benefits of the Act ethnic Koreans who had migrated to China and the former Soviet Union prior to 15 August 1948, and ordered the National Assembly to take legislative action to remove the unconformability by 31 December 2003.

Notes

1 I am grateful to Sangmee Bak, In-Seop Chung, Sang Ik Eom, Young-im Kim, Jeanyoung Lee, June J. H. Lee, Keun-Gwan Lee, Kyeyoung Park, Dong-Hyun Seok, Dong-Hoon Seol, and Phil S. Yang for their help at various stages of writing this chapter. Any errors are of course my responsibility.

2 Overseas Korean Foundation, *Segye hanminjok bunpo hyeonhwang* [The Distribution of Koreans in the World], http://www.okf.or.kr. In Korea, the designation *joseonjok* is now avoided in official usage and replaced by *jaejung dongpo* (ethnic Koreans in China). Nowadays the term *joseonjok* is often thought to carry pejorative connotations. Yet it is widely used in practice, and I choose to use it here as a first-order term, which I think will better serve the descriptive purpose of this study. The transliteration of Korean language in this study follows the method recently adopted by South Korea's Ministry of Education.

3 National Intelligence Service, *Jungguk dongpo hyeonhwang* [The Situation of Koreans in China], http://www.nis.go.kr/menu/m09000000/m09010100.html.

4 A complex question arises from the Nationality Act and the Provisional Rules on Nationality. According to the Nationality Act before its 1997 revision, a person was a national of the Republic of Korea if his father was a national of the republic when the person was born. How could one become a national of the Republic of Korea if he was born before the birth of the republic? According to the Provisional Rules, a person was a Korean national if his father was a Korean (*joseonin*) at the time of his birth. Both the Nationality Act at the time of its enactment and the Provisional Rules seem to have presupposed as the basis for Korean nationality a community of Koreans, to which the Provisional Rules applied the term *joseonin* and the Nationality Act retrospectively extended the application of the name Republic of Korea. Whatever term was applied to that community of Koreans, neither the Provisional Rules nor the Nationality Act gave a clear definition as to the membership and boundaries of that community. While this is a significant question in itself, this study cannot afford to inquire into it in its limited space.

5 While Japan's Nationality Law provided for termination of Japanese nationality as a result of acquisition of foreign nationality, Japan did not apply the law to Korea, and interpreted that Koreans were Japanese nationals according to custom and reason. This was to prevent Koreans in Manchuria from escaping from Japanese control by obtaining Chinese or Russian nationality. See Egawa Eibun, Yamada Ryōichi and Hayada Hōrō, *Kokuseihō* [Nationality Law], 2nd edn (Tokyo: Yūbigaku, 1989) pp. 191–2; Jeong Inseop [In-Seop Chung], 'Beopjeok gijun eseo bon hangugin eui beomwi' [The Range of Koreans on the Basis of Legal Criteria], in *Sahoegwahak eui Jemunje* [Problems in Social Science], Festschrift for Professor Im Wontaek (Seoul: Beommunsa, 1988), pp. 653–4. Yet opinions differ as to whether the fact that renunciation of nationality was disallowed under the Joseon dynasty and Japanese rule is an effective ground for recognizing the continuation of the Korean nationality of the emigrants. Jeong Inseop, unlike No Yeongdon, is in the negative because the Provisional Rules on Nationality presupposed the loss of nationality of those who had acquired foreign nationality. See the writings of Jeong and No cited in the next note.

6 Jeong Inseop, 'Uri gukjeokbeop sang choecho gungmin hwakjeong gijun e gwanhan geomto' [A Review of the Initial Criteria for Defining Korean Nationals

Under Korean Nationality Law], *Gukjebeophakhoe nonchong* [Korean Journal of International Law], vol. 43, no. 2 (1998) pp. 243–6; 'Jaeoe dongpo eui churipguk gwa beopjeok jiwi e gwanhan beomnyul eui naeyong gwa munjejeom' [The Content and Problems of the Act on the Immigration and Legal Status of Overseas Koreans], *Seoul gukjebeop yeongu* [Seoul International Law Journal], vol. 6, no. 2 (1999) pp. 315–16; No Yeongdon, 'Jaejung hanin eui gukjeok e gwanhan yeongu' [A Study of the Nationality of Koreans in China], *Gukjebeophakhoe nonchong*, vol. 44, no. 2 (1999) pp. 87–8; Seok Donghyeon, 'Hyeonhaeng gukjeokbeop eui munjejeom gwa gaejeong banghyang yeongu' [Inquiry into Problems in the Present Nationality Act and Directions for Amendment], *Beopjo* [Judiciary], vol. 46, no. 1 (1997) pp. 52–3.

7 Supreme Court, 31 October 1973, 72na2295; Supreme Court, 10 February 1981, 80da2189. See summaries and a comparison of the two cases, which involve Korean emigrants to the United States during Japanese rule, in Jeong Inseop (ed.) *Hanguk pallye gukjebeop* [Korean Cases on International Law] (Seoul: Hongmunsa, 1998) ch. 2. See also Constitutional Court, 31 August 2000, 97heonga12, which denied the Korean nationality of a person whom the court found to have acquired Chinese nationality before 1948.

8 See Ministry of Foreign Affairs/Institute of Foreign and Security Policy, *Jungguk gyopo sahoe waeui gyoryu mit jiwon bang-an* [Interchange and Assistance Scheme for Koreans in China] (1989) p. 9.

9 'Oeguggin ipguk jangnyeon 294 man myeong' [2,940,000 Foreigners Entered Last Year], *Joseon ilbo* [Chosun Daily], 15 February 1992, p. 2.

10 'Jungguk dongpo 50 myeong yeongju heoyong' [Fifty Koreans from China Granted Permanent Residence], *Joseon ilbo*, 2 May 1995, p. 37.

11 For an account of the background of the 1997 revision of the Nationality Act, see Seok Donghyeon [Dong-Hyun Seok], 'Singukjeokbeop eui seongnip gyeonggwa mit gaejeong eui gaeyo' [An Overview of the Course of the Revision of the Nationality Act], *Justice*, vol. 32, no. 2 (1999) pp. 140–81.

12 See Gim Byeongcheon, 'Gim Yeongsam jeongbu eui jaeoe dongpo jeongchaek' [The Overseas Koreans Policy of the Kim Young Sam Government], *Jaeoe hanin yeongu* [Studies of Koreans Abroad], no. 8 (1999) pp. 317–58.

13 See Yi Jonghun, 'Jaeoe dongpo jeongchaek eui gwaje wa jaeoe dongpo gibonbeop eui jejeong munje' [Tasks of Overseas Koreans Policy and the Problem of Making the Basic Law for Overseas Koreans], *Ipbeop josa yeongu* [Legislation Studies], no. 249 (1998) pp. 146–72.

14 'Oegyo tongsangbu, *jaeoe* dongpo teungnyebeop bandae ipjang pyomyeong' [MOFAT Opposes the Special Law on Overseas Koreans], *Jung-ang ilbo* [Joongang Daily], 28 August 1998; 'Jaeoe dongpo teungnye beoban jungguk deungseo yugam pyomyeong' [China and Other Countries Express Uneasy Feelings Towards the Special Law on Overseas Koreans], *Jung-ang ilbo*, 3 September 1998, online at http://news.navers.com.

15 Article 2, Overseas Koreans Act; Article 3, Presidential Order Implementing the Overseas Koreans Act.

16 On the other hand, the Overseas Korean Foundation Act of 1997, on the basis of which the Overseas Korean Foundation was set up, adheres to the definition of *jaeoe dongpo* (overseas compatriots/overseas Koreans) that embraces 'residents in foreign states who are of Korean descent regardless of nationality'.

17 See Jeong Inseop, 'Jaeoe dongpo eui churipguk gwa beopjeok jiwi e gwanhan beomnyul eui naeyong gwa munjejeom' [The Content and Problems of the Act on the Immigration and Legal Status of Overseas Koreans], p. 306.

18 *Ibid.*, pp. 313–15; see a similar critique during the legislative deliberation in Baek Chunghyeon, Mun Junjo and Kim Deokju, *Jaeoe dongpo gwallyeon ipbeop eui naeyong*

gwa hyeongsik e gwanhan geomto [Inquiry into the Content and Form of Legislation Concerning Overseas Koreans] (Seoul: Overseas Koreans Foundation, 1999) pp. 11–12.

19 'Jaeoedongpobeop, mueosi munje inga?' [What Problems Are There in the Overseas Koreans Act?], *Joseon ilbo*, 24 August 1999, p. 29.

20 Ministry of Justice, *Jaeoe dongpo beomnyul sangdam* [Legal Advice for Overseas Koreans], online at http://www.moj.go.kr/board; Embassy of the Republic of Korea in China, *Joseonjok sajeung balgeup jeolcha gaeseon: jaeoedongpobeop bowan daechaek* [Improvement of the Visa Issuance Procedure for joseonjok: Supplementary Measures to the Overseas Koreans Act], reproduced at http://hometown.weppy.com/sansaya/99–873.htm.

21 Ministry of Justice, *Churipguk gwalli tonggye nyeonbo* [Annual Immigration Statistics] (2000) pp. 246–7, 296–7; 356–7, 384.

22 See Gim Yongchan, Gim Taeyeong, Go Byeongguk and Gang Gwonchan, 'Jaehan oegugin' [Foreigners in Korea], *Minjok yeongu* [Studies in Ethnicity], no. 4 (2000) p. 11; 'Jung-Reo dongpo cheryu gigan yeonjang yogu' [Demands for a Lengthened Period of Sojourn for Koreans from China and Russia], *Joseon ilbo*, 22 November 1999, online at http://www.chosun.com/w21data/html/news.

23 The industrial trainees thus counted comprise all kinds of D-3 visa holders, of which the trainees this study focuses on form a large majority. Other than the industrial trainees, over 24,000 foreigners are working in Korea on D- and E-type visas. Most of them are either in Korea for business purposes or working in financial and hi-tech industries, research institutions, and schools. See Ministry of Justice, *Churipguk gwalli tonggye nyeonbo* [Annual Immigration Statistics] (2000) pp. 246–7.

24 'Oegugin bulbeop cheryu 61,000 myeong singo' [61,000 Illegal Aliens Reported], *Joseon ilbo*, 4 August 1992, p. 22.

25 Gim Seonsu, 'Hanguk eseoeui oegugin nodongja ingwon munje' [Human Rights Problems Concerning Foreign Workers in Korea], *Simin gwa byeonhosa* [Citizens and Lawyers], no. 12 (1995) pp. 140–1.

26 Ministry of Justice, *Churipguk gwalli tonggye nyeonbo* [Annual Immigration Statistics] (2000) p. 247; Yi Hyegyeong, 'Oegugin nodongja eui sahoe gyeongjejeok sanghwang' [The Socio-Economic Situation of Foreign Workers], in Seok Hyeonho, Yi Hyegyeong, Jeong Giseon, Gang Sudol and Seol Donghun, *Hanguk sahoe wa oegugin nodongja* [Korean Society and Foreign Workers] (Seoul: Mirae illyeok yeongu Center, 1998) pp. 41, 47.

27 Seol Donghun [Dong-Hoon Seol], *Oegugin nodongja wa hanguk sahoe* [Foreign Workers and Korean Society] (Seoul: Seoul National University Press, 1999) pp. 121–2. As we shall see, the illegality of those I describe as 'illegal workers' lies in their immigration status and not in their labor contracts. Seol prefers to use the term 'undocumented workers' to 'illegal workers'. Dong-Hoon Seol, 'Past and Present of Foreign Workers in Korea 1987–2000', *Asia Solidarity Quarterly*, vol. 2 (2000) pp. 6–31.

28 Seol Donghun, *Oegugin nodongja wa hanguk sahoe* [Foreign Workers and Korean Society] (Seoul: Seoul National University Press, 1999) pp. 331–2.

29 'Urido saram daejeop haedala' [Treat Us as Human Beings], *Joseon ilbo*, 10 January 1995, p. 39 and other articles. Detailed reports are available on newspapers between 10 January and 18 January 1995.

30 See Nam Donghi, *Oegugin geulloja eui beopjeok munje* [Legal Problems of Foreign Workers] (Seoul: Garim M&B, 1999) ch. 4.

31 Supreme Court, 22 December 1995, 95nu2050.

32 Choe Hongyeop, 'Oegugin geulloja eui nodongbeop sang jiwi e gwanhan yeongu' [A Study of the Status of Foreign Workers Under Labor Law], unpublished Ph.D. dissertation, Seoul National University (1997) p. 106.

33 Gim Jun, *Saneop yeonsu jedo* [Industrial Training System], National Assembly Network (2000) online at http://www2.nanet.go.kr:8080/lkmeta/intro/a0296_intro.htm. According to a survey by the Ministry of Finance and Economy, the average productivity of foreign workers is 72 per cent of that of Korean workers. Nam Donghi, *Oegugin geulloja eui beopjeok munje* [Legal Problems of Foreign Workers], p. 93.

34 A recent court conciliation ended up with the payment of a severance pay to a trainee, which may lead to a new rule in the future. 'Oegugin saneop yeonsusaeng toejikkeum jura' [Give Foreign Trainees Severance Pay], *Hangyeore sinmun* [Hangyore Times], 26 April 2001, http://korean.hani.co.kr/section-005100008/

35 Yi Hyegyeong, 'Oegugin nodongja eui sahoe gyeongjejeok sanghwang' [The Socio-Economic Situation of Foreign Workers], in Seok Hyeonho, Yi Hyegyeong, Jeong Giseon, Gang Sudol and Seol Donghun, *Hanguk sahoe wa oegugin nodongja* [Korean Society and Foreign Workers] (Seoul: Mirae illyeok yeongu Center, 1998) pp. 50–1; Gim Jun, *Saneop yeonsu jedo* [Industrial Training System], National Assembly Network (2000).

36 According to one study, the ratio between the estimated average wages for illegal workers and the average allowances for trainees reached 100:98.6 for male and 100:84.9 for female by 1996. According to another, illegal workers still earn 20 per cent more than trainees. Yi Hyegyeong, 'Oegugin nodongja eui sahoe gyeongjejeok sanghwang' [The Socio-Economic Situation of Foreign Workers], in Seok Hyeonho, Yi Hyegyeong, Jeong Giseon, Gang Sudol and Seol Donghun, *Hanguk sahoe wa oegugin nodongja* [Korean Society and Foreign Workers] (Seoul: Mirae illyeok yeongu Center, 1998) p. 58; 'Jeongbu bucheo, oeguguin nodongja daechaek e igyeon' [Government Ministries Voice Different Opinions About the Foreign Workers Question], *Jung-ang ilbo*, 24 May 2000, p. 23.

37 Jeong Gwisun, 'Yeong-wonhan ibang-in, iju nodongja' [Eternal Foreigners, Migrant Workers], in Oegugin nodongja daechaek hyeobeuihoe [Joint Committee for Migrant Workers in Korea] (ed.) *Oegugin nodongjaeui beopjeok jiwi e gwanhan gongcheonghoe* [Proceedings of a Workshop on the Legal Status of Foreign Workers] (1999) p. 24.

38 See Yi Hyegyeong, 'Oegugin nodongja eui sahoe gyeongjejeok sanghwang' [The Socio-Economic Situation of Foreign Workers], in Seok Hyeonho, Yi Hyegyeong, Jeong Giseon, Gang Sudol and Seol Donghun, *Hanguk sahoe wa oegugin nodongja* [Korean Society and Foreign Workers] (Seoul: Mirae illyeok yeongu Center, 1998) p. 59; 'Oegugin nodongja ju 12 sigan deo ilhae' [Foreign Workers Work 12 Hours Longer Per Week], *Jung-ang ilbo*, 6 October 2000, reproduced at http://www.migrantworkers.or.kr/2000/20001102s-news.txt.

39 Seoul High Court, 26 November 1993, 93gu16774; 3 December 1993, 93gu19995; Supreme Court, 15 September 1995, 94nu12067.

40 Yet the Supreme Court left a caveat that, although one's illegal status under immigration law does not retrospectively invalidate one's labor contract, the parties are not bound by the contract towards the future. For a critical analysis of this decision, see Choe Hongyeop, 'Oegugin geulloja eui nodongbeop sang jiwi e gwanhan yeongu' [A Study of the Status of Foreign Workers Under Labor Law], pp. 74–82.

41 See Hanguk hyeongsajeongchaek yeonguwon [Korean Institute of Criminology], *Gungnae cheryu oegugin eui beomjoe pihae mit boho siltae* [Crimes Against and Protection of Foreigners in Korea] (1996) pp. 78–9.

42 'Segye reul chingu ro mandeupsida (7)' [Let's Make Friends with the World (7)], *Joseon ilbo*, 1 January 1995, p. 2.

43 'Jeongbu bucheo, oeguguin nodongja daechaek e igyeon' [Government Ministries Voice Different Opinions About the Foreign Workers Question], *Jung-ang ilbo*, 24

May 2000, p. 23; Dong-Hoon Seol, 'Past and Present of Foreign Workers in Korea 1987–2000', *Asia Solidarity Quarterly*, vol. 2 (2000) pp. 6–31.

44 Gim Jun, *Saneop yeonsu jedo* [Industrial Training System], National Assembly Network (2000).

45 Seol Donghun, *Oegugin nodongja wa hanguk sahoe* [Foreign Workers and Korean Society] (Seoul: Seoul National University Press, 1999) pp. 329–31.

46 Yi Hyegyeong, 'Oegugin nodongja eui sahoe gyeongjejeok sanghwang' [The Socio-Economic Situation of Foreign Workers], in Seok Hyeonho, Yi Hyegyeong, Jeong Giseon, Gang Sudol and Seol Donghun, *Hanguk sahoe wa oegugin nodongja* [Korean Society and Foreign Workers] (Seoul: Mirae illyeok yeongu Center, 1998) pp. 52–7.

47 'Oegugin yeonsusaeng, inni e choeda baejeong' [The Largest Foreign Trainee Quota Given to Indonesia], *Joseon ilbo*, 3 May 1995, p. 9; Seol Donghun, *Oegugin nodongja wa hanguk sahoe* [Foreign Workers and Korean Society] (Seoul: Seoul National University Press, 1999) pp. 124, 145–6.

48 *Ibid.*, pp. 266, 296–7, 334.

49 *Ibid.*, pp. 390–403.

50 *Ibid.*, pp. 396, 403–7.

51 Federation of Korean Trade Unions, *Oegugugin illyeok jeongchaek banghyang* [The Direction of Foreign Manpower Policy] (2000) reproduced at http://www.migrant.or.kr/kindex.htm.

52 Visit http://www.fktu.or.kr and http://www.nodong.org for declarations, resolutions and press releases of the two national leagues of unions.

53 Visit http://jcmk.jinbo.net for information of the activities of the Joint Committee and links to the websites of its member associations.

54 See Bak Seogun, 'Geudeul ingwon musihamyeon gukjehwa sidae e nagohanda' [Ignoring Their Human Rights, We Will Fall Behind in the Age of Internationalization], *Wolgan jung-ang* [Monthly Joongang], no. 216 (January 1994) pp. 298–305.

55 Oh Cheongeun, *Jungguk joseonjok dongpo munje eui hyeonhwang gwa haegyeol bang-an* [The Question of Koreans from China and Solutions for the Problem], at http://www.migrant.or.kr/kindex.htm; 'Segye reul chingu ro mandeupsida (6)', *Joseon ilbo*, 9 January 1995, p. 2.

56 See Bak Seogun, 'Hangugeui oegugin nodongja ingwon munje wa daechaek' [Human Rights Problems of Foreign Workers in Korea and How to Cope with the Problems], *Beop gwa sahoe* [Korean Journal of Law and Society], no. 11 (1995) pp. 288, 293; Gim Seonsu, 'Hanguk esoeui oegugin nodongja ingwon munje' [Human Rights Problems Concerning Foreign Workers in Korea], *Simin gwa byeonhosa* [Citizens and Lawyers], no. 12 (1995) pp. 137–8; Seol Donghun, *Oegugin nodongja wa hanguk sahoe* [Foreign Workers and Korean Society] (Seoul: Seoul National University Press, 1999) pp. 371–8.

57 See Yi Namju, 'Jugaek dwibaggwin goyongheogaje' [The Employment Permit System Getting Things the Other Way Around], *Hanguk kyeongje sinmum* [Korea Economic Times], 5 September 2000, http://hksearch.hankyung.com/cgi-bin.

58 Accounts of the history of the *hwagyo* in Korea and their current situation are available in Bak Eungyeong [Eun-Kyung Park], 'Hanguk hwagyo sahoe eui yeoksa' [A History of Chinese Society in Korea], *Jindan hakbo* [Jindan Academic Journal], no. 52 (1981) pp. 97–128; Eun-Kyung Park, 'The Various Phases of Ethnicity: The Chinese Minority in Korea', *Minjok gwa munhwa* [Nation and Culture], no. 3 (1995) pp. 39–53; Yi Hyojae and Bak Eungyeong, 'Hanguk hwagyo mit hwagyo idong e gwanhan yeongu' [A Study of Chinese in Korea and Their Migration], *Hanguk munhwa yeonguwon nonchong* [Journal of the Korean Culture Institute, Ewha Women's University], no. 37 (1981) pp. 211–53; Go Seungje, 'Hwagyo daehan imin eui sahoesajeok bunseok' [Social-Historical Analysis of Chinese

Immigrations to Korea], *Baeksan hakbo* [Baeksan Academic Journal], no. 13 (1972) pp. 136–75; Bak Gyeongtae, 'Hanguk sahoe eui injong chabyeol: oeguguin nodongja, hwagyo, honhyeorin' [Racial Discrimination in Korean Society: Foreign Workers, Chinese Immigrants and Mixed-Blood People], *Yeoksa bipyeong* [Historical Critique], no. 48 (1999) pp. 195–8; Yang Pilseung [Phil S. Yang], 'Hanguk hwagyo eui eoje, oneul mit naeil' [The Past, Present and Future of Chinese in Korea], *Gukje ingwonbeop* [International Human Rights Law], no. 3 (2000) pp. 139–58.

59 Sheena Choi, 'Educational Choices of Ethnic Chinese Minorities in Korea: Trends and Policy Implications', *Proceedings of the ISSCO Seoul Conference 2000 on Chinese Overseas and Asia-Pacific Rim Countries: Opportunities and Challenges in the New Millennium*, 12–13 June 2000, Yonsei University, p. 7.

60 According to Sheena Choi, the misunderstanding comes from the fact that, whereas district offices send notices to the Korean parents of children reaching the compulsory school age, they do not do so to Chinese residents, who are not required by Korean law to send their children to school (*ibid.*, p. 8).

61 The information on the aspects of education discussed here relies mainly on Sheena Choi's study.

62 Yi Hyojae and Bak Eungyeong, 'Hanguk hwagyo mit hwagyo idong e gwanhan yeongu' [A Study of Chinese in Korea and their Migration], *Hanguk munhwa yeonguwon nonchong* [Journal of the Korean Culture Institute, Ewha Women's University], no. 37 (1981) pp. 235–6.

63 See *ibid.*, pp. 236–47.

64 *Hwagyo* complain about higher interest rates on bank loans, the requirement of extra guarantees when applying for mobile phone services, and frequent refusal of department store membership.

65 Sheena Choi, 'Educational Choices of Ethnic Chinese Minorities in Korea: Trends and Policy Implications', *Proceedings of the ISSCO Seoul Conference 2000 on Chinese Overseas and Asia-Pacific Rim Countries: Opportunities and Challenges in the New Millennium*, 12–13 June 2000, Yonsei University, p. 5.

66 'Gungnae e saneun oegugin' [Foreigners in Korea], *Dong-a ilbo* [Dong-a Daily], 13 September 1999, http://www.donga.com/fbin/searchview?n=199909130227; interview on 8 December 2000 with Phil S. Yang [Yang Pilseung], a university professor and leading figure in the *hwagyo* rights campaign.

67 For an analysis of the Permanent Residence Act and the Foreign Residents' Local Election Right Act, see Yi Cheoru [Chulwoo Lee], 'Janggi geoju oegugin eul wihan ipbeop eui donghyang' [The Current Trend of Legislative Efforts for Long-Term Foreign Residents], *Beop gwa sahoe* [Korean Journal of Law and Society], no. 20 (2001) pp. 372–85.

68 'Gungnae geoju oegugin ingwon sagak sineum' [Foreign Residents in Korea Suffer in Want of Human Rights], *Dong-a ilbo*, 11 December 2000, http://www.donga.com/fbin/searchview?n=200012110035; Choe Hong-yeop, 'Nodongja roseoeui gwolli' [Rights as Workers], in Oegugin nodongja daechaek hyeobeuihoe [Joint Committee for Migrant Workers in Korea] (ed.) *Oegugin nodongja gongcheonghoe* [Proceedings of a Workshop on Foreign Workers] (1999) p. 17.

69 See, for example, Gim Bong-u, 'Joseon ilbo saseol 'Chinatown i eomneun nara' e daehan ballon' [Objection to the *Joseon ilbo* Editorial 'A Country Without a Chinatown'], *Dong-a ilbo*, 30 June 2000, reproduced in the BK Human Rights Research Team, College of Law, Konkuk University (ed.) *Segyehwa sidae e isseoseoeui ingwon* [Human Rights in the Age of Globalization] (2000) pp. 134–7.

70 See Anthony Smith, *The Ethnic Origins of Nations* (Oxford: Blackwell, 1986) ch. 2; Gi-Wook Shin, James Freda and Gihong Yi, 'The Politics of Ethnic Nationalism in Divided Korea', *Nations and Nationalism*, vol. 5, part 4 (1999) pp. 465–84; Michael Weiner, 'The Invention of Identity: Race and Nation in Pre-war Japan', and Kosaku

Yoshino, 'The Discourse on Blood and Racial Identity in Contemporary Japan', in Frank Dikötter (ed.) *The Construction of Racial Identities in China and Japan* (London: Hurst and Co., 1997).

71 No Yeongdon, '1997 nyeon gukjeokbeop gaejeong eui geomto' [Examining the 1997 Amendment Bill for the Nationality Act], *Seoul gukjebeop yeongu* [Seoul International Law Journal], vol. 4, no. 2 (1997) p. 34.

72 Seoul High Court, 20 August 1997, 97bu776.

73 Constitutional Court, 31 August 2000, 97heonga12.

74 I am grateful to Gim Yeong-im [Young-im Kim], head of the Kosian Shelter of the Ansan Migrant Shelter, for giving me helpful information on this issue.

75 Cases are available in Jeong Gwisun, 'Yeong-wonhan ibang-in, iju nodongja' [Eternal Foreigners, Migrant Workers], in Oegugin nodongja daechaek hyeobeuihoe [Joint Committee for Migrant Workers in Korea] (ed.) *Oegugin nodongja gongcheonghoe* [Proceedings of a Workshop on Foreign Workers] (1999) pp. 22–33.

76 Visit http://www.migrant.or.kr.

77 See Bak Gyeongtae, 'Hanguk sahoe eui injong chabyeol: oeguguin nodongja, hwagyo, honhyeorin' [Racial Discrimination in Korean Society: Foreign Workers, Chinese Immigrants and Mixed-Blood People], *Yeoksa bipyeong* [Historical Critique], no. 48 (1999) pp. 198–202.

78 For a more detailed discussion of the *talbukja* issue, see Chulwoo Lee, ' 'Us' and 'Them' in Korean Law: The Creation, Accommodation and Exclusion of Outsiders in South Korea', in *Rule of Law and Group Identities Embedded in Asian Traditions and Cultures*, Proceedings of the Wagatsuma Hiroshi Memorial Conference, 19–20 January 2001, University of California, Los Angeles.

79 See the title of the book by Im Jihyeon, *Minjokjueui neun banyeok ida* [Nationalism is Treason] (Seoul: Sonamu, 1999).

7

INTERNAL MIGRANTS AND THE CHALLENGE OF THE 'FLOATING POPULATION' IN THE PRC

Dorothy J. Solinger

Why should we link the internal migrants of China with the word 'challenge'? Indeed, that people moving about across their own native terrain should be dubbed 'migrants' is already a bit of a puzzle. This is especially the case for the ones in China, since they are very much viewed and dealt with as if outsiders, even outcasts, surely as elements who do not 'belong' where they have arrived.

This chapter considers a double challenge surrounding their persons – one not just for the Chinese state and metropolitan communities, but also facing the urban-situated Chinese peasant transients themselves. These peasants away from home are the occupants of an awkward category, the 'floating population', whose members populate a nebulous space that is neither their home nor their host, and who yet must negotiate an existence somewhere in between the two.

Even to survive in this bedevilling domain – much less to thrive there – these sojourners need to navigate amidst a sobering array of contradictory poles. These are the antinomies of nationalism and localism, citizenship and foreignness, community and officialdom, the rhetoric of rights and the reality of an absence of rights, the socialist superstructure still lingering about and the base of capitalism now closing in on its landscape, and, perhaps most challenging of all, between two realms that ought not be mutually conflicting at all, but which surely are in China today: the market and the law.

At the heart of the plight of the incoming peasants in cities is the immaturity – or, less optimistically but conceivably more accurately – one might say the stubborn, nagging, ongoing inadequacy of that elusive element, law, in Chinese society today. For could it come of age, could it fulfil its function, law could stand as the bridge that links up the nation with local exclusivism, the full citizen with the sojourning denizen, the subcommunity of the sidelined with the sphere of officialdom. Thus it is up to the law to bring together the discourse of rights with their delivery, and to bend the institutional legacies of socialism to fit the immediacy of capitalism. It could also probably manage to tame the madness of the current Chinese marketplace.

I proceed by reviewing in turn each of these conflicts characterizing the challenges of (in the double sense of 'posed by' and 'for') the floating population, as they affect the triangular tie between state, local society and alien in Chinese cities today, and as they have been affecting it over the past two decades, without much of a fundamental alteration. But first I need to supply some background, so that the reader can comprehend just why so much bother surrounds the movement into the municipalities of their own nation by ethnic Chinese from the countryside.

A bit of background

How have Chinese peasants, treated as so out-of-place, come to be found in the cities, and why is this an issue? In the socialist times of Mao Zedong, following the institution of the Communist Party's reign (1949), Party leaders almost immediately essayed to keep the cities clear of rural folk.[1] At first, in the 1950s, their effort was meant to ensure order, keep better track of the populace, and guarantee that the numbers of urbanites would be manageable, thereby reserving urban resources for the pursuit of heavy industrialization and the city workers who engaged in it.[2] Probably too, in cities, potential popular discontent would have been deemed much more serious; also there, the hope of building a modernized economy seemed within reach, if only the numbers of people residing there could be kept within strict bounds.

This quotation from the 1950s, of the then Minister of Public Security Luo Ruiqing, reveals concerns about chaos and criminality that disposed early, post-1949 Communist Party elites to attempt to dispel farmers from crossing the urban frontier:

> During the last few years the phenomenon of rural migrants blindly flowing into the cities has become a comparatively serious problem. This type of thing [recruiting people without urban household registrations to work in city enterprises] helped to make a bad situation really chaotic and created enormous difficulties for various aspects of city planning and the maintenance of social order. It led to a whole series of problems emerging in the areas of city transportation, accommodation, supply, employment, study, etc. … and thus created a very tense situation. The rural population that blindly drifts into the city is unable to find work and consequently suffers great difficulties. Some of these people roam idly in the streets, and some even go as far as to be enticed into evil activities, becoming pickpockets or swindlers or adopting other criminal activities, all of which destroy the social order of the cities.[3]

After the disastrous Great Leap Forward of the late 1950s, concerns over food grain shortages and potentially serious urban hunger led the leadership to banish back to the countryside tens of millions of country workers who had somehow slipped into town in the previous decade, or been recruited during the Great Leap Forward.[4] For the urban population had increased by 31.7 million, or 32 per cent in just the three years of the Leap, with 90 per cent of the increase the result of migration.[5]

Repatriation of peasants back to the countryside had occurred in 1955 and again in 1957. But the forced exodus after 1960 was totally unprecedented.[6] John P. Emerson cites figures of 20 million for 1961 and 30 million for the following year.[7] These deportations were not just more sizable than earlier ones; they were also far more successful.[8] Most importantly, they set down the model for migration control that lasted for the next two decades.

And so, once repatriated, these farmers languished in field labor for the next twenty years. The early 1960s saw the start of a most rigid enforcement of a system of household registration (the *hukou* system), which consigned peasant households to the region of their birth and deprived them of rations and of the entitlements of employment, housing, medical care, education and pensions paid out to city inhabitants. That system of distinction had been pushed rather gingerly and ineffectively beginning in 1955,[9] but gained real force with the failure of the Leap. The evolution of the resultant status order is captured in this quotation:

> Just after liberation, peasant households did not feel lower-rank [*diren yideng*] and urban households did not feel higher ... Later, a great difference in interests came from the difference in where one lived. ... A ranking structure was gradually established with the peasant household at the lowest level.[10]

Thus, within a short time after 1960, the following situation began to prevail:

> There are two social classes; [the difference between] the agricultural and non-agricultural *hukou* makes the rural population exert its utmost strength to squeeze onto the rolls of the urban *hukou*.[11]

As illustration of the extremity of the lifestyle distinctions involved, a popular ditty had it that it is 'better [to have] a bed in the city than a house in the suburbs' (*ning yao shiqu yizhang chuang, buyao jiaoqu yitao fang*).[12]

But, in the early 1980s, with the shift at the doctrinal level (at first, and gradually at the level of practice, little by little) away from allegiance to the orthodox, socialist planned economy to one granting legitimacy to market forces, China's leaders let the ruralites leave the villages, where they had been quite literally landlocked onto the fields. Peasant workers, freed from the farms, unceasingly poured into the cities, driven by the sudden, headlong and steadily marketized industrialization that got underway within just a few years of

Chairman Mao's demise in 1976, and the frantic building in the cities, combined with the ending of the socialist era's starvation of the service sector.

But even as the economy became steadily more marketized, even as planning and rations fell away bit by bit, the cumbrous shadows of socialist-era institutions and biases, especially the stigma attached to farmhands, have not easily been eradicated. So despite the hefty contribution to urban prosperity of the peasant-workers' toil, and the rather questionable nature of the actual drain they truly put on urban resources, they have remained pariahs for the most part up to the present, once ensconced in town.[13] I proceed to consider the six contradictions noted above that are posed by Chinese rural people's social exclusion from urban Chinese society, even as they live beside it, challenging it and its state and being challenged by them.

Nationalism and localism; citizenship and foreignness

In spite of the raucous nationalism emanating from China in recent years, internally the country is – and has historically been – replete with many restrictive local identities, each of them the foundation for fierce loyalties to place. Emily Honig has even likened these region-based particularisms, with their lasting power and mutual suspicions, and their antagonistic inter-relations, to ethnic differences, even though all the people involved are properly speaking Han Chinese.[14]

The concept of a separation between a permanent residence and a temporary abode has a venerable pedigree in China. Sojourning was common in historical times; while the wanderer traveled, and even settled away from home, his family would remain at the old homestead.[15] The term *jiguan* referred to the place of residence that defined a person's origin, and both social custom and government policy emphasized this attribute.[16]

Scholars have termed regional groupings within the historical Chinese labor market an 'ethnic division of labor'.[17] Writing of the eighteenth century, Susan Naquin and Evelyn Rawski report that 'native place was the principle most often invoked as grounds for affiliation and assistance by men who left their homes to work in an alien environment'.[18] Work on the late nineteenth and early twentieth centuries similarly identified native place bonds that structured residence, work experiences, mutual aid, conflict, and power formation in the urban areas of that time.[19]

And yet, in these historical cases, the principle of exclusion was purely interprovincial; no sharp distinction was ever drawn between urban and rural, either in acknowledging or in assigning identities.[20] Instead, city and country were perceived as linked in a seamless web of comings and goings, by family diversification strategies in which roles and assets could be split between different locales.[21]

It was only in the early twentieth century when what Myron Cohen has termed 'a major crisis of cultural integration and national identity' occurred –

sparked in large part by China's brush with the West and its urban-based imperialistic 'treaty ports' – that there arose a novel style of urban 'elite intellectual nationalism'. Cohen goes on to explain that this new elite 'reject[ed] and condemn[ed] the traditional culture of the Chinese masses', thus disdaining to make common cause with its fellow nationals. This elite also invented a new word to set them apart, namely *nongmin* (literally, 'rural folk'), a term with a pejorative twist still in use today. This movement can be said to have paved the way for combining the much more timeworn xenophobic stance toward extra-locals with a new, equally disparaging one toward peasants, a position that the communists' policies later nurtured and expanded upon.[22]

Even as Chinese people may unite today against the American bombing of their embassy, or perceived current slights from and distant shameful memories of the Japanese, relations between Chinese 'floaters' and Chinese urban dwellers remain tinged with vigilance, with sub-segments of the same Han Chinese ethnic family divided by distrust, and even, it has been discovered, disgust.[23] Either in spite of or because of the very limited interaction between these two groups, 97 per cent of an educated sample of Shanghai natives admitted in a 1995 survey that they felt disturbed by the outsiders in regard to at least one of four issues (transportation, security of property, the environment or employment), while as many as 71 per cent believed themselves to be threatened either somewhat or seriously by the migrants.[24] The quotations from popular journals below illustrate the clannish separatism practiced by both parties:

> Lots of outside construction teams have come into Shanghai from [the nearby provinces of] Jiangsu, Shandong, etc. ... these people use their work sites as their home. Their mobility is great and their quality is lacking; they're without any legal knowledge or concept of the law. Their livelihood customs and speech are each different and they display a thick hue of local cliquism. If one suffers a loss, all will attack. ... They protect each other if there are problems. ... This can even lead to disturbances. They provoke quarrels: a team at a local glass factory's construction site provoked a brawl with a Shanghai team, leading the Shanghai team not to dare even to go to work.[25]

Another:

> In feuds, local people get more supporters among the onlookers; there are few dissuaders. The contradiction between local and outside people has now become a social contradiction. ... They treat outsiders as second-class citizens and see them as the snatchers of local people's interests.[26]

And yet one more:

> Their thinking, morality, language, and customs are all different, their quality is inferior. The places they inhabit are very likely dirty places. … They lack a concept of public morality … so that behavior that harms prevailing social customs occurs time and time again. City residents are dissatisfied because they disturb normal life and livelihood.[27]

Given their outrage against the outsiders, it is unremarkable that members of the urban 'host society' harass their guests:

> When they ask the way, Beijing people intentionally send them in the opposite direction; if they carelessly bump someone getting off the bus, it can lead to a brutal attack. When they enter a restaurant, the waiter creates difficulties. When they knock on the door and ask for old things to buy, the owner might fiercely spit![28]

In the very typical words of one of my own interviewees in the major northern city of Tianjin in 1992, 'We couldn't possibly [*buhuide*] accept them as regular urban people … people look down on them as peasants … Tianjin people don't want to marry outsiders'.[29]

Besides this discrimination against extra-locals at the level of city folks' feelings, urbanized peasants' historical exclusion from benefits and entitlements once the birthright of urbanites (but no longer so, with the now rapid incursion of the market into the world of welfare) surely makes it possible to argue that only locals native to a given city have had the status of 'citizens'. Here I am drawing on the conceptualization I gave of this notion in my 1999 book, where I state that

> as a Chinese scholar remarked, the *hukou* – very much as a badge of citizenship in a Western society would do – [before about 1995] determined one's entire life chances, including one's social rank, wage, welfare, food rations, and housing.[30] … These are the kinds of 'goods and opportunities that shape life chances' which only citizenship can guarantee.[31]

I further justified my somewhat unusual use of the concept of citizenship in this context because the term has, after all, been variously defined.[32] In the words of Brian S. Turner, for instance, 'The modern question of citizenship is structured by two issues': The first of these has to do with social membership, or, one might say, with belonging to a community; the second concerns the right to an *allocation of resources*.[33] Interestingly, these conditions are much the same as those that pertained to the possession of the urban register (*hukou*) in China through the early 1990s, and still carry some influence today. Also in the broader literature, a number of scholars find that the hallmark of citizenship is exclusivity, as it 'confers rights and privileges' (again, as has the urban *hukou*) just to those legally living within specifically designated borders.[34] Though the boundaries that define 'members' (namely citizenship) are most typically drawn around the urban (or national) geographical community, historically and even sometimes today around the world, they have also delineated only some of the groups within such geopolitical spaces.

Working with such a formulation, I was able to argue that 'the values and behaviors that citizenship endorses in a society will reflect the norms of whatever might be the dominant participatory and allocatory institutions in the community with which the citizen is affiliated', and to emphasize 'not the political but just the identity/membership and distributive components of citizenship'. Given this understanding, I considered as full, official, state-endorsed urban citizens only those who enjoyed a form of valid, official membership in or affiliation to the city, and who consequently were the recipients of state-disbursed goods. Even up to the present, officially ruralites in big cities are still denied genuine membership, namely the right to belong officially.[35]

If law were to intervene in this battle of localisms and city versus country folk, it could override the prejudice and discrimination that consigns peasants to a lower order, thereby allowing them to take their place as equals under the urban administration, and among those who are now judged full-fledged urban residents. For, after all, the current version of the Chinese state constitution, adopted in 1982, announces in Article 33 that '[a]ll persons holding the nationality of the People's Republic of China' are citizens, equal before the law, and enjoying the rights while performing the duties prescribed in the constitution and the law'.[36]

Subcommunity and officialdom

But this issue is actually more complex. As I contended in my 1999 book, migrants in Chinese cities are by no means all of a kind. I differentiated between those from the less prosperous inland, who tended to become sorted into manual laborers (employed, usually in comparatively short-term slots, in construction, hauling or transport teams, or else in some form of household labor) or manufacturing (often in the foreign-invested firms along the coast, but some in state-owned enterprises, too). A second category was those from the wealthier, coastal provinces, who were heirs to a legacy of marketing or specialized crafts and skills (such as tailoring, shoe repair or barbering), who took up these tertiary-sector occupations once having arrived in a town. And a third group was comprised of indigent drifters who might end up as scrap collectors or beggars, and who largely hailed from very poor locales.[37]

In my book, I went on to show that the state of belonging in urban society was a variable condition. Most of the incomers were unable to create any kind of connection at all to the original urban society – that is, to establish any personal bond with the people who had long lived in the city where the migrants had landed and who possessed urban registration there. But, by the early and mid-1990s some had contrived, either through their affluence – acquired in urban commerce, which eventually enabled them to accumulate enough funds to purchase an urban registration – or else via some form of prior personal tie to local officialdom, to find an entrée for themselves. Still, the overwhelming majority of the newcomers were treated just as transients by the locals, no matter how lengthy their period of time in the town. They were, upon their appearance there, and forever after, quite clearly outsiders, with no hope or pretense of being a part of the municipal populace.

But just because most could not become urban or members, not every migrant remained a single unit within an anomic mass. Migrants of the second, more skilled group with coastal roots, I demonstrated, frequently congregated in what the Chinese term urban 'villages', spaces within cities where, at the extreme end, the residents in them live by their own rules and mores, communicate in their original local dialects, run their own shops and services for their co-provincials, and even organize business networks. Among the Wenzhouese,[38] who are the most successful of the migrants of this type, such networks have developed an international scope. Since their communities are constructed over time by chain migration and bonds of interpersonal patronage (as are those of migrants the globe around), their operative mode in managing their internal affairs is not the state's laws or its informal regulations (which, granted, they flaunt at their peril), but the trust they can generate among themselves.[39] Indeed, the rules they live by lack any reference to the laws of the state.

True, migrants of the first type (the inland manual workers) might pass substantial periods laboring and traveling in a particular team. Frequently the contractors who gathered them into a company, however, were an arrogant and peremptory lot, wielding enormous arbitrary and fearsome command over their underlings.[40] Similarly, those of the third, drifter, category were occasionally combined into beggar bands, or collected their garbage and scraps under orders from a tyrannical chieftain. But the internal relations in crews of this kind tended, like those of the manual workers, to be steeply hierarchical, with bosses lording it over frequently shifting and rank-ordered underlings.[41] So we cannot conclude that genuine communities cohered with shared understandings and common goals and responsibilities, as they could among the skilled and more monied migrants.[42]

Yet the one thing shared by a great many of the incomers – of whatever type – is that they simultaneously inhabited two different spaces: the immediate and more or less known one of their own subcommunity, and the more nebulous and distant one of officialdom and the larger society beyond their own nested realm. In that greater, all-encompassing space, most migrants were at the mercy of urban administrators' caprice, without being able to cry out for any compelling legal appeal that could serve as a bridge between this more foreign space and the one to which they had been consigned by native place and occupation.

Standing against the trust that made business thrive for the community and the successful itinerants, and enabled its arteries to extend across continents, were two other principles of contemporary Chinese urban life, neither relying on mutual confidence, and both nearly wholly lawless. These are, first, market precepts undergirding profit and greed, eventuating of late in China in the crassest and grossest breeds of corruption, a 'market' run wild; and second, the remnants of the worst of the maxims of socialism, including official privilege and perquisites, making for an easy milieu for rent-seeking by the empowered, along with politicized statuses for the underdogs which are carved in concrete.

All three of these realms have some overlapping regions, but most of the participants of the first realm, the enclave community, are totally barred from the third, the official one. Only an effective societally-wide, all-inclusive and serviceable legal process – which, alas, is currently absent in China for these people in all but the very most rudimentary of forms – could have the power to brake the utter licentiousness of these two latter worlds, and to include in a larger frame, not to mention a fair one – the members of the first, the 'floating' urban farmers.

The rhetoric and the reality of rights[43]

An important current in the study of globalization[44] and its impacts holds that the spread of economic liberalism and of the concept of human rights globally has led to new notions of citizenship. What has been termed a 'postnational' citizenship, granted 'on the basis of personhood', has increasingly offered to immigrants the rights and privileges once granted just to nationals, in this view. Whether the mechanism at work is said to be principally ideational – as, by 'changes in the institutional and discursive order of rights at the global level'[45] – or ideational-cum-material – as, in the words of another author, through the dissemination of notions of social justice and human rights which accompany the spread of market relations, both domestically and internationally – this analysis claims to see underway a new 'extension of rights to individuals who are not full members of the societies in which they reside'.[46]

In another, similar formulation, the proliferation of international human rights law, which 'recognizes the individual as an object of rights regardless of national affiliations or associations with a territorially-defined people', has meant in recent years that 'states [have] had to take account of persons qua persons as opposed to limiting their responsibiities to their own citizens'.[47] Whether or not these claims are valid, one could make a very different argument as well: this is that the 'globalization' of economic and market entanglements among states has probably done as much to *minimize* the granting of citizenship and membership rights and privileges to individuals as it has done to extend it.

Thus, although with the onset of marketizing reforms in China in 1979 myriad new laws were written to suit an economy progressively more and more fully engaged in worldwide commercial relations,[48] even at the turn of the century the country continued to lack a legal system capable of governing a truly market-driven economy.[49] A pervasive rhetoric of rights, which does obtain, is rarely realized in practice, and defendants have often lost their cases before they begin.

As for the migrants, despite much discussion and debate, and even talk of fundamental reform, the basic features of the *hukou* policy itself hang on. A few notable alterations were the availability of a new, 'temporary' household registration in the cities in the mid-1980s, the *zhanzhuzheng*;[50] a widespread resort to the sale of the urban *hukou*, on black markets by the late 1980s,[51] and, by the early 1990s, openly by city administrations themselves, in the form of a 'blue *hukou*'. But these *hukou* are only affordable for those who have amassed a fair amount of wealth and who are thus no longer living at subsistence level.[52] And most lately, an important provision passed by the State Council in summer 1998, permitting permanent residence rights to be accorded 'qualified investors' and to an urban citizen's spouse, parents and children.[53]

But ongoing reluctance to eliminate the household registration system entirely, with its very unequal granting of citizenship rights, even in the face of widespread marketization, seems to signify that there may be at the root a persisting and even heightening official paranoia in the face of mobile peasants. This appears to be the case in that, beginning in 1995, the issue of the floating population was described as

> No longer a question of the transfer of surplus rural labor, but a major economic and political issue which has a direct bearing on economic development and social stability.

This was a formula that has been repeated thereafter on many occasions.[54] In one formulation, this stark statement of apprehension was, suggestively, combined with a warning that

> Infringements on the legitimate rights and interests of migrant workers and businesspeople are serious and signs of migrant workers becoming a source of trouble have appeared in some places.[55]

That statement explicitly links anxiety about public order to a movement toward legal rhetoric. It seems that this fear may have paired the two in leaders' minds.

Migrants themselves started to display a concern with rights and injustice – if mainly economic rights – almost as soon as they had made their way into the municipalities. One of the earlier manifestations was their feeling of unfairness over the blatant inequality they were forced to confront there. Journalists picked up the anger this engendered, much of it directed against the permanent population of the city. As an example:

> The peasants and semi-peasants who enter the city feel comparatively deprived by the tightly locked city walls. Peasants coming in want to enjoy this fat meat with city people. When in the countryside, they feel that everyone is poor, so [their poverty] can be tolerated. But differences in wealth become obvious after entering the city. They feel, 'The more you city people look down on me, the more I oppose you'.[56]

With time, members of the floating population came to demand legal protection against the treatment they were receiving on the job, by remonstrating at public security stations and by calling in the press at least as early as 1988 for the authorities to 'please support our rights and interests' (*qing weihu women quanyi*).[57] In 1989 two roving journalists quoted a peasant informant who raised her lament to the level of the law:

> 'They say everyone is equal before the law', complained a glass seller bullied and beaten up by thugs sent by a native competitor in Lanzhou, then given little solace by the local police. 'Why can't we outside peasant workers be equal too?' she seemed to be howling.[58]

In response to these feelings, organized agitation had already begun to appear by the mid-1980s, with the emergence of unauthorized unions and illicit strikes. By 1986, work stoppages and strikes were frequent among the temporary workers of the Shenzhen Special Economic Zone, home of a multitude of foreign-funded firms.[59] Issues of treatment, hours, contract violation and unsafe working conditions often figured in the resistance, though by far the majority of grievances – as many as 86 per cent – in at least one city where statistics on this were recorded, were about pay.[60] There were also reports that many of the strikes specifically had revenge as a motive, surely evidence of feelings that rights had been wronged.[61]

There were also scattered stories of migrant workers agitating for the right to form their own unions. For only the official All-China Federation of Trade Unions was recognized by the government, and its cadres were much more likely to suppress rather than to support signs of worker discontent,[62] while any other association of workers was automatically labeled illegal.[63] In one case employees in a joint-venture hotel in Shanghai attempted to set up their own organization in the summer of 1993.[64] In addition, some bold members of the floating temporary workers went ahead without permission and created unregistered unions of their own. These organs sprang up mainly at foreign-invested, joint-venture plants.[65]

By 1994, according to a survey undertaken among transient factory hands in the Pearl River Delta, at least 10 per cent and sometimes as many as 61 per cent of the workers in the firms there expressed each of the following demands: a guarantee of basic livelihood, higher wages, improved livelihood conditions, better working conditions, and equality of various sorts.[66] And, remarkably, in an early 1995 survey of leavers in 318 villages, as many as 79 per cent of the respondents admitted that they felt that they lacked any guarantee of their rights and interests (*quanyi*).[67] But in nearly all cases of worker protest that found voice in the printed media, attempts at relief met with varying degrees of repression or rejection. Given how easily these efforts to express and realize rights were generally squelched,[68] it seems fair to judge that even as of the year 2000 the discourse of rights – for urban workers and rural farmers, as well as for peasants sojourning in cities – was well developed, but distribution of such rights to them nonetheless remained denied.

Socialist superstructure and capitalist base

Certainly, since 1980 the Chinese politico-economy has been moving steadily further from the former Maoist regime. Yet with the continuing rule of the Communist Party, not only the repressiveness but also the values, alliances and allegiances of that regime – the culture and politics of socialism – have proven far stickier, harder to outgrow or discard than have the material practices of the old planned economy. Ironically, the superstructure has outlived the base. Indeed, these socialist behavioral and belief patterns serve to enhance any impediments to migrants' welfare and rights introduced by the new market regime. These impediments, the residue of China's socialist past, make the plight of the excluded and legally unprotected even more serious in China than it would be from the impact of untrammeled market customs alone.

In particular, behavioral remnants from a couple of the central institutions that the nation's rulers installed long ago in order to implement their socialist system linger on, even as the more material dimensions of the institutions weaken and atrophy. These institutions include the socialist-era legal system (or, one might say, the absence of one), recently revamped to appear more predictable, procedural and just, but still quite unreliable, and as we have seen, socialism's household registration system. The free-wheeling, free-market economic habits of today – the capitalist analog of what I just referred to as 'the [socialist] material practices of the old planned economy' – that make for 'efficiency', competitiveness, and 'flexibility' are easily enough incorporated into a still-authoritarian regime. But, to the contrary, the prior legal, management and control systems of socialism are much more difficult to dislodge and replace than is the slower, more 'comradely' and rigid workstyle of the past.

Under the reign of Mao Zedong, from 1949 to 1976, law was considered to be a 'bourgeois' construct, inapplicable – at least in its Western incarnation – to a socialist society.[69] Nonetheless, China's often harsh socialist version was enshrined up until the Cultural Revolution, which began in 1966. With that movement, all legal institutions were dismantled for over a decade. But regardless of the many laws on the books today, the style of implementing them is still quite reminiscent in many ways of the one under Mao. For mistreated migrant laborers, this means that the 1994 Labor Law and its promises of protection and inclusion are almost always honored only in the breach.[70] Thus, despite the attempt of the past two decades to bolster legality, authoritarian and lawless habits from the past persist.

The aspect of this situation relevant to my purposes here is twofold: first, migrant rural labor makes up the great bulk of the workforce in foreign-invested firms, especially those along the coast. Here, their willingness to toil under often seemingly intolerable circumstances effectively places these workers outside a rights regime of any kind. Second, as local urban managers, even in Chinese state firms, grew increasingly profit- and competition-conscious as the 1990s wore on, they more and more turned to the recruitment of peasants migrating into town – people who could safely be hired with lesser or no benefits than urban folk, and who, with their impermanence in town and lesser education, were seemingly less likely to struggle for legality.[71]

In addition, as the numbers of laid-off and idle urbanites mounted after the mid-1990s (partly for domestic economic reasons but also, arguably, in preparation for China's entry into the World Trade Organization), city officials bent on worker quietude in their domains clashed with firm managers hungry for the profits made possible by cost-cutting measures. For urban officials were demanding that higher-paid local city labor be privileged over peasants when hiring and firing occurred,[72] much as foreign migrant workers were pushed out of Southeast Asian communities in the midst of the late-1990s financial crisis in that region.[73]

The manifestations of this bias are multifold: besides being let go with more arbitrariness than before, peasants-in-cities have not been encompassed within the regular rules of the contract system for city labor. And even a regulation that was to apply to them alone, which specified a three-to-five-year contract as the norm, was far from fully honored,[74] with many so-called contracts lasting under a year. Unemployment insurance has yet to apply to these workers,[75] nor does a national Reemployment Program that aims to place only the furloughed city laborers.

Beginning in 1995, major cities such as Beijing and Shanghai began publicly requiring that certain occupations be reserved for city people (though the repetition of these demands a few years later raises questions about the extent of compliance they commanded).[76] Thus rural migrants' now forty-plus-year-old lack of an urban *hukou*, or household registration, an institution established under socialism, continues to mark them as excluded noncitizens when they work in cities. In the words of a laid-off Chinese worker – words which fit the urbanized farmers even more – 'Workers today suffer under both socialism and capitalism'.[77]

Conclusion: market and law

The final contradiction that the Chinese migrant worker brings to mind is one that may appear odd from a broader perspective. After all, it is often argued that the state is necessary in order for the market to operate effectively, to underwrite contracts, enforce regulations and standardize procedures, thereby easing transaction costs, as well as to offer predictability and stability to those in business. Surely the state is best equipped to provide these services dependably where a reliable legal infrastructure guides its moves in these regards.

In the case of the People's Republic, however, market and law (in the modern, Western sense) arrived on the scene more or less in tandem, both of them subsisting to this day in their most infantile versions. This means that neither can nascent legal institutions truly govern market transactions, nor, until the law develops much further, can the marketplace mature into a site of safety. Migrants who are ill treated and excluded economically cannot call upon a calculable politics or a stable law to bail them out.

Because there is no commonly accepted, legitimized, statutory structure in China that could support the 'strangers' in its cities – persons who, oddly enough, are ethnically identical to those who reject them – the 'floating population' from the country's farms is indeed challenged. But at the same time, in its very essence as a social form, it furnishes both the state and Chinese urban society with contradictions to resolve – between nationalism and localism; citizen and outcast; community and officialdom; rhetoric and reality when it comes to rights; the socialist superstructure and the capitalist base – thereby challenging the state and its more privileged city people as well.

Notes

1 See my book, *Contesting Citizenship in Urban China: Peasant Migrants, the State, and the Logic of the Market* (Berkeley: University of California Press, 1999) pp. 36–9.

2 Cheng Tiejun and Mark Selden, 'The Origins and Social Consequences of China's Hukou System', *China Quarterly*, no. 139 (1994) pp. 644–68; Lynn T. White, *Careers in Shanghai* (Berkeley: University of California Press, 1978) p. 90.

3 Zhang Qingwu, 'Basic Facts on the Household Registration System'. *Chinese Economic Studies*, vol. 22, no. 1 (1988) pp. 96–7.

4 Kam Wing Chan, *Cities With Invisible Walls: Reinterpreting Urbanization in Post-1949 China* (Hong Kong: Oxford University Press, 1994) p. 76; Wang Feng, 'Invisible Walls Within Cities: Migration and the Emergence of a Dual Society in Urban China', paper prepared for Conference on the Social Consequences of Chinese Economic Reform, Harvard University, 23–4 May 1997, pp. 5–6.

5 Andrew G. Walder, *Communist Neo-Traditionalism: Work and Authority in Chinese Industry* (Berkeley: University of California Press, 1986) p. 36.

6 For relevant documents, see Lu Feng, 'The Origins and Formation of the Unit (Danwei) System', *Chinese Society and Anthropology*, vol. 25, no. 3 (1993) p. 68.

7 John P. Emerson, 'Employment in Mainland China: Problems and Prospects', in US Congress, Joint Economic Committee (ed.) *An Economic Profile of Mainland China* (Washington DC: Government Printing Office, 1967) vol. 2, p. 422; and *idem*, 'The Labor Force of China, 1957–80', in US Congress, Joint Economic Committee (ed.) *China Under the Four Modernizations: Part I* (Washington DC: U.S. Government Printing Office, 1982) p. 242. This latter article cites Deng Xiaoping as having admitted to 'more than 20 million' thrown out of cities between 1959 and 1961.

8 R. J. R. Kirkby, *Urbanisation in China: Town and Country in a Developing Economy, 1949–2000 AD* (London: Croom Helm, 1985) pp. 27, 49.

9 Sulamith Heins Potter and Jack M. Potter, *China's Peasants: The Anthropology of a Revolution* (Cambridge: Cambridge University Press, 1990) pp. 296–310.

10 Gong Xikui, 'Zhongguo xianxing huji zhidu toushi' [A Perspective on China's Present Household Register System], *Shehui Kexue* [Social Science], no. 2 (1989) p. 32.

11 Zhongguo nongcun laodongli liudong yu zhuanyi ketizu [Chinese rural labor forces' mobility and transfer study group], 'Zhongguo nongcun laodongli jiuye xiankuang ji fazhan qingjing yanjiu' [Investigation of China's Rural Labor Forces' Employment Situation and Development Prospects], *Nongcun wenti* [Rural issues], vol. 12, no. 7 (1989) pp. 12–20.

12 'Huji yanjiu' ketizu ['Household Registration Research' Task Group], 'Xianxing huji guanli zhidu yu jingji tizhi gaige' [The Present Household Registration Management System and Economic System Reform], *Shanghai shehui kexueyuan xueshu jikan* [Shanghai Academy of Social Science Academic Quarterly], no. 3 (1989) p. 85.

13 D. J. Solinger, *Contesting Citizenship in Urban China: Peasant Migrants, the State, and the Logic of the Market* (Berkeley: University of California Press, 1999) ch. 4.

14 Honig, Emily, *Creating Chinese Ethnicity: Subei People in Shanghai, 1850–1980* (New Haven: Yale University Press, 1992) ch. 1; *idem*, 'Regional Identity, Labor, and Ethnicity in Contemporary China', in Elizabeth J. Perry (ed.) *Putting Class in Its Place: Worker Identities in East Asia* (Berkeley: Institute of East Asian Studies, University of California, 1996) p. 241.

15 G. William Skinner, 'Mobility Strategies in Late Imperial China: A Regional Systems Analysis', in Carol A. Smith (ed.) *Regional Analysis, vol. 1* (New York: Academic Press, 1976) p. 335.

16 Wong Siu-lun, *Emigrant Entrepreneurs: Shanghai Industrialists in Hong Kong* (Hong Kong: Oxford University Press, 1988) p. 110.

17 G. William Skinner, 'Introduction: Urban Social Structure in Ch'ing China', in G. William Skinner (ed.) *The City in Late Imperial China* (Stanford: Stanford University Press, 1977) p. 544.

18 Susan Naquin and Evelyn S. Rawski, *Chinese Society in the Eighteenth Century* (New Haven: Yale University Press, 1987) p. 47.

19 William T. Rowe, *Hankow: Commerce and Society in a Chinese City 1796–1889* (Stanford: Stanford University Press, 1984); David Strand, *Rickshaw Beijing: City People and Politics in the 1920s* (Berkeley: University of California Press, 1989); Gail Hershatter, *The Workers of Tianjin, 1900–1949* (Stanford: Stanford University Press, 1986); Elizabeth J. Perry, *Shanghai on Strike: The Politics of Chinese Labor* (Stanford: Stanford University Press, 1994); Bryna Goodman, *Native Place, City, and Nation: Regional Networks and Identities in Shanghai, 1853–1937* (Berkeley: University of California Press, 1995).

20 F. W. Mote, 'The Transformation of Nanking, 1350–1400', in G. William Skinner (ed.) *The City in Late Imperial China* (Stanford: Stanford University Press, 1977) pp. 102, 103, 114, 117; and Myron L. Cohen, 'Cultural and Political Inventions in Modern China: The Case of the Chinese "Peasant"', *Daedalus*, vol. 122, no. 2 (spring 1993) p. 156.

21 Myron L. Cohen, *House United, House Divided: The Chinese Family in Taiwan* (New York: Columbia University Press, 1976).

22 Myron L. Cohen, 'Cultural and Political Inventions in Modern China: The Case of the Chinese 'Peasant' ', *Daedalus*, vol. 122, no. 2 (spring 1993) pp. 153, 156.

23 Jinhong Ding and Norman Stockman, 'The floating population and the integration of the city community: A survey on the attitudes of Shanghai residents to recent

migrants', in Frank N. Pieke and Hein Mallee (eds) *Internal and International Migration: Chinese Perspectives* (Richmond: Curzon Press, 1999) p. 120.

24 *Ibid.*, pp. 123–5.

25 Wang Yanling, Wu Yekang and Jiang Jianping, 'Cong xue di jiaoxunzhong dedao qishi' [Get Enlightenment from a Bloody Lesson], *Shehui* [Society], no. 8 (1990) p. 2.

26 Zhang Youren, 'Zunzhong 'waidiren' yingdang chengwei shehui gongde' [Respecting 'Outsiders' Should Become Social Public Morality], *Shehui*, no. 6 (1987) p. 25.

27 Wang Jianmin and Hu Qi, 'Zhongshi tiaojie wailai liudong renkou jiekou di duice yanjiu' [Research on Policy Measures to Regulate the Structure of the Floating Population from Outside], *Zhongguo renkou kexue* [Chinese Population Science], no. 6 (1988) p. 72.

28 Liu Bingyi, 'Liudong di 'shimin' ' [Floating 'City People'], *Qing Chun* [Youth], no. 6 (1989) p. 32.

29 Interview in Tianjin, 8 June 1992.

30 Gong Xikui, 'Zhongguo xianxing huji zhidu toushi' [A Perspective on China's Present Household Register System], *Shehui Kexue* [Social Science], no. 2 (1989); see also Michael Dutton, 'Editor's Introduction', in Zhang Qingwu, 'Basic Facts on the Household Registration System', *Chinese Economic Studies*, vol. 22, no. 1 (1988) p. 8; Rogers Brubaker, *Citizenship and Nationhood in France and Germany* (Cambridge MA: Harvard University Press, 1992) p. 24. In *ibid.*, p. 180, he lists as crucial elements of citizenship 'not only political rights but the unconditional right to enter and reside in the country, complete access to the labor market, and eligibility for the full range of welfare benefits'.

31 This comes from D. J. Solinger, *Contesting Citizenship in Urban China: Peasant Migrants, the State, and the Logic of the Market* (Berkeley: University of California Press, 1999) p. 4.

32 *Ibid.*, p. 6.

33 Bryan S. Turner, 'Contemporary Problems in the Theory of Citizenship', in Bryan S. Turner (ed.) *Citizenship and Social Theory* (London: Sage, 1993) pp. 1–18. p. 2.

34 Yasemin Nuhoglu Soysal, *Limits of Citizenship: Migrants and Postnational Membership in Europe* (Chicago: University of Chicago Press, 1994) p. 119; Elizabeth Meehan, *Citizenship and the European Community* (London: Sage, 1993) p. 22; Rogers Brubaker, *Citizenship and Nationhood in France and Germany* (Cambridge MA: Harvard University Press, 1992) p. 21; and Zig Layton-Henry, 'The Challenge of Political Rights', in Zig Layton-Henry (ed.) *The Political Rights of Migrant Workers in Western Europe* (London: Sage, 1990) p. 12.

35 D. J. Solinger, *Contesting Citizenship in Urban China: Peasant Migrants, the State, and the Logic of the Market* (Berkeley: University of California Press, 1999) p. 7.

36 Constitution of the People's Republic of China (adopted on 4 December 1982 by the Fifth National People's Congress, Fifth Session) (Beijing: Foreign Languages Press, 1982) p. 31.

37 D. J. Solinger, *Contesting Citizenship in Urban China: Peasant Migrants, the State, and the Logic of the Market* (Berkeley: University of California Press, 1999) chs 5 and 6.

38 This is a district in Zhejiang province, from several counties of which most migrants from that province originate. For a study of the social relations in Beijing's now famous 'Zhejiang Village', see Li Zhang, *Strangers in the City* (Stanford: Stanford University Press,2001); and Frank N. Pieke and Hein Mallee (eds) *Internal and International Migration: Chinese Perspectives* (Richmond: Curzon, 1999) for case studies of the migrants from that region.

39 Of course, as Li Zhang shows (see note 38 above), the personal charisma possessed by some migrant leaders, raw power, and wealth also play a role in ordering these local sub-societies.

40 These impressions are ones I gleaned during several unpleasant encounters with such bosses at worksites, in Nanjing, 19 May 1992, and in Wuhan, 10 August 1994. Yuan Yue, *Luoren: Beijing liumin di zuzhihua zhuangkuang yanjiu baogao* [The Exposed: A Research Report on the Condition of the Organization of Migrants in Beijing] (Beijing: Beijing Horizon Market Research and Analysis Company, 1995) p. 47, concur.

41 Chai Junyong, 'Liudong renkou–chengshi guanli di yi da kunrao' [The Floating Population: The Puzzle in Urban Management], *Shehui*, no. 10 (1990) p. 9; *China Daily*, 30 July 1991, p. 6; Zeng Jingwen, 'Dadushi di 'shihuangzhe' ' [Big Cities' 'Trash Collectors'], *Nanfang Chuang* [Southern Window] (Guangzhou) no. 1 (1988) p. 24; Liu Hantai, Zhongguo di Qigai Qunluo [China's Beggar Community] *Wenhui Yuekan* [Encounter Monthly] (Shanghai) no. 10 (1986) pp. 198, 205–10; Foreign Broadcast Information Service (FBIS) 17 October 1994, p. 80 (from Zhongguo xinwenshe [Chinese news agency]); and interview, 10 June 1992, with a cadre from Tianjin's public security office.

42 My information about these latter two kinds of groupings comes mainly from Yuan Yue, *Luoren: Beijing liumin di zuzhihua zhuangkuang yanjiu baogao* [The exposed: a research report on the condition of the organization of migrants in Beijing] (Beijing: Beijing Horizon Market Research and Analysis Company, 1995).

43 Much of the following comes from D. J. Solinger, 'Conclusion', in *Contesting Citizenship in Urban China: Peasant Migrants, the State, and the Logic of the Market* (Berkeley: University of California Press, 1999).

44 For a small but critical segment of the literature on globalization in recent years, see Suzanne Berger and Ronald Dore (eds) *National Diversity and Global Capitalism* (Ithaca NY: Cornell University Press, 1996); James H. Mittelman (ed.) *Globalization: Critical Reflections* (Boulder: Lynne Rienner, 1996); William Greider, *One World Ready or Not: The Manic Logic of Global Capitalism* (New York: Simon and Schuster, 1997); Philip Gummett (ed.) *Globalization and Public Policy* (Cheltenham: Edward Elgar, 1996); Dani Rodrik, *Has Globalization Gone Too Far?* (Washington DC: Institute for International Economics, 1997).

45 Yasemin Nuhoglu Soysal, *Limits of Citizenship: Migrants and Postnational Membership in Europe* (Chicago: University of Chicago Press, 1994) pp. 3, 12.

46 James F. Hollifield, *Immigrants, Markets, and States: The Political Economy of Postwar Europe* (Cambridge MA: Harvard University Press, 1992) pp. 170, 216; there is a similar argument made in Wayne A. Cornelius, Philip L. Martin and James F. Hollifield, 'Introduction: The Ambivalent Quest for Immigration Control', in Wayne A. Cornelius, Philip L. Martin, and James F. Hollifield (eds) *Controlling Immigration: A Global Perspective* (Stanford: Stanford University Press, 1995) pp. 3–41.

47 David Jacobson, 'New Border Customs: Migration and the Changing Role of the State', *UCLA Journal of International Law and Foreign Affairs*, vol. 3, no. 2 (fall/winter 1998–9) p. 453; also see *idem*, *Rights Across Borders: Immigration and the Decline of Citizenship* (Baltimore: Johns Hopkins University Press, 1996).

48 Pitman B. Potter, 'Riding the Tiger: Legitimacy and Legal Culture in Post-Mao China', *China Quarterly*, no. 138 (1994) pp. 325–58; and Pitman B. Potter (ed.) *Domestic Law Reforms in Post-Mao China* (Armonk: M. E. Sharpe, 1994).

49 This is an argument in Stanley B. Lubman's book on the law, *Bird in a Cage: Legal Reform in China After Mao* (Stanford: Stanford University Press, 2000).

50 See Michael R. Dutton, *Policing and Punishment in China: From Patriarchy to 'The People'* (New York: Cambridge University Press, 1992) p. 336.

51 Anthony Kuhn and Lincoln Kaye, 'Bursting at the Seams', *Far Eastern Economic Review*, 10 March 1994, pp. 27–8, and Ding Shuimu, 'Xianxing huji guanli zhidu chuyi' [A Preliminary View of the Present Household Registration Management System], *Shehui*, no. 1 (1987) p. 19.
52 For instance, Cao Jingchun, 'Lanpi lanyin hukou yinfa di sikao' [Some Deliberations on the Blue Seal Household Registration Permit], *Renkou yu jingji* [Population and Economy], no. 5 (1993) pp. 38–42; and Ma Chenguang, 'Cities Set Looser Rules on Residency', *FBIS*, 4 March 1994, p. 22, from *China Daily* of the same date, p. 3.
53 *China Daily Business Weekly*, 6 September 1998, p. 1.
54 For instance, Vice Premier Wu Bangguo voiced it at a meeting in early 1996. See Huang, Haixia, 'How to Ensure the Orderly Flow of the Rural Surplus Labor Force? Interviewing Labor Minister Li Boyong', *Liaowang*, no. 13 (1996) p. 30, in *FBIS*, 5 June 1996, pp. 30–1.
55 *Liaowang*, no. 30 (1995) pp. 4–5, in *FBIS*, 8 August 1995, p. 14.
56 Tang Xiaotian and Chen Donghu, 'Qiangxing jiju yu chengshi shehui fanzui' [Forced Residence Away from Home and Urban Society's Criminals], *Shehui*, no. 9 (1989) p. 20.
57 *Nanfang ribao* [Southern Daily] (Guangzhou) 14 December 1988, p. 2.
58 Ge Xiangxian and Qu Weiying, *Zhongguo Mingongchao: 'Mangliu' Zhenxianglu* [China's Tide of Labor: A Record of the True Facts about the 'Blind Floaters'] (Beijing: Chinese International Broadcasting Publishing Co., 1990) p. 103.
59 *FBIS*, 23 August 1988, p. 41, from Beijing Domestic Service, 19 August 1988.
60 The 'defensive' nature of these strikes bears out the point made in Elizabeth J. Perry, *Shanghai on Strike: The Politics of Chinese Labor* (Stanford: Stanford University Press, 1994) pp. 60ff, that unskilled workers (in that study, in late nineteenth- and early twentieth-century Shanghai) tend to strike over purely economic grievances, and do not raise political demands.
61 *FBIS*, 31 March 1994, p. 27, from *Eastern Express*, 31 March 1994, p. 9.
62 According to a report from 1994, 'Workers are discriminated against by official unionists'. This is from an interview with a researcher at the Trade Union Education Center in Hong Kong, who spoke on the basis of his own experience with these workers in China, and reported in the *South China Morning Post*, 14 June 1994, p. 5, reprinted in *FBIS*, 14 June 1994, p. 31. See also Ching-kwan Lee, 'Production Politics and Labour Identities: Migrant Workers in South China', in Lo Chi Kin, Suzanne Pepper and Tsui Kai Yuen (eds) *China Review 1995* (Hong Kong: The Chinese University Press, 1995) p. 15.12.
63 Willy Wo-Lap Lam, 'Party Circular Warns of Spread of Illegal Trade Unions', *South China Morning Post*, 4 June 1996, p. 1, in *FBIS*, 5 June 1996, p. 20; Ching-kwan Lee, 'Production Politics and Labour Identities: Migrant Workers in South China', in Lo Chi Kin, Suzanne Pepper and Tsui Kai Yuen (eds) *China Review 1995* (Hong Kong: The Chinese University Press, 1995) p. 15.14.
64 *South China Morning Post*, 9 July 1993, reprinted in *FBIS*, 9 July 1993, p. 25.
65 *Ibid.*
66 Ba jia <Nongxun laodongli liudong yanjiu> keti weituo nongyebu nongcun jingji yanjiu zhongxin ketizu bianji [Eight 'Rural Labor Force Mobility Research' Tasks Commissioned by the Ministry of Agriculture Rural Economic Research Center Task Groups] (ed.) *Nongcun laodongli jingji yanjiu tongxun* [Bulletin of Rural Labor Mobility Studies] (n.p., 1995) pp. A-02, A-07.
67 Zhang Xiaohui, Zhao Changbao and Chen Liangbiao, '1994: Nongcun laodongli kuaquyu liudong di shizheng miaoda' [1994: A Real Description of Rural Labor's Cross-Regional Flow], *Nanfang Chuang*, no. 6 (1995) p. 28.

68 Anita Chan, 'Briefing to the Australia/China Parliamentary Friendship Group', Canberra, 12 September 1996; and *idem*, 'The Changing Ruling Elite and Political Opposition in China', in Garry Rodan (ed.) *Political Oppositions in Industrialising Asia* (London and New York: Routledge, 1996) p. 178.

69 Jerome Cohen, *The Criminal Process in the People's Republic of China, 1949–1963* (Cambridge MA: Harvard University Press, 1968).

70 This law was adopted on 5 July 1994, at the eighth session of the Standing Committee of the Eighth National People's Congress, translated in *FBIS*, 19 July 1994; Hilary K. Josephs, 'Labor Law Reflects New Realities', *China Rights Forum* (fall 1996) pp. 24–7.

71 Sun Changmin, 'Floating Population in Shanghai: A Perspective of Social Transformation in China', in Thomas Scharping (ed.) *Floating Population and Migration in China: The Impact of Economic Reforms* (Hamburg: Institut fur Asienkunde, 1997) p. 211.

72 Cao Jingxing, 'A Good Trend or a Reason for Worry?', *China Focus*, vol. 5, no. 8 (August 1997) p. 8; Lin Lean Lim and Gyorgy Sziraczki, 'Employment, Social Security, and Enterprise Reforms in China', in Gregory K. Schoepfle (ed.) *Changes in China's Labor Market: Implications for the Future* (Washington DC: US Department of Labor, Bureau of International Labor Affairs, 1996) p. 53; and Summary of World Broadcasts, FE/3162 (227/98) p. G/5 (from *Xinhua*, 20 February 1998) for an official source.

73 See David Lamb, 'Migrant Asians Now Out of Work', *Los Angeles Times*, 3 March 1998, pp. A3, A9; and Margot Cohen, 'Deport and Deter', *Far Eastern Economic Review*, 23 April 1998, pp. 16–20.

74 'Provisions on Employing Contract Workers from Among the Peasants by State-owned Enterprises', in *Zhonghua renmin gongheguo guowuyuan gongbao* [Bulletin of the State Council of the Chinese People's Republic] (Beijing) no. 28 (18 October 1991) pp. 1001–16.

75 Lin Lean Lim and Gyorgy Sziraczki, 'Employment, Social Security, and Enterprise Reforms in China', in Gregory K. Schoepfle (ed.) *Changes in China's Labor Market: Implications for the Future* (Washington DC: US Department of Labor, Bureau of International Labor Affairs, 1996) pp. 61, 64.

76 *FBIS*, 23 February 1995, p. 68; 16 March 1995, p. 33; 28 June 1995, p. 81. See also Loraine A. West, 'The Changing Effects of Economic Reform on Rural and Urban Employment', paper presented at the conference on the 'Unintended Social Conequences of Chinese Economic Reform', Harvard School of Public Health and The Fairbank Center for East Asian Studies, Harvard University, 23–4 May 1997, p. 11; and Xiao Lichun, 'Shanghai shiye, xiagang renyuan xianzhuang ji fazhan qushi' [Shanghai Unemployment, Laid-off Personnel's Situation and Development Trend], *Zhongguo renkou kexue*, no. 3 (1998) pp. 26–37.

77 Antoine Kernen, 'Surviving Reform in Shenyang: New Poverty in Pioneer City', *China Rights Forum* (summer 1997) p. 10.

8

THE HISTORICAL ROOTS OF STASIS AND CHANGE IN JAPANESE LEGAL EDUCATION

Kahei Rokumoto

Legal education in Japan is now being re-examined, and is likely to be overhauled within a decade. This reexamination forms part of a more comprehensive scheme of restructuring the judicial system and the legal profession as a whole, proposed by the Judicial Reform Council (JRC). The JRC was established directly in the Cabinet in July 1999. By law, its mission is 'to consider fundamental measures necessary to reform the judicial system and its infrastructure by defining the role of the administration of justice in Japan in the twenty-first century'.[1] Based on its own intensive research and deliberations, the JRC released a Final Report in June 2001 that includes a recommendation to establish a new regime of legal education by the year 2004. This recommendation was coupled with a proposal to expand the number of new recruits to the legal profession annually from the present 1,000 to 3,000.[2]

According to the plan, a new graduate school of law, ***Hoka-daigakuin***, popularly called 'the Japanese style law school', will be established subject to periodic accreditation by an appropriate third party body. The graduate school will offer a three-year program, successful completion of which would be the prerequisite for taking the national Legal Examination.[3] The Legal Examination itself will have to be refurbished to reflect the teaching program of the new graduate law school. The existing Institute of Legal Research and Training will continue to function and will admit those who pass the Legal Examination, and will confer on its graduates their qualification as lawyers. Although the present law faculties and departments with their undergraduate programs of legal education will continue to operate, their curricula would have to be modified to fit the new regime of higher education. It is contemplated that on average 70 to 80 per cent of the annual graduates from the law schools would be admitted to the Institute, a big leap from the current pass rate of 3 per cent in the Legal Examination.[4] On the basis of the target number of 3,000 passes per year,[5] this would mean that the number of annual enrollments of all law schools combined would be something like 5,000 students.

The proposal calls for major restructuring, involving not only the university law faculties and their curricula, but also the whole mechanism of training and qualifying all legal professionals. Why do we need to undertake such radical changes in legal education? The need for radical reforms lies not only in the state of legal education itself, but also in the legal profession as a whole, comprised of judges, prosecutors and practicing attorneys. The proposed reform of legal education thus forms a package plan affecting the basic structures of the judicial system.[6] Moreover, judicial reform was called for by a growing consensus that it is time to change the operative character of the legal system to bring it more in line with the principle of the rule of law that underlies the Constitution of 1946. Indeed, the JRC formulated its basic mission in terms of finding out

> what we ought to do to make the rule of law form the flesh and blood of this nation and define 'the shape of this nation', a task that this country has been continuously bearing for the past 130 years since the beginning of its modern era.[7]

Accordingly, to appreciate the significance of this extraordinary reform project, as well as the difficulties that it may face, it is indispensable to view it in broad historical context and to place it against the background of the basic characteristics of the Japanese judicial system that are rooted in history. Therefore, this chapter first summarizes the main features of the present system of legal education and the legal profession that form the target of the JRC reforms, and then goes back to the pre- and post-Meiji Restoration period to trace the political processes by which the modern judicial system was fashioned.[8]

The present legal education and the need for reform

Presently in Japan, legal education is part of the undergraduate curriculum. There are about thirty law faculties or departments housed in national or municipal universities. In addition, there are sixty-five private university law faculties. The total number of undergraduate students studying law at those faculties and departments is about 45,000 per year.

Few students of these programs will ultimately become members of the legal profession. To take the example of the University of Tokyo Law Faculty: of the 650 students in a class, about 100 become bureaucrats, mainly for the national government, and 200 or more pass the Legal Examination. The rest find jobs with private firms. This rate of 200 students out of 650 becoming lawyers is exceptionally high. If we take the total student population, just a handful, 1,000 out of 45,000, pass the examination. Table 8.1 compares the annual enrollment and the total number of graduates (regardless of the year of graduation) who passed the Legal Examination in 1999 for top-ranking state and private universities.

Of the many law faculties or departments that exist, a great majority produce only a few lawyers, or none at all. In 1999 the top ten law faculties accounted

Table 8.1 Annual enrolment and total number of graduates passing the Legal Examination

	Annual enrolment	*Total number of graduates passing Legal Exam in 1999*
University of Tokyo	650	230
University of Kyoto	400	110
Waseda University	1,200	140
Keio University	1,200	100
Chuo University	1,700	90

for 85 per cent of the 1,000 successful candidates. Those 1,000 candidates had spent an average of 4.8 years (after graduating from the university) before being admitted to the Legal Research and Training Institute.

The small proportion of undergraduate law students who become members of the legal profession is partly the result of the stringent pass rate of the Legal Examination, which was 2.9 per cent. There were 34,000 candidates (only a small minority – probably less than 20 per cent – of whom are fresh graduates of universities) sitting for the examination in 1999. A substantial number of students may wish to become lawyers, but quit after one or two trials at the Legal Examination. Another reason is that not all law students even aspire to become lawyers. Many of them choose to become civil servants (in national or local government) or to enter private business firms.

A typical law faculty is composed of a department of political science as well as a department of law, and offers courses in economics as well as political science. It also offers courses in what is called 'the basic science of law', which includes foreign laws, legal history, legal philosophy and legal sociology. Generally speaking, major law faculties attract the best of the students who are oriented to social studies and the humanities, who wish to attain leadership positions in government, business or law. Above all, the faculties of national universities have traditionally considered themselves responsible for educating good bureaucrats, who play principal roles in national policy making, administration and legislation. As it is often said, the education at Japanese law faculties and departments is generalist education, aiming at preparing the students for managing an organization, whether in government or business. It is not concerned to educate or train professionally qualified persons equipped with specialist knowledge and skill. Supposedly, this generalist orientation of Japanese legal education was originally based on the Confucian idea that 'the gentleman is not a vessel'.

It has been a normal pattern since university legal education started, that only a minority of law students become members of the legal profession. It is also an established tradition that instruction at law faculties and departments is given primarily in the form of lectures to a class of as many as 500 students or more. The students are encouraged to raise their hands to ask questions, but they rarely do so and remain passive listeners and note-takers, although there are some who come up to the instructor with questions after the lecture. The instructors in the core subjects of law typically try to cover in lectures systematically the codes or statutes relevant to the subject in question within the prescribed hours of the semester. Professors take pride in that their lectures reflect the high academic quality of their own research in some specialized topics, as well as incorporate the standard, up-to-date knowledge in the field, but they rarely care much for the educational efficacy of their teaching. Evaluation of students' coursework is made solely on the basis of the written examination given at the end of the semester. Seminar courses are offered, in which students sometimes show an exceptionally high ability of self-motivated research work. But seminar courses constitute only a small, elective portion of the total units required for the diploma.

Over the past few decades, the field of law has become intensely specialized and ramified. Many new subjects have been added to the law curriculum, such as securities law, intellectual property law, etc. On the other hand, the general academic standard of students entering the university has been in decline, undoubtedly reflecting the cumulative effects of the elaborate system of selecting students solely on the basis of paper tests at every stage of their school education leading to university. As a result, students have become even more passive in their studies than before. Survey research shows that many law students find it difficult to follow and digest the lectures, even if they attend lectures regularly.

For those students who are interested in the legal profession, commercial schools have emerged to offer efficient programs for training students in examination techniques geared specifically to the types of question asked in the Legal Examination. As a result, it has become usual for those students who seriously want to pass the Legal Examination to regularly attend such cram schools during much of the time they have to devote to preparation for the Examination – including the time they are enrolled in universities as law students. Thus complaints began to be heard about the poor quality of many of the students who enter the Institute of Legal Research and Training. Against this general background, the call to improve the quality of university legal education by means of more student participation in smaller classes has been gaining support.

The structure of the legal profession

The issues of legal education are closely related to the structure of the legal profession. The Japanese legal profession may be characterized as a divided profession. The division is threefold, because judges, prosecutors and attorneys have traditionally tended to be seen as belonging to separate occupations, pursuing different career paths, and even as living in different worlds. In a sense, though, the division is twofold, because judges and prosecutors are career officials, whereas attorneys are private practitioners. In the formative era of the legal profession, judges and prosecutors were bundled together as 'judicial officers' and came to be called 'the lawyers of the government camp' as opposed to the attorneys, 'the lawyers of the opposition camp'. It is easy to see that this structure necessarily affects the fundamental character of legal education in many ways, and that introducing changes to it is a matter of vital importance not only to legal education, but also to the judicial system as a whole.[9]

The Japanese judiciary is characterized by the system of career judges. Most of the current judges were first appointed assistant judges straight from the Institute. After five years, assistant judges are allowed to sit alone on the bench, and after another five years, they are appointed as regular, fully fledged judges, with only rare exceptions. Thereafter, every ten years they are re-appointed until they reach the mandatory retirement age of sixty-five.[10] Throughout their career, judges are transferred every three years or so from court to court around the country, some assuming administrative positions in the General Secretariat of the Supreme Court and the Ministry of Justice, as well as the position of chief judge in various courts. Judges' remuneration is finely graded, and the various courts and posts to which they may be assigned are also (unofficially) ranked according to importance and desirability. Administrative positions tend to be ranked high on the scale. At each transfer, judges are selectively promoted and climb the career ladder step by step; their career pattern looks very similar to that of other public servants in the ministries. In fact, the judiciary as a whole looks like a hierarchically organized bureaucracy, comprised of all the judges of all the courts of various ranks. This career system is centrally administered by the Secretariat of the Supreme Court, whose key posts are manned by those judges who are appointed to them in the course of their career.[11]

This kind of career for judges in Japan is undoubtedly the product, and perhaps an inevitable outcome, of the historical processes by which the legal profession was created and developed. Japan has succeeded in establishing a legitimate and stable court system manned by competent and incorruptible judges who are well versed in the Western techniques of legal interpretation and application. The result is an independent and autonomous judiciary, an organization manned by judges who, individually, look more like bureaucrats than independent judges.[12] This system has been criticized for its tendency to produce many judges who are passive and remote from the reality of the world, as well as for providing judges who are often accused of being immature. Japanese judges have been criticized on grounds that even though they are not fossil-like, they tend to lean toward formal correctness and to lag behind the changing values of society in their evaluation of substantive policy issues. In any event, it is clear that these features do not help to enhance their prestige in the eye of the general public.

The issue of the career judge began to be debated within a decade of the reform of the entire judicial system during the postwar period. The criticisms were made against the career system of judges in the name of the Constitution of 1946 itself, but the task of re-reforming the judiciary in response to those criticisms has not made much progress.

In 1962 the Ad Hoc Committee for the Investigation into the Judicial System, *Rinji Shiho-seido Chosakai*, or *Rinshi*, was established in the Cabinet in similar fashion to the present JRC. The main task of this Committee was to investigate whether the career system of judges should be maintained or should be replaced by an alternative scheme called the 'unitary system of the legal profession'. This latter term refers to the system of recruiting fully fledged judges from among experienced attorneys, and not from among assistant judges. This alternative scheme is based on the idea that judges, prosecutors and attorneys should constitute one unified legal profession as they do in Britain or in the United States, instead of forming separate professions. This scheme would also eliminate the inbred system of judges, as well as limit judges' long careers.

After deliberating for two years, the Committee concluded in its 1964 final report that the unitary system was a desirable method of recruiting judges, but that the preconditions indispensable for adopting it were not yet fulfilled. The main inadequacy discussed in the report was that the number of practicing attorneys was insufficient as well as that their geographical distribution was uneven. It would be difficult to find adequate numbers of candidates for judicial posts, particularly in jurisdictions other than the large metropolitan areas. The report also pointed out that the attorneys' patterns of work, based predominantly on individual practice and concentrating on court work, would hinder the recruitment of judges from their ranks.[13]

The *Rinshi* Committee recognized that behind the voices demanding the 'unitary system', there was persistent and pertinent criticism of the regime of career judges. However, the committee pointed out that this system has the great advantage of being able to procure judges capable of making fair, neutral and stable judgments, and to provide honest judges of high quality throughout the country. At the same time, the final report was equally firm in stressing a major disadvantage, namely that a bureaucratically organized judiciary deviates from the model of the judiciary presupposed by the Constitution of 1946, which gave each judge the power to declare any law or governmental act unconstitutional and void. It also recognized that this regime tends to produce a judiciary that lacks a popular basis, and judges who are remote and insulated from society. Such judges would often be overly concerned with technical and formal logical correctness and legal stability, while unable to arrive at mature judgments based on a discerning appreciation of the case in dispute.[14]

Thus, even though its conclusion was negative on the adoption of the 'unitary system', the *Rinshi* Committee's report left an important legacy. It publicly recognized that the reforms of the judicial system under the

Constitution of 1946, purporting to establish the 'rule of law' in Japan, had failed to take root in the institutional reality of the judicial system. In other words, it left open to further debate the issues of the structure of the legal profession and the quality of the judiciary. The Judicial Reform Council of 1999 represents a renewed attempt to deal with the same basic issues under different political and social circumstances, and many of its reform proposals, including that concerning the Japanese style law school, can only be properly understood in terms of the basic mold in which the legal profession and judicial system are cast at birth.

Genesis of the modern judicial system: nation-building struggles

The basic and persistent mold of the judicial system of Japan was set during the few decades following the Meiji Restoration of 1868, which marked the emergence of a modern nation-state out of a feudal regime based on an agrarian economy and secluded from the outside world. It is true that its structure underwent substantial modifications since, especially under the US-led Allied Occupation after 1945, a major turning point in the modern legal history of Japan. However, it is also undeniable that some of the principal characteristics of the judicial system, as well as those of the legal profession, have remained up to the present. It goes without saying that the judicial system forms part of the structure of government. The modern judicial system took shape in the precarious processes by which the feudal political regime under the Tokugawa Shogunate (*bakufu*) was replaced by a set of entirely new state institutions. Accordingly, in order to understand the basic characteristics of the Japanese judicial system, it is necessary to look at the overall political circumstances in which it gradually emerged a century ago,[15] just as it is important today, in looking at the processes of its restructuring, to understand the political forces as well as the rational, intellectual motives that are driving it.

Inevitably, we will find in these processes and outcomes the intricate interplay between the traditional and the modern, the institutional and the cultural elements. However, the principal driving force required for achieving such drastic changes within a short period of time must come from the political sphere. The Meiji Restoration was not the product of a sustained movement organized by a particular group of people or led by a particular ideology or vision. It was rather the end result of desperate struggles and outbursts of energy with which the body politic reacted to the unprecedented demands of its environment for change. Various status groups and leaders took turns in leading those processes, until finally a small group of young warriors, who came mainly from the Satsuma and Choshu fiefs, succeeded by coup in establishing a new state structure and controlling the modernizing reforms. Throughout those revolutionary struggles, all the existing intellectual and institutional resources had to be tested, mobilized and exploited.

In spite of the great deal of Western learning that the Tokugawa warrior intellectuals had accumulated and utilized for the rebuilding of the nation,[16] it was Confucian learning that provided the basic framework for their view of the world.[17] The Tokugawa Shogunate had developed a well ordered, centralized bureaucratic system of government run by a well disciplined corps of warrior officials. It also had developed its own notion of 'law' that emphasized the guiding and controlling of behavior – primarily that of its civil servants, and secondarily and indirectly that of its subjects – by means of a comprehensive system of codified norms, rather than by adjudication of open disputes.[18] Public and private schools based on Confucian ethics had been widespread throughout the nation and had produced the world's most literate subjects[19] to provide the underlying human resources for the construction of a new state, together with a well developed domestic commercial economy.

The Japanese term *Meiji Ishin*, coined by its own instigators, is usually translated as 'restoration', but its literal meaning is closer to 'renovation'.[20] In fact, it was introduced in tandem with another term, *Oosei Fukko* (return to the imperial rule), for the Meiji Restoration as a political process had dual aspects of revolutionary innovation and reactionary falling back on an ancient institution. The Meiji Restoration overturned the entire system of absolute domination by the warrior class composed of the Shogun and his vassals, as well as the domain chiefs and their vassals (the *bakuhan* system), replacing it with modern Western institutions and principles. Western ideas and technologies were indispensable, but a consensus existed that at stake was nothing less than national survival, and the whole collective enterprise was motivated and driven by culturally embedded ideologies, and had to be carried out within the existing framework of political and legal institutions.

The appearance in 1853 of Commodore Perry with his fleet off the Bay of Tokyo graphically illustrated the mounting pressure from the West for the opening-up of the hitherto closed country of Japan, under the threat of overwhelming military force. It was a powerful reminder of the Opium War of 1839–42 that had led to the humiliating disintegration of the revered empire of China and its civilization. The task of reacting promptly to the crisis and defending national security fell in the first instance on the shoulders of the Shogun, who ruled the country under the title of *Seii Taishogun* ('Generalissimo who Conquers Barbarians') bestowed by the Emperor. He was counseled by a small number of domain chiefs, but only those who held privileged positions on account of blood ties or hereditary allegiances to the Shogun. Some powerful and enlightened domains located on the southwestern coasts, and occupying marginal positions in the *bakuhan* regime, began their own reform efforts, adopting Western industrial and military technologies. The enlightened chiefs of those domains, as well as their warrior officials, were increasingly critical of the Shogunate and competed for leadership. This crisis created the opportunity for the contenders to invoke the authority of the Imperial Court, which reemerged as the symbol of unity and identity of the nation.

In 1858 the Treaty of Commerce was signed with the United States and other Western powers. It demanded the opening of some major ports and cities for foreign trade, but the Shogunate had to make this fateful step without authorization by the Emperor. The political process from this event up to 1868 is well documented, and may be summarized in the following schema. The initial slogan, 'support the Shogunate' (*sabaku*) was taken over by the call for 'union of the Court and Shogunate' (*kobu gattai*), which was advocated by some enlightened chiefs of powerful domains such as Tosa, Satsuma and Choshu in alliance with some able staff officials of the Shogunate. However, the Shogunate, whose power had been built upon delicate mechanisms of control and balance based on a decentralized feudalalism, proved incapable of coping with the crisis. The dominant cry was initially 'revere the Emperor and expel barbarians' (*sonnoo joi*), and soon changed to 'overthrow the Shogunate' (*toobaku*).

As Marius Jansen aptly summarizes, 'pressures posed by opening and reconstruction revealed to friend and foe alike the impossibility of long continuing with the institutional structure of the *bakuhan* system and the need to replace it with the structure of a central state'.[21] In 1863 the powerful southwestern domains, Choshu and Satsuma, equipped with their own modernized military forces, tried their hands in turn at fighting the Western warships. Their defeat in these wars made it obvious to everyone that it was simply impossible to put expulsion (*jooi*) into practice. At the same time the domestic economy had been suffering from chronic crises for decades and was in need of fundamental reforms.

But the Shogun and the enlightened domain chiefs were not capable of shouldering the task of reconstruction. It was a small group of young activists from the lower warrior ranks in the southwestern domains who quickly emerged as rescuing heroes. These people had been educated in domain schools in Confucian learning, and had experienced in their teens the first visits of foreign warships to Japanese ports. They acquired Western knowledge, some being sent abroad for study by their domain chiefs, and worked as domain officials under and in support of their respective domain chiefs, moving freely between their home domain capitals, the national capital Edo, and the old imperial capital Kyoto. They associated with and disputed with fellow warriors of other domains. They were primarily motivated by the Confucian sense of loyalty, whose ideational mechanism enabled them to justify revolt against their own domain chiefs or the Shogun in terms of admonishing their lord for errors in promoting the latter's cause, and switching their loyalty to the highest lord, the Emperor.[22]

This was a revolution 'from above', executed by members of the ruling class itself that in turn constituted only 5–6 per cent of the population. The revolutionary leaders, coming from the lower and best educated ranks of the ruling warrior class, fully exploited the overwhelming authority and privilege of their warrior status, driven by the Confucian sense of mission to enlighten and lead the people, and paid due respect to those of higher rank. They eventually succeeded in tearing down the regime of domination by the warrior class itself in the name of 'protection of the innocent and illiterate people at large'. The 'people' feared, rejoiced, complained, derided, protested, and even revolted, but on the whole remained passive recipients of the benefits as well as the costs of the revolution.

The primary goal of these young makeshift politicians, working in cooperation with some shrewd court nobles under the authority of the young Emperor Meiji (who was enthroned in 1866 at the age of sixteen), was to maintain the independence and unity of the nation against the threat of Western encroachment. They later came to run the state under the rather abstract slogan of 'enrich the country and strengthen the military', but they came to power without any pre-conceived policy program or ideological vision. They had before them a series of formidable tasks that had to be accomplished in turn: to destroy the feudal domains, to establish a centralized government with a unitary tax system as well as unified armed forces, to promote industry by creating a capitalistic economy based on private ownership and abolition of the entire feudal status system, and to develop the education system in order to enlighten and educate the people. It was also believed that, in order to build a modern nation and to ensure a respectable place in the world order, it was necessary to have a modern legal system, and to renegotiate the unequal treaties of 1858 that accorded the Western powers extraterritorial jurisdiction over matters concerning their nationals and deprived Japan of tariff autonomy. In the process of tackling all these tasks, the first and paramount requirement was to establish and maintain an effective apparatus of government. It was necessary to start with a set of *ad hoc* arrangements and to proceed on a trial-and-error basis, modifying them as new issues and conflicts arose, and responding to the internal divisions that inevitably appeared within the small group of ruling leaders, until a permanent form of government could eventually be established.

Establishing a central government within an ancient legal framework

The first phase of the Restoration was to create the structure for a centralized government. The initial processes of putting together the new political structure in the early years of Meiji were carried out mainly in accordance with the existing, traditional framework for the political and legal order. Japan had a well established legal framework for government, the *Ritsuryo* system, which was first imported from China in the seventh century and had been maintained intact throughout the feudal periods. This was a status-based, hierarchically organized system of government offices which served the rule of the Emperor. The system was embodied in innumerable written codes, with the Great Governing Office, *dajokan*, at the top. The Tokugawa Shoguns, even though they were usurpers of the effective ruling power of the Emperor, formally occupied the office of the Generalissimo under the *Ritsuryo* system. They developed in turn a highly sophisticated bureaucracy to maintain domination and control of the 260 fiefs (domains) based on the decentralized feudal principles of vassalage. This system of bureaucratic government was duplicated in each of the 260 domains.[23]

The *Ritsuryo* system, which provided the basic legal framework for various political maneuvers during the pre-Restoration period, should be seen in light of the fact that the Emperor, who had long been regarded as a mere figurehead, began to move toward center stage as a potent alternative to the Shogun as an object of political allegiance. In 1863 the desperate Shogun Iemochi actually requested the Imperial Court – unsuccessfully – to exempt him from the impossible task of expelling barbarians. Four years later, in 1867, the next Shogun, Yoshinobu, obtained 'permission' to return, first his rule, and then his title of Shogun to the Emperor. After this it was possible for the Emperor to legitimately declare war on Yoshinobu, now reduced to a mere feudal lord, as an enemy of the Emperor, and to confiscate the territories that were directly governed by the Shogun and place them under Meiji rule.[24]

The Meiji Restoration itself, in legal terms, started as a *coup d'état* at the Imperial Court, instigated by young warrior activists such as Okubo (Satsuma), Goto (Tosa), and the shrewd court noble Iwakura, backed by an army of forces assembled from several allied domains including Choshu, under the command of Saigo (Satsuma). At a Court conference they passed a resolution to have the Emperor declare, 'Return to the imperial rule' (*taisei hokan*). The Emperor complied, and went on to declare the abolition of the existing *dajokan* offices of Court ministers as well as the Shogunate. The revolutionary junta instituted under the same *dajokan* a set of new governing structures, which consisted of a president (*sosai*), senior councilors (*gijo*), and junior councilors (*san'yo*) and seven ministries thereunder. The President must be a member of the imperial family; Iwakura, Okubo and Saigo, who were the real decision makers, were among the twenty junior councilors appointed from among the young nobles and activists of the allied domains who participated in the coup.[25] Even though the Shogunate disappeared, the decentralized domain-based government structure remained intact, except for those territories that were confiscated from the Shogun in addition to those originally belonging to the Emperor. The famous Charter Oath of Five Articles (*gokajo no goseimon*) of March 1868, with which the Meiji government proclaimed its ruling principles, was an oath that was taken by the Emperor to the gods, combined with the oaths taken by all the domain chiefs to the Emperor.

The structure of *dajokan* was reformed several times thereafter, becoming at each step more centralized, until it was finally abolished and replaced by the Cabinet (*naikaku*) in 1885. The Constitutional Declaration (*seitaisho*), issued in 1868, incorporating the Charter Oath of a month earlier, proclaimed that all powers come under *dajokan*, and would be divided into three powers, namely the legislative, the administrative and the judicial. One ministry was assigned the legislative function, five the administrative, and another (the Ministry of Criminal Law) the judicial. This idea of the separation of powers obviously reflected the Western learning of its drafters.[26] However, later developments revealed that this was only a piece of on-the-table borrowing from the most advanced institution of the civilized world known to them.

In 1869 the structure of government was reformed, so that the two Great Ministers of Left and Right (*sadaijin* and *udaijin*) were exclusively to report to the Emperor, and to govern the entire *dajokan* that comprised all the ministries other than the Office of Rites (which was in charge of Shintoism). Two years later, another reform abolished the Office of Rites, making *dajokan* the sole inclusive office, under which three chambers were placed. Moreover, the Left Chamber (*sa-in*) that was in charge of legislative functions and the Right Chamber (*u-in*) that governed all the ministries were both to report to the Central Chamber (*sei-in*), whereas the Central Chamber was presided over by the Emperor himself, counseled by the Great Minister (*dajo-daijin*), the Junior Minister (*nagon*), and the Councilors (*sangi*). The first two of these positions were reserved for former Court nobles, while former warrior activists were to be appointed Councilors or chiefs of ministries, respect being thus duly paid to the old status system.

This central government reform of 1871 was concomitant with the fundamental restructuring of the national political system that was realized in the same year: the abolition of domains and the introduction of prefectures (*haihan chiken*). This was the most important of all the reconstruction tasks of the new government, and was again achieved stepwise in accordance with the *ritsuryo* principles. As suggested earlier, each of the numerous domains, large and small, had kept its feudal administrative prerogatives within its own territories intact, including those concerning finance, tax, currency and military forces. At this time, the combined rice yields from the territories that were directly controlled by the government and its prefectures amounted to less than a third of the national total. The overwhelming expenses for the expeditions against the Tokugawa forces (the Boshin War, which involved a force of 120,000 on the Imperial Court side and took 3,500 lives) constituted heavy burdens for all the domains that participated in the war on either side. Those that were on the losing side also had to worry about showing allegiance to the new regime.

In 1869 some of the domain chiefs who had been the main supporters of the Meiji Restoration took the initiative, under the slogan of 'Emperor's land, Emperor's subjects' (*oodo oomin*) to voluntarily return their domain territories and inhabitants to the Emperor. Other domains followed suit, and eventually the remaining domains were forced to do so (*hanseki hokan*). Then, all the former domain chiefs were appointed non-hereditary governors of their own former domains. They were allowed to take one tenth of the domain revenues; another tenth of the domain revenues went to the central government to cover military expenses. Their former vassals were to receive annual stipends out of the remaining domain revenues. All this meant that the feudal bond that had bound these warriors to their domain chiefs was permanently broken.[27]

These truly revolutionary measures naturally invited tenacious resistance from members of the warrior class, and led to several outbreaks of armed rebellion. The opening of domestic markets to international commerce, as well as civil wars, brought economic hardship to the warriors and to the rest of the population. The government had to keep peasant uprisings under control. In 1871 an Imperial Army was established, consisting of 8,000 former warriors, drawn from the three most powerful prefectures or domains represented in the government – Kagoshima (formerly Satsuma), Yamaguchi (formerly Choshu) and Kochi (formerly Tosa). With this force at his back, the Emperor convoked all the domain governors and proclaimed the edict to abolish domains and replace them with prefectures.

Thus the former 260 domains were consolidated into seventy-five prefectures, and the government became the sole provider of stipends for the former warriors. It was this reform that laid the foundation for the centralized Meiji government and for its execution of the further tasks of building a modern nation. Numerous modernizing social reforms were made around this time. In 1871 former non-warriors were allowed to marry with former warriors and nobles, while the nobles were allowed to take up any profession. In 1872 the government began to issue land certificates (*chiyken*) to private landowners that proved the ownership of land as well as the tax duty attached to it. This was to pave the way for the revision of land taxation that immediately followed. A national money tax system was introduced. In the same year, a nationwide system of schools was introduced with the slogan 'Learning is a capital asset for getting on in the world; would it do for any human not to learn?'. Also in the same year, the imperial edict on universal conscription (*chohei kokuyu*) was announced.

Formation of a unified judicial system

The judicial system of modern Japan was gradually built up in the process of the formation of the Meiji government. Its basic characteristics were inevitably determined by the political circumstances of this process.

Immediately after the new government was born, it started to compile a criminal code. The first products of this effort were the Provisional Criminal Code *kari keiritsu* of (presumably) 1868 and the Outline of the New Criminal Code *shinritsu koryo* of 1870. Both codes were based on the Chinese tradition,[28] as opposed to Western law. The government began attempts at a similar codification of civil law, but soon abandoned the undertaking, as it was too formidable a task to be tackled at this stage. For decades, many civil law matters were left to customary norms and *jori*, or the sense of reasonableness.[29] Obviously, tackling criminal law was a more urgent task for the new government, since it concerned the maintenance of social order as well as the suppression of political crimes and revolts. Thus, in the formation of the legal system, crime control and criminal prosecution tended to take precedence over the treatment of private disputes.

This tendency can also be seen in the fact, mentioned earlier, that for the first few years the judicial functions of government were assigned to the Ministry of 'Criminal Law'. The adjudication of litigation was left in the hands of prefectures and domains, where administrative officials in their own litigation sections heard the case just as they did under the old regime. Initially the Ministry of Domestic Affairs (*minbusho*) of the central government was charged with making decisions on difficult cases involving land or persons referred to it by domains and prefectures. This function was later transferred to the Ministry of Finance.[30]

It was after *haihan chiken* of 1871 that the Ministry of Justice (*shihosho*) was first introduced as an agency with comprehensive jurisdiction over matters related to law and order, including judicial administration (i.e. the administration of personnel, financial and other matters within courts), interpretation of law, administration of criminal and civil justice, and criminal investigation.[31] It was given the power to oversee all matters concerning litigation (civil or criminal) and imprisonment, including those handled by prefectures. In the next year 1872, the Statute for Regulation of Judicial Offices (*shiho shokumu teisei*), drafted by Shinpei Eto, was promulgated. Prior to the promulgation of the Statute, Eto had obtained from *dajokan* the ruling that 'the Ministry of Justice controls all the courts of the land and assumes the administrative work concerning the courts, but does not engage in the administration of justice'. This ruling is generally interpreted as providing for the autonomy of the courts in the administration of justice, separated from judicial administration.[32] On that basis the Statute provided that the Ministry of Justice be comprised of three branches: the courts, the office of prosecutors (*keiji kyoku*) and the Institute for Legal Studies (*meiho ryo*). For the courts it prescribed five ranks of court together with rules of appeal.

Accordingly, the Ministry of Justice began to requisition judicial power from the prefectures. However, this could not be done in one shot, but rather took many years. It was not easy to establish the ministerial courts all around the country, not only because it was difficult, in the absence of any tradition of professional training in Western law, to find competent persons to be appointed judges and prosecutors, but also because of strong resistance exercised by the prefectures.[33] In many prefectures the local officials administered justice until this practice was formally abolished in 1876.

On the other hand, the Statute introduced the office of prosecutor, charged with the very broad responsibility of 'protecting the legal order as well as the rights of the people, supporting good and eliminating evil, and supervising the correctness of the judgment of the court'.[34] This reveals the heavy influence on the Statute of its author's academic learning in the French legal system. The

Statute also introduced the advocate and the scrivener, although it did not contain any specific provisions as to their rights and duties.

The establishment of the Ministry of Justice was part of the political efforts of the new government to establish a centralized state structure by placing all former domains and jurisdictions under its own aegis. The political aspect of the establishment and the position of the justice ministry are well illustrated in the fate of Shinpei Eto, who was the chief advocate for the autonomous development of the judicial sphere. Eto was a low-ranking warrior intellectual of the Saga domain, which contributed its modernized military forces to the birth of the Meiji Restoration and became the fourth of the major domains that provided the core group of leaders who ran the Meiji government. Eto was instrumental in drawing his own domain into the restoration campaign, but he was not involved in the national politics of the pre-Meiji period. Instead, he was a renowned advocate of radical reforms in his own domain. Soon after the success of the Meiji Restoration, Eto was quickly recruited by the new government. He took command of the military rule of the conquered Edo, and was then appointed chief research officer in legal matters in the central government. It is believed that it was Eto who was working behind the scenes for Iwakura and Okubo in drawing up the vision of a centralized government under the Emperor, as well as the concrete plans for replacing domains with prefectures.[35] He served as Vice-minister of Education for a short time before becoming Minister of Justice in 1872.

Around the time when the Statute for Regulation of Judicial Offices of 1872 was passed, several political scandals came to light involving two leading members of the government, Minister of the Army Aritomo Yamagata and Minister of Finance Kaoru Inoue. The two were both of Choshu origin, later becoming eminent members of the Meiji oligarchy that emerged. Eto's determined attempts to prosecute them according to law was not acceptable to the core leaders of the government. In addition, there was another legal case, in which Kyoto Prefecture was sued by a merchant based on the legal rule, which had been introduced by Eto himself, which accorded citizens the right to sue local officials for infringement of their rights.[36] In the midst of the political conflicts over these issues, the government decided to cut Eto's budget request for the Ministry of Justice, while accepting that of the Army, whereupon Eto submitted his resignation. Although this resignation was not accepted and Eto was soon made Councilor instead, he was already marginalized. He was soon involved in the issue of 'punishing Korea' taken up by the Councilors' meeting. In this well known meeting of 1873, conducted with intricate political manipulations in the background, the Councilors Saigo, Itagaki, Goto and Soejima, as well as Eto, were defeated and forced to leave office. After this confrontation, known as the 'Coup of Meiji Six', Okubo became a virtual dictator in the government, and within a short time he was to execute Eto on charges of leading a rebellion of dissatisfied former warriors in Saga in 1874.[37]

Eto's intellectual radicalism, based on a knowledge of the liberal French law, served the purpose of centralizing the structure of national governance. But when it was directed toward the conduct of the central government itself, it was not tolerated. Presumably, the young Meiji government was preoccupied with the task of establishing the governing structure and promoting its policy to 'enrich the nation and strengthen the army'. It had no capacity to embrace the idea of the separation of powers and the rule of law and put it into actual operation. The same basic stance of the Meiji government of this period was evident at the next stage, when the *taishin-in* or Great Court of Judicature (GCJ) was introduced. This reform came to be realized as a concession made by the core government leaders to the dissenting elements that were gradually being pushed out of the original group who had participated in founding the Meiji government.

Some of the former Councilors who left the government along with Eto in 1873 formed the first political parties in Japan,[38] criticizing what they claimed was the dictatorial style by which the government, led by the Satsuma and Choshu group, had come to rule the country. In 1874 they submitted to the government a proposal to establish a house of representatives. This marked the beginning of the Popular Rights Movement (*jiyu minken undo*). It was as a result of negotiations conducted between the government led by Okubo and the dissenting group of influential politicians such as Kido (of Choshu origin) and Itagaki, that the Great Court of Judicature was established in 1875, together with a legislative organ called the Chamber of Seniors (*genro-in*). As a result, the judicial courts around the country that were in the hands of the Ministry of Justice now became integrated under the GCJ, constituting an entity separate from any administrative organ of government. However, the position of Chief Justice of the GCJ was deliberately placed below that of a minister in ranking order, and the Minister of Justice's control over judges was maintained. Judges were not guaranteed tenure until 1886.

The formation of the legal profession and legal education

During the pre-Meiji era the warrior officials of the Shogunate and the domains administered justice in their capacity as general administrators. However, no legal profession independent of officialdom had developed, nor had any professional education in law, even though there developed a group of officials (of junior positions) who possessed specialized knowledge and skills. These officials specialized in conducting hearings and interrogations in court, and also in drafting judgments for their superiors in accordance with statutory norms and precedents.[39] Apparently, in the early years of Meiji, many such officials were appointed judges or continued to work in local government as *de facto* judges.[40] It was inevitable, though, under the modern legal system, that they were a dying species, although it is an open question as to whether the influence of the skills and outlooks of those former bureaucrat judges disappeared from the Japanese judiciary as quickly. The Meiji government had to 'create', by statutory pronouncements, a whole new breed of legal professionals, or rather a set of new professions. In the absence of any tradition of independent professional activities in the private sector, the government had also to take initiatives in the education and training of future members of the bar.

Modern legal education in Japan formally began with the establishment of the School of the Institute of Legal Studies (*meihoryo gakko*) in the Ministry of Justice in 1871.[41] The main purpose of the School was to produce judges and prosecutors schooled in Western law to man the Ministry's courts around the country. The method adopted for achieving this was to invite a number of French lawyers (Georges Bousquet, Gustave Boissonade and several others) to teach French law in French.[42] The school started with about twenty students, who passed the tests in French and Chinese studies, and who were provided with free dormitory accomodation and food, as well as allowances.[43] The Institute was closed in 1875, and the School was incorporated into the Law School of the Ministry of Justice (*shihosho hogakko*) that was created in the same year. The students of the first class graduated in 1876, and some were sent abroad for further studies. The Law School of the Ministry of Justice then recruited students for the second class, and thirty-six of those admitted graduated in 1884. The number of lawyers produced was small, and it took them about six years to finish the program. The system did not look very effective.

Another line of legal education was started by the Ministry of Education. In 1874 the Ministry of Education opened a law department within its Tokyo Kaisei Gakko, a predecessor of the University of Tokyo. Its law program emphasized English law and admitted nine students.[44]

The private sector of the legal profession developed later, but received only perfunctory treatment. The Tokugawa Shogunate had prohibited any activities of advocacy or representation for litigants in court. It is noteworthy that this situation continued to exist even after the Meiji Restoration, until the prohibition was formally lifted in 1876 for civil matters and in 1882 for criminal matters. The profession of 'advocate' was introduced in 1872 under the title of *daigen-nin*, which was again a straight borrowing from the French legal system. Specific rules concerning the exercise of this profession were not provided until the introduction of the Regulation on Advocates (*daigennin kisok*u) of 1876. Under this Regulation, advocates were to obtain annually from the Ministry of Justice a practice certificate for a particular court, on the basis of a test for summary knowledge of law and procedures as well as good behavior, but each local government administered the test in its own way. Advocates were subjected to the disciplinary authority of judges for professional misconduct.[45]

The Regulation of Advocates was revised in 1880 to introduce a uniform national test and to make the certificate valid nationwide. At the same time, advocates were now required to join the association of advocates formed for each District Court jurisdiction, and were prohibited from forming any other association. The associations of advocates were placed under the control of prosecutors.[46]

In the process of the creation of the private sector, we encounter another instance of the political constellation exerting its lasting influence on the characteristics of the legal profession in Japan. Recall the political situation within the government regarding to Shinpei Eto's Statute of 1872 which introduced the profession of advocate (*daigen-nin*). Just after the introduction of the Statute, many people began to carry the new title of *daigen-nin* and to act as advocates. This happened to coincide with the beginning of the Popular Rights Movement, which stressed the importance of people knowing the law in order to defend their legal rights, and the importance of advocates. *Daigen-nin* formed associations to facilitate their professional practice and studies, as well as to promote public enlightenment. Their associations were often linked with the Popular Rights Movement. These circumstances made the government oligarchy suspicious of the profession. The prohibition of private association in 1880 must be understood against the background of this political confrontation between government and opposition forces. In the same year the Code of Criminal Instruction (*chizaiho*) authorized advocates (though not exclusively) to act as counsel for criminal defendants to compensate for the prohibition. Significantly enough, it is in this context that private law schools began to be established, representing a new stream of legal education. The prohibition of private association, combined with the professional need to rise to the challenge of a new public role, paved the way for the emergence of private law schools.[47]

The formative or preparatory period of Japan's modern legal system came to an end with the promulgation of the Meiji Constitution in 1889, which marked the beginning of the second period of consolidation of the Meiji government.[48] However, on the way to this culmination, there was another turning point in 1881 in the political confrontation between core members of the government and dissident groups. Minister of Finance Okuma, who was of Saga origin and one of the most prominent and influential figures in the government, was ousted from the government after making a public appeal for an early opening of the Diet. He was also openly attacking the government for its scandalous plan, prepared by another Choshu politician, Matsukata, to dispose of government properties.[49] As soon as he left office, Okuma joined the Popular Rights Movement and later formed his own political party. The government conceded to Okuma by halting its property disposal plan, and announced the imperial promise to open the Diet by the year 1890. This event, the 'Coup of Meiji Fourteen', was another of several successive concessions that the government made to dissident, more liberal elements within the small group of leaders who had joined forces in the realization of the Meiji Restoration.

It was Hirobumi Ito who began to prepare the draft of a constitution within a few years of the Coup of Meiji Fourteen. Ito came from Choshu, was a junior member of the founding group of the Meiji Restoration, and survived in government to succeed Okubo (who was assassinated in 1878) as leader of the oligarchy that formed the mainstay of the state. At this point, the government made the crucial decision to shift from the French to the German model for reconstructing the legal system of the new nation. Whereas the French model had been adopted on the basis of intellectual learning at the time of the Restoration, the choice of Prussian Germany was a product of systematic studies based on the actual political experience of ruling the newly born polity of the Far East for a few decades. This shift was crucial in completing the structure of the Meiji Government and forming the 'shape of this country'.

As a first step, Ito abolished the entire system of *dajokan* and introduced in its place a formal legal institution, a Cabinet (*naikaku*), consisting of Prime Minister and other chiefs of ministries, each directly appointed by and responsible to the Emperor. Ito himself became the first Prime Minister. The structure of the Cabinet was kept intact by the Constitution that was promulgated in 1889.

The time was ripe for the system of legal education to take its final shape. Somewhat earlier, in 1877, the University of Tokyo had been created under the Ministry of Education to succeed the *Tokyo Kaisei Gakko*, and its Faculty of Law had begun with a small number of students. The law faculty's teaching staff had a few English and Americans, but the majority were Japanese. Then, the Law School of the Ministry of Justice was transferred to the Ministry of Education in 1884, to be annexed to the University of Tokyo. Private law schools began to appear around this time. The law faculties of the present Hoosei, Senshu and Meiji universities were all founded in 1880, and Waseda (1882) and Chuo (1885) followed, and were soon placed under the supervision of the Imperial University Law School.

In 1886, with the preparatory work for the Constitution in view, and as part of the plan for the reconstruction of the nation, the government established the Imperial University, 'to meet the essential needs of the state'. The former University of Tokyo was reorganized to form part of the Imperial University.[50] The Faculty of Law, renamed the Grand School of Law (*hooka daigakko*) of the Imperial University, was given the new role of educating state officials on the German model of state bureaucracy. The number of its students was dramatically increased and instruction began to be given in Japanese. The institutionalization of legal education at the Imperial University corresponded to the introduction of the national examination for higher civil servants in 1888, from which graduates of the Imperial University were exempted. A qualifying examination for judicial officers, judges and prosecutors was introduced by the Regulation for the Appointment of Judges (*hanji toyo kisoku*) in 1884. Judges were guaranteed tenure in 1886. Codes of law were promulgated one after another, such as the Code of Criminal Procedure, the Code of Civil Procedure, and the Law of Organization of Courts, all of 1890. The Commercial Code and the Civil Code were published in the same year, although these had to be revised to become laws several years later.

Advocates came later. The Attorneys Law (*bengoshi ho*) of 1893 gave them a new title of *bengoshi*, but kept them under control of the Minister of Justice. The law introduced a qualifying examination for attorneys that was separate from the examination for judges and prosecutors. Judges and prosecutors, along with graduates of the University of Tokyo Law Faculty, were exempted from the attorneys' examination. The first choice of University of Tokyo law graduates was to become civil servants, next came judges and prosecutors, and only a minority became attorneys. With the graduates of private law schools, this ranking was exactly reversed.[51]

Conclusion

This brief historical review clearly shows that the initial political processes that gave birth to the legal profession in Japan have determined its fundamental features. Already in the early Meiji period the idea of the separation of powers was known in the abstract by the architects of the new state structure, but in the absence of any tradition of an autonomous legal profession, the system of courts and lawyers indispensable for the implementation of that ideal had to be created by the new-born government. Its first task was to institute a unitary system of courts and jurisdictions, and to produce judges and prosecutors responsible for administering justice and maintaining order. After the initial attempt at a straight importation of the French legal education system in a government law school, the Meiji oligarchy adopted a system of university education on the German model. Thus was created the tradition of university legal education being primarily aimed at training civil servants, legislators, administrators, judges and prosecutors. The education and qualification of advocates was relegated to a secondary item on the agenda, and in the context of the newly created political parties' opposition to the oligarchic government, the new profession of 'attorneys' was suspected of belonging to the forces opposing the government.

The way in which the legal profession was born corresponded to the basic structure of Meiji polity, embodied in the Meiji Constitution, that emerged at the end of the initial period of trial and error. It was constructed by a handful of former warrior statesmen, representing the extremely small ruling class, who – we might well recall that they were originally the brightest of bureaucrats in the former domain governments – ingeniously manipulated the existing legal and ideological framework of the *Ritsuryo* government under the authority of the Emperor. They started by building on the inherited culture of law and government, and ended up producing a new version of it adapted to the modern environment. This structure served them and and their bureaucratic successors well for leading the nation through the initial period of 'enriching the country and strengthening the military', until it failed catastrophically to cope with the global economic depression of the late 1920s and early 1930s. Despite the fact that journalism flourished and political parties began to be formed, again led by former warriors, and vigorously attacking the oligarchic government, the mass of the people were left as passive subjects, with minimal opportunities to participate actively as citizens in matters of law and government through legislative and judicial processes.

The basic mold in which the Japanese legal profession and legal education system was cast seems to have exerted a lasting influence on the profession, despite the various institutional modifications that were made in subsequent decades. The democratizing reforms after 1945, in particular, brought about significant changes by according each judge the power of judicial review, and by introducing the common qualifying examination, as well as practical training at the Institute for Legal Research and Training, for all the three branches of the legal profession. Nevertheless, this profession remained divided as before, and even though the position of private attorneys has been enhanced remarkably, both in quality and quantity, during the course of the following fifty years, the fundamental features have persisted until today. The principle features, as discussed in the first two sections of this chapter, may be summarized as:

1 a divided legal profession
2 a bureaucratically organized career judiciary
3 a private legal sector which carries much less prestige than the public sector, though it may be its equal in quality
4 a system of legal education oriented primarily to providing state officials and government lawyers who legislate, interpret and apply the law, and only secondarily train professional lawyers for private practice

It may be said that this structure allowed the institutionalizing of a legitimate legal order characterized by a stable and honest judiciary and a low crime rate, conditions that were undoubtedly favorable for economic development. On the other hand, the weak development of the private sector implied inadequate provision, in areas other than the large metropolitan centers, of law services to protect and promote the legal rights of individuals and firms.

The task of the Judicial Reform Council of 2001 is to alter these basic features of the Japanese judicial system by buttressing its main body, which is threatening to crumble under growing social demands, with major reconstructions. In fact its mission is defined in terms of a third pivotal reform project of recent years, following the political and administrative reforms. It is for this reason that the JRC's Final Report contains far-reaching and wide-ranging proposals. Within the field closely related to the legal profession discussed in this chapter, it proposes not only the introduction of the Graduate School of Law and reform of the Legal Examination, but also some reforms to the judiciary. It has not endorsed a wholesale shift to the 'unitary system' for recruiting judges, but proposes to vigorously promote the appointment of judges from among attorneys, as well as from among other groups such as prosecutors, administrators and legal academics. It also proposes the establishment of an independent committee to advise the Supreme Court on the nomination of candidates to be appointed judges. In addition, the JRC proposes, as a measure of broadening the popular basis of the judicial authority, a new system of lay judges in which randomly selected members of the public sit on the bench alongside professional judges to decide serious criminal cases.

The JRC's proposal for the reform of legal education, coupled with the plan to triple the size of the legal profession in fifteen years, constitutes a crucial component of its overall scheme for changing the 'shape of this nation'. However, there is a host of difficult issues and problems yet to be addressed and solved before this ambitious scheme can become a reality, and questions such as: Which of the existing institutions, and who else, would be authorized to establish a law school? What would be the content of their new teaching programs that are required to be professionally oriented, unlike the traditional generalist approach? How would the new law schools be financed? How would they conduct their admission tests? and so on. The situation is precarious, but one lesson we can draw from our brief excursion into history is that the major driving force must come from the political sphere.

Notes

1 Law to Establish the Shiho Seido Kaikaku Shingi-kai [Council on Judicial Reform] (JRC) Article 2. For the writer's own view on the political circumstances of the establishment of the JRC, see Kahei Rokumoto, 'Law and Culture in Transition' (revised draft), keynote speech for the Fourth *Sho Sato* conference on 'Japanese and US Law: Legal Reform and Socio-Legal Change in Japan', 4 November 1999.

2 JRC, 'Saishu Ikensho' [Final Report], *Shiho Kaikaku* [Journal of Judicial Reform in Japan], no. 22 (2001) pp. 65–81.

3 The report recognizes the need to make exceptions to this rule in order to allow, for financial and other reasons, certain candidates to take the legal examination without going through the graduate school.

4 Strictly speaking, the two rates are different. The pass rate is calculated on the basis of the total students who sit for the bar exam, not those who graduate.

5 The Final Report sets this figure as a goal to be achieved by around 2010, so that the size of the legal profession will be expanded to be 50,000 or more by 2018. It is important to note here that the Final Report makes it clear that these figures are presented not as any kind of ceiling, but as goals to be attained within the shortest period of time possible.

6 The Final Report, consisting of five chapters and more than 100 pages, is a comprehensive diagnosis of the Japanese judicial system and legal profession. Its main body covers three areas: (1) the institutions of the administration of justice, (2) the legal profession, and (3) the popular basis for the judicial system, and proposes many fundamental reforms in each of these. In this chapter only a few of those reform proposals, related to legal education, will be examined.

7 JRC, 'Chukan Hokoku' [An Interim Report], *Shiho Kaikaku*, no. 15 (2000) p. 173.

8 There is no lack of literature describing existing institutions of the Japanese judicial system and the historical development of those institutions. See among other sources in English, Takaaki Hattori (assisted by R. Rabinowitz) 'The Legal Profession in Japan? Its Historical Development and Present State', in Arthur Van Mehren (ed.) *Law in Japan: The Legal Order in a Changing Society (Cambridge MA: Harvard University Press, 1963);* Hideo Tanaka (ed.) assisted by Malcolm D. H. Smith, The Japanese Legal System: Introductory Cases and Materials *(Tokyo: University of Tokyo*

Press, 1976); and Meryll Dean, Japanese Legal System: Text and Materials *(London: Cavendish Publishing, 1997). There is an even larger accumulation of legal historical research based on documentary analyses. However, legal historical studies tend to concentrate on specific institutions and statutes. Little is available that presents the historical development of the Japanese judicial system in the politico-ideational context in which it was formed. This chapter is a modest attempt at filling this gap, albeit only for the initial period of its formation.*

9 Another aspect of the reform plan of the legal education that directly concerns the structure of the legal profession is that it aims at a radical expansion of the notoriously small size of the legal profession, especially that of the bar. For lack of space, I will not go into it here, except to note that the number of attorneys is closely related to the issue of the recruitment of judges that is mentioned in the main text.

10 There is a sizable number of judges (and prosecutors for that matter) who resign from the office mid-way to become attorneys.

11 The appointment and reappointment of all judges and assistant judges except for the Supreme Court Justices is made by the Cabinet from 'a list of persons nominated by the Supreme Court' (Article 8 of the Constitution). In practice, the list is prepared by the Secretariat, and accepted as it is by the Cabinet.

12 Article 76 (3) of the Constitution provides that 'judges shall be independent in the exercise of their conscience and shall be bound only by this Constitution and the laws', and Article 48 of the Courts Act provides that 'judges shall not be transferred to another post against their will'. Nonetheless, judges are regularly given an offer from the Supreme Court which they regularly accept as expected.

13 Rinshi (Rinji Shiho Seido Chosa-kai) [Ad Hoc Commission on Judicial System], *Rinji Shiho Seido Chosa-kai Iken-sho* [Opinions of the Ad Hoc Commission on the Judicial System] (Tokyo: 1964) pp. 38–41; 47. Behind this issue lies obviously an antagonistic stance taken by practising attorneys against judges and prosecutors as status groups. The bar has been demanding the 'unitary system' as a way of enhancing their status even since prewar times. However, they face a dilemma in the sense that the unitary system logically requires a radical increase in the number of attorneys, which they view as contrary to their professional interests (expressed in terms of 'increase the quantity, decrease the quality'). Up to 1999, there was a semi-formal agreement that every legislation changing the state of the legal profession must be made on the basis of the prior agreement among the three parties: the Supreme Court, the Justice Ministry (prosecutors) and the Japanese Federation of Bar Associations (JFBA). In 1999 the JRC was established based upon an explicit discarding of this tripartite consensus scheme. On 1 November 2000, The Japanese Federation of Bar Associations crossed the Rubicon when its extraordinary general meeting voted, after a long and turbulent session, to accept the executive board's proposal for a radical expansion of lawyers' numbers along the lines being discussed in the JRC.

14 Rinshi (Rinji Shiho Seido Chosa-kai) [Ad Hoc Commission on Judicial System], *Rinji Shiho Seido Chosa-kai Iken-sho* [Opinions of the Ad Hoc Commission on the Judicial System] (Tokyo: 1964) 19–22.

15 We may recall Bellah's suggestion that the Tokugawa regime, in terms of the analytical framework of social systems, exhibited primacy of the political values over the economic, the educational, or the legal. See Robert Bellah, *The Tokugawa Religion* (Chicago: Free Press, 1960).

16 See Koyo Matsuzawa, *Kindai Nihon no Keisei to Seiyo Taiken* [The Formation of Modern Japan and the Western Experience] (Tokyo: Iwanami Shoten, 1993) p. 58. It is estimated that 150 people went abroad for studies or study trips and 300 persons were sent abroad in formal missions either by the Shogunate or domains.

17 Koyo Matsuzawa, *Kindai Nihon no Keisei to Seiyo Taiken* [The Formation of Modern Japan and the Western Experience] (Tokyo: Iwanami Shoten, 1993) p. 72.
18 See Meryll Dean, *Japanese Legal System: Text and Materials* (London: Cavendish Publishing, 1997) pp. 64–5, referring to Henderson's works.
19 Ronald P. Dore, *Education in Tokugawa, Japan* (Berkeley and Los Angeles: University of California Press, 1965) ch. X: 'The Legacy', pp. 291–316.
20 J. A. A. Stockwin, *Governing Japan: Divided Politics in a Major Economy*, 3rd edn (Oxford: Blackwell, 1999) p. 14; Meryll Dean, *Japanese Legal System: Text and Materials* (London: Cavendish Publishing, 1997) 307.
21 Marius B. Jansen (ed.) *The Emergence of Meiji Japan*, (Cambridge: Cambridge University Press, 1995) p. 202.
22 See *ibid.*, referring to Maruyama's analysis of the concept of *renso*. See also Masao Maruyama, 'Chusei to Hangyaku' [Loyalty and Rebellion] (1960) reprinted in *Maruyama Masao Shu* [Collected Writings of Maruyama Masao], vol. VIII (Tokyo: Iwanami Shoten, 1996) pp. 163–277.
23 See Dan Fenno Henderson, *Conciliation and Japanese Law: Tokugawa and Modern*, vol. 1 (Seattle: University of Washington Press, 1965) ch. VI: 'Conciliation in Tokugawa Civil Trials', pp. 127–70. Tokugawa had a centralized political order despite the decentralized feudal system.
24 Ryosuke Ishii, *Taikei Nihon-shi Sosho 4: Hoseishi* [History of Legal System (Systematic Japanese History vol. 4)] (Tokyo: Yamakawa Shuppan-sha, 1964) pp. 257–8.
25 Toshihiko Moori, *Okubo Toshimichi* [Toshimichi Okubo] (Tokyo: Chuokoron-sha, 1969) pp. 123–6.
26 This was drafted by the young warrior intellectuals Yuri and Fukuoka. Fukuoka later wrote in his memoir that they referred to Bridgman's History of the United States and Fukuzawa's 'Western Affairs' (*Seiyo jijo*) besides numerous classic Japanese and Chinese legal literature.
27 Masahito Matsuo, *Haihan Chiken* [The Establishment of Prefectures in place of Feudal Domains] (Tokyo: Chuokoron-sha, 1986) pp. 27–38.
28 Paul H. Ch'en, *The Formation of the Early Meiji Legal Order* (London: Oxford University Press, 1981).
29 See Meryll Dean, *Japanese Legal System: Text and Materials* (London: Cavendish Publishing, 1997) p. 153.
30 Nobuyoshi Someno, 'Saiban Seido' [The Judicial Court System], in *Nihon Kindai-ho Hattatsu-shi Koza* [A Series of Lectures on the Development of Japanese Modern Law], vol. 6 (Tokyo: Keiso Shobo, 1959) pp. 23–4.
31 Masaaki Kikuyama, *Meiji-kokka no Keisei to Shiho-seido* [The Formation of the Meiji State and the Legal System] (Tokyo: Ochanomizu Shobo, 1993) pp. 130–1. It is to be noted, however, that the authority for ultimate decision making about all these matters was retained by *dajokan*.
32 Ryosuke Ishii, *Taikei Nihon-shi Sosho 4: Hoseishi* [History of Legal System (Systematic Japanese History vol. 4)] (Tokyo: Yamakawa Shuppan-sha, 1964) p. 305.
33 Nobuyoshi Someno, 'Saiban Seido' [The Judicial Court System], in *Nihon Kindai-ho Hattatsu-shi Koza* [A Series of Lectures on the Development of Japanese Modern Law], vol. 6 (Tokyo: Keiso Shobo, 1959) pp. 64–9.
34 Hyo Mizubayashi, 'Shin-ritsukoryo Kaitei-ritsuryo no Sekai' [The World of the Outline of the New Criminal Code and the Revised Ritsuryo], in *Kindai Shiso Taikei: Ho to Chitsujo* [System of Modern Thoughts – Law and Order] (Tokyo: Iwanami Shoten, 1992) pp. 454–551. This reflected the persistence of the Tokugawa notion that judges (*hanji*) are officials combining the functions of prosecutor and judge responsible for investigating and punishing wrongdoers, p. 463.
35 Toshihiko Moori, *Eto Shinpei* [Shinpei Eto] (Tokyo: Chuokoron-sha, 1987) pp. 67–75; 107–8.

36 This is the case known as 'Ono gumi tenseki jiken'. Hirobumi Ito, the first Prime Minister and the architect of the Meiji Constitution, criticized this institution of administrative lawsuit later in his commentary on the Constitution.

37 It is considered doubtful that Eto was really committed to the cause of the dissatisfied former warriors. It is also probable that the whole of 'Coup of Meiji Six' may well have been a plot designed to thwart the aggressive judicial policy advanced by Eto. See Toshihiko Moori, *Okubo Toshimichi* [Toshimichi Okubo] (Tokyo: Chuokoron-sha, 1969).

38 Another eminent member of this group, Saigo, openly defied the government, fell back on his home domain forces in Kagoshima, and perished in the civil war (*senan senso*) of 1877.

39 These legal materials were used within the Shogunate or domain governments as administrative directives and were not made public. For a detailed description of Tokugawa apparatus for handling litigation and its processes, see Dan Fenno Henderson, *Conciliation and Japanese Law: Tokugawa and Modern*, vol. 1 (Seattle: University of Washington Press, 1965).

40 Masaaki Kikuyama, *Meiji-kokka no Keisei to Shiho-seido* [The Formation of the Meiji State and the Legal System] (Tokyo: Ochanomizu Shobo, 1993) p. 61; Eiichi Takikawa, *Nihon Saiban-seido-shi Ronko* [On the History of Japanese Court System] (Tokyo: Shinzan-sha, 1991) p. 20.

41 The Institute was established not only for legal education, but also as an institute for legal research, charged with the compilation and translation of materials of legal history, as well as with drafting codes of law.

42 This idea is attributed to Shinpei Eto. This may be seen as representing the efforts of the government quickly to obtain officials needed for the ministries by themselves promoting the specialized fields of their competence. A similar school was established in the same year in the Ministry of Civil Engineering. Shigeru Nakayama, *Teikoku Daigaku no Tanjo* [The Birth of Imperial Universities] (Tokyo: Chuokoron-sha, 1978) p. 14.

43 Many of the first students were those who transferred from the government School of the South, the descendant of the former Shogunate school for Western learning. Masahito Matsuo, *Haihan Chiken* [The Establishment of Prefectures in place of Feudal Domains] (Tokyo: Chuokoron-sha, 1986) p. 124.

44 Tokyo Daigaku Hogaku-bu [Faculty of Law of The University of Tokyo] (ed.) *Tokyo Daigaku Hyaku-nen-shi: Hogaku-bu* [One Hundred Years of the University of Tokyo: Faculty of Law] (Tokyo: 1985): p. 9.

45 Masamizu Okudaira, *Nihon Bengoshi Shi* [A History of Japanese Lawyers] (Tokyo: Gennando Shoten, 1914) pp. 170–4.

46 *Ibid.*, pp. 297–310.

47 Hosei Daigaku Daigaku-shi Shiryo Iinkai [Committee on the History of Hosei University] (ed.) *Hosei Daigaku 1880–2000: sono Ayumi to Tenbo* [A Pictorial History of Hosei University 1880–2000] (Tokyo: Hosei University, 2000) p. 23.

48 Revision of treaties with the Western countries was still pending until 1896–9.

49 This is known as the *hokkaido kaitakushi kanyuubutsu haraisage* affair.

50 The Imperial University of Kyoto was established in 1897 (M30). At that time the original Imperial University was renamed as the Imperial University of Tokyo. Other imperial universities followed: Tohoku (1907) Kyushu (1910) Hokkaido (1918) Keijo (in Korea, 1924) Taipei (in Taiwan, 1928) Osaka (1931) and Nagoya (1939). The seven of these that were established within Japan form the seven leading national law faculties today.

51 Ikuo Amano, *Gakureki no Shakai-shi: Kyoiku to Nihon no Kindai* [Social History of Academic Credentials: Education and Japanese Modern Era] (Tokyo: Shincho-sha, 1992) pp. 235–7; 249.

References

Amano, Ikuo, *Education and Examination in Modern Japan* (Tokyo: University of Tokyo Press, 1990).

Fukushima, Masao, 'Shiho-Shokumu-Teisei no Seitei to sono Igi' [Enactment/Establishment of judicial duties and its significance], in Fukushima Masao Chosaku-shu [Collected Works of Masao Fukushima], vol. 1 (Tokyo: Keiso Shobo, 1993).

Fukushima, Masao (ed.) Nihon Kindai-ho Taisei no Keisei [Formation of the Modern Japanese Legal System], 2 vols (Tokyo: Nihon Hyoron Sha, 1981, 1982).

Henderson, Dan Fenno, 'Japanese Law in English: Reflections on Translation', *Journal of Japanese Studies*, no. 119 (1980).

——'Law and Political Modernization', in Robert E. Ward (ed.) *Political Development in Modern Japan* (Princeton: Princeton University Press, 1968).

Hosei Daigaku Daigaku-shi Shiryo Iinkai [Committee on the History of Hosei University] (ed.) *Hosei Daigaku 1880–2000: sono Ayumi to Tenbo* [A Pictorial History of Hosei University 1880–2000] (Tokyo: Hosei University, 2000).

JRC (Shiho Seido Kaikau Shingi-kai) [Judicial Reform Council] 'Chukan Hokoku' [An Interim Report], *Shiho Kaikaku* [Journal of Judicial Reform in Japan], no. 15 (2000) pp. 170–98.

Kusunoki, Seiichiro, *Meiji Rikken-sei to Shiho-kan* [The Meiji Constitutional System] (Tokyo: Keio-Tsushin, 1989).

Moori, Toshihiko, *Eto Shinpei* [Shinpei Eto] (Tokyo: Chuokoron-sha, 1987).

——*Meiji Rokunen Seihen* [The Coup of the 6th Year of Meiji] (Tokyo: Chuokoron-sha, 1979).

Rabinowitz, Richard W., 'The Historical Development of the Japanese Bar', *Harvard Law Review*, vol. 70 (1956) 61.

Rokumoto, Kahei, *Nihon no Ho-shisutemu* [The Legal System in Japan] (Tokyo: Hoso Daigaku Kyoiku Shinko-kai, 2000).

——'Law and Culture in Transition' (revised draft) keynote speech for the fourth Sho Sato conference on Japanese and US law: 'Legal Reform and Socio-Legal Change in Japan', 4 November 1999 (*American Journal of Comparative Law*, forthcoming).

——'The Heisei Reform of the Japanese Judicial System: Its Background and Prospects', public speech delivered at the University of California at Berkeley Law School, 7 November 2000.

Rokumoto, Kahei and Shozo Ota, 'The Issues of Lawyer population in Japan', in Kahei Rokumoto (ed.) *The Social Role of the Legal Profession: Proceedings of the International Colloquium of the International Association of Legal Science, ICCLP* (Tokyo: The University of Tokyo, Faculty of Law, 1993) pp. 193–209, 293–4.

Teters, Barbara, 'The Otsu Affair: The Formation of Jappan's Judicial Concience', in David Wurfel (ed.) *Meiji Japan's Centennial* (Lawrence: University Press of Kansas, 1971) pp. 36–62.

Ward, Robert E. and Denkwart A. Rustow (eds) *Political Modernization in Japan and Turkey* (Princeton: Princeton University Press, 1964).

9

OF LAWYERS LOST AND FOUND

Searching for legal professionalism in the People's Republic of China

William P. Alford

> 'I was impressed by the extent to which lawyers had penetrated the process', he [Anthony Kronman] said. 'They are on their way to a very different system of adjudication'.
>
> Sara Leitch, 'Law Dean Advises Chinese Law Reform', *Yale Daily News*, 16 September 1998, p. 1.

American scholars and policy makers concerned with legal development in the People's Republic of China share a deep faith in the value of China developing a legal profession that operates as we would like to think our own does. Indeed, this idea is so deeply ingrained that it is rarely broken out for critical examination, but instead is treated as an obvious good, the attainment of which is essentially a matter of time. Virtually all such observers seem to assume that lawyers, whether out of idealism or self-interest or some blend thereof, will prove to be a principal force leading the PRC toward the rule of law and a market economy, while some go so far as to treat the development of an indigenous legal profession as crucial to the promotion in China of a more liberal polity.

The hidden assumptions regarding the Chinese legal profession[1] found in both US academic writing and policy papers provide a fitting focus for an essay commemorating the seventy-fifth anniversary of the birth of the distinguished late Japanese legal anthropologist Professor Hiroshi Wagatsuma. Lurking not too far beneath the surface of such portrayals are further assumptions about the inexorability of convergence along a common path, remarkably (surprise) similar to our own, of the very type that Professor Wagatsuma so insightfully sought to puncture in his own writing regarding the interplay of culture and law.[2] Unexamined, such assumptions run the risk of leaving us with an impoverished understanding, not only of the role that the emerging legal profession is playing in China, but also of both the complexity of legal development there more broadly and the limits of the ideology of professionalism in law. This, in turn, may generate unwarranted expectations on our part as to the manner in which change may come in China, while reinforcing the inflated sense that far too many of us in the American legal world have of our own profession's historic importance.

This chapter consists of three sections. After a brief discussion of the manner in which the PRC's legal profession has been portrayed, the first section endeavors to depict, in more balanced terms, its growth over the past twenty years and its current situation, drawing in part on a series of interviews I conducted among Chinese practitioners between 1993 and 2000, as well as more conventional research sources. The second section then seeks to explain why scholars and policy makers, particularly in the United States, have so misunderstood the development of the Chinese legal profession, suggesting that the problem may have as much to do with their appreciation of their own legal profession as with the difficulties of comprehending China's. The final section of the chapter offers further thoughts regarding the challenges that we need to confront in thinking about the place of lawyers and legal development in the PRC.

The growth of the Chinese legal profession

American portrayals of Chinese legal development, whether for scholarly or more policy-oriented ends, have tended to take as a given the model of legality generally believed to be in effect in our country today. Only infrequently are its fundamental assumptions questioned or even scrutinized through balanced accounts of its historical development, careful consideration of the interplay of law with other norms and institutions in contemporary American society, or rigorous comparison with the experience of other nations. The result, all too often, is a faith that scrupulous adherence to what is presented as the American model will suffice to bring about major and desirable legal and perhaps political reform in China. These observers also tend to take an approach toward Chinese legal development that sometimes overly exalts modest steps made in emulation of the model, or more typically, bemoans China's failure better to appreciate and absorb the lessons we provide.[3]

Nowhere is this cast of mind more evident than in treatment of the legal profession. At its most pronounced, this leads scholars of considerable reputation to make what this chapter will argue are extravagant claims about the character and potential (at least in present circumstances) of the profession. Consider, for instance, the following assertion from *Dealing in Virtue*, a celebrated 1996 book by Bryant Garth, President of the American Bar Foundation (the United States' preeminent center for socio-legal research) and Yves Dezalay, the leading disciple of Pierre Bourdieu in legal studies.

> Law may begin to rival Communism – perhaps more precisely, the legal profession may rival the Party – as the leading legitimating authority. Law may provide a kind of neutral ground between

> competing national elites. As we shall see, there is also evidence that the US version of law and legal practice is of particular importance.[4]

Garth and Dezalay's views may be among the more fulsome, but they find echoes in the writings of some of our more astute and otherwise sober analysts of China, as well as in the words of leaders of American legal education (such as those of Dean Kronman quoted at the beginning of this essay), pillars of our bar and bench, and shapers of pertinent dimensions of American foreign policy. So it is, for example, that Jonathan Hecht of Yale, the author of an influential study on criminal justice, assumes that the growing involvement of lawyers will perforce advance the rule of law and human rights.[5] Or that Pei Minxin, who has taught at Princeton, posits that the legal system could be the '"back door" through which a gradual process of democratic transition could be introduced' and the party's power 'contested and constrained' with China's 'emerging professional legal community', potentially constituting 'an autonomous social group capable of concerted political action' in the attainment of these goals.[6] Or that Randall Peerenboom of UCLA, among the most accomplished of Americans who has written about lawyers in China, suggests that, whatever problems may now afflict the profession, at a minimum, the desire of competent attorneys to replace *guanxi* (roughly, 'connections') with legal substance will, in time, be a significant factor in promoting the rule of law more broadly within China.[7] Much the same positive reading of the development of the Chinese profession to date and considerable faith in it future prospects underlie the very considerable funding and energies that multilateral organizations (such as the World Bank and the Asian Development Bank),[8] foundations (most notably Ford),[9] and governmental bodies (including the European Community and the United States government via the State Department's rule of law initiative) are expending on it.[10] A similar sense of the profession informs the strategy of important human rights organizations, such as the Lawyers Committee for Human Rights, which recently lauded the PRC bar and wrote of its potential 'to play a vital role in encouraging more far-reaching reforms'.[11] It is also echoed in much trumpeted announcements by the American Bar Association and similar actors about their recently discovered PRC brethren.[12]

So, what is wrong with this picture? How, I have been asked when venturing ideas of the type this chapter will discuss (especially in the halls of American legal academe or other such precincts), could one not share the aforementioned enthusiasm? Isn't this the very thing that those of us who have long toiled in the obscurity of Chinese legal studies have been waiting for and have something of an obligation to cultivate?

The answer, at least to the academic dimension of these questions, has three principal components. The first is that, as a simple descriptive matter, the role of the profession, if not of legal development in China more generally, has been significantly overstated to date. The second is that the character of the Chinese legal profession has been badly misunderstood, with considerable consequences for assessment of what it may (or may not) have done to foster a rule of law and liberalism more generally. The third is that while change of the type that many American and other observers desire may be possible over the long run, we lack an empirical foundation or even strong theoretical underpinnings for the tone of assurance that, consciously or otherwise, infuses such sentiments. The remainder of this section will address these three issues.

It would certainly be erroneous to ignore either the exponential growth in the size of the Chinese legal profession over the past twenty years, or the accompanying changes in its manner of organization, educational attainments or relationship to officialdom, let alone the very substantial ways in which the Chinese legal system more generally has developed since the end of the Cultural Revolution in the mid-1970s. In little more than a generation, the Chinese bar has expanded from 3,000 members to more than 125,000, with the state continuing to make noises about its plans for China to have 300,000 lawyers by the end of the current decade.[13] Whereas the operative legal framework in 1981 spoke of state legal workers, the current principal governing national statute describes lawyers as professionals with duties to society as well as to the state.[14] Nor, it is fair to say, are we dealing only with issues of size and nomenclature here, as more than a third of China's law firms, all of which previously were under direct state ownership, are now organized as partnerships or collectives, and there is considerable evidence, at least at the anecdotal level, of lawyers wishing to shield their practice from intensive state scrutiny, if for no other reason than to avoid taxes as well as unlawful exactions.

Even as we recognize such changes in the Chinese profession, however, we would do well not to overstate the impact that they are making. Resort to law and lawyers remains very much the exception in Chinese affairs both large and small. This is so notwithstanding the inordinate publicity accorded such matters, particularly in the western media (where they have a bit of the dancing bear quality that also greets foreigners who manage to utter more than a few garbled phrases in Mandarin). Perhaps most tellingly, the Communist Party, which is not only the nation's leading repository of political power, but which also continues to be its single most consequential actor economically and in many other respects, remains above the state's law, both as a formal and as a practical matter, as has been borne out all too painfully by those who have sought through the courts to cabin it,[15] even as the Party remains intimately involved in the selection and oversight of judicial personnel.[16] The same insulation from the state's law holds true for individual members, particularly those of consequence, who have been far more likely to be called to task for corruption (whether in their governmental or Party guises) via the Party's internal disciplinary processes than through public positive law, save for those unlucky enough to be singled out for exemplary punishment.[17]

It is not only important cadres or others within the Party, however, who have yet to acquire a taste for lawyers. Litigation in the PRC rose steadily over the past decade to the current level of approximately six million cases per annum,[18] but, even before we scrutinize the content of such actions, their number needs to be set in context. To a far greater extent than most outside observers appreciate, China remains fundamentally an administrative state, with administrative recourse (whether for routine civil matters or to address deviance, as through reeducation through labor[19]) being the norm, rather than exception, and with respect to which lawyers essentially have scant role representing clients. Beyond this, lawyers have had little, if any, part to play in vital avenues through which tens of millions of individuals routinely seek redress, including the letters and visits (*xinfang*) process,[20] extrajudicial mediation,[21] resort to rice roots legal workers (*falugongzuozhe*) and other yet more informal processes.[22] But, of course, we do need to scrutinize litigation; if so, we can see that not more than approximately one out of every ten litigants appears to have been using legal counsel.[23] And, if we press our inquiry further, we may do well to question the simple equation that virtually all observers make between litigation and legality,[24] by asking precisely what it is that lawyers are doing even when present, given the near certainty of conviction in criminal cases (the area in which citizens are, by far, most likely to be represented by counsel),[25] the fact that the judiciary continues to be characterized by a relatively low level of legal training,[26] and the proliferation of accounts of lawyers and judges using litigation as a pretext for bribery.[27]

One might respond to criticisms regarding the frequency with which citizens use lawyers by suggesting that it does not necessarily diminish the core argument of those who have been relatively sanguine about the building of a legal profession in China and its implications, but instead shows simply that the process is more time-consuming than many assumed, or perhaps that more resources ought to be devoted to the task than they had initially thought. But as the aforementioned account suggests, rather than presuming that the changes of recent years *a fortiori* have been a boon for the rule of law, we need more thoroughly to probe what is underway in China. That type of research, in part regarding illicit behavior, some of which may carry severe criminal sanctions (including the death penalty) is not easy to conduct, most especially in a society in which many matters, particularly concerning the administration of justice, remain off-limits, especially for foreigners. There are, however, growing numbers of articles to be found in Chinese media regarding widespread corruption in legal processes (which lawyers are inclined to blame on judges and judges on lawyers – but few, at least in print, on the Party as an institution). My own interviews of scores of Chinese and foreign lawyers, judges, legal academics and businesspeople working in Beijing, Shanghai and other major cities suggest that the expansion of the Chinese bar has been accompanied by increasing corruption, with lawyers often a conduit for, if not the instigators of, such behavior.[28] Indeed, although the list of questions I developed for these interviews did not specifically address corruption, the lawyers interviewed brought up this topic themselves, with some expressing regret at what they described as the need to engage in such behavior in order to stay competitive, and others boastful about what they claimed was their capacity to reach virtually any Chinese judge. My sampling, to be sure, makes no pretense of being broadly representative of the nation's bar as a whole. If anything, however, it drew disproportionately on urbanites with elite legal educations (whether obtained in China or abroad or both), whose predominantly business-oriented law practices and broader life experience generally involve a greater exposure to the sort of international norms typically lauded by those who vest considerable hope in China's developing a domestic counterpart to the bar in this country.

Presumably, without minimizing such problems, some outside analysts may be tempted to view them as likely to abate substantially as increasingly professionalized lawyers (and others) with an interest in the cleaner administration of justice make their presence felt. That may happen, but then again, it may not – for reasons having to do with the degree to which the Chinese legal profession remains interwoven with the Party/state. Western, and especially American, observers remain far too ready to read the Communist Party's ebbing enthusiasm for the ideology and economics of Marxism as encompassing either a concomitant receptivity to competing sources of authority or a naive ignorance or obliviousness on the part of the Party's leadership to the potential impact of forces set in motion by the policies of the reform era.[29] We need to guard against underestimating either the Party's desire to retain power or the self-interest of those who are benefitting from the manner in which power is now held and exercised.[30]

The Party/state remains far more involved in the professional lives of lawyers than most foreign observers (perhaps blinded by what I have elsewhere described as the 'tasselled loafers' phenomenon[31]) recognize, or than Chinese attorneys, conscious of appearances, would wish to acknowledge.[32] Through the Ministry of Justice (MOJ) and its sub-national counterparts, it continues directly to have the authority to determine such vital indicia of professional independence, as that term is understood in the West, as the size of the profession, admission, educational requirements, modes of organization, official fee schedules, and disciplinary proceedings, among others. Nor have the MOJ's much vaunted efforts to assume a posture of macro (*hongguan*) oversight while leaving day-to-day governance to the bar associations done much to promote professional autonomy, given the ways in which, for example, the MOJ has filled the leadership ranks of the All China Lawyers Federation (*Quanguo lushi xiehui*) with its own personnel and has displayed little interest in supporting the calls that have arisen for malpractice measures that might make lawyers more subject to the discipline of the marketplace.[33]

The foregoing links have important implications for thinking about the independence of lawyers from the Party/state, some such lines having the potential for direct political influence and others constraining the bar in more subtle, but ultimately more consequential, ways. So it is, for example, that notwithstanding the tendency of most foreign observers to view the Party/state as largely having written off direct ideological control, there are scores of regulatory measures governing law practice in Beijing that, *inter alia*, require that law firms form Communist Party cells and senior lawyers provide junior colleagues with ideological as well as practical training. And so it is that the lawyers bureau of the Beijing municipal government, which oversees the annual renewal of lawyers' licenses, in 1999 instructed attorneys not to represent persons detained during the crackdown on the Falungong movement.

To heed the state's on-going presence in the affairs of Chinese lawyers is not to suggest that the nature of its involvement is unchanged from the days when socialism was more than an adjective used to justify whatever economic measures the Party might wish to promote. Senior partners interested in maximizing revenues may be none too keen to spend time in empty ideological exercises, while warnings against representing the Falungong and other activists are, as one of the more outspoken members of Beijing's legal community put it, utterly superfluous. But before we break out the *maotai* and celebrate the ways in which the profit motive may be sapping the ideological content of the Party/state's efforts at political control, we need soberly to consider the possibility that it may be reinforcing the Party's hold on power, and impeding, rather than facilitating, movement toward the rule of law specifically and liberalism more generally.

There are undoubtedly exceptions, but it could be argued that at least some in the Chinese bar, and perhaps most especially elite business practitioners in the capital, have struck a Faustian bargain with the Party/state, willingly accepting a good life materially and in terms of prestige and security in return for foregoing certain of the attributes (most notably, a considerable measure of independence from the state) generally associated with legal professionalism in liberal democratic states, and for acquiescing in the role the Party has accorded itself in Chinese political and legal life. This is perhaps most readily apparent in the array of corporatist alliances formed between the Party/state and lawyers.[34] At their most extreme, these may include links between officialdom and law firms in which work is directed, foreign study opportunities granted, licenses for specialized tasks awarded, and permits clients need doled out in return for pecuniary gain. We ought not, for instance, be any more mesmerized by the proliferating forms of ownership of PRC law firms than we would be by those of industrial enterprises. For as is the case in the latter, so too, in the former, placards suggesting that a firm is non-state may still mask close financial and other ties to pertinent officials, while an on-going designation as state-owned does not necessarily mean that we can rest assured that all proceeds are, at the end of the day, finding their way into state coffers.

But even if such practices are not as widespread as my interviewing would seem to suggest, there is the arguably more vexing dilemma presented by the ways in which lawyers benefit from the current distribution of power. This is neither to paint all PRC lawyers with a single brush,[35] nor to ignore challenges that legal professionals may face worldwide, but rather to demand that those of us who consciously target China's lawyers as likely to be a major force in promoting greater liberality, confront such institutional factors and associated collective action problems (e.g. the strong disincentive, noted by many lawyers I interviewed, to eschew bribery if one wishes to retain clients). These factors surely present a daunting and very concrete set of challenges that noble visions of the place of legal professionals in other societies alone cannot will away.

Why observers misunderstand the development of the Chinese legal profession

Why is it, then, that we are so inclined to see lawyers in the PRC as, in effect, junior colleagues – cut from the same cloth as their American brethren, but needing a bit more tailoring before their professional attire fits them as smartly as we like to think ours fits us (or at least once did)? The answer is in some respects quite obvious, in others appreciably less so. Ironically, the more obvious respects are those concerning the supposedly exotic Orient, the less apparent those much closer to home, linked to the ways in which we American lawyers and legal academics think of the very profession we seek to propagate.

There is no particular mystery to or instructive novelty about many of the difficulties that impede the conduct of research into topics such as the place of the legal profession in China. In this, as in many other areas, it is rarely easy to examine facets of Chinese life that might be politically sensitive because they touch directly on either the Party's power or abuses thereof (as with corruption at high levels). Notwithstanding a movement toward greater transparency made in conjunction with various bilateral trade agreements or with accession to the World Trade Organization (WTO), Chinese authorities continue to limit access to potentially pertinent materials. Normative documents that may override positive laws are often limited to *neibu* or 'internal circulation' (i.e. no foreigners, and in some instances few Chinese, need apply). An example is the Beijing rules on the formation of party cells in law firms (e.g. all cells must have at least three Party members).[36] On top of this, there are the endemic problems of working with official Chinese statistics – which in this area purport to tell us precisely how many times lawyers negotiated contracts (down to the last *renminbi*), drafted opinion letters, and provided other forms of legal guidance, but which differ between their public and internal versions and provide no information as to how many citizens were executed or sent to reeducation through labor, with (or, more typically, without) the benefit of counsel.[37] There is little new or intriguing about such impediments to scholarly understanding.

More interesting are the ways in which prominent figures in the scholarly and policy community in this country have read, or misread, the Chinese landscape. The point here is not that one expects that all who would venture to work with or write about China must possess the equivalent of an area studies background; so steep an entry price would deter many who may have contributions of value while privileging others whose vision may suffer constraints of their own, including insufficient disciplinary depth or comparative breadth.

Rather, it is to decry the ignorance or arrogance of those who would deign to prescribe for another society without first taking the trouble to consider basic issues of historical experience, institutional structure, political power and the like – to wit, the type of due diligence that we would demand of any foreign observer deigning to suggest ways in which our society might better itself. In some instances, this may be a product of what Bruce Ackerman of Yale recently bemoaned in the *Harvard Law Review* as the stunning lack of knowledge of the world beyond our borders demonstrated by American legal academics, even relative to our brethren in political science.[38] In other situations, it may result from the soothing sound of one's Chinese interlocutors invoking language that we, not always listening closely, may associate with liberal legality, as figures ranging from Jiang Zemin through members of the dissident community, speak of ruling the country through law (*yi fa zhi guo*).[39] In yet others, it may have to do with the desire on the foreign side to disseminate values deeply cherished here or to use China as a staging ground to re-fight our own ideological battles or otherwise vindicate signature theoretical positions in the manner Richard Madsen so artfully describes in more general terms in *China and the American Dream*.[40] And in yet others, it may be driven by a need to undertake 'legal exportation projects', designed as much with an eye toward satisfying domestic American political concerns or economic interests as with the recipient country in mind.[41]

However interesting such concerns may be, ultimately they sound very much in the familiar comparativist's key of non (area) specialists not knowing as much as they need to about something that is removed from their principal line of endeavor. There is, however, a more novel and engaging focus, whether from the vantage point of those wishing to probe more deeply into the reasons why the transplantation of foreign institutions into China is so problematic, or from the vantage point of those who are far more concerned with American legal thought than with anything Chinese. It is that the Chinese case can help us to see limitations of a fundamental nature in the non-China-related work of those who are seeking to foster the growth of an American-style legal profession in China. The remainder of this section supports this point with a consideration of the understanding of the legal profession portrayed in Dean Kronman's landmark book, *The Lost Lawyer*.[42] Kronman, to be sure, has not written about China specifically, but as the epigraph introducing this chapter illustrates, he has, in his role as Dean of the Yale Law School and as US chair of a bilateral conference on legal education, launched under the auspices of the State Department in conjunction with President Clinton's 1998 trip to the PRC, played a role both in disseminating American norms to China and in portraying China's norms here.[43] Perhaps even more importantly, whatever Kronman's direct involvement in things regarding China, the conception of the lawyer set forth in his book – which one commentator termed 'a major document in the history of American law' and which has generally been treated as one of the most important books of its generation regarding the legal profession[44] – not only surely has made its influence felt in efforts to propagate American models of lawyering in China, but also exemplifies a central strand of thinking in this country about what the legal profession should be.[45]

At first blush, a book entitled *The Lost Lawyer: The Failing Ideals of the Legal Profession* might seem an odd choice in a discussion of efforts to foster American notions of lawyering overseas. But then again, Kronman clearly did not write his nearly 400-page book simply to mark the imminent passing of a golden age. Rather, very much in the manner of Confucian argumentation (even if not recognized as such), *The Lost Lawyer* is better understood as invoking the past in order both to make points about the deficiencies of the present and to suggest what a better future might be.

A complex book, to be sure, *The Lost Lawyer*'s central proposition is that over the course of the second half of the twentieth century, the legal profession in the United States experienced a falling away from the ideal of the lawyer-statesman, with serious ramifications for our polity and society in general. To understand why this is, we need briefly to consider Kronman's vision of politics. For him, politics ought not to be construed only as the battling out of previously defined sets of interests, but instead as a potential act of fraternity in the course of which, through reasoned deliberation, interests can be developed, refined and either reconciled for the larger good or, if truly incommensurate, accommodated in as an intelligent and fair a manner as reason permits.

The lawyer-statesman, Kronman argues, has a singular role to play in this all-important enterprise, so central to a sense of community, because the lawyer-statesman, by definition, 'excels at the art of deliberation … [and] is a paragon of judgement'.[46] That means that even as he represents private interests vigorously, the lawyer-statesman is able to discern their impact on the public interest and to work with his or her clientele to define the former in a manner consistent with the latter, to the longer-term benefit of both interests. So, too, in public life the lawyer-statesman is able to assist members of the polity to transcend parochialism and to realize their deeper interests as part of a larger community.

The attributes that make one a lawyer-statesman, contends Kronman, are 'trait[s] of character' further cultivated through appropriate study to produce a prudence or 'practical wisdom'. In effect, says Kronman in words that unwittingly echo the Confucian *Analects*, we should 'look to him for leadership … [and] praise him for his virtue and not just his expertise'.[47] That course of study, continues Kronman, in words that do not echo the *Analects*, is rooted in the case method classically employed in American law schools, in which students, by virtue of being forced to imagine themselves as judges in exceptionally close appellate cases, learn not only to see issues from many sides, but, in so doing, also learn to cultivate the art of being simultaneously sympathetic and rigorous, and to understand that politics, and, indeed life generally, prizes the art of blending that which is ideal with that which is practical.

Alas, bemoans Kronman, forces in both the world of ideas and that of affairs, have over the past half-century increasingly militated against realization of the lawyer-statesmen ideal. In the former regard, the legal academy has increasingly abandoned the very thing that set law apart from other disciplines – namely the common law case method – in favor of what he describes as a belief in 'scientific law reform', that may have begun at the end of the nineteenth century with Harvard Law School Dean Christopher Columbus Langdell and that may have grown further through the legal realists. Today this belief finds expression in schools of thought as seemingly varied as law and economics and critical legal studies. Whatever the virtues of economics or philosophy (or social science in general), they are, to his way of thinking, inferior to the law for the nurturing of the 'practical wisdom' Kronman so prizes. This is because they stress an abstract and, in his mind, excessively ideological approach toward the resolution of problems that need to be understood in a more nuanced manner if one is to strike a prudential balance between the desirable and the attainable, or between the general rule and individual circumstance. In effect, the growing reliance on these disciplines beyond the law has 'encouraged lawyers to view themselves as "social engineers" engaged in the structural design of institutions ... focused on more-abstract concerns ... in contrast to the common lawyer of the past, who built by indirection and without a conscious plan in view'.[48] Compounding this trend in the world of ideas has been a transformation in the nature of law jobs, whether at the bar or on the bench (or in the academy), which in an atmosphere of increasing commercialization and complexity have become almost too specific – as exemplified by their growing concern with technique and specialized knowledge that have dulled, rather than sharpened, the traits of character that when properly honed may yield the qualities of deliberation he so prizes.

But the seeming bleakness of parts of *The Lost Lawyer* notwithstanding, all is not despair, for why, otherwise, would Kronman have taken the trouble to write so substantial a book? We can indeed, he argues, recapture the ideal of the lawyer-statesman if we reshape our institutions accordingly (which presumably is how he would justify accepting the deanship of a law school known more for its commitment to social scientific and philosophical inquiry than to traditional doctrinal analysis).[49] And perhaps in China, which, as fortune would have it, has embarked in our lifetime on an epic effort of singular magnitude wholly to reconstruct itself legally, we have a critical role to play in helping to implement this ideal – which may also provide us with the opportunity, perhaps not easily available in our own society, to acquit ourselves as lawyer-statesmen of historic note.

Kronman's devotion to the ideal of the lawyer-statesman may in some respects seem excessive, but the general sentiment it expresses informs a good deal of both academic work and policy efforts concerning the development of a legal profession in China. We advocate the profession's further growth in China not so much to produce technicians (though there is, no doubt, some element of that desired by business and others who regularly need to deal with the

PRC), but more so because we see lawyers as especially well equipped to advance concerns that we value – such as the rule of law, devotion to a market economy, and even democratic government – be it through active propagation or simply the power of the example of their daily professional lives.

Ironically, however, some of the very same qualities that Kronman extols for the part they play in the nurturing of the lawyer-statesman bear a measure of responsibility for the misunderstanding of the Chinese profession reflected in Kronman's own observations and in both scholarly and policy circles more broadly. We can see this in Kronman's (repeated) statements, upon which he places great weight, of the nature and genesis of the habits of mind and traits of character that warrant our vesting leadership in the lawyer-statesman. The qualities of practical wisdom and political fraternity that we (should) so cherish, Kronman tells us, are not primarily about 'the structural design of institutions' of the type fostered through immersion in economics or philosophy and the capacity they promote to see things in broad, abstract, and perhaps ideological terms. Rather, they involve a more Solomonic interstitial, incremental balancing of potentially incommensurate ends that is imparted by the type of analysis and way of thinking that the case method fosters.

Structure, however, does matter. Kronman, and virtually all others who would share what they take to be the ideals of liberal legal professionalism in the US with China, seem to be assuming that these ideas are so powerful they will not only blossom in the PRC, but will also play a critical role in the liberalization of distinctly illiberal institutions there. As Dezalay and Garth put it at one point in a prognosis that, one suspects, echoes the thinking of many Americans engaged in legal transplantation, soon 'the legal profession may rival' the Communist Party. As recounted in the first section of this chapter, the record so far suggests the opposite – namely that it is the Communist Party, and China more generally, that is doing the far larger part of the shaping, judging from the ways in which the PRC profession has assisted the Party/state in legitimating its position[50] and, perhaps even more tellingly, from the role that lawyers appear to be having in exacerbating the corruption that so afflicts judicial and administrative life in China.[51]

That this is so ought not necessarily to be surprising if one were to realize that the qualities Kronman prizes would be better served were they to be informed by a greater appreciation of structure, not to mention a healthy dose of humility. The history in China of Buddhism, Christianity, Marxism – and many other ideas possessed of a longer history, more innate power and more effective proselytizing than legal professionalism has – underscores the fact that we do not need to see context as static in order to appreciate the ways in which it shapes that which would shape it.[52] And to take a more contemporaneous illustration that would seem obvious, but that has largely been ignored in consideration of the value of external cultivation of the legal profession, lawyers in the PRC function in an institutional setting quite different from that of our own society.[53] The Chinese bench has, at least in theory, been cast in a civil law frame (albeit quite different from that of liberal democratic states with a continental system), while we promote a distinctly common law model of the profession, typically with utter obliviousness to how things function in civil law jurisdictions.[54] And to put it mildly, PRC authorities have not yet come to prize independence in any major dimension of public life.[55] In addition there are massive and immediate incentives for lawyers, among others, to accept a system arrested between plan and market, with many a bottleneck (and concomitant opportunities for rent-seeking), rather than to push for more thorough-going reform and accompanying competition.[56]

But the failure of Kronman and others like him to engage in the type of inquiry that might elicit such an understanding, raises broader questions, reaching beyond the PRC to our own society. For example, as a normative matter, how do we know that the values Kronman so strongly advocates are worthy of broader adoption or even of retention here if, as our own society and bar have become more democratic, pluralistic and prosperous, each, along with the bench and the legal academy, has, by Kronman's own account, largely rejected them? More practically, how do we know that the ideal Kronman sketches, centered around a call for a small legal-aristocratic leadership, is not so linked to the conditions (including a far more homogeneous elite) of the period within which Kronman suggests it flourished (i.e. this nation's first century) that even if desirable, it is unsustainable, given the current structure of American life, economically, politically and socially? And, to take but one more illustration, if we are so uncertain about the links between this ideal and the society from which it has emerged, how are we (or those whose lives it would shape) to determine its feasibility in another society that presumably differs in important respects from our own?

In one sense, Kronman's relative slighting of what he terms the structural in favor of practical wisdom seems odd, given that he earlier produced a book-length study of Weber's approach to law,[57] and given that *The Lost Lawyer* describes itself as a work of philosophy and sociology that states quite explicitly that philosophical argument is the only remaining hope for recapturing the ideals embodied by the lawyer-statesman.[58] Yet, in another sense, it is very much of a piece with the great majority of American writing about the sociology of the legal profession which, whether by lawyers, sociologists, or others, tends to present its theoretical findings as having universal validity, even if they emerge from work principally concerned with the United States.[59] This approach is taken in discussions of schools as seemingly different as the functionalism of Talcott Parsons,[60] the professionalization project of Magali Sarfatti Larson,[61] the market-driven focus of scholars running the political gamut from Richard Abel[62] to Richard Posner, and the knowledge-centered inquiry of Andrew Abbott,[63] David Trubek,[64] Bryant Garth[65] and others. It has produced a sociology of the profession that assumes the US-specific backdrop of a weak executive (relative to a parliamentary system), a highly independent bench, and a strong profession largely distinct from the state but less so from commerce. It also assumes a vibrant civil society to such a degree that the theoretical signposts emerging from it do not map comfortably even onto liberal democratic states with a civil law heritage, let alone societies such as the PRC.[66] Perhaps even more crucially, because it takes our institutions so much as a given, such work, in the end, does not probe as thoroughly as it might into the relationship, even here, between the particular institutions of our society and the nature and role of our legal profession. As such, it is far less illuminating academically and far less empowering for those engaged in legal development than is work that is of a more nuanced historical or richly comparative bent.[67]

The challenge of thinking about lawyers in the PRC

Appearances to the contrary, the principal purpose of this paper has not been to follow in the Harvard tradition of faulting legal scholarship emanating from Yale. Instead, it has been to utilize the phenomenon of Dean Kronman's hope of finding (or implanting) in China the ideals of legal professionalism that he believes we are losing here as a focal point for reflecting on what is, assuredly, the most concerted effort in world history to spawn a legal profession. For, as this brief concluding section will endeavor to suggest, the Chinese experience raises difficult but essential questions not only about China, but about legal professionalism, legal academe, and law more generally.

For all its use of the tools of sociology and philosophy, Kronman's book does not yield as much insight as at least this observer wishes it had into the broad implications of professionalism from the vantage point of either discipline as we turn to the Chinese case. From a sociological perspective, we need to know far more than we can glean from *The Lost Lawyer* (and most other writing regarding the legal profession) about the interplay between ideas of professionalism and broader institutions and norms. If, for example, Robert Gordon is correct in his provocative hypothesis that the patterns of American liberalism made themselves felt not only in tangible form, such as the manner in which the late nineteenth-century elite New York bar organized itself for the practice of law, but also in the very ways in which those lawyers thought through legal problems, what does this suggest for our consideration of lawyers in the as yet decidedly illiberal PRC setting?[68] Or, to use Kronman's frame of analysis, what does it mean to speak of the lawyer-statesman as possessing a singular capacity to formulate and articulate a society's interests through politics, in a setting where the range of views that might be given voice remains sharply constrained, and where behind the state and its law lurks the Party? Or, if what Kronman describes as the qualities that distinguish lawyers from other intellectuals in our society can only be cultivated through the common law case method, what does that suggest about the prospects for the bar in civil law jurisdictions, even in liberal democratic civil law states, let alone China? And what are the implications of promotion of a legal profession for the access of citizens, particularly among society's more vulnerable groups, to dispute resolution, especially if historically grounded alternatives to formal legal processes (such as mediation) are cut back as the bar and the state's law grow?

Nor are the questions we need explore from a philosophical viewpoint any easier. If we believe that the high ideals undergirding our profession are failing here, what is the moral basis for our seeking to persuade the Chinese or anyone else to adopt them? If we believe that the ideals of legal professionalism are linked to or dependent upon the institutions and values of liberalism, does that obligate us to push first or simultaneously for broader political change and, if so, on what moral foundation? And if so sweeping a course is either inappropriate or impractical, what are the implications of our placing so great an emphasis on legal professionals, if not legal reform more generally, in the absence of broader political change?

Lurking beneath many of these questions, both sociological and philosophical, are fundamental tensions in the nature of lawyering and law (and, for that matter, legal academe), at least in this society, that Kronman slights in his hope of promoting the ideal of the lawyer-statesman and of which most American observers seem essentially oblivious as they seek to foster legal development in the PRC. Kronman, reflecting, one imagines, the pride that a great many Americans who would export our legal institutions have had in at least the ideals of our legal profession, clearly is taken with the sentiment expressed in de Tocqueville's statement that 'it is at the bar or the bench that the American aristocracy is found' – which he both quotes on the first page of his book and affirms with the observation that 'judging by the wealth and influence of lawyers in contemporary America, one might conclude that his famous dictum is as true today as when he uttered it a hundred and fifty years ago'.[69] Kronman, however, does not quote de Tocqueville's accompanying admonition – that although lawyers

> value liberty, they generally rate legality as far more precious; they are less afraid of tyranny than of arbitrariness, and provided that it is the lawgiver himself who is responsible for taking away men's liberty, they are more or less content.[70]

This important dimension of de Tocqueville's thinking is instead captured, if at all, in a fleeting acknowledgment well into *The Lost Lawyer* that 'the observation that American lawyers tend to be conservative … [has] been made before most famously by Tocqueville', and Kronman's statement that our bar has tended to be 'closely connected to the propertied class' and to have a disdain, coming from 'above all, the discipline of legal reasoning … for the unruly proceedings of democratic assemblies'.[71] American lawyers as a whole may (or may not) be conservative in the sense Kronman suggests, but that proposition, I would argue, fails adequately to convey the grave danger – regarding lawyers' potential proclivity to sacrifice liberty and embrace tyranny – against which de Tocqueville sounded his warning, both in the above-cited passage and in his further observation that a ruler 'faced by an encroaching democracy' would do well to bring lawyers into his government, for 'having entrusted to them a despotism taking its shape from violence, perhaps he might receive it back from their hands with features of justice and law'.[72]

My point here is not to deny the good that lawyers can do. Our history and that of other nations contains many an admirable example of lawyers deeply dedicated to the promotion of liberty through law.[73] Rather, it is to urge that we not lose sight of de Tocqueville's prescient observation regarding the profession's double-edged capacity, borne out in our history and with analogs elsewhere, to facilitate very different ends. One need not lapse into a relativism that would equate the US and PRC to observe that even as we take note of a 98–99.5 per cent conviction rate in China in our discussion of the role of counsel there, we might also want to remain mindful, as we consider the profession here, of the fact that some 90 per cent of criminal cases in this country are resolved through plea bargaining (on which formal constitutionally oriented procedural protections cast at best a distant shadow). An awareness of the complex picture de Tocqueville actually paints would seem to require that those who speak only of the profession's promise in China explain both why we would have reason to expect more of it there[74] and why the Chinese leadership, which is quite committed to maintaining its distinctly non-democratic hold on power, seems so intent on promoting the growth of the legal profession.[75] The recognition that law may be dual-edged should, in turn, prompt us to stay attentive (as de Tocqueville also observed regarding the American experience) to the subtle and not always self-conscious ways in which lawyers and law may channel energies for political change into legal avenues, often to the fundamental preservation of the status quo and, not coincidentally, the enrichment of lawyers themselves. That may be one thing in a state that is essentially liberal democratic, and quite another in a nation that remains highly authoritarian.[76]

The foregoing presents a stiff challenge to lawyers and others concerned with the legal profession and legal development in the PRC, particularly if we also seek to remain cognizant of the ways in which legalization may privilege some members of society, and the impact it may have on less formal modes of dispute resolution and citizen redress. Dedicated to the good that lawyers and law can do, we need to understand their pitfalls, even as we extol their potentialities. And, at least for those of us primarily situated in professional schools, we must not allow the allure presented by the opportunity to promote our ideals (or ourselves) to divert us from striving fairly to critique such endeavor. If we hope to see our ideals and ideas penetrate others' legal processes. We owe it to them and to ourselves to be no less penetrating about ourselves and our history.

Notes

1 As will be suggested herein, I use the word 'profession' in conjunction with the PRC advisedly – simply to refer to those Chinese citizens who have been certified by the state to engage in the practice of law.

2 See, for example, Hiroshi Wagatsuma and Arthur I. Rosett, 'The Implications of Apology: Law and Culture in Japan and the United States', *Law and Society Review*, vol. 20 (1986) p. 461; and Hiroshi Wagatsuma and Arthur I. Rosett, 'Cultural Attitudes Toward Contract Law', *UCLA Pacific Basin Law Journal*, vol. 2 (1983) p. 76.

3 Faith in what can be accomplished through embracing the American model is not, of course, limited to China or to the legal profession. Consider, for example, Steven Calabresi's recent call for emulation of American constitutionalism ('[T]he Federalist Constitution has proved to be a brilliant success, which unitary nation states and parliamentary democracies all over the world would do well to copy') or Reinier Kraakman and Henry Hansmann's declaration that, in corporate law, history has culminated in the American model. See, respectively, Steven G. Calabresi, 'An Agenda for Constitutional Reform', in William N. Eskridge Jr and Sanford Levinson (eds) *Constitutional Stupidities, Constitutional Tragedies* (New York: New York University Press, 1998) p. 22; and Henry Hansmann and Reinier Kraakman, 'The End of History for Corporate Law', John M. Olin Center for Law, Economics and Business, Discussion Paper no. 280 (2000).

4 Yves Dezalay and Bryant G. Garth, *Dealing in Virtue: International Commercial Arbitration and the Construction of a Transnational Legal Order* (Chicago: University of Chicago Press, 1996) p. 258.

5 Jonathan Hecht, *Opening to Reform? An Analysis of China's Revised Criminal Procedure Law* (New York: Lawyers Committee for Human Rights, 1996).

6 Pei Minxin, 'Political Changes in Post-Mao China: Progress and Challenges', in Ted Galen Carpenter and James A. Dorn (eds) *China's Future: Constructive Partner or Emerging Threat?* (Washington DC: Cato Institute, 2000) pp. 301–5.

7 Lawyers Committee for Human Rights, *Lawyers in China: Obstacles to Independence and the Defense of Rights* (New York: Lawyers Committee for Human Rights, 1998).

8 I discuss efforts of multilateral organizations to promote legal development in China in William P. Alford, 'The More Law, the More … ? Taking the Measure of Legal Reform in the People's Republic of China', Stanford Center for Research on Economic Development and Policy Reform Working Paper no. 59 (2000).

9 See, for example, Aubrey McCutheon, 'Contributing to Legal Reform in China', in Mary McClymont and Stephen Golub (eds) *Many Roads to Justice: the Law Related Work of Ford Foundation Grantees Around the World* (New York: Ford Foundation, 2000).

10 See William P. Alford, 'Exporting the "Pursuit of Happiness"', *Harvard Law Review*, vol. 113 (2000) p. 1677, for further discussion of the rule of law initiative and of governmental democracy promotion programs more generally.

11 See the preface to William P. Alford, 'The More Law, the More … ? Taking the Measure of Legal Reform in the People's Republic of China', Stanford Center for Research on Economic Development and Policy Reform Working Paper no. 59 (2000).

12 See, for example, Robert A. Stein, 'Two Billion Reasons to Cooperate', *American Bar Association Journal*, vol. 85 (February 1999) p. 86.

13 William P. Alford, 'Tasselled Loafers for Barefoot Lawyers: Transformation and Tension in the World of Chinese Legal Workers', *The China Quarterly*, vol. 141 (1995) pp. 22–39. But see below, note 33.

14 *Zhongguo Renmin Gongheguo Lushi Fa* [The Lawyers Law of the People's Republic of China] (1997).

15 William P. Alford, 'Double-Edged Swords Cut Both Ways: Law and Legitimacy in the People's Republic of China', *Daedalus*, vol. 122 (1993) pp. 45–63. For a telling account of the shadowy involvement by the family of one of China's most senior leaders in the management of a major joint venture, see Henny Sender, 'For Morgan Stanley, a Chinese Headache', *Wall Street Journal*, 14 November 2000, p. A21.

16 Stanley B. Lubman, *Bird in a Cage: Legal Reform in China after Mao* (Stanford: Stanford University Press, 1999).

17 Luo Bing, 'Mijian Xielu Zhonggong Zuzhi Fulan' [Secret Document Exposes Decay in Communist Party Organization], *Cheng Ming* [Contend], vol. 225 (1996) p. 6.

18 Zhongguo Sifa Xingzheng Nianjian Bianji Bu [The Editorial Department of the China Yearbook of Judicial Administration], *Zhongguo Sifa Xingzheng Nianjian* [The China Yearbook of Judicial Administration] (Beijing: Falu Chubanshe, 1999).

19 China's police are authorized by the provisions on reeducation through labor to sentence citizens to periods of up to four years in labor camp for deviant behavior that falls short of warranting criminal prosecution. Such confinement may be extended if the police deem the individual not to have made sufficient progress in redeeming himself. It is now possible for citizens to appeal such determinations to the courts, but there is little evidence of many having done so.

20 This process, which involves petitioning officials for discretionary relief in a manner reminiscent of imperial days, and which is a far more active channel for citizen grievances than the much touted Administrative Litigation Law, has barely been studied by foreign (or Chinese) scholars.

21 The PRC has over one million neighborhood mediation committees, with over six million official mediators.

22 The role of lawyers in counseling and negotiation is discussed in William P. Alford, 'Lawyers in China', unpublished manuscript (1998).

23 I discuss in detail the statistics for representation through the mid-1990s in *ibid.*

24 Typical of this is the writing of Pei Minxin. See above, note 6.

25 Conviction rates run between 98 and 99.5 per cent, according to the *Falu Nianjian* [The Law Yearbook]. In weighing this statistic, it helps to be mindful of a comparably high conviction rate in Japan (J. Mark Ramseyer and Eric Rasmussen, 'Why the Japanese Conviction Rate is So High', John M. Olin Center for Law, Economics and Business, Discussion Paper no. 240 [1998]) and of the fact that the overwhelming majority of criminal cases in the United States result in plea bargains. In the PRC, approximately 40 per cent of criminal defendants are represented by counsel, although often they have little involvement in the all important pre-trial stage.

26 Many are ex-soldiers, re-assigned in the 1990s when it was determined that the army had too many people and the courts too few and that the requisite skill sets are somewhat comparable. 'He Weifang, Fuzhuan Junren Jin Fayuan' [Retired Soldiers in the Courts], *Nanfang Zhoumo* [Southern Weekend], 2 January 1998. To be sure, the court system has made extensive efforts in recent years to provide on-the-job training.

27 As the noted social critic He Qinglian recently observed, 'Among Chinese lawyers, there is a saying that "to bring a litigation is to use one's connections"' ["da guan si jiu shi da guanxi"]. He Qinglian, 'Dangqian Zhongguo Shehui Jiegou Yanbian de Zongtixing Fenxi' [An Overall Analysis of the Current Change of China's Social Structure], *Dangdai Zhongguo Yanjiu* [Modern China Studies], vol. 68, no. 3 (2000) p. 86. See also Frank Ching, 'Rough Justice', *Far Eastern Economic Review*. 20 August 1998, p. 13. Also confirmed in author's interviews, July 2000, Beijing.

28 William P. Alford, 'Lawyers in China', unpublished manuscript (1998).

29 For an example of such smugness about the naivety of China's leaders (and a disturbing inattentiveness to the possible consequences of pointing this out on the

op-ed page of the *New York Times* – which the PRC Embassy, no doubt, monitors) from an otherwise thoughtful writer, see Anthony Lewis, 'The Engine of Law', *New York Times*, 6 July 1998, p. A11.

30 The pervasiveness of corruption is discussed in Hu Angang (ed.) *Zhongguo: Tiaozhan Fubai* [China: Fighting Against Corruption] (Hangzhou: Zhejiang Renmin Chubanshe, 2000). This volume, put together by one of China's most distinguished economists, estimates that some 16–17 per cent of China's GDP (running at well over 100 billion dollars) is lost annually to corruption and associated behavior. See also Craig S. Smith, 'Graft in China Flows Freely, Draining the Treasury', *New York Times*, 1 October 2000, p. 4; 'China Handling 9,000 Corruption Cases', *Agence France-Presse*, 11 December 2000 (indicating from official sources that more than 500,000 cases of corruption have been investigated during the past decade and that at present, some 9,000 regarding banks and other state enterprises are underway); and James Kynge, '"Personal Conduct" Costs Chinese Minister His Job', *Financial Times*, 5 December 2000. The last article concerns the PRC's Minister of Justice, Gao Changli, who was supposedly placed under house arrest for, *inter alia*, misuse of state resources after an investigation said to have been carried out by the party's central disciplinary authorities, rather than by the judiciary or a state administrative organ.

31 By this, I mean the tendency of some foreign observers to mistake appearances for substance. William P. Alford, 'Tasselled Loafers for Barefoot Lawyers: Transformation and Tension in the World of Chinese Legal Workers', *The China Quarterly*, vol. 141 (1995) pp. 22–39.

32 There is, to be sure, some quite sophisticated writing by PRC scholars about the situation of Chinese lawyers. See, for instance, Du Gangjian and Li Xuan, *Zhongguo Lushi De Dangdai Mingyuan* [The Contemporary Fate of Chinese Lawyers] (Beijing: Gaige Chubanshe, 1997); Zhang Zhimin, 'Dangdai Zhongguo de Lushi Ye, Yi Minquan Wei Jiben Chidu' [Lawyers in Contemporary China: A Civil Rights Perspective], *Bijiaofa Yanjiu* [Journal of Comparative Law], vol. 9 (1995) p. 1.

33 To be sure, the Lawyers Law acknowledges the possibility of malpractice actions (without providing a mechanism for them). The All China Lawyers' Federation recently prepared a report denouncing corruption and incompetence on the part of lawyers, and called for a reduction in the number of persons admitted annually to the bar.

34 A comparable point has been made with respect to the emerging business community in the PRC. See, for example, Margaret Pearson, *China's New Business Elite: the Political Consequences of Economic Reform* (Berkeley: University of California Press, 1997); David L. Wank, 'The Institutional Process of Market Clientelism: Guanxi and Private Business in a South China City', *The China Quarterly*, vol. 147 (1996) p. 820. He Qinglian has expressed a good deal of disappointment with the ways in which businesspersons, lawyers, accountants, and the middle class more generally have exacerbated China's endemic problems. See He Qinglian, 'Dangqian Zhongguo Shehui Jiegou Yanbian de Zongtixing Fenxi' [An Overall Analysis of the Current Change of China's Social Structure], *Dangdai Zhongguo Yanjiu* [Modern China Studies], vol. 68, no. 3 (2000) pp. 86, 85–87 and generally. As Robert Bianchi's work of the 1980s on Egypt and Turkey suggests, we may want to guard against the pervasive assumption that the middle class will always be a force for liberalization. See Robert Bianchi, *Unruly Corporatism: Associational Life in Twentieth Century Egypt* (New York: Oxford University Press, 1989).

35 There are, to be sure, isolated figures such as Zhang Sizi and Guo Jianmei, who on behalf of political dissidents and abused women respectively, have posed noteworthy challenges to the authorities. And, as previously indicated, my interviews have focused predominantly on business practitioners in Beijing, for whom the stakes may

be higher than for their provincial brethren engaged in more mundane areas of practice. I would also note, as discussed above in note 51, that we ought not to allow our focus on the legal profession to overshadow the ways in which ordinary citizens may seek to avail themselves of the protections to which the law suggests they are entitled.

36 Compliance with Article X of the General Agreement on Tariffs and Trade (concerning transparency) would seem to require far more extensive adjustment in Chinese rule making and application processes than appears generally to be appreciated. For a thoughtful essay on the challenges posed by China's integration into the WTO, see Robert Herzstein, 'Fitting China into the WTO: Can China Function in a Law Governed Trading System?', *Harvard China Review*, vol. 2 (2000) p. 63.

37 See William P. Alford, 'Double-Edged Swords Cut Both Ways: Law and Legitimacy in the People's Republic of China', *Daedalus*, vol. 122 (1993) pp. 45–63. The law yearbooks do indicate that approximately 200,000 people resided in such camps during the mid-1990s, but neither they nor other official sources I have found indicate how many citizens are annually committed or re-committed. Nor is this system a relic of the past, as some are inclined to suggest. Human rights groups believe that as many as 10,000 followers of the Falungong may have been consigned to reeducation through labor camps in recent years.

38 Bruce Ackerman, 'The New Separation of Powers', *Harvard Law Review*, vol. 113 (2000) p. 633.

39 See, for example, 'President Tells Legal Profession to Help Promote Reform', *Xinhua*, 27 January 1997.

40 Richard Madsen, *China and the American Dream: a Moral Inquiry* (Berkeley: University of California Press, 1995).

41 See William P. Alford, 'Exporting the "Pursuit of Happiness"', *Harvard Law Review*, vol. 113 (2000) p. 1677.

42 Anthony T. Kronman, *The Lost Lawyer: Failing Ideals of the Legal Profession* (Cambridge MA: Belknap Press of Harvard University Press, 1993).

43 See Sara Leitch, 'Law Dean Advises Chinese Law Reform', *Yale Daily News*, 16 September 1998, p. 1.

44 The words are those of David Kornstein of the *New York Law Journal*, reproduced on the back cover of the paperback edition of Kronman's book, along with lavish praise from Charles Fried, Robert Gordon and other noted scholars of the legal profession. Even the book's critics treat it as a major work.

45 For instance, see Gordon's comments in note 44 above, or the insightful critique by David B. Wilkins, 'Practical Wisdom for Practicing Lawyers: Separating Ideals from Ideology in Legal Ethics', *Harvard Law Review*, vol. 108 (1994) p. 458.

46 Anthony T. Kronman, *The Lost Lawyer: Failing Ideals of the Legal Profession* (Cambridge MA: Belknap Press of Harvard University Press, 1993) p. 15.

47 *Ibid.*, p. 16.

48 *Ibid.*, p. 22.

49 See, for example, Richard Falk, 'Casting The Spell: The New Haven School of International Law: Jurisprudence for a Free Society', *Yale Law Journal*, vol. 104 (1995) p. 1991. Of course, some have expressed skepticism about the depth of Yale Law School's commitment to social science inquiry. Mark Tushnet, 'Critical Legal Studies: A Political History', *Yale Law Journal*, vol. 100 (1991) p. 1515.

50 Many persons concerned with China policy take considerable comfort in the fact that the PRC now often responds to criticisms of its rights record in the language of the law. While I, too, think it significant that the Chinese government has taken up this discourse (and happily acknowledge that there are serious Chinese scholars working on rights issues) we need also to take account of the ways in which the state (and some scholars) have used such rhetoric in a highly instrumental fashion to defend acts

that would seem deeply problematic from the vantage point either of Chinese law or of international human rights, and to fend off foreign criticism. Consider, for example, the uses of law to justify the state's harsh crackdown on the Falungong movement. In that regard, see materials in Danny Schechter, *Falun Gong's Challenge to China: Spiritual Practice or 'Evil Cult'?* (New York: Akashic Books, 2000).

51 To note this is not to ignore the ways in which citizens have sought to hold the state to its own law – the 'double-edged' phenomenon about which I first wrote in 1993. See William P. Alford, 'Double-Edged Swords Cut Both Ways: Law and Legitimacy in the People's Republic of China', *Daedalus*, vol. 122 (1993) pp. 45–63. To the contrary, it is in part to point out the ways in which lawyers may be blunting, as well as facilitating this phenomenon.

52 Jonathan D. Spence, *To Change China: Western Advisors in China 1620–1960* (New York: Penguin Books, 1980).

53 Kronman, to be sure, does acknowledge in passing that in some societies 'there is no room ... for civic friendship or the statesmen's art ... because they [the statesmen] stand at the boundaries of political life and, if they lead anywhere at all, it can only be to revolution'. Anthony T. Kronman, *The Lost Lawyer: Failing Ideals of the Legal Profession* (Cambridge MA: Belknap Press of Harvard University Press, 1993) p. 107. Judging from the nature of his involvement in and comments about the PRC, it would not seem that Kronman could fairly include the PRC in this category.

54 He Weifang, 'Tongguo Sifa Shixian Shehui Zhengyi: Dui Zhongguo Faguan Xianzhuang de Yige Toushi' [The Realization of Social Justice Through Judicature: A Look at the Current Situation of Chinese Judges], in Xia Yong (ed.) *Zou Xiang Quanli De Shidai: Zhongguo Gongmin Fazhan Yanjiu* [Toward a Time of Rights: a Perspective on the Development of Civil Rights in China] (Beijing: Zhongguo Zhengfa Daxue Chubanshe, 1995).

55 As Ken Lieberthal has put it, 'all nonofficial organizations exist only at the sufferance of the party'. Kenneth Lieberthal, *Governing China: From Revolution Through Reform* (New York: W. W. Norton, 1995). This is not to denigrate the serious efforts, nicely documented by Tony Saich, of a growing number of citizens' groups to carve out space for themselves in the interstices. Tony Saich, 'Negotiating the State: The Development of Social Organizations in China', *The China Quarterly*, vol. 161 (2000) p. 125.

56 Author's interviews, Beijing, September 1997, August 1999, July 2000.

57 Anthony T. Kronman, *Max Weber* (Stanford: Stanford University Press, 1983).

58 Anthony T. Kronman, *The Lost Lawyer: Failing Ideals of the Legal Profession* (Cambridge MA: Belknap Press of Harvard University Press, 1993) p. 14.

59 This may be most obvious in the writing of Richard Posner. Although his writing on the legal profession is principally concerned with the experience of the United States, he treats the lessons he draws from this as having far broader application. Richard Posner, 'Professions', *Arizona Law Review*, vol. 40 (1998) p. 1. See also Richard Posner, 'Creating a Legal Framework for Economic Development', *World Bank Research Observer*, vol. 13 (1998) p. 1. I discuss Posner in William P. Alford, 'Exporting the "Pursuit of Happiness"', *Harvard Law Review*, vol. 113 (2000) p. 1677.

60 See, for example, Talcott Parsons, 'The Legal Profession', in William Evans (ed.) *Law and Sociology* (New York: Free Press of Glencoe, 1962).

61 Margali Sarfatti Larson, *The Rise of Professionalism: A Sociological Analysis* (Berkeley: University of California Press, 1977).

62 See, for example, Richard Abel, 'Comparative Sociology of the Legal Profession', in Richard Abel and Philip Lewis (eds) *Lawyers in Society: Comparative Theories* (Berkeley: University of California Press, 1988).

63 Andrew Abbott, *The System of Professions: An Essay on the Division of Expert Labor* (Chicago: University of Chicago Press, 1988).

64 David Trubek, Yves Dezalay, Ruth Buchanan and John Davis, 'The Future of the Legal Profession: Global Restructuring and the Law: Studies in the Internationalization of Legal Fields and the Creation of Transnational Arenas', *Case Western Reserve Law Review*, vol. 44 (1995) p. 407.

65 See Yves Dezalay and Bryant G. Garth, *Dealing in Virtue: International Commercial Arbitration and the Construction of a Transnational Legal Order* (Chicago: University of Chicago Press, 1996) p. 258.

66 Interestingly, scholarly writing about the legal profession in Europe tends to be more self-conscious about the significance of institutional context, perhaps a reflection of the vicissitudes of the German legal profession over the past century, or of the likelihood that those who write about societies other than the US cannot help but be mindful of the American experience and the ways in which it differs from what they discern to be the case elsewhere (in a manner that does not have a direct counterpart for those whose principal focus is the American profession). See, for example, Dietrich Rueschemeyer, 'Comparing Legal Professions: A State-Centered Approach', in Richard Abel and Philip Lewis (eds) *Lawyers in Society: Comparative Theories* (Berkeley: University of California Press, 1988); Kenneth F. Ledford, *From General Estate to Special Interest: German Lawyers 1878–1933* (New York: Cambridge University Press, 1996); Terence C. Halliday and Lucien Karpik (eds) *Lawyers and the Rise of Western Political Liberalism* (New York: Oxford University Press, 1997).

67 This argument is further developed in William P. Alford, 'Exporting the "Pursuit of Happiness"', *Harvard Law Review*, vol. 113 (2000) p. 1677.

68 Robert W. Gordon, 'Legal Thought and Legal Practice in the Age of American Enterprise', in Gerald L. Geison (ed.) *Professions and Professional Ideology in America* (Chapel Hill: University of North Carolina Press, 1983).

69 Anthony T. Kronman, *The Lost Lawyer: Failing Ideals of the Legal Profession* (Cambridge MA: Belknap Press of Harvard University Press, 1993) p. 1.

70 Alexis de Tocqueville, *Democracy in America* (New York: Vintage Books, 1990 [1848]) p. 266.

71 Anthony T. Kronman, *The Lost Lawyer: Failing Ideals of the Legal Profession* (Cambridge MA: Belknap Press of Harvard University Press, 1993) p. 155.

72 Alexis de Tocqueville, *Democracy in America* (New York: Vintage Books, 1990 [1848]) p. 266.

73 With respect to the United States, the work of the legal team in *Brown v. Board of Education*, the famed 1954 school desegregation case, comes readily to mind. See Richard Kluger, *Simple Justice: the History of Brown v. Board of Education and Black America's Struggle for Equality* (New York: Knopf, 1975). Examples of heroic lawyering abroad are discussed in a number of the essays in Austin Sarat and Stuart Scheingold (eds) *Cause Lawyering: Political Commitments and Professional Responsibilities* (New York: Oxford University Press, 1998).

74 It might also require that we take note of the observation of many Chinese lawyers I interviewed, to the effect that American business lawyers in China present a more variegated picture than we might imagine. Even as they acknowledge that the expatriate bar there may be introducing new norms of professionalism, there is considerable resentment among my sampling of PRC lawyers that many foreign lawyers routinely provide advice about local law in contravention of PRC legal and ethical requirements. For an account of one American lawyer's unwitting efforts to circumvent PRC requirements in order to work as a legal professional, see Peter Wonacott, 'As China Opens the Door, Foreign Lawyers are Poised to Rush In', *Wall Street Journal*, 15 November 2000, p. A23.

75 As indicated earlier (see above, note 29 and accompanying text) we should be wary of suggestions that authorities in the PRC are too naive to understand the implications of their actions. This is not to deny that China's top leadership has relatively little direct experience with the institutions of liberal democracy. Nor is it to ignore the possibility that the Party's top echelon may in desperation be tolerating changes that it appreciates present some risk to its tight grip on power, or that there may even be some persons of rank who would welcome a modest degree of liberalization, whether for reasons of philosophy or factionalism. Instead, it is to urge that persons who portray foreign legal assistance as a Trojan Horse demonstrate why they think they have a better understanding than China's ruling elite of how particular institutions may play out on Chinese soil, given the arduous political gauntlet through which those leaders have passed to reach and retain their present positions, their greater access to information about current Chinese circumstances, and the earnestness with which Beijing has dissected the experience of Eastern Europe and Taiwan over the past decade.

76 For a recent account of the potential for foreign assistance in legal development to legitimate problematic activity such as Beijing's crackdown on the Falungong, see Ian Johnson, 'UN Helps Sponsor China Conference on "Evil Cults"', *Wall Street Journal*, 22 November 2000, p. A19.

10

CHINESE COURTS AND LAW REFORM IN POST-MAO CHINA

Stanley Lubman

The economic reforms that began in 1979 to transform China have caused law to become more important than it has been at any time in Chinese history: law has been incorporated into the governance of the Chinese Party-state, a legal framework for a marketizing economy has been constructed by an astounding outpouring of legislation, and the courts have been rebuilt.[1] The bar has been revived,[2] as has legal education. This chapter summarizes the state of China's courts after twenty years of reform efforts, and speculates on the prospects for further necessary reforms of the judicial system. It emphasizes some forces that influence law reform and legal institutions in China today, and suggests, now that China has acceded to the World Trade Organization (WTO) it will have difficulty in meeting the standards that membership in that body will impose on its legal institutions.

The growing activity of the courts

The courts, formerly scorned as 'rightist' institutions at the end of the 1950s and as 'bourgeois' during the Cultural Revolution, have been rebuilt in a four-level hierarchy, and are increasingly being used as the fora in which rights created by legislation are asserted by citizens against each other and, to some extent, against state agencies.

The number of civil and economic disputes brought to the courts yearly has risen, from 2.4 million cases in 1990 to over five million in 1999, with most of the increase attributable to the rise in contract and property disputes and suits arising out of what would be considered as torts in the West, such as claims for personal damages for injuries caused by negligence.[3] The increasing activity of the courts reflects the slowly increasing willingness among many Chinese, especially in the coastal cities, to bring their disputes to court rather than to resort to extra-judicial mediation, which has traditionally been the preferred means for settling most civil disputes. Still, more than half of the cases brought to the courts are currently resolved through judicial mediation rather than adjudication of competing claims and rights. This represents a decline from the mid-1980s, when the rate of judicially mediated cases may have been as high as 80 per cent in some courts.

The relationship of mediation to adjudication is changing slowly. A system of local committees created for the express purpose of mediating civil, family and some property disputes has been active in China since 1949. Today, the greater accessibility and credibility of the courts is reflected in a decline in the number of disputes brought to the mediation committees, from 7.4 million in 1990 to 5.18 million in 1999.[4] Current Party-state policy emphasizes that mediation should yield to adjudication that clearly defines the rights, duties and liabilities of parties in disputes; growing reliance on contracts and the increase in litigation suggests increasing acceptance of concepts of law-based rights. At the same time, Chinese institutions for dispute resolution continue to reflect the traditional emphasis on group harmony and put less stress on rights than the West.

Continuing problems

As impressive as the efforts to build new institutions have been, the tasks of deepening their power and broadening their reach continue to face critical difficulties. Some of these difficulties arise out of Maoist ideology and unreformed Maoist institutions. Others reflect new forces unleashed by the economic reforms themselves. A third group of challenges has its sources in traditional Chinese legal culture. Amidst the welter of conflicting values, the courts operate against a background of extraordinary confusion in the hierarchy of norms that are issued at central and local level, and in the face of vast discretion exercised by the Chinese bureaucracy at all levels.

Legislative disorder

During the reform era the legislative power of provincial governments has expanded, along with the parallel legislative power of more than twenty functional bureaucracies of the central government. The State Council, which heads the central government bureaucracy, supervises more than sixty departments (including ministries), commissions, administrations and offices. These exercise authority to issue regulations that implement specific legislation, either under a specific grant of power by a legislative body such as the National People's Congress Standing Committee, or by wielding a general rule-making power that is deemed to be inherent in the agencies and enables them to issue any rule that is necessary to carry out their functions.[5] In practice (not unlike agencies in other countries!), Chinese administrative agencies wield their law-making powers to protect or increase their jurisdiction and to advance their policies. The wide array of 'departmental rules' that they issue, all of which have general binding authority, are superior to all local enactments.[6] No procedural rules exist to govern enactment of these important rules, which may be issued or modified by any agency with exclusive jurisdiction over the subject matter of the rule.

Furthermore, crucial to the future of the role of courts and the rule of law itself, local governments and central bureaucracies alone possess the power to interpret the rules they issue. Chinese administrative agencies, then, have the power both to issue and interpret their own rules, and to require the courts to enforce them.[7] This power is extensive, because most laws originate in the state bureaucracy rather than the legislative bodies.

This distribution of legislative power suggests that China suffers from 'legal fragmentation',[8] and that no legal institution in China currently has 'either the authority or the desire to impose order on the legal system'.[9] Moreover, the broad discretion that Chinese bureaucrats exercise in making and implementing general rules is wielded in a system in which agencies are arrayed in parallel hierarchies of equal (and poorly defined) authority, often overlapping in jurisdiction, and marked by a cellularity that encourages consensus decision-making. The courts are formally denied power other than to apply laws, although in practice the unavoidability of their involvement in interpretation is coming to be recognized,[10] and the Supreme People's Court has asserted a strong role in the interpretation of laws and administrative rules.[11]

The language and phrasing of Chinese legislation and rules create wide scope for administrative discretion in interpretation because a major goal of Chinese legislative drafting is 'flexibility'. As a result, at all levels Chinese legislation is intentionally drafted in 'broad, indeterminate language' that allows administrators to vary the specific meaning of legislative language with circumstances.[12] Standard drafting techniques include the use of general principles, undefined terms, broadly worded discretion, omissions, and general catch-all phrases.[13]

No wonder that one writer concludes that

> The disparate mass of laws and regulations which makes up the formal written sources of Chinese law does not possess sufficient unity to be regarded as a coherent body of law. In their disarray, the sources of Chinese law seem barely capable of providing the basic point of reference which all complex systems of law require.[14]

Another, and deep-rooted cause of disorder is a persistent tendency to interpret and apply Chinese laws as if they were identical to the policies they are meant to replace. Formerly, many policies had to be complied with in spirit only,[15] and bureaucrats may have difficulty distinguishing the current proliferation of normative documents from policy documents, a distinction that did not exist before reform. That task is made more difficult by the existence of a large gray area of 'policy laws' – policy statements, administrative regulations, meetings, notices, instructions and speeches that are given legal effectiveness because they emanate from authoritative government and Party bodies.[16] A Chinese legal scholar argues that reliance on 'policy laws' is undemocratic, disorderly and a source of instability, because they neither set precise limits between legal and illegal behavior nor define the legal consequences of failure to comply, and they are procedurally unclear.[17]

Curbing bureaucratic discretion

Nowhere is the difficulty of improving Chinese legality better illustrated than by the hesitantly developing field of administrative law. The 1990s saw the beginning of what could eventually prove to be a significant wave of further legal reform, when the Chinese leadership addressed the need to create legal institutions that might curb bureaucratic arbitrariness by defining the scope of administrative authority and providing remedies for the exercise of arbitrary power.

An Administrative Litigation Law (ALL, effective in 1990) gives affected persons or organizations the right to sue in the Chinese courts those agencies that have acted unlawfully.[18] Almost 100,000 suits were brought against administrative agencies under the ALL in 1999 (double the number of such cases in 1995) – although plaintiffs lost in considerably more than 50 per cent of the cases.[19] An Administrative Punishments Law (effective in 1996) defines the wide assortment of punishments that may be imposed by administrative agencies,[20] and an Administrative Compensation Law (effective in 1995) defines the situations in which governmental agencies may be liable for injurious consequences of their acts.[21]

The jurisdiction of the courts and the extent to which they may vindicate rights, and their power to restrain arbitrariness, all remain very limited.[22] The actions of administrative agencies in applying rules in specific situations may be reviewed only if the agency has violated a law, but this is difficult to show when the rule in question, like most Chinese laws and administrative rules, has been very generally and broadly framed and has given an agency broad – and unreviewable – discretion.[23] Under the ALL the courts can neither review the validity of general rules issued by administrative agencies, nor decide that they improperly used their discretion, although a law adopted in 1999 empowered the courts to review certain general rules.[24] Moreover, even when individual citizens or organizations go so far as to challenge agency acts in court, the possibility that the agency will retaliate in some form causes a considerable number of them to withdraw their suits.[25] Clearly, Chinese administrative law is still very much in a nascent state, a condition that is being slowly addressed by ongoing legislative drafting efforts at both the State Council and the Legislative Affairs Commission of the National People's Congress.

Constraints on judicial autonomy

Although the caseload of the courts is rising, their independence, powers and effectiveness are constrained by a number of forces.

External influence on courts by the national Party-state

Courts are still expected to follow policy as it is articulated by the CCP, most obviously in the campaigns against crime that have frequently been launched since the 1980s. Although the links between judicial decisions and general policies are much less explicit and less often emphasized than they were before the onset of reform, the courts are expected to apply the laws within whatever boundaries are set by such policies, and must also respond to changing emphases. The principal affairs of the court are directed by the Party organization within the court, which is itself subject to the leadership of the local Party committee. Important roles in the selection of judges are played by the Party committee at the court, the local Party committee and its personnel department. Party leadership is reflected in the handling of some important and difficult cases. In such cases, one Chinese law professor writes,

> [the court] often reports ... to the local Party committee and solicits opinions for solution ... and if contradictions arise among different judicial organs, the Party's political-legal committee often steps forward to coordinate.[26]

External influences on courts by the local Party-state

The strongest and most insidious type of extra-judicial influence on the outcomes of non-criminal disputes is interference by local officials in pending litigation and in the enforcement of judgments. Judges are appointed, and the courts are financed, by the local governments in the jurisdictions in which they serve. The extensive decentralization promoted by the economic reforms has reinforced localism in China. The increasing stakes of local governments in economic enterprises have stimulated 'local protectionism' that does not appear to be responding to central government criticisms and appeals to desist. Economically driven pressures are exerted on the courts to persuade complaining parties to withdraw suits, to issue judgments not in accord with law and facts, and to punish with transfers those judges who try to be impartial.[27]

'Local protectionism' consistently makes it difficult to enforce judgments of the courts when the successful litigants must attempt to obtain payment in a place where defendants live or do business. In 1988, China's Supreme Court President said that around 30 per cent of all judgments that had some executable content were not enforced, and other estimates are even higher.[28] A judge from Yangzhou wrote in 1994 that whenever disputes involve parties from outside Yangzhou, the policy of the local courts was to mediate such disputes as a matter of course because a mediated solution to which the local party had agreed would deflect local resistance to resist enforcing a judgment.[29] An extensive 'outline' of a program for judicial reform issued in October 1999 placed 'local protectionism' at the head of a list of problems faced by the Chinese courts.[30]

The use of *guanxi* (relationships) to influence outcomes is common enough to cause Chinese judges to refer to cases whose result was influenced by a relationship between judges and local officials or others as '*guanxi* cases' (*guanxi an*), as if they were an entirely separate type of case. Such 'back-door' influences on outcomes shade into downright corruption and bribery, potent causes of perversions of justice.[31]

Adjudication with Chinese characteristics

The judges

When we turn to the staffing, organization and operation of the courts, other significant problems appear. The educational level of China's judges is low. When rebuilding of the courts began, most of the judges appointed were transferred to the courts from Party and military posts. Many were former People's Liberation Army officers, who lacked not only legal education, but also any university education. Considerable efforts have been made to train these judges by means of on-the-job training, courses at the courts and courses at centers for judicial training at Beijing and People's Universities. The percentage of judges with college or college-equivalent educations has risen, but most judges still have not had a legal education. In 1994, a provincial higher court president wrote that 'about half of the judges in the country have not reached the level of university-level legal education'.[32] Moreover, not only are judges selected and paid by local governments, but, unlike their Anglo-American counterparts, they have never previously worked as lawyers.

Slow progress has been made in raising the quality of judges. Objective qualifications for all judges were not formally established until a Judges Law[33] was promulgated in 1995, and judges then in office who did not meet the qualifications were given an undetermined amount of time to attain them.[34] Nonetheless, the Judges Law does set academic qualifications for judges. It provides that Chinese citizens who have reached the minimum age of twenty-three, uphold the Constitution, and 'possess good political and professional quality and good conduct' may become judges if they have graduated from an institution of higher learning where they specialized in law as undergraduates or graduates or, if they have graduated from such an institution with a specialization other than law, have 'professional legal knowledge' and have worked for two years.

The Judges Law provides for examinations of judges, with grades on such examinations to be the basis for 'rewards, punishments, training, dismissals and readjustment of grades and wages' (Article 13). Each People's Court is required to establish examination and appraisal committees, and the committee at the Supreme People's Court is to organize national examinations for newly appointed judges and assistant judges (Article 46). Judges face annual performance reviews and can be dismissed for, among other reasons, having been rated as 'incompetent' in two consecutive years. In July 2001, steps were taken to raise the professional qualifications of judges: sitting judges would be required to take an examination, and, beginning in 2002, new judges would have to take the nation-wide examination required for all prospective members of the Chinese bar.[35]

The judicial process

Certain characteristics of the Chinese judicial process itself present obstacles to the growth of legality. Judges often prefer to resolve cases by mediation because they are unsure of their legal competence and fear reversal by a higher court. Judges ordinarily bear the sole responsibility for deciding cases only in very minor matters, and a high degree of consultation within and between courts is a sign of serious weakness. The courts are subdivided into 'departments' (*ting*) according to subject matter, and a judge may consult a department head, senior judges, the Chief Judge, or all of them, when deciding a case. Cases deemed 'difficult' or 'complicated' (including those that have attracted the attention of local officials because the outcomes may adversely affect local government revenues) are regularly decided by an 'adjudication committee' of senior judges. Procedure may be consultative in a different manner: lower courts, apprehensive about possible reversal, sometimes request instructions from a higher court before they issue a judgment, which renders meaningless the right of unsuccessful parties to appeal.

Chinese civil procedure undervalues the finality of judgments, which in the West provides stability to the expectations of disputants and reinforces the popular credibility of the courts, thereby strengthening the rule of law itself. Under current Chinese law, however, any noncriminal decisions may be reopened within two years after they become final.[36] Even after appeals have been exhausted and judgments have technically become final, a discontented litigant may bring about a review by applying again to the court that rendered the judgment, and may also try to involve higher courts or local officials. Moreover, the higher courts themselves, in supervising the quality of the work of lower courts, from time to time conduct reviews of batches of their decisions even though the judgments have already taken legal effect. Moreover, since the Chinese courts are subject to the supervision of the people's congresses – the legislative bodies that appoint them – inspection by those bodies of the work of the courts includes review of decisions in specific cases identified by 'the masses'.[37] In recent years, widespread public concern about judicial corruption led a number of provinces to adopt regulations providing for legislative requests by provincial people's congresses to the courts to reexamine cases that had already been decided, and NPC Chairman Li Peng was a prominent adherent of the view that legislative supervision of the courts should be increased.[38] Chinese legal scholars with whom these developments were discussed during July 2001, expressed concern about the obvious implications of such legislation for the independence of the courts.

These aspects of civil procedure should be viewed together with other insights into the Chinese courts: for one thing, the role of the judge has been defined only ambiguously. In a noteworthy essay,[39] one Chinese law professor who has analyzed the content of the internal newspaper of the courts concludes that judges are celebrated for being good soldiers of the state, not wise dispensers of justice. In the same essay he points also to a second aspect of the role of judges, by characterizing their behavior as that of bureaucrats. Chinese judges, in this view, do not make decisions in a significantly different manner than their counterparts in administrative agencies when they are administering policies. Seen together with the consultative nature of decision-making, the links between the courts and local officials, and the relatively small number of cases that are actually adjudicated rather than mediated, this perception that Chinese judges act primarily as bureaucrats seems to explain their role and decision-making style today.

Chinese courts as bureaucratic institutions

This brief summary highlights some significant ways in which Chinese courts differ from Western courts, both in ideals and in practice. What emerges is the weakness of the concept of adjudication, which becomes clearer when Chinese courts are seen from the perspective of adjudication in the West. Marc Galanter has enumerated criteria of the phenomenon known as 'adjudication'.[40] A contrast between the elements of his 'adjudication prototype' and Chinese practice suggests that

- individuated treatment of cases is impaired by judicial campaigns;
- the formal rationality of Chinese adjudication is low because judicial decisions
    - (i) are often shaped by political or localistic considerations external to the body of legal rules that courts are supposedly engaged in applying;
    - (ii) some rules applied by Chinese courts are available only in internal publications; and
    - (iii) the vagueness of many normative rules weakens their clarity and suggests a lack of differentiation from general policies.

- the finality of judicial decisions is low;
- although in the Western ideal adjudication is differentiated from other activities, is conducted by professional specialists, and in general is 'insulated from general knowledge about persons and their histories and status', as I have discussed here, Chinese adjudication remains closely tied to politics and policy;

- although in the Western ideal the forum is impartial and 'is not the agent of any entity outside the forum, with responsibility to further policies other than those crystallized in the decision', the responsibility of the Chinese courts to advance policies of the Party-state and their dependence on local governments affects the outcomes of cases.

Chinese adjudication has a special characteristic thrust on it by political doctrine: adjudication is not a society-wide phenomenon, since most of the activities of other Chinese agencies lie beyond the reach of the courts. Most controversies arising out of the exercise of power by a Chinese agency of government, central or local, to which affected persons may wish to object as a matter of law, may not and do not come to the attention of the courts at all. Other agencies of the Party-state deal with – or do not deal with – issues that are often the ordinary work of courts elsewhere.[41]

Today Chinese courts and law are far less politicized than at any time since the PRC was founded. Otherwise there would be no point in writing about them in such detail, but they still remain so functionally undifferentiated from the rest of the Party-state that they should be characterized as bureaucratic rather than adjudicatory organs. The Chinese courts may outwardly resemble those of civil law systems more than their Anglo-American counterparts because 'the emphasis on career service, explicit hierarchy of posts, precise application of codes, the elaboration of files, and correction and supervision by superiors matches the bureaucratic model fairly closely'.[42] However, the extent of hierarchical review of judicial decisions, within and between courts – often before decisions are final – suggests that Chinese judicial decision-making is more of an administrative process than a judicial one, especially if the criteria are judicial independence and the judge's individual responsibility for the decision.[43] These aspects of the judicial hierarchy reflect its position as only one of many bureaucratic 'systems' (*xitong*) existing in parallel with, but not superior, to all others. This integration of courts into the entire Chinese bureaucracy[44] causes adjudication to be organized like the work of any other governmental agency – such as issuing permits, establishing production targets for state-owned enterprises, or making safety rules for the roads.

The view of Chinese courts that has been proposed here is resonated with research by Professor He Weifang of the Beijing University Law Faculty that captures the views of some judges on the position of their courts in Chinese society. The characteristics of the courts described by a county court judge before enactment of the Judges Law is particularly telling:

> The management style of our courts is a kind of unprofessionalized form of management. Why is it so difficult to reform the style of adjudication? Because Chinese law is mass-oriented (qunzhong hua) and anti-professionalized. ... Judges of grassroots and intermediate courts with low levels of legal professionalization handle many cases ... why is

> it for a long time there has been no change in the situation in which a large number of demobilized soldiers become judges? I once worked in a county ... the director of the county personnel department said: 'What is the PLA for? It serves as a tool of proletarian dictatorship. And what is a judicial organ for? It is also a tool of proletarian dictatorship. It's the same thing'. Apart from this, anyone from any profession can join judicial organs ... the best cadres will not be assigned to work at the court, only those without a profession will be assigned to the courts because anyone can do the job. Can this profession have any authority? ... This is a systemic problem, and cannot be solved by the judicial organs alone.[45]

Based on such interviews, He Weifang concludes that 'as long as the judge fulfills a kind of administrative or non-judicial function, there will be no possibility or necessity to attain professionalism in the selection of judges'.[46] He quotes a judge describing the current problems faced by one vice president of a provincial court:

> The operational mechanism of the court isn't scientific, it's 'just a copy from the same old Political-Legal department mold'; [it] lacks a mechanism that would guarantee independent adjudication by law and mixes Party and governmental functions with adjudication; [it provides] no legal guarantee of occupation, position, or salary for the judge, [and] no legal guarantee of financial support, [so that] the courts are restricted by administrative agencies.[47]

These interviews suggest the continuing challenge to legal reform presented by organizational patterns antedating reform. Under Mao, Chinese law was assimilated to administration, and the principal doctrinal controversy contrasted only two different views of bureaucracy, 'Red' and 'Expert'. Today Chinese law reformers must make fundamentally different distinctions. As totalitarianism ebbs and functional specialization increases, speculation has begun in China about a view of judicial activity centered on upholding the rule of law, and about the professional orientation in the courts that is appropriate in light of this goal.

Linking the activity of the courts to the rule of law would require an entirely different perspective from that underlying the courts' current status. The rule of law is an ideology, even if its content is contested.[48] Courts truly dedicated to promoting that ideal cannot be instruments of a government that uses them to promote changing political tasks; they must have a more passive interest in solving conflict to attain a social equilibrium. Because the rule of law implies a very different view of the state, movement in the PRC toward legality remains hobbled. It puts into question a fundamental element of current Party policy – insistence that the boundaries of reform must be set by the CCP without changing its position in the Party-state. A metaphor that may be appropriate here was suggested early in the reforms by the call of a senior Chinese economist to keep the non-state sector of the economy as a 'bird in a cage'. That expression no longer fits the economy, but it does describe law reform today, which is still enclosed by the bars of a cage.

Proposals for reform

Little in Chinese history suggests any model for an appropriate relationship between courts, the government that created them and the society they serve. The Chinese leadership, and legal professionals, are groping for a formula. In 1999 judicial reform became a topic commonly discussed in the Chinese press.

Reappraisal of the courts as bureaucratic institutions has just perceptibly crept into official policy. In late 1999, a 'five-year outline of reform of the People's Courts' was issued by the Supreme People's Court.[49] It began by citing the problems that confront the courts today: local protectionism, corruption, and a low quality of work at the lowest level. It stressed adherence to the principles of independent adjudication based on law, and a unified national legal system, 'while proceeding from China's national conditions'. It also noted that 'the model of administrative management of adjudicative work is not suited to the special characteristics and regular patterns of adjudication work'. The significance of this thrust becomes apparent in certain of the measures that are advocated, such as public adjudication, raising the analytic quality of judicial decisions, publishing typical cases to be taken as 'reference' by local courts, enforcing the plaintiff's burden of coming forward with evidence, limiting the role of the adjudication committees, assuring participation by senior judges in hearing and deciding cases, and strengthening the enforcement of judicial decisions. In addition, the 'outline' emphasizes legal training for judges, and states that judges for upper levels should come from lower-level courts, and that judges should be selected from 'lawyers and upper-level legal talent'.

Concern for raising the ethical level of judges is manifested, in a clause promising the issuance of regulations on relations among litigants, defendants and lawyers on the one hand, and court personnel on the other. Such regulations were issued in early 2000.[50] Closer supervision of lower courts by higher-level courts is called for, as well as a new system of discipline based on a 'supervisory system' to strengthen the 'professional morality' of judges, that is not expounded.

For all its emphasis on rationalizing and professionalizing the activities of the courts, the 'outline' also emphasizes clearly political themes: while emphasizing the 'fundamental plan of ruling the country by law' it also stresses that the courts must adhere to the leadership of the CCP and the system of 'the people's democratic dictatorship'. In personnel matters, it is quite specific in calling for management of lower-court personnel by CCP organizations at higher-level courts.

Since the 'outline' was issued, the Chinese press has carried speeches by leaders and commentaries urging judicial reform,[51] denouncing various forms of corruption,[52] and praising the institution of structural reforms,[53] including a system of personal responsibility of judges for their intentional violations of law in rendering decisions.[54] Judges have replaced their military-style uniforms for robes or western suits with badges.[55] The extent to which these reforms can be carried out will depend on a number of factors.

Forces in Chinese society affecting legal reform

Changes in the Chinese economy and in Chinese society wrought by economic reform since 1979 could impel further legal reform, but they also create new difficulties for it. Here I note only some of the most obvious changes, and some of their possible implications for the deepening and strengthening of law reform.

Political

Leadership ambivalence in policy toward law

Since 1979 and the beginning of economic reform, China's leaders have wrestled with defining the role of law. Although they have emphasized the importance of law in governing the nation, they also insist on maintaining the dominant role of the CCP in Chinese society, and cannot resolve the contradiction between these two policies. Thus, when President Jiang Zemin proclaimed, at an important meeting in 1996, that the country should be ruled by law, he immediately added a qualifying phrase emphasizing the need to 'protect the long-term peace and stability of the country', a shorthand reference to maintaining the rule of the CCP.[56]

The contradiction between simultaneous emphasis by the Chinese leadership on legality and on the dominance of the Chinese Communist Party was underlined in March 1999, when the National People's Congress (NPC) adopted an amendment to the Chinese Constitution that states, 'The People's Republic of China shall be governed according to law and shall be built into a socialist country based on the rule of law'. At the same time, however, the NPC also amended the Constitution in a different manner. Prior to the amendment, Article 12 had affirmed 'the leadership of the Chinese Communist Party and Marxism-Leninism and Mao Zedong Thought' as 'guiding principles'. To these sources of Communist ideology was added 'Deng Xiaoping Theory'. Ideology remains a potential and self-contradictory inspiration, both for further and far-reaching reform and for the continued maintenance of Communist authoritarianism. The CCP continues to use law as an instrument to punish and suppress dissent or any movements or tendencies that seem to threaten CCP rule, such as the attack launched by the leadership on the Falun Gong sect in

1999. Paralleling the exhortations of high officials to raise the quality of judicial work are reminders that Party members must 'oversee' the work of the courts[57] and 'strengthen political and ideological work'.[58]

Leadership ambivalence about the role of the courts stands in contrast to the perceptible appearance, among legal professionals and the general population, of an incipient belief in the legitimacy of formal institutions for dispute resolution. For these trends to continue, they must be nourished by popular perceptions that the courts function meaningfully to foster substantive justice. Policy, however, remains ambivalent about the functions of the courts.

The decline of the power of the central Party-state

When the leadership granted more power to local authorities to promote economic reform, 'they probably did not anticipate that diffusion of economic decision-making to the local areas and regions would concentrate less political power in Beijing'.[59] The control and influence of local governments over economic resources and local business activity that has been so critical to the success of the economic reforms is not decreasing, but rather seems to be deepening over time. At the same time, the decline of the state sector has reduced the economic resources available to the center. More fundamentally, the growth of regionalism has weakened the 'Leninist structure' of the Party-state. Central directives and exhortations are 'ignored or superficially followed',[60] deviation from central state policies is encouraged, and the overall power of the state is undermined.[61]

Economic

An emergent non-state economic sector in uncertain transition; a backward state sector

The economic reforms have created a growing and increasingly differentiated non-state sector, composed of enterprises under varying degrees of control by local governments and private owners. Chinese economic reform has proceeded without careful definition of property rights,[62] and local officials have benefited from the ambiguous legal status of private firms to form alliances with them and to peddle influence and protection in forms such as subsidies and favorable tax treatment. By the end of the 1980s, 'many rural firms that were nominally collective had in fact become private firms operated with the cooperation of local officials'.[63]

Local governments influence enterprises directly, as in the licensing process, and also support some enterprises with credit, tax breaks or exemptions, allocations at market prices of scarce goods and access to information about new products, technology and markets.[64] In the 'interpenetration' of government and business at the local level, bargains are struck daily between business and bureaucrats who may be disguised owners or simply accepting payoffs and bribery.[65]

Patterns of local government involvement in enterprises are in a state of flux. In some places local enterprises were increasingly privatized during the mid-1990s, as local governments decided that privatization did not diminish their control. The Chinese leadership continues to declare its commitment to further reform and the economy's future trajectory will take it far from its Maoist origins, but the goals of the Chinese leadership remain undefined, and the journey will certainly be shaped by forces beyond its control. In the near term, the economy is 'marketized but not privatized'.[66]

Meanwhile, the state sector of the economy, long recognized as failing, continues to face difficult obstacles to economic and legal reform.[67] Half of all state-owned enterprises may be insolvent, dependent on generous bank loans to keep them afloat; the banks that have lent to them would be close to bankruptcy if the loans were not rolled over; unfunded pension liabilities are enormous; and assets are being stripped by managers.[68] Legal rules are essentially irrelevant. Relations between center and locality and between administrative superiors and inferiors are currently based on bargaining.[69] In this environment, enterprises and their superiors 'face a vast realm of indeterminacy, in which everything – price, plan, supply, tax, credit – is subject to change and negotiation'.[70] In the state sector, the enterprise and its superior are locked in an inextricable embrace in which they must bargain with each other, while accountability fades away. Reform of the state sector, long a goal of the Chinese leadership, presents enormous difficulties, but until reform is accomplished the state sector will remain outside the legal realm.[71]

Cultural

The crisis of values

Reform has dramatically enlarged the personal freedom of many Chinese. Now, Chinese are better able to communicate without fearing surveillance, criticism or denial of access to social welfare for political reasons by agents of the police in their work unit. The state is beginning to channel social services such as housing, social security and medical services through local governments rather than through work units. Privatization has encouraged many to 'jump into the sea' (*xiahai*) of private enterprise and entrepreneurship, and has created employment alternatives in the non-state sector. The social values and intellectual life of many Chinese, especially in the cities along the coast, have moved farther from government and Party control than could have been deemed possible in 1979.[72]

At the same time, the profound political and economic changes that are taking place have unsettled the beliefs and values of China's people. While the material lives of many have been improved by ten years of an extraordinary rate of economic growth, both traditional values and values promoted during decades of Communism have been threatened by the effects of the economic reforms. With dramatic improvement in material and personal life have come changes in China's social fabric that are both momentous and irreversible. Income disparity is growing, both as a general phenomenon and between urban and rural areas. Demographic pressures and the lure of increased income have prompted a huge number of peasants to leave the countryside in search of employment in the cities. This population flow, formerly forbidden, has created a 'floating population' of as many as 100 million in China's cities, people unattached to work units and who constitute 'swelling armies of impoverished rural floaters'.[73] Reports continue to emerge about discontent among peasants angry at their exploitation by local cadres, an increasing number of spontaneous protests by unemployed workers, and considerable alienation among young people.[74] Environmentally related social protests have become increasingly more common.[75] Since the beginning of economic reform, crime, violent and otherwise, has risen, provoking widespread concern about social order and provoking the Chinese leadership to launch numerous campaigns against crime.

Distinctions between state and non-state property and rights are vague, and standards of appropriate conduct whether ideological, legal or moral are lacking.[76] Relations among Chinese are changing, as new networks of personal relationships appear as means of getting things done. The weakening of the totalitarian grip on individual lives has fostered the reemergence of an emphasis on personal relationships. Although traditionally the foundation of *guanxi* has not been pecuniary, in China today the concept is often transmuted into highly instrumental behavior. The success of economic reforms has led many Chinese to lose what little faith they may have had in the ideology of Marxism-Leninism-Mao Zedong Thought. The consequences of Maoist rule and the Cultural Revolution had already begun to weaken belief in the ideology, and the economic reforms have further accelerated its decline. While the ideology to which the leadership constantly proclaims loyalty is eroded from below, it is also being hollowed out from above. The leadership repeatedly changes policy while maintaining its ostensible consistency with established ideology, as when it changed the goal of economic reform from a 'socialist commodity economy' to a 'socialist market economy', without clearly defining the characteristics of either. The Party's legitimacy will, as a result, increasingly be questioned.

Even as the ideology that justifies the Party's rule declines, the opening of China to the rest of the world has exposed the Chinese people to new values and ideas. Interest in politics and belief in the virtue of the officials of the Party-state have declined, and the leadership's calls to create a 'spiritual civilization' elicit little popular enthusiasm. No alternative system of belief has appeared to challenge an increasingly empty communism, and China is drifting ideologically.

In the midst of this enormous flux of values and institutions, corruption is growing, despite continued efforts by the leadership to check and punish its many manifestations. The US-China Business Council has commented

> The corruption problem seems only to worsen. So tightly knit are corrupt practices into the fabric of modern Chinese society that they are almost invisible. Invoice fraud, diversion of government investment capital, bribery and misappropriation of central and local government funds all seem to have become a way of life. ... The universal assumption that all officials and corporate managers are corrupt is probably responsible for the speed with which disgruntled workers take to the streets; civil protest, mostly peaceful, is reported almost daily by the foreign (not Chinese) press in China.[77]

Chinese legal culture: continuity and change

The future development of Chinese legal reforms will be influenced by various and disparate elements of Chinese legal culture. The term 'legal culture' is used here to mean, in the words of one scholar, 'those parts of general culture – customs, opinions, ways of doing and thinking – that bend social forces toward or away from the law and in particular ways'.[78] Traditional Chinese attitudes toward law still prompt many to avoid and fear involvement with formal legal institutions, while new values emergent from economic and legal reforms are increasing the acceptability of formal legal institutions.

The continuing force of tradition

Traditionally in China, the emphasis on social harmony and avoidance of conflict interacted with family, social structure and political institutions to form a rich and mutually reinforcing blend of attitudes that shaped Chinese 'legal culture' as it influenced the resolution of disputes. When disputes arose, widely held values discouraged persons from invoking formal legal rules or the agencies, judicial or otherwise, charged with formally enforcing and applying such rules.[79] Today a venerable tradition of emphasizing compromise in the context of long-standing relationships continues to exert its influence. The traditionally dominant attitudes were reinforced by decades of Communist rule, during which formal legal institutions were insignificant except as vehicles to demonstrate for the Chinese masses the CCP policies of the moment. Many Chinese, especially in the countryside, remain unwilling to take their disputes to court, and would rather find less contentious solutions to problems that would center on adjusting the relationships of the disputants without reference to legal rights and duties. Tradition continues to generate social pressures even as the non-state economy develops. For example, a recent village study notes the continuing importance of face (*lian* or *mianzi*) in the settlement of disputes in the context of a 'recycling' of tradition in which decollectivization has fuelled the expansion of new *guanxi* networks;[80] a press report tells of the existence of a new profession of debt collectors, who shame debtors publicly in order to induce them to pay.[81] Even though much Chinese legislation since 1979 has created new rights and obligations, the assertion of rights is still relatively novel in much of Chinese society.

New rights, new means of enforcing them

The new legal relationships and transactions created by the economic reforms have been defined, even if often incompletely, by an enormous amount of legislation that has created a framework for contract and other commercial transactions and defined new rights in many other areas. For example, an inheritance law that took effect in 1985 aims to protect private rights over property that formerly would have been considered 'means of production' that could be owned only by the state.[82]

Changing attitudes among the populace toward law and legal institutions are suggested, as already noted, by the slight decline in the number of cases handled by mediation committees and the rise in the number of disputes that are being taken to the courts. Legal scholars and press reports alike tell of successful lawsuits in which new principles of tort liability have been asserted in an increasing number of suits for injury to a variety of personal rights, including rights to life and health, personal names, image and reputation.[83] The Supreme People's Court has expanded the definition of rights arising under the provisions of the General Principles of Civil Law, as by listing examples of conduct that should deemed to be injurious of reputation.[84] Consumers have asserted their rights to sue retailers for knowingly selling counterfeit goods.[85]

Notably, too, class actions have been brought to enforce a wide and growing range of rights, such as failure to pay dividends, breach of contract, damage to crops caused by inferior seed or fertilizer, and violation of environmental antipollution regulations.[86] Class actions present burdens on the courts, already suffering from a lack of resources and trained judges. Some judges may discourage such cases as too time-consuming, and some lawyers may not welcome class actions because of their complexity or difficulty and because the regulations on legal fees give them little incentive to take on such cases. Despite these obstacles, the use of class actions is growing as a means by which citizens can try to force local governments to obey national laws; more generally, they suggest that 'the ways in which litigants use the legal system to pursue their own interests may be increasingly important in shaping the evolution of law in China'.[87] The growth of legal aid services has further made the courts more accessible to individuals and groups with legal claims.[88] Also, despite the leadership's ambivalence toward the rule of law, the development of administrative law reflects their concern about the need to curb official arbitrariness.

Changing attitudes toward law

Some Chinese legal scholars, officials and intellectuals have called for a legal system that embodies standards of procedural fairness. Although there have been no public demonstrations in the name of democracy since 1989, published discussions of political and legal reform have increasingly called for the rule of law. In addition to intellectuals who appreciate the importance of the rule of law in the West, other elements of Chinese society would also like to see stronger legal institutions. Research suggests that despite the continuing vitality of *guanxi* and increasing corruption, some of the growing number of entrepreneurs would like their economic transactions to be protected by rules enforced meaningfully and consistently by the power of the Chinese state.[89] Chinese government and Party officials who suffered hardships during the Cultural Revolution are well aware of the need to check and punish official arbitrariness, and many ordinary Chinese would prefer to see a legal system that would deter and punish arbitrary conduct by officials. Scholars have noted that some Chinese peasants rely on published laws and policies to resist official behavior that they consider to be unjust,[90] and that protests against environmental abuses began to appear after environmental laws were promulgated.[91] These are indigenous Chinese sentiments, not the creations of Western scholars, and they signify that the issue of whether China is to strengthen the rule of law is becoming a truly Chinese problem.

Chinese attitudes toward law are also influenced by increasingly frequent encounters between Chinese and visitors from abroad and exposure to foreign media. Especially along the China Coast, it is not unusual to meet Chinese who tell of something they have learned about law from watching American television or discussing differences between East and West with foreign visitors. Overseas Chinese are a particularly important conduit for Western values, although often Overseas Chinese from Hong Kong and Southeast Asia prefer to undervalue formal legality and do business in a relatively traditional manner, relying on relationships to particular places such as an ancestral village or rural county, or to persons whether related or linked by alliance.

While the outcome of the conflicting trends described here cannot be predicted, it is apparent that ideas about law are moving from abroad into China in a forceful stream that cannot be stopped by government or Party. It is also impossible to measure or predict the impact of those ideas, and the extent to which they may contribute to the modernization of Chinese law. What is certain is that institutional change is necessarily a process that, even with the strongest political support, can only work slowly at best.

Legal culture in flux

Several aspects of current judicial practice illustrate the complexity of the forces that are acting on the courts. More and more case decisions are being published, some under the authority of the Supreme People's Court. While the appearance of these cases reflects the growth of the courts, the accretion of their experience and the lengthening of the reach of the laws they apply, they must be read, however, in light of the strong local government involvement in the outcomes of court decisions that has been mentioned above. Two studies by Western scholars of dispute resolution during the 1980s concluded that the courts treated current policies and the views of local officials as more important to the outcomes than relevant laws.[92] Even when the courts emphasized contractual rights, this emphasis derived 'from an insistence upon observing the Party's current policy'.[93] On balance, although published reports of judicial decisions reflect some development of the courts during the past decade, they cannot yet not be taken as accurate representations of the daily work of the judicial system.

Although the number of contract disputes brought to the courts is rising, current Chinese sources underline the existence of fundamental problems in the quality of Chinese adjudication and the ability of the courts to enforce their decisions. Their opinions, usually written in a formalistic and conclusory manner, not only give no hint of their underlying reasoning but also conceal doctrinal and structural difficulties produced by the disorder among the sources of the rules and standards that Chinese courts apply in their decisions.

We know nothing yet about the impact of reported cases. Private conversations with a small number of judges and law professors suggest that in practice they have not frequently been consulted by lower courts. As for the lawyers, since cases are not supposed to have precedental value, might they feel less need to keep abreast of Chinese court decisions than their Western counterparts? My conversations with Chinese lawyers suggest that some, in litigation, are beginning to cite previous cases in arguments to the courts. Under Chinese doctrine, cases are not supposed to have any precedental value, but the 'reform outline' mentioned above provides that 'typical cases ... which have been discussed and decided by the Supreme People's Court Adjudication Committee will be published, providing references for lower levels of court for their adjudication of similar types of cases'.[94]

Other evidence suggests that regardless of the extent to which the opinion of a court may be couched in legalistic terms, the many different values that coexist in Chinese society – traditional, Maoist, reformist – shape both the arguments of parties to civil litigation and the judicial decisions that resolve disputes. Sociologists Isabelle Thireau and Hua Linshan examined courtroom debate in Guangdong courts during a few weeks in 1995, as a means of investigating changing norms in Chinese society.[95] The 130 cases that were examined were all civil cases, involving such issues as rights over houses or commercial spaces, tort suits for damages, debts, divorce and custody, and other matters not involving conflict with governmental authorities. The authors noted that in over 58 per cent of the cases, no lawyers were involved, although in many cases other representatives assisted the parties. Even when lawyers participated in courtroom debates, they asserted arguments based not on law but on values derived from traditional society or pre-reform 'collectivist society'. Discrepancies between the requirements of legal rules and social practice were often not explicitly addressed. In most sessions, note the authors, judges acted as mediators, and often pressed the parties to adopt conciliatory attitudes: 'To accept a compromise is still highly valued, as the analysis of court sessions reveals, making it sometimes difficult for the parties to reject such an offer'.[96] The authors conclude by noting that the various 'historical ruptures' that have confronted Chinese society during the last decades have 'introduced a certain plurality of principles and values' that are integrated into the settlement of legal disputes. This, they say, helped to reinforce the 'traditional perception ... that laws are first of all a governmental instrument and not a reflection of ongoing social debate about norms, rights and obligations'.[97]

The uncertain future of Chinese law reform

There is, at base, the question of whether the Chinese leadership wishes to build a legal system. Quite apart from the weaknesses of the courts that have been discussed above, I have thus far emphasized that ideology and lack of political will highlight the leadership's failure or unwillingness to choose to establish a meaningful rule of law. Institutional weakness is another powerful factor: Chinese legislative institutions are weak and stand alongside, not effectively superior to, the administrative bureaucracy; as already noted, Chinese courts are at best only at the same level of authority as the other institutions of the state apparatus; their limited reach reflects the subordination of law to the bureaucracy, and continuing weakness in their power to enforce their decisions. Substantial changes in this configuration of institutions would require major political decisions, little sign of which has appeared.

Even if the central leadership were firmly committed to more vigorous promotion of legality, it faces serious limits on its capacity. Two principal characteristics of the Chinese economic reforms, creation of a parallel economy and devolution of power to the localities, have benefited economic reform, but their combined force may also retard and deflect Chinese legal development because they make problematic the standardized application of law and implementation of policies. Enough power has been devolved downwards to lead frequently to downright defiance of central government policies that, at least in the short run, promotes a particularism inimical to the growth of national regulation and law-making.

The new business/government alliances and *guanxi* networks could mark an intermediate stage between the breakdown of old bureaucracies and the emergence of markets, but the weight of Western scholarship is more pessimistic.[98] Rather than seeing a post-totalitarian separation between state and society, scholars perceive the emergence of a 'corporatist' state[99] in which non-governmental actors reflect the motives and actions of the state. The pattern is not uniform. Although state corporatism may bring stability to local polities in wealthy areas, 'significant parts of rural China lack the political institutions or party authority to maintain a stable political order'.[100] In the face of the fluidity and the variety of configurations of local power that have been sketched here, the impact on the evolution of legal institutions of the identifiable forces in Chinese society that have been discussed here cannot be predicted.

Individuals, businesses and local governments alike might begin to desire greater nationwide uniformity in the implementation of law. In the short run, however, the prospects for the sustained development of meaningful legal institutions seem doubtful. Their current weakness and the moral vacuum in which they operate encourage opportunistic behavior. The organizational challenge presented by the task of building effective institutions that have been noted here is formidable. The immense size and poverty of large portions of China make any administrative tasks difficult, and the task of revising the allocations of power within the Chinese bureaucracy and between government and Party presents enormous difficulties. The expansion of economic opportunities and relationships, together with the decline of the work unit and the multiplication of other routes for the delivery of social services, could, perhaps, increase pressure, especially from economic actors in the non-state sector, to make implementation of law more regular. At the moment, however, the difficulties stated here threaten to retard Chinese legal development unless fundamental changes are made in the current structure of the Chinese state and the state sector of the Chinese economy. Somehow the CCP will have to retreat, quietly or otherwise, from its determined opposition to the emergence of values and social organizations that it perceives as threats to its dominance over Chinese society.

Twenty years of legal reform have aroused new concerns, which are a luxury impossible to imagine not long ago. Indeed, the sheer volume of legislation, its undeniable growing importance, and the institutions that have been created sometimes generate excessive optimism among some Chinese and foreign observers alike. So, for example, to say that '[T]he Chinese know how to enact laws, they have a good process for doing it ... and they will be able to make the kinds of legal changes that WTO entry requires', seems to ignore the normative chaos in Chinese law-making today and to exaggerate the progress that has been made toward transparency.[101]

A force that promises to accelerate legal reform is China's accession to the WTO. As accession drew near, discussion by Chinese scholars and officials reflected growing recognition that accession will entail not only manifold economic obligations but will also require legal institutions to be modified to meet standards of governance and transparency that are very generally expressed in Article X of the GATT, and in other treaties that are implemented by the WTO. Among the troublesome issues in the lengthy negotiations between representatives of the PRC and a working party representing the WTO were the extent and definition of China's obligation to bring a new transparency to the adoption and implementation of trade-related laws. In the Draft Protocol of

Accession, China agreed to enforce only laws on goods, services, TRIPS and foreign exchange control that have been published; to establish an official journal for publication of such laws and allow a reasonable period for comment before they are implemented; and to establish an enquiry point at which information on such laws could be obtained. China also agreed to establish and maintain 'tribunals, contact points and procedures for the prompt review' of administrative actions related to laws and decisions covered by GATT Article X, GATS Article VI and relevant portions of TRIPS; such tribunals must be 'impartial' and there must be opportunity to appeal to a judicial body.[102] These commitments are encouraging – but they also contain the seeds of further friction between China and its trading partners. Frustration by foreign traders and investors at perceived slowness or incompleteness in Chinese reform could provoke an increase in the volume of disputes brought to the WTO's dispute settlement institutions, as well as pressure on China during the annual reviews of its trade policies to which it has agreed – and resentment in Beijing at foreign pressure.

On balance, the overall thrust of the past twenty years of reform efforts has been positive, and further encouraging efforts are underway to advance judicial reform, add coherence to Chinese law-making and continue the development of administrative law.[103] Chinese legal institutions are slowly becoming increasingly differentiated and functionally specialized, and promise to expand rights and rights-consciousness. Further reform continues to be deterred or slowed, however, by formidable obstacles that arise out of both the Chinese Party-state and Chinese society.

Notes

1 This chapter draws on analysis that I have presented in Stanley Lubman, *Bird in a Cage: Legal Reform in China After Mao* (Stanford: Stanford University Press, 1999), which retains copyright in respect of all excerpts and adapted sections.

2 See generally, Lawyers Committee for Human Rights, *Lawyers in China: Obstacles to Independence and the Defense of Rights* (New York: Lawyers Committee for Human Rights, 1998). China now has well over 150,000 lawyers and 8,000 law firms, most of which are state-run, although the number of 'cooperative' firms is growing. The new profession faces many problems. The state continues to regulate and scrutinize lawyers' activities, and a major unresolved contradiction exists between a legal profession and the CCP opposition to autonomous organizations and professions. China's lawyers are still few, and their professional qualifications and educational standards remain low. Legal ethics are emerging only slowly. The sudden expansion of the legal profession has created enormous temptations for lawyers, judges and officials to engage in bribery and a variety of corrupt practices that currently pervade their professional activities. The use of personal contacts with judges or other officials to attempt to influence the outcomes of cases, for example, is pervasive. I have discussed below the concerns of the leadership about judicial corruption.

3 Source: *Zhongguo Falü Nianjian* [China Law Yearbook]: 1991 (pp. 934–5); 1992 (p. 855); 1993 (p. 936); 1994 (p. 1028); 1995 (p. 1064–5); 1996 (pp. 958–9); 1997 (p. 1056); 1998 (p. 1239); 1999 (p. 1021); 2000 (p. 1209). Chinese theory

distinguishes between 'economic' legal relationships in which any of the parties are state-owned entities, and 'civil' legal relationships involving privately owned entities and individuals.

4 Department of Grass-Roots Work, Ministry of Justice, *People's Mediation in China* (*c.*1991); *Zhongguo Falü Nianjian* [China Law Yearbook]: 1991 (p. 956), 1992 (p. 875), 1993 (p. 956), 1994 (p. 1047), 1995 (p. 1081), 1996 (p. 977), 1997 (p. 1075), 1998 (p. 1257), 1999 (p. 1041), 2000 (p. 1230). Discrepancies in figures appear in originals.

5 Peter Howard Corne, *Foreign Investment in China: The Administrative Legal System* (Hong Kong: Hong Kong University Press, 1997) p. 56.

6 *Ibid.*, pp. 68–83.

7 Perry Keller, 'Sources of Order in Chinese Law', *American Journal of Comparative Law*, vol. 42 (1994) pp. 711, 734. Anthony Dicks, 'Compartmentalized Law and Judicial Restraint: An Inductive View of Some Jurisdictional Barriers to Reform', in Stanley Lubman (ed.) *China's Legal Reforms* (Oxford: Oxford University Press 1996) pp. 82, 99–103.

8 *Ibid.*, p. 108.

9 Perry Keller, 'Sources of Order in Chinese Law', *American Journal of Comparative Law*, vol. 42 (1994) p. 740.

10 Perry Keller, 'Legislation in the People's Republic of China', *University of British Columbia Law Review*, vol 23, (1989) pp. 653, 668. See also Peter Corne, '"No Pain, No Gain": Steps Toward Securing the Future of China's legal System', in *The Rule of Law: Perspectives From the Pacific Rim* (Washington DC: Mansfield Center for Pacific Affairs, 2000) pp. 55, 56–9.

11 See Stanley Lubman, *Bird in a Cage: Legal Reform in China After Mao* (Stanford: Stanford University Press, 1999) pp. 282–4 and sources cited therein; Jianfu J. Chen, *Chinese Law: Towards an Understanding of Chinese Law, Its Nature and Development* (The Hague: Kluwer Law International, 1999) pp. 106–9.

12 See Perry Keller, 'Sources of Order in Chinese Law', *American Journal of Comparative Law*, vol. 42 (1994) pp. 750–2.

13 See Peter Corne, '"No Pain, No Gain": Steps Toward Securing the Future of China's legal System', in *The Rule of Law: Perspectives From the Pacific Rim* (Washington DC: Mansfield Center for Pacific Affairs, 2000) pp. 95–104. See also Claudia and Lester Ross, 'Language and Law: Sources of Systemic Vagueness and Ambiguous Authority in Chinese Statutory Language', in Karen G. Turner, James V. Feinerman and R. Kent Guy (eds) *The Limits of the Rule of Law* (Seattle: University of Washington Press, 2000) pp. 221, 223, hereinafter *Limits of the Rule of Law*.

14 Perry Keller, 'Sources of Order in Chinese Law', *American Journal of Comparative Law*, vol. 42 (1994) p. 711.

15 See Peter Howard Corne, *Foreign Investment in China: The Administrative Legal System* (Hong Kong: Hong Kong University Press, 1997) p. 90.

16 Meng Qinguo, 'Some Issues Relating to Policy Law', *Tianjin Shehui Kexue* [Tianjin Social Science], no. 2 (1990) p. 55, translated as 'Shortcomings of Policy Law', *Joint Publications Research Service*, no. 90038, 17 May 1990, p. 21.

17 *Ibid.*

18 Administration Litigation Law of the People's Republic of China (adopted 4 April 1989) CCH China Laws for Foreign Business (hereafter CCH) §§19–558.

19 *Zhongguo Falü Nianjian* [China Law Yearbook], 2000 (p. 1211).

20 Administrative Punishment Law of the People's Republic of China (adopted 17 March 1996) published in *Xinhua News Service*, 21 March 1996 (hereafter *Xinhua*), available in *Foreign Broadcast Information Service*, Daily Report, China (hereafter FBIS) no. 96–071 (11 April 1996).

21 State Compensation Law of the People's Republic of China (adopted 12 May 1994) translated in *Reuter Textline BBC Monitoring Service Far East.*

22 See e.g. Peter Howard Corne, *Foreign Investment in China: The Administrative Legal System* (Hong Kong: Hong Kong University Press, 1997) pp. 246–8.

23 An excellent brief discussion of administrative rule-making is Xixin Wang, 'Rule of Rules: An Inquiry into Administrative Rules in China's Rule of Law Context', in *The Rule of Law: Perspectives From the Pacific Rim* (Washington DC: Mansfield Center for Pacific Affairs, 2000) p. 71.

24 Administrative Reconsideration Law, *FBIS*, no. 1999–0512 (29 April 1999).

25 See, e.g., Veron Hung, 'Judicial Practice and Judicial Reform in the People's Republic of China: Lessons From Administrative Litigation in Guangdong Province', thesis submitted to the Stanford Law School in partial fulfillment of requirements for the MSL degree, May 1999, 85–9; David Zweig, 'The "Externalities of Development": Can new political institutions manage rural conflict?', in Elizabeth J. Perry and Mark Selden (eds) *Chinese Society: Change, Conflict and Resistance* (London and New York: Routledge, 2000) pp. 120, 125 (hereafter *Chinese Society*). In 1999, almost 45 per cent of administrative cases were withdrawn, *Zhongguo Falü Nianjian* [China Law Yearbook]: 2000 (p. 1023).

26 He Weifang, 'Tongguo Sifa Shixian Shehui Zhengyi: Dui Zhongguo Faguan Xianzhuang de Yige Toushi' [The Realization of Social Justice Through Judicature: A Look at the Current Situation of Chinese Judges], in Xia Yong (ed.) *Zou Xiang Quanli de Shidai: Zhongguo Gongmin Quanli Fazhan Yanjiu* [Toward a Time of Rights: A Perspective of the Civil Rights Development in China] (hereinafter *Toward a Time of Rights*) (Beijing: Zhong Guo Zhong Fa Da Xue Shu Ban She, 1995) pp. 209, 249.

27 See e.g. Zhou Dao, 'Shiying shehui zhuyi shichang jingji tizhi xuyao jiakuai fayuan tizhi gaige bufa' [To Adapt to the Socialist Market Economy, the Pace of Reform of the Court System Must be Quickened], in *Zhongguo Sifa Zhidu Gaige Zongheng Tan: Quanguo Fayuan Xitong Diliu Jie Xueshu Taolun Hui Lunwen Xuan* [A Free Discussion of the Reform of China's Judicial System: A Collection of Essays from the Sixth Academic Conference of the National Court System] (Beijing: Ren Min Fa Yuan Shu Ban She, 1994) pp. 1, 10.

28 See Donald C. Clarke, 'Power and Politics in the Chinese Court System: The Enforcement of Civil Judgments', *Columbia Journal of Asian Law*, vol. 10 (1996) pp. 28–34.

29 Yangzhou shi zhongji renmin fayuan [Yangzhou Municipal Intermediate Level People's Court], 'Kefu difang baohu zhuyi, jianchi yansu gongzheng zhifa' [Overcome Local Protectionism, Resolve to Seriously and Justly Uphold the Law], in Supreme People's Court Economic Chamber (ed.) *Jingji shen pan canyuan celiao yu xinleixing anli pingxi* [Economic Adjudication Reference Materials and Analysis of New Types of Cases] (1994) p. 113 at p. 115.

30 The 'Five Year Outline of Reform of the People's Courts' appeared on 23 Oct. 1999, in the *Fazhibao* [Legal Daily], published under the aegis of the Ministry of Justice, and was accessed at http://www.china-judge.com/fnsx386.htm. It was issued by the Supreme People's Court.

31 He, *Toward a Time of Rights*, pp. 266, 272; see also Margaret Y. K. Woo, 'Law and Discretion in Contemporary Chinese Courts', in *Limits of the Rule of Law*, pp. 169–170.

32 He, *Toward a Time of Rights*, p. 228 (citing Zhou Dunhe, 'Cong "zhongshi jiaoyu, zhongshi rencai" tan faguan jiaoyu, peixun wenti' [Discussing Education and Training of Judges from the Perspective of 'Emphasizing Education, Emphasize Human Resources'], *Renmin Fayuan Bao* [People's Court Journal], 12 May 1994.

33 'Law of the People's Republic of China on Judges', in British Broadcasting Corporation – Summary of World Broadcasts (hereafter BBC-SWB) (23 March 1995).
34 Donald C. Clarke, 'Dispute Resolution in China', *Journal of Chinese Law*, vol. 5 (1991) pp. 245, 258n44.
35 'China Introduces national exams for entry to legal profession', *Xinhua* News Agency, 16 July 2001, BBC World Monitoring, 16 July 2001.
36 Civil Procedure Law of the People's Republic of China (9 April 1991) CCH, *Zhongguo Falü Nianjian* [China Law Yearbook]: 2000, §§19–201, Articles 178, 182, 189; on the lack of finality generally, see Nanping Liu, 'A Vulnerable Justice: Finality of Civil Judgements in China', *Columbia Journal of Asian Law*, vol. 13 (1999) p. 35.
37 Margaret Y. K. Woo, 'Law and Discretion in Contemporary Chinese Courts', in *Limits of the Rule of Law*, pp. 180–1.
38 'Chinese leader Li Peng visits Zhejiang Province, discusses role of local congresses', *Xinhua* News Agency, BBC Worldwide Monitoring, 17 April 2001.
39 He Weifang, 'Tongguo Sifa Shixian Shehui Zhengyi: Dui Zhongguo Faguan Xianzhuang de Yige Toushi' [The Realization of Social Justice Through Judicature: A Look at the Current Situation of Chinese Judges], in *Toward a Time of Rights*, pp. 209, 249.
40 Marc Galanter, 'Adjudication, Litigation and Related Phenomena', in Leon Lipson and Stanton Wheeler (eds) *Law and the Social Sciences* (New York: Russell Sage, 1986) p. 151.
41 See, noting that the Chinese courts share their responsibilities 'with other "courts" – ministries, commissions and other bodies', Anthony Dicks, 'Compartmentalized Law and Judicial Restraint: An Inductive View of Some Jurisdictional Barriers to Reform', in Stanley B. Lubman (ed.) *China's Legal Reforms* (Oxford: Oxford University Press, 1996) pp. 82, 86.
42 Marc Galanter, 'Adjudication, Litigation and Related Phenomena', in Leon Lipson and Stanton Wheeler (eds) *Law and the Social Sciences* (New York: Russell Sage, 1986) p. 172.
43 Hikota Koguchi, 'Some Observations About 'Judicial Independence' in Post-Mao China', *Boston College Third World Law Journal*, vol. 7 (1987) pp. 195–213.
44 Perry Keller, 'Sources of Order in Chinese Law', *American Journal of Comparative Law*, vol. 42 (1994) p. 753.
45 *Toward a Time of Rights*, pp. 233–4.
46 *Ibid.*, p. 245.
47 *Ibid.*, 254–5, citing *Renmin fayuan bao* [People's Court Journal] 6 June 1994.
48 See e.g. Edward J. Epstein, 'Law and Legitimation in Post-Mao China', in Pitman B. Potter (ed.) *Domestic Law Reforms in Post-Mao China* (Armonk: M. E. Sharpe, 1994) p. 17. Randall Peerenboom's chapter in this volume (Chapter 4) explores alternative conceptions.
49 See above, note 30.
50 'New rules to help clean up judicial system', *Xinhua* News Agency, 31 Jan. 2000, in BBC World Monitoring, 3 Feb. 2000. Under the new regulations, judges were forbidden to try cases before courts in which they had served. *Ex parte* meetings with litigants were forbidden, as were 'accepting bribes, attending parties hosted by litigants, or borrowing money from them'.
51 '*Xinhua* Commentary on Judicial Reform', *Xinhua*, 31 Aug. 2100, in FBIS-CHI-000–0831; 'Li Peng Speaks on PRC Judicial Reform', *Xinhua*, 26 Oct. 2000, in FBIS-CHI-2000–1026.
52 'China Issues Rules to Prevent Nepotism in Judicial Reform', *Xinhua*, 31 Jan. 2000, in FBIS-CHI-2000–0205, 31 Jan. 2000; 'China's Chief Justice Targets 'Lax

Discipline', in Judiciary', *Xinhua*, 25 May 2000, in BBC-SWB 25 May 2000; 'PRC's Guangdong Justice Issues Tough Corruption Prevention Guideline', *Xinhua*, 16 Aug. 2000, in FBIS-CHI-2000–0816, 16 Aug. 2000.

53 E.g. '*Xinhua* Commentary on Selecting Presiding Judges for Hearing Legal Cases', *Xinhua*, 16 Aug. 2000, in FBIS-CHI-2000–0816.

54 'Courts to Promote Accountability System, for Verdicts', *Xinhua*, 1 March 2000, in BBC-SWB, 30 March 2000.

55 'Beijing Judges Replace Military-style Uniforms', *Xinhua*, 10 May 2000 in FBIS-Chi-2000–0510, 10 May 2000.

56 Liu Hainian, 'Yifa Zhiguo Jianshe Zhuyi Fazhi Guojia Xueshu Yantao Hui Jiyao' [Summary of Forum on Ruling the Country According to Law and Constructing a Nation of Socialist Legality], *Faxue Yanjiu* [Legal Studies], vol. 18, no. 3 (1996) p. 3.

57 'China: People's Courts Urged to Follow President's "Three Representations"', *Xinhua*, 22 June 2000, in BBC-SWB, 24 June 2000.

58 'Supreme People's Court Urges All Courts to Strengthen Ideological Work', *Xinhua*, 19 Sept. 2000, in FBIS-CHI-2000–0919.

59 Merle Goldman and Roderick MacFarquhar, 'Dynamic Economy, Declining Party-State', in Merle Goldman and Roderick MacFarquhar (eds) *The Paradox of China's Post-Mao Reforms* (Cambridge MA: Harvard University Press, 1999) pp. 3, 25.

60 *Ibid*., p. 26.

61 One study describes how in Xiamen entrepreneurs provide bribes and other benefits to officials in return for use of their personal ties within the bureaucracy, creating patron/client relationships that shift power downward to the lowest levels in society at which business and bureaucracy intersect in order to benefit local interests. David L. Wank, 'Bureaucratic Patronage and Private Business: Changing Networks of Power in Urban China', in Andrew G. Walder (ed.) *The Waning of the Communist State* (Berkeley: University of California Press, 1995) p. 153.

62 See generally, Jean C. Oi and Andrew G. Walder (eds) *Property Rights and Economic Reform in China* (Stanford: Stanford University Press, 1999).

63 Barry Naughton, *Growing Out of the Plan: Chinese Economic Reform 1978–1993* (Cambridge: Cambridge University Press, 1995) p. 157.

64 Jean Oi, *Rural China Takes Off: The Political Basis for Economic Reform* (Cambridge MA: Harvard University Press, 1999). Another interpretation regards TVEs not as necessarily strengthening formal state power at the local level, but as a form of local 'dictatorship' dominated by 'family links'. David Zweig, *Freeing China's Farmers: Rural Restructuring in the Reform Era* (Armonk: M. E. Sharpe, 1997) p. 24, summarizing the conclusions of Nan Lin, 'Local Market Socialism', *Theory and Society*, vol. 24 (1995) p. 301, at pp. 301–54.

65 See e.g. Dorothy Solinger, 'Urban Entrepreneurs and the State: The Merger of State and Society', in Arthur Lewis Rosenbaum (ed.) *State and Society in China: The Consequences of Reform* (Boulder: Westview Press, 1992) pp. 121, 136; and David L. Wank, 'Bureaucratic Patronage and Private Business: Changing Networks of Power in Urban China', in Andrew G. Walder (ed.) *The Waning of the Communist State* (Berkeley: University of California Press, 1995) p. 153.

66 The distinction is used by Robert F. Dernberger, 'China's Transition to the Future: Mired in the Present, or Through the Looking Glass to the Market Economy?', in *China's Economic Future: Challenges to U.S. Policy, Study Papers submitted to the Joint Economic Committee, Congress of the United States, 104th Congress, 2nd Session* (1996) p. 57, at p. 58.

67 Summarizing the problem, two scholars noted 'the bankruptcy or stagnation of over 60 per cent of China's relatively inefficient and obsolete state industries', and observe that although state industries employed over two thirds of the work force, they

produced less than half of China's economic production. Merle Goldman and Roderick MacFarquhar, 'Dynamic Economy, Declining Party-State', in Merle Goldman and Roderick MacFarquhar (eds) *The Paradox of China's Post-Mao Reforms* (Cambridge MA: Harvard University Press, 1999) pp. 3, 9.

68 See e.g. Nicholas P. Lardy, *China's Unfinished Economic Revolution* (Washington DC: Brookings Institution, 1998) pp. 21–58; X. L. Ding, 'The Illicit Asset Stripping of Chinese State Firms', *China Journal*, no. 43 (1995) p. 1.

69 See e.g. Barry Naughton, 'Hierarchy and the Bargaining Economy: Government and Enterprise in the Reform Process', in Kenneth G. Lieberthal and David M. Lampton (eds) *Bureaucracy, Politics, and Decision Making in Post-Mao China* (Berkeley: University of California Press, 1992) pp. 245–89.

70 *Ibid.*, p. 270.

71 See, generally, Edward S. Steinfeld, *Forging Reform in China* (Cambridge: Cambridge University Press, 1998).

72 See e.g. Charlotte Ikels, *The Return of the God of Wealth* (Stanford: Stanford University Press, 1996); Richard Baum, *Burying Mao: Chinese Politics in the Age of Deng Xiaoping* (Princeton: Princeton University Press, 1994) pp. 376–80.

73 *Ibid.*, p. 380.

74 See, generally, *ibid.*, pp. 376–80. On labor protests, see e.g. Feng Chen, 'Subsistence Crises, Managerial Corruption and Labour Protests in China', *The China Journal*, July 2000, p. 41; Ching Kwan Kee, 'Pathways of Labor Insurgency', in *Chinese Society*, p. 41.

75 Jun Jing, 'Environmental Protests in Rural China', in *Chinese Society*, p. 143.

76 Within the business sector,

> [g]ranting licenses and loans, forgiving debts, allowing tax breaks, and providing access to needed electricity, water, telephones, and transportation are only a few of the types of decisions for which PRC officials now expect 'tea money', or bribes.
>
> (Kenneth G. Lieberthal, *Governing China: From Revolution Through Reform* [New York: W. W. Norton, 1995] p. 268)

77 US-China Business Council, 'China's Political Developments in US-China Business Council' (comp.) *China Operations '98* (unpublished materials from China Operations '98, a conference held in Beijing, 17–18 Feb. 1998) p. 5. On the link between labor protests and managerial corruption, see Feng Chen, 'Subsistence Crises, Managerial Corruption and Labour Protests in China', *The China Journal*, July 2000, p. 41.

78 Lawrence Friedman, *The Legal System, A Social Science Perspective* (New York: Russell Sage, 1975) 15.

79 A recent discussion by a Chinese scholar of this subject is Liang Zhiping, 'Explicating "Law": A Comparative Perspective of Chinese and Western Legal Culture', *Journal of Chinese Law*, vol. 3 (summer 1989) p. 55. Recent scholarship suggests that during the eighteenth and nineteenth centuries, at least, a significant number of disputes may have been brought before local magistrates, whose judicial functions formed part of their administrative duties, see e.g. Philip Huang, *Civil Justice in China: Representation and Practice in the Qing* (Stanford: Stanford University Press, 1996). Nonetheless, dominant cultural attitudes discouraged persons from taking their disputes to courts.

80 Yunxiang Yan, *The Flow of Gifts I* (Stanford: Stanford University Press, 1996) pp. 136–8 (disputes), 237–8 ('recycling' of tradition).

81 'Chinese Deadbeats Cringe at the Sound of Mr Li's Gong', *Wall Street Journal*, 21 Sept. 2000.

82 Michael Palmer, 'China's New Inheritance Law: Some Preliminary Observations', in Stephan Feuchtwang, Athar Hussain and Thierry Pairault (eds) *Transforming China's Economy in the Eighties, Volume 1: The Rural Sector, Welfare and Employment* (Boulder: Westview Press, 1988) pp. 169–97.
83 Wang Liming, Yang Lixin and Zhao Hui (eds) *Renge quan fa* [Law of Personality Rights] (Beijing: Falü chubanshe [Legal Publishing House] 1997).
84 *Ibid.*, p. 18.
85 'He Shan Incident Represents Consumer Rights Issue', *Zhongguo qingnian bao* [China Youth Daily], 17 Oct. 1996, in FBIS 96-252 (17 Oct. 1996).
86 This discussion of class actions is based on Benjamin L. Liebman, 'Note: Class Action Litigation in China', *Harvard Law Review*, vol. 111 (1998) p. 1523.
87 *Ibid.*, p. 1541.
88 See e.g. Benjamin L. Liebman, 'Legal Aid and Public Interest Law in China', *Texas International Law Journal*, vol. 34 (1999) p. 211.
89 See e.g. Pitman B. Potter, 'Guanxi and the PRC Legal System: From Contradiction to Complementarity', in Pitman B. Potter and Michael W. Dowdle, *Developing Civil Society in China: From the Rule by law Toward the Rule of Law?*, Woodrow Wilson Center Asia Program Special Report no. 4, March 2000; Doug Guthrie, *Dragon in a Three-Piece Suit* (Princeton: Princeton University Press, 1999) pp. 175–97. Potter argues that *guanxi* and law are not necessarily seen in conflict with each other, but mutually complementary.
90 Li Lianjiang and Kevin J. O'Brien, 'Villagers and Popular Resistance in Contemporary China', *Modern China*, vol. 22 (1996) p. 28; Kevin O'Brien and Li Lianjiang, 'The Politics of Lodging Complaints in Rural China', *China Quarterly*, no. 143 (1995) p. 756.
91 Jun Jing, 'Environmental Protests in Rural China', in *Chinese Society*, p. 143.
92 Phyllis Chang, 'Deciding Disputes: Factors That Guide Chinese Courts in the Adjudication of Rural Responsibility Contract Disputes', *Law and Contemporary Problems*, vol. 53 (1989) p. 101; David Zweig, Kathy Hartford, James Feinerman and Deng Jianxu, 'Law, Contracts, and Economic Modernization: Lessons from the Recent Chinese Rural Reforms', *Stanford Journal of International Law*, vol. 23 (1987) p. 319.
93 *Ibid.*, p. 362.
94 'Five Year Outline', above, note 30, para. 14.
95 Isabelle Thireau and Hua Linshan, 'Legal Disputes and the Debate about Legitimate Norms', in Maurice Brosseau, Kuan Hsin-chi and Y. Y. Kueh (eds) *China Review 1997* (Hong Kong: Chinese University Press, 1997) p. 349.
96 *Ibid.*, p. 371.
97 *Ibid.*, p. 376.
98 See e.g. Steven M. Goldstein, 'China in Transition: The Political Foundations of Incremental Reform', *China Quarterly*, no. 145 (1995) p. 1105.
99 Jean C. Oi, 'Fiscal Reform and the Economic Foundations of Local State Corporatism in China', *World Politics*, no. 45 (1992) p. 99; Margaret M. Pearson, 'The Janus Face of Business Associations in China: Socialist Corporatism in Foreign Enterprises', *Australian Journal of Chinese Affairs*, no. 31 (1994) p. 25.
100 David Zweig, *Freeing China's Farmers: Rural Restructuring in the Reform Era* (Armonk: M. E. Sharpe, 1997) p. 25.
101 Jerome Cohen, remarks at Columbia Business School conference, 'China's Accession to the World Trade Organization: Implications for the United States, Japan and the World' (9 April 1999) p. 14; Center on Japanese Economy and Business and APEC STUDY Center, Columbia University Business School. Compare the remarks of Pitman Potter at the same conference, *ibid.*, pp. 8–9.

102 World Trade Organization, Working Party on the Accession of China, Report of the Working Party, 1 October 2001, Document No. WT/ACC/CHN/49.

103 E.g. the 'Outline of the Five-year Reform of the People's Courts' (text above, note 30); a Law on Legislation, see 'Full Text of PRC Legislation Law', FBIS-CHI-2000–0403, 18 March 2000; Peter Howard Corne, 'The New PRC, Legislation Law: The Emperor's New Clothes?', *China Law and Practice*, vol. 14 (May 2000) p. 30; and the ongoing efforts at administrative law that have been mentioned above.

INDEX

Abbott, Andrew 194
Abel, Richard 194
Ackerman, Bruce 190
adjudication 212–13
administrative discretion 17, 54, 63, 206–8
administrative law 17, 55, 63–4, 67, 186, 208
Alford, William P. vii, 14, 15–17, 182–204
American Bar Association 184
American Bar Foundation 183
American Law Institute 3
Anderson, Benedict 91
Aristotle 52
Asian Development Bank 2, 184
Asian values: China 52–4, 59, 74–5; Singapore 5
Australia 39, 87

Bangladesh 111–13
Belgium 54
Boissonade, Gustave 172
Bourdieu, Pierre 183
Bousquet, Georges 172
Burma 41, 44

Cambodia 44
Cameroon 40
Canada 39, 87, 109
capitalism: China 13, 53, 137, 148–9; democracy 35, 52; developing countries 34, 45; economic disparities 8; laissez-faire 38, 45, 56; Taiwan 12; United Kingdom 45
Castles, Stephen 86
Chen Shui-bian 101
Cheng, Lucie vii, 1–21, 33, 45, 85–105
China: courts, (adjudication) 210–16; (adjudication committees) 211, 215; (bureaucratic institutions) 212–15; (continuing problems) 206–7; (enforcement of judgments) 209; (growing activity) 205–6; (hierarchy) 211, 213; (judicial process) 211–12; (legal culture in flux) 222–4; (legislative order) 206–8; (litigation) 185–6, 205, 212, 221; (local protectionism) 209–10, 215; (politicization) 213; (post-Mao era) 17–18, 205–33; (reform proposals) 215–16; (Supreme People's Court) 207, 209, 215, 221–23 economy, (capitalism) 13, 53, 137, 148–9; (economic development) 219; (economic reform) 17, 66, 73, 216, 217–19; (economic regime) 55–7; (ethnic division of labor) 140; (floating population) 13, 137–38, 141, 146, 147, 219; (foreign investment) 143, 146–47, 149; (Great Leap Forward) 60, 138–9; (household registration [*hukou*]) 138–39, 142, 144, 146, 149; (industrialization) 138–39; (insolvency) 218; (liberalization) 39, 60, 188, 204; (licensing) 188–217; (market capitalism) 53; (market economy) 17, 52, 53, 56, 139–40, 182, 219; (market-dominant majority) 39; (market/law) 13–14, 137, 149–50; (marketization) 139–40, 145–6, 205, 218; (poverty) 60; (privatization) 218; (public ownership) 57, 218; (Shenzhen Special Economic Zone) 147; (socialism) 13, 137, 148–9; (sojourners) 140; (unemployment) 60, 149, 219; (urban subcommunities)

143–5; (Wenzhouese) 144 judiciary, (administrative decisions) 67–8, 208; (army officers) 199, 210, 214; (corruption) 186–7, 210, 211, 215, 216; (external influences) 209–10; (independence/autonomy) 208–9, 212; (rule of law) 54, 62–4, 214; (supervision) 64, 185, 209, 211, 215; (training) 186, 199, 210–11 law reform, (changing attitudes) 222; (continuity and change) 220–4; (courts) 215–16; (crisis of values) 218–20; (culture) 218–24; (economic reform) 217–18; (political leadership) 187, 197, 200, 204, 216–17; (tradition) 220–1; (uncertain future) 224–6 legal profession, (All China Lawyers Federation) 187; (American perceptions) 16–17, 182–5, 187, 189–95; (attorneys) 184; (bribery) 186, 189, 210; (civil law) 193–4; (corruption) 16, 186–7, 210, 211, 215, 216; (expansion) 15, 16, 185, 186, 226; (independence) 63, 64, 187–8; (law firms) 15–16, 185, 188–89, 226; (licensing) 188; (Ministry of Justice [MOJ]) 63, 64, 187; (party cells) 188–89; (professionalism) 15–17, 182–204; (rice roots legal workers) 186; (state legal workers) 15, 63, 185 legal system, (administrative law) 17, 55, 63–4, 67, 186, 208; (changing attitudes) 222; (civil law) 193–4, 213, 221; (class actions) 221; (constitutional law) 52, 66–7, 89, 143, 216; (conviction rates) 186, 197, 199; (criminal law) 65, 68, 186, 189, 197, 199, 219; (dispute resolution) 56, 62, 186, 195–6, 205–6; (labor law) 11, 148–9; (legal institutions) 13, 62–4, 69, 220; (mediation) 62, 186, 196, 205–6, 209, 211–12, 221; (normative documents) 189; (policy laws) 207; (re-education through labor) 68, 186, 189, 199, 201; (rule by law) 55, 56, 57, 59, 62, 69; (rule of law) 9–10, 16, 51–84, 182, 184, 188, 214, 221 peasants, (migration) 13, 137–55, 219; (protests) 222; (region of birth) 139; (repatriation) 139; (social class) 139 politics and government, (administrative discretion) 17, 63, 206–8; (civil service) 63–4; (civil society) 55, 57, 58, 59, 63; (clientalism) 56–7, 63–4; (Communist Party [CCP]) 16, 57, 59, 63, 66, 71, 90, 138, 185, 187, 193, 216–17, 219; (community/officialdom) 13, 137, 143–5; (corporatism) 56–7, 224; (corruption) 63–4, 145, 189, 200, 219–20, 222; (Cultural Revolution) 55, 60, 62, 66, 148, 185, 205, 219; (democracy) 53; (dissidents) 68, 201; (elections) 57, 61–4, 67; (four cardinal principles) 57, 64, 66, 216; (Legislative Affairs Commission) 208; (Leninism) 57, 66, 216, 217, 219; (local government) 61, 206, 207, 217–18; (Mao era) 15, 55, 59, 62–3, 66, 138–39, 148, 214; (Maoist ideology) 17, 57, 206, 216, 219; (Marxism) 57, 66, 187, 193, 216, 219; (multinationalism) 87; (nation and state) 89–92; (National Peoples Congress [NPC]) 63–4, 208, 216; (National Peoples Congress Standing Committee) 17, 206; (nationalism/localism) 13, 137, 140–3; (nationality) 88–9, 109; (political order) 57–8; (Qing dynasty) 60, 90; (socialism) 4–5, 13, 137, 148–9; (socialist rule-of-law state) 52, 57, 216; (sovereignty) 59; (stability) 60–1, 68; (State Council) 17, 206, 208; (thought control) 55, 59; (trade unions) 147; (transparency) 189 rights, (Asian values) 52–4, 59, 74–5; (citizenship) 13, 14, 88–9, 137, 142–3; (civil rights) 13, 52, 58–9, 60, 65, 68; (enforcement) 221; (human rights) 184, 201–02; (property rights) 217, 219, 221; (rhetoric/reality) 13, 137, 145–8 society, (crime) 65, 68, 186, 189, 197, 199, 219; (environment) 219, 222; (ethnic groups) 39, 140; (Falungong) 67, 188, 201–02, 216; (foreignness) 13, 137; (*guanxi* [connections]) 5, 184, 210, 219, 221–22, 224; (Koreans) 106, 107, 111, 130; (permanent residence) 140; (spiritual civilization) 219 World Bank 184; World Trade Organization (WTO) 149, 189, 205, 225–6 Chinese:

Chinatowns 121, 124; diaspora 92–3, 101; education 121–2; Han 39, 140–41; Indonesia 40–4, 49, 121, 122; legal formality 222; market-dominant groups 39–40, 41, 42–4; Singapore 90; South Korea (*hwagyo*) 13, 88, 106, 111, 113, 117, 120–4, 129; Taiwan, citizenship 97, 102–3; diaspora 92, 93; market-dominant groups 39, 40; other-izing 12, 98; South Korean 121–22
Thailand 121–22; United States 86
Chua, Amy L. vii, 7–8, 33–50
citizenship: allocation of resources 142; China 13, 14, 88–9, 137, 142–3; descent (*jus sanguinis*) 87–8, 92, 97, 102, 123, 125, 126; Germany 87,102; globalization 85, 145; Japan 87–9; place of birth (*jus soli*) 87, 102, 125; place of residence (*jus domicili*) 87, 92, 97, 102; South Korea 12, 14, 88; Taiwan 12, 14, 87, 89, 92, 97, 102–3; United States 102
civil rights: China 13, 52, 58–9, 60, 65, 68; liberal democracy 65–6, 68; migrant labor 87, 99–100, 102; Taiwan 87, 99–100, 102
civil society: China 55, 57–9, 63
clientalism: China 56–7, 63–4; developing countries 38
Cohen, Myron 140–1
Commonwealth of Independent States (CIS) 107
communitarianism: Japan 70; nationalism 4; particularization 3; rule of law 9, 52–62, 64–5, 67, 68; South Korea 70; Taiwan 70
Confucianism: *Analects* 191; doing right 61; duty/custom/discretion 5; education 158, 163–64; Japan 158, 163–65; loyalty 24; new Confucianism 53–4; Tokugawa warriors 163, 165
constitutional law: China 52, 66–7, 89, 143, 216; Japan 14, 88, 161–2, 166–7, 173–75; liberal democracy 65–6; parliamentary supremacy 54; separation of powers 54, 64, 167, 171, 175; socialism 65–6; South Korea 126, 128–9; Taiwan 89, 93
corruption: China, (judiciary) 186–7, 210–11, 215, 216; (legal profession) 16, 186–7, 210–11, 215, 216; (politics and government) 63–4, 145, 189, 200, 219–20, 222 developing countries 37, 38; Indonesia 49
courts: China 17–18, 185–6, 205–33; Japan 30, 31, 171
criminal law: China 65, 68, 186, 189, 197, 199, 219; Japan 167, 168–9, 172–74
critical legal studies 6, 62, 192
cultural meanings 2, 5–6
Cultural Revolution 55, 60, 62, 66, 148, 185, 205, 219
cultural theorists 3
culturally embedded practices: Japan 7, 22–3; legal institutions 14–18; migrant labor 11
culture: critical legal studies 6; East Asia *see* local culture; legal culture 218–24

democracy: capitalism 35, 52; China 53; developing countries 8, 33–4, 45; economic development 33; markets 7, 8, 9, 33, 35–7; pro-market retreat 42–4; property rights 35
democratization: axes 45; developing countries 33–4, 38, 45; Japan 176; market-dominant minorities 42; meaning 34; Taiwan 89
Deng Xiaoping 66, 80, 216
developed world: markets and democracy 35–7; poverty 35, 36; wealth redistribution 35, 36
developing countries: capitalism 34, 45; clientalism 38; corruption 37, 38; democracy 8, 33–4, 45; democratization 33–4, 38, 45; economic disparities 38, 46; ethnic conflict 33, 44; ethnicity 8, 33; legal reform 45; liberalization 34, 40–1; market democracy 37–8; market-dominant minorities 40–1; marketization 34, 41, 45; markets 8, 33–4; markets/democracy conflict 42, 44–5; population growth 37; poverty 37, 38, 45; privatization 34, 37–8, 40, 41; property rights 38; rule of law *see* rule of law; suffrage 34, 38, 45; wealth redistribution 37
Dezalay, Yves 183, 184, 193

East Asia: Asian values 5, 52–4, 59, 74–5; culture *see* local culture; economy *see*

economic development; tiger economies 39–40
Easterbrook, Frank 25
economic development: China 219; culture 1; democracy 33; markets 2, 33; role for law xi, 1–21; Taiwan 12, 91, 95, 100
education: Japan *see* Japan; South Africa 40–1; South Korea 121; Taiwan 121, 122
Edwards, Jonathan 22
elections 57, 61–4, 67
Emerson, John P. 139
enfranchisement *see* suffrage
Engels, Friedrich 8
Epstein, Richard 26, 32
Eritrea 44
ethnic conflict: developing countries 33, 44; Indonesia 42, 43;
marketization 41
ethnic groups: China 39, 140; economic dominance 40–1; Filipinos 93–4, 111–13, 117; Han *see* Chinese; Hong Kong 39, 40; Indians 40; Indonesians 93, 94, 99, 111, 113; Japan 39–40, 88; Japanese 88; Koreans *see* Koreans; market-dominant 39–41; nationalism 13; Singapore 39; South Korea 13, 39, 118; superior entrepreneurialism 40–1; Taiwan 39–40, 90; Thais 93–4, 99, 111; United States 39; Vietnamese 88, 111–13
ethnicity: developing countries 8, 33; markets 7–8, 9, 38–41; meaning 34
ethnie 125
Eto, Shinpei 169, 170–71, 173
European Union (EU) 86

Faist, Thomas 86
Falungong 67, 188, 201–02, 216
Filipinos: South Korea 111–13, 117; Taiwan 93–4
Ford Foundation 184
foreign investment: China 143, 147, 149; liberalization 40, 41, 43
Franck, Thomas A. 11, 19, 21

Galanter, Marc 212
Garth, Bryant 183–84, 193–94
General Agreement on Tariffs and Trade (GATT) 225–26
General Agreement on Trade in Services (GATS) 226
Gerchenkron, Alexander 23, 32
Germany 87, 102, 173–75
globalization: citizenship 85, 145; human rights 145; migrant labor 11, 85, 101, 119, 122; rule of law xi, 18
Goodwin, Robert E. 4, 20
Gordon, Robert 195
Goto 166, 170
Grafstein, Robert 6
Great Leap Forward 60, 138–9
guanxi (connections) 5, 184, 210, 219, 221–22, 224
Guatemala 40–1

Hart, H.L.A. 72
He Weifang 213–14
Hecht, Jonathan 184
Hirschman, Albert 9
Hong Kong: economic regime 56; ethnic groups 39–40; formal legality 222; rule of law 70–1
Honig, Emily 140
human rights: China 184, 201–02; global norms 11; globalization 145;

Indonesia 44; international law 145; rule of law 52, 58–9, 60; South Korea 106, 129; universal values 3, 19

identity politics 3
ideology: markets 45–6
Indians: market-dominant groups 40
individual self-interest 8–9
Indonesia 40–1, 42–4, 49, 121–22
Indonesians: South Korea 111, 113; Taiwan 93, 94, 99
Inoue, Kaoru 170
International Convention on the Elimination of All Forms of Racial
Discrimination 119
International Covenant on Civil and Political Rights 125
International Covenant on Economic, Social and Cultural Rights 119
International Labor Organization (ILO) 100
international law: human rights 145
International Monetary Fund (IMF):

economic development 46; Indonesia 43, 44; rule of law 2
Itagaki 170–71
Ito, Hirobumi 173
Iwakura 166, 170

Jansen, Marius 164
Japan: advocates 172–74; agency slack 25–6; attorneys 159, 160, 174–5, 176; banking 27–9, 32; Cabinet (*naikaku*) 166, 174; Charter Oath of Five Articles 166; citizenship 87–9; Civil Code 26, 174; colonization 11, 13; Commercial Code 24–5, 174; communitarianism 70; Confucian ethics 158, 163–65; constitutional law 14, 88, 161–2, 166–7, 173–75; corporate charters 7, 25, 26; corporate investment 23–6; corporate law 24–6, 27; corporate market control 26; courts 30, 31, 171; culturally embedded practices 7, 22–3; democratization 176; domains 166, 167–8, 170; employment contracts 7, 26; equity 7, 23–4; ethnic groups 39–40, 88; French model 169, 170, 172–75; German model 173–75; government role 27–9; Great Court of Judicature (GCJ) 171; indigenous arrangements 30–2; Industrial Bank of Japan (IBJ) 28–9; Institute for Legal Studies 169, 172; Institute of Legal Research and Training 15, 156, 158–59, 176; Japanese style law school 15, 156; Judicial Reform Council (JRC) 15, 156–57, 161–62, 176–7; judiciary, (legal history) 168–71, 172, 174–75; (structure) 160–2 Kagoshima (Satsuma) 162, 164, 166, 168, 171; Kochi (Tosa) 164, 166, 168; Koreans 88, 107, 123–24; labor policy 24–5; law and custom 30–1; law faculties 157–8; Law School (Ministry of Justice) 172, 174; law student enrolment 157–8, 172, 174; legal education 14–15, 156–81; Legal Examination 15, 156–59, 176; legal institutions 7, 14, 26–7; legal profession, (formation) 171–7; (structure) 159–62 local culture 6; Meiji period, (centralized government) 165–8, 170; (civil war) 167–8; (coups) 170, 173; (criminal law) 167, 168–9, 172–74; (judicial system) 168–72, 175; (nation-building) 14–15, 162–5; (Restoration) 162–63, 165–67, 170, 172–74 migrant labor 88; Ministry of Education 172, 174; Ministry of Justice 169, 170–72, 174; *minzoku* 125; nationality 130; off-the-rack governance 27; Opium War 163; Osaka stock exchange 7, 24; Popular Rights Movement 171, 173; prefectures 167–70; private arrangements 30, 31; private law schools 173–75; property rights 31; prosecutors 159, 160, 169, 174–75; *Rinshi* Committee 161, 178; *Ritsuryo* system 165–6, 167, 175; rule of law 6–7, 22, 32; Saga 170, 173; separation of powers 167, 171, 175; state-building 162–5; Taiwan 90; Tokugawa Shogunate 14, 30, 31, 162, –64, 166–67, 171–72; Tokyo stock exchange 7, 24; United States, commerce 163–64; university education 157–9, 172, 174, 175, 180; Yamaguchi (Choshu) 162, 164, 166, 168, 170–71, 173
Japanese: Latin America 88
Jayasuriya, Kanishka 5, 20, 75, 82
Jiang Zemin 52, 53, 57, 61, 76, 190, 216
Johnson, Chalmers 27, 32
Jones, Carol A.G. 5, 20
judiciary: administrative decisions 67–8, 208; appointment 54, 62–3; Chinese *see* China; independence/impartiality 62–4, 160; Japan 160–2, 168–71, 172, 174, 175; legal convergence 3

Kaplow, Louis 31–2
Kazakhstan 107, 111
Kenya 40, 44
Kido 171
Kim Dae-jung 123
Kim Young-Sam 109
Korean War 120
Koreans: China 106, 107, 111, 129, 130; ethnic nationalism 13; Japan 88, 107, 123–24; *joseonjok* 107–12, 116–20, 125, 128–29; North America 109, 111; North Koreans 12, 120, 128–9; South Koreans *see* South Korea; Soviet Union 107, 111
Kronman, Anthony T. 184, 190–6, 201–02

labor law: China 11, 148–9; migrant labor 11; North Korea 11; South Korea 11; Taiwan 11; United States 30
Langdell, Christopher Columbus 192
Larson, Magali Sarfatti 194
Latin America: Japanese 88
law: cultural meanings 2, 5–6; embedded identities 1, 6–10
law and economics 192
law firms: China 15–16, 185, 188–89, 226
Lawyers Committee for Human Rights 184
Lebanese: market-dominant groups 40
Lee, Chulwoo vii, 11–3, 88, 106–36
legal convergence: global/local dichotomy 1; judiciary 3; local practices 2–4, 70
legal education: Japan 14–5, 156–81
legal institutions: China 13, 62–4, 69, 220; culturally embedded practices 14–18; Japan 7, 14, 26–7; shifting involvements 9
legal profession: China 15–16, 63, 64, 182–204; common law case method 192; Japan 159–62, 171–7; lawyer-statesman 191–3, 195; regulation 54; sociology 194–96; specialization 192; United States 16–17, 191, 194–5, 196–7
Leninism 57, 66, 216–17, 219
Li Denghui 98
Li Peng 211
Li Shenzhi 61
liberal democracy: civil rights 65–6, 68; constitutional law 65–6; economic regime 55–6; elections 57; freedom 58, 61; rule of law 9, 10, 52–3, 57, 59–62, 68–70
liberalism: universal values 4
liberalization: China 39, 60, 188, 204; developing countries 34, 40–1; foreign investment 40, 41, 43; Indonesia 43
Linshan, Hua 223
local culture: economic development 1; familism 5; global/local dichotomy 1; *guanxi* (connections) 5, 184, 210, 219, 221–22, 224; Japan 6; role of law 5; rule of law 1, 2; special case 4–5
Locke, John 72
Lockwood, William W. 28, 32
Lubman, Stanley vii, 14, 17, 80, 205–23
Luo Ruiqing 138
Macaulay, Thomas Babington 35, 47
Madison, James 35, 47
Madsen, Richard 190
market democracy: developed world 35–7; developing countries 37–8; paradox 35–8
market economy: China 17, 52–3, 56, 139–40, 182, 219; Scandinavia 34; United States 34–5
market system 34
market-dominant majorities 39–40
market-dominant minorities: anti-market backlash 42–4; atrocities 42; democratization 42; economic dominance 40–2; economic restrictions 42, 43; eliminationism 43–4; expulsions 42 marketization: China 139–40, 145–6, 205, 218; developing countries 34, 41, 45; ethnic tension 41 markets: compatible ideologies 7, 36, 38; democracy 7–9, 33, 35–7; developing countries 8, 33–4; economic development 2, 33; ethnicity 7–8, 9, 38–41; ideology 45–6; modernization theorists 4; pro-market retreat from democracy 42–4
Marx, Karl Friedrich 8
Marxism 57, 66, 187, 193, 216, 219
Matsukata, Kojiro 28
mediating devices 7, 36, 37–8
Megawati Sukarnoputri 44
migrant labor: civil rights 87, 99–100, 102; culturally embedded practices 11; dirty/difficult/dangerous (3-D) industries 88, 95, 99, 112; foreign workers 101; framework of analysis 96; globalization 11, 85, 101, 119, 122; identity 101; ideologies of incorporation 87–9; Japan 88; labor law 11; naturalization 87; non-governmental organizations (NGOs) 11; political status 86; professional services 122; settlers 86, 101; Singapore 95; sojourners 86; South Korea 12, 14, 111–20, 124; Taiwan 12, 14, 92–105; territoriality 87, 101; transnationals 12, 14, 85–6, 101; UN Convention 89
Migrante International 89
Minxin, Pei 184
Miwa, Yoshiro viii, 6–8, 22–32
modernization theorists 4

multiculturalism 3
Muto, Sanji 24
Myanmar 111, 113

Naquin, Susan 140
nationalism: China 13, 137, 140; communitarianism 4; ethnonationalism 8; particularization 3, 19
nationality: China 88–9, 109; Japan 130; South Korea 13, 107–11, 122–8, 130;*see also* citizenship
nationalization: ethnically targeted 42–4
neo-authoritarianism: rule of law 9, 53, 56–9, 61–8
Nepal 111, 113, 119
new Confucianism 53–4
New Zealand 39
Nigeria 40
non-governmental organizations (NGOs) 11
North Korea 11
North Koreans 12, 120, 128–9

Okazaki, Tetsuji 29
Okubo 166, 170–71, 173
Okuma 173
Okuno-Fujiwara, Masahiro 29
oppression: economic dominance 40–1
Organization for Economic Cooperation and Development (OECD) 122

Pakistan 44, 111–13
Parsons, Talcott 194
particularization: communitarianism 3; global/local dichotomy 1; nationalism 3, 19
path-dependence: economic dominance 41
Peerenboom, Randall viii, 9–10, 51–84, 184
Peng Ming-min 91
Peoples Republic of China (PRC) *see* China
Perry, Matthew Galbraith (Commodore, USN) 163
Philippines 41, 44
Posner, Richard 194, 202
poverty: China 60; developed world 35–6; developing countries 37–8, 45; indigenous majorities 41–2
privatization: China 218; developing countries 34, 37–8, 40, 41; Indonesia 43
property rights: China 217, 219, 221; confiscation 35, 36; democracy 35; developing countries 38; Japan 31; rule of law 8; Russian Federation 30; suffrage 35–6, 45

racism: market compatible ideologies 7, 36; markets/democracy conflict 42
Ramseyer, J. Mark viii, 6–7, 8, 22–32
Rawls, John 4, 20
Rawski, Evelyn 140
religious fundamentalism 3
Ricardo, David 35
Roh Tae-woo 107–08, 112
Rokumoto, Kahei viii, 14, 156–81
Rosett, Arthur viii, 1–21, 33
rule by law 55–7, 59, 62, 69
rule of law: Asian Development Bank 2, 184; central/local relations 60–1; China 9–10, 16, 51–84, 182, 184, 188, 214, 221; communitarianism 9, 52–62, 64–5, 67–8; competing conceptions 9, 51–84; globalization xi, 18; human rights 52, 58–9, 60; ideal types 53–5; initiatives 45; International Monetary Fund (IMF) 2; Japan 6–7, 22, 32; liberal democracy 9–10, 52–3, 57, 59–62, 68–70; local culture 1, 2; mediating devices 7; neo-authoritarianism 9, 53, 56, 57–9, 61–5, 67–68; outcomes in specific cases 65–9; pluralism 2; political succession 60; property rights 8; purposes 59–62; rent seeking detritus 7, 32; stability 60–1, 68; statist socialism 9, 52–3, 56–68; thick conceptions 9, 10, 51–2, 55, 74; thin conceptions 9, 10, 51–2, 55, 74; universal values xi; World Bank 2, 184
Russian Federation 30, 44
Rwanda 40

Saigo 166, 170
Scandinavia 34, 39
Sen, Amartya 9, 21
Seol Donghun 118
Shavell, Steven 31–2
Singapore: Asian values 5; Chinese 90; ethnic groups 39; migrant labor 95; rule of law 70–1

Smith, Adam 35, 47
Smith, Anthony 125
social identity 8–9
Soejima 170
Solinger, Dorothy J. ix, 11–4, 137–55
South Africa 40
South Korea: abandoned children 125; aliens, (illegal sojourners) 111–18, 126–7, 128; (industrial trainees) 111–16, 117–18; (Korean descent) 110; (land ownership) 121–22; (permanent residence) 123; (registered) 111; (residence visas) 120, 122, 123, 127 anti-communism 122, 124; Chinese (*hwagyo*) 13, 88, 106, 111, 113, 117, 120–4, 129; citizenship 12, 14, 88; communitarianism 70; compatriots 110, 118;constitutional law 126, 128–9; Democratic Party for the New Millennium 117, 123; dispatching companies 114–16; dual nationality 109, 125; education 121; elections 123–4; ethnic groups 13, 39, 118; Federation of Small and Medium Enterprises (FSME) 113–15; Filipinos 111–13, 117; foreign policy 107, 108; Gim Gwangho case 126; *goryeoin* 107, 111, 128; human rights 106, 129; incomes 113–18; Indonesians 111, 113; industrial injuries 116–17; Japanese rule 12–3, 111, 120; Joint Committee for Migrant Workers 119; *joseonjok* 107–12, 116–20, 126, 128, 129; Kosians 128; labor law 11; marriage 116, 122, 125–8; migrant labor 12, 14, 111–20, 124; Ministry of Commerce 112; Ministry of Justice 109, 110; Ministry of Labor 114, 116, 117; *minjok* 125; mixed blood 122, 128; nationality 13, 107–11, 122–8, 130; nationality adjudication 108; naturalization 108, 109, 123, 127; Nepalese 111, 113, 119; New Overseas Koreans Policy 109; North Koreans 12, 120, 128–9; outsiders 106; Overseas Koreans Foundation 109, 130–31; patrilateralism 125–26; Pearl Buck Foundation 128; permanent resident returnees 108; refugees 120, 128–9; Thais 111; trade unions 118–19; trainee allowances 113–15, 117–18; Vietnamese 111, 113; working conditions 113–16, 120
sovereignty 59
Soviet Union 88, 107, 111
Soysal, Yasemin 86
Sri Lanka 40, 44, 111
state aids 34
state-building: assimilation 87, 102; exclusion 87; ideologies of incorporation 87–9; Japan 162–5; multiculturalism 87; multinationalism 87; Taiwan 86; transnationalism 87
statist socialism 9, 52–3, 56–68
Stigler, George 26
suffrage: developing countries 34, 38, 45; property rights 35–6, 45
Suharto 43, 49
Sukarno, Achmed 43
Sun Yat-sen 89
Sweden 45

Taiwan: bureaucratic practices 100–1; capitalist competition 12; Chinese persons *see* Chinese; citizenship 12, 14, 87, 89, 92, 97, 102–3; civil rights 87, 99–100, 102; class 12, 93; communitarianism 70; constitutional law 89, 93; Council on Labor Affairs 97, 98, 100; democratization 89; DPP 98; economic development 12, 91, 95, 100; education 121; ethnic groups 39, 40, 90; Filipinos 93, 94; foreign labor, (alternative labor) 99; (background) 95; (demographics) 93; (differentiation) 98; (domestic service) 93–5, 99; (framework of analysis) 96; (legalization) 95–9; (restrictions) 98, 99; (*wailao*rights) 99–100 independence claim 90–1; Indonesians 93–4, 99; Japan 90; Kuomintang (KMT) 90, 98; labor law 11, 95–101, 103; local labor 92–3, 100; mainland labor 93; marriage 99, 103; migrant labor 12, 14, 92–105; other-izing 12, 98; racism 99; Republic of China (ROC) 89–90, 93, 97–8, 102–3; state-building 86; Thais 93–4, 99; Vietnamese 88; wage differentials 97, 99–101
Tay, Alice 62
Thailand 41, 44, 121–22
Thais: South Korea 111; Taiwan 93–4, 99

Thireau, Isabelle 223
Tocqueville, Alexis de 196–7
trade unions: China 147; South Korea 118–19
transnational labor *see* migrant labor
TRIPS agreement 226
Trubek, David 194
Tsurunen, Marutei 89
Turner, Brian S. 142

Uganda 44
United Kingdom 45, 54
United Nations 19, 89
United States: assimilation 87, 102; China, (perceptions of legal profession) 16–17, 182–5, 187, 189–95; (rule of law initiative) 184, 190 Chinese 86; citizenship 102; communitarianism 4; ethnic groups 39; Koreans 109, 111; labor law 30; legal profession 16–17, 191, 194–5, 196–7; market economy 34, 45; plea bargaining 197; separation of powers 54, 64; upward mobility 36
universal values: critique 3; economic principles 7–8; human rights 3, 19; liberalism 4; local practices 18–19; rule of law xi
upward mobility 7, 36, 38
Uzbekistan 107, 111

Vietnam 41, 44, 99
Vietnamese 88, 111, 113

Wagatsuma, Hiroshi xi, xii, 182
Wahid, Abdurrahman 44
Weber, Max 62, 194
welfare state 7
Western values: liberalism 4
Winn, Jane Kaufman 5, 20
Woo, Margaret Y.K. ix, 1–21, 33
World Bank: China 184; economic development 46; economic disparities 8; Indonesia 43; population growth 37; rule of law 2, 184
World Trade Organization (WTO) 122, 149, 189, 205, 225–6

Yamagata, Aritomo 170
Yu Keping 61

Zimbabwe 40

For Product Safety Concerns and Information please contact our EU representative GPSR@taylorandfrancis.com
Taylor & Francis Verlag GmbH, Kaufingerstraße 24, 80331 München, Germany

www.ingramcontent.com/pod-product-compliance
Ingram Content Group UK Ltd.
Pitfield, Milton Keynes, MK11 3LW, UK
UKHW022133190926
475702UK00013B/1795
* 9 7 8 0 3 6 7 0 2 6 9 2 9 *